Co-curating the City

Co-curating the City

Universities and urban heritage past and future

edited by Clare Melhuish, Henric Benesch,
Ingrid Martins Holmberg and Dean Sully

First published in 2022 by
UCL Press
University College London
Gower Street
London WC1E 6BT

Available to download free: www.uclpress.co.uk

Collection © Editors, 2022
Text © Contributors, 2022
Images © Contributors and copyright holders named in captions, 2022

The authors have asserted their rights under the Copyright, Designs and Patents Act 1988 to be identified as the authors of this work.

A CIP catalogue record for this book is available from The British Library.

This book contains third-party copyright material that is not covered by the book's Creative Commons licence. Details of the copyright ownership and permitted use of third-party material is given in the image (or extract) credit lines. If you would like to reuse any third-party material not covered by the book's Creative Commons licence, you will need to obtain permission directly from the copyright owner.

This book is published under a Creative Commons Attribution Non-commercial Non-derivative 4.0 International licence (CC BY-NC-ND 4.0), https://creativecommons.org/licenses/by-nc-nd/4.0/. This licence allows you to share, copy, distribute and transmit the work for personal and non-commercial use providing author and publisher attribution is clearly stated. If you wish to use the work commercially, use extracts or undertake translation you must seek permission from the author. Attribution should include the following information:

Melhuish, C et al. (eds). 2022. *Co-curating the City: Universities and urban heritage past and future*. London: UCL Press. https://doi.org/10.14324/9781800081826

Further details about Creative Commons licences are available at
http:// creativecommons.org/ licenses/

ISBN: 978-1-80008-184-0 (Hbk.)
ISBN: 978-1-80008-183-3 (Pbk.)
ISBN: 978-1-80008-182-6 (PDF)
ISBN: 978-1-80008-185-7 (epub)
ISBN: 978-1-80008-186-4 (mobi)
DOI: https://doi.org/10.14324/9781800081826

Contents

List of figures	vii
List of contributors	xv
Acknowledgements	xix

Introduction   1
Clare Melhuish, Henric Benesch, Ingrid Martins Holmberg and Dean Sully

I. Critical perspectives

1   The evolving role of universities in framing critical urban heritage discourse in regeneration contexts   15
Clare Melhuish

2   Universities curating change at heritage places in urban spaces   43
Dean Sully

3   Historic urban buildings in the university curriculum: the re-evaluation of Haga, Gothenburg, as urban heritage   66
Ingrid Martins Holmberg

4   Deferred heritage: digital renderings of sites of future knowledge production   90
Adam Brown

II. Sites and historical contexts, past and future
Part 1: University of Gothenburg and UCL East (London)

5   From dispersed multi-site to cluster and campus: understanding the material infrastructure of University of Gothenburg as urban heritage   113
Claes Caldenby

6   The dis-, mis- and re-membering of design education:
     understanding design education as urban heritage   132
     Henric Benesch

7   London's mega event heritage and the development of
     UCL East   154
     Jonathan Gardner

8   Building back better? Hysterical materialism and the role
     of the university in post-pandemic heritage making: the case
     of East London   177
     Phil Cohen

Part 2: Elsewhere: Lund, Rome, Beirut and São Paulo

9   Big Science and urban morphogenesis: the case of   200
     Lund University
     Mattias Kärrholm and Albena Yaneva

10   The university as regeneration strategy in an urban heritage
     context: the case of Roma Tre   220
     Ola Wetterberg and Maria Nyström

11   Heritage from a neighbourhood perspective: reflections from the
     American University of Beirut   248
     Cynthia Myntti and Mona El Hallak

12   From Red São Paulo to Brazilian neofascism: urban, political and
     cultural heritage in the making of a public university 269
     Pedro Fiori Arantes

Postscript: a collective reflection by the contributors   296

Index   304

List of figures

1.1 Aerial view of Olympic Park from south, with UCL East site lying between the Olympic Stadium and Aquatics Centre on South Lawn. Courtesy of UCL East Figure ... 30
1.2 View of existing Faculty of Humanities and Library (to left of image), University of Gothenburg, with Näckrosen construction site and hoarding to right. Photo: C. Melhuish, 2017 ... 32
1.3 Site hoarding showing visualisation of new four-storey faculty building and formal façade, Näckrosen development, University of Gothenburg. Photo: C. Melhuish, 2017 ... 33
1.4 UCL East Final draft masterplan section. Courtesy of UCL East ... 37
1.5 UCL East illustrative masterplan. Courtesy of UCL East ... 37
1.6 UCL East, visualisation of Phase 1 (Pool St West, left, and Marshgate, right, either side of Waterworks River), looking south towards Stratford. Courtesy of UCL East ... 38
2.1 Island of Continuity: House Mill on Three Mills Island (2017). Source: Dean Sully ... 44
2.2 Urban landscape in flux: View from House Mill toward the Queen Elizabeth Park (2017). Source: Dean Sully ... 44
2.3 Heritage as understood in twentieth century. Source: Dean Sully ... 47
2.4 Heritage as understood in the early twenty-first century. Source: Dean Sully ... 48
3.1 The invisibility of historic urban buildings in the imaginary geography of attraction. This postcard of the early 1900s clearly illustrates how the imaginary geography of attraction set its entire focus upon the monumental features of the city. Accordingly, the postcard shows monumental buildings at the edge of Haga together

with the historical fortlet from the seventeenth century in the background. This imaginary geography consequently omitted the city's heterogenous vernacular historic building-stock. To take this shot of Haga, one must keep at the outside from where none of these buildings can appear. Note that not even the name of the area is mentioned: 'The Caponnière street with the public library, the Renström's Public Bath and the fortlet "The Crown" in the fund' [*Kapuniergatan med folkbiblioteket, Renströmska Badanstalten och Skansen "Kronan" i fonden*]. Photo: City Museum, Gothenburg 71

3.2 The monumentalisation of vernacular buildings of the urban fringe in the imaginary geography of commemoration. This photo is taken at a public debate on the future of the fringe settlement Green Street in 1955. In front of a model of some of the buildings stands, at the far left, the museum director Dr Stig Roth (promoting maintenance) in company of the city's planning manager (promoting demolition) and other prominent men. Shortly after, the area was demolished after thoroughgoing historical documentation by the museum, and transplant of some buildings to a reserve. Photo: City Museum, Gothenburg 73

3.3 The stigmatisation of the urban vernacular historic buildings in the imaginary geography of sanitisation. The idea of urban sanitisation gradually radicalises when, during the mid-twentieth century, the claims on renewal gain political power. The imaginary geography of sanitisation builds upon the two parallel imaginary geographies (focus on monuments and/or historical buildings in the urban periphery) and develops it into making Haga appear as the epitome of 'old-and-ugly'. The city's planning manager, Tage William-Olsson, in a 1943 daily newspaper interview states that 'Haga lacks the idyll found in for example Majorna [that is, Gröna Gatan] where there are several preservation-worthy buildings. From a cultural-historic point of view I cannot find any reason to keep away from sanitisation of Haga […] The proper and rational thing to do is to demolish the old hovels and build new.' [*Haga saknar sådana idyller som exempelvis Majorna där det finns åtskilligt man vill bevara.*

	Ur kulturhistorisk synpunkt kan jag inte finna att det finns något som hindrar en sanering av Haga. [...] Det enda man kan göra i Haga är att rationellt riva ned de gamla rucklena och bygga nytt. (Stadsplanechef Tage William-Olsson, in Göteborgs-Posten 1943, "Sanering av Haga ...."] Photo: Lars Mongs	76
3.4	The imaginary geography of maintenance brought a conversion of Haga's moral geography from the former 'nice-new-outer', to the 'nice-old-inner'. The previously invisible as well as despised inner part of Haga, with low-rise wooden construction and mainly of dwelling function, now became the main bearer of identity, through the means of the narrative of 'the city's oldest workers' area. This narrative was the guideline for the preservation project. Photo: Lars Mongs	81
4.1	Zaha Hadid, rendering of HKPU Jockey Club Innovation Tower, 2012. © Zaha Hadid Architects	97
4.2	Swansea University Bay Campus, Hopkins and Porphyrios (Architects), St Modwen (Developers), screenshot from flythough, 2014. Reproduced with permission of Swansea University.	107
4.3	Swansea University Bay Campus, Hopkins and Porphyrios (Architects), St Modwen (Developers), screenshot from flythough, 2014. Reproduced with permission of Swansea University.	107
5.1	Main building from 1907, the only protected building of University of Gothenburg. Withdrawn from the street, in a park and reached by stairs. Photo: Krister Engström	115
5.2	City and university library from 1901, reopened as university library in the 1990s after a period as city archive. In a park but not withdrawn from the street. Photo: Krister Engström	115
5.3	Map of University of Gothenburg and Chalmers in the early 1990s. A centrally located dispersed university from the 1970s transformed into faculty size 'clusters'. Credit: Claes Caldenby	120
5.4	Faculty of Education in the 1970s. A flexible structure around interior courtyards in an external location in the neighbour municipality Mölndal. Photo: White architects.	121
5.5	New faculty of Education, built in 2006 as an addition to an 1850s hospital. The only externally located faculty now	

	became the only one inside the moat of the former fortifications. Photo: Krister Engström	122
5.6	'Samvetet', Faculty of Social Sciences, built in the early 1990s in a central location and closely integrated with new housing in an old workers' housing district. Photo: Krister Engström	126
5.7	School of Economics from early 1990s in a block of its own next to the faculty of social sciences. On the corner the library with a large 'urban window'. Photo: Krister Engström	127
7.1	The Carpenters Arms and housing blocks of the Carpenters Estate, Stratford, East London, January 2016. Site of the now cancelled UCL Stratford scheme. Photo: Jonathan Gardner. CC BY 4.0	157
7.2	One of the few photographs of the Crystal Palace in Hyde Park in 1851, which hosted the Great Exhibition. Attributed to Claude-Marie Ferrier. Public Domain. Available at: https://commons.wikimedia.org/wiki/File:Crystal_palace_1851.jpg	165
7.3	The models of dinosaurs and extinct animals that remain as one of the few surviving traces of the Crystal Palace at Sydenham. Photo: Jonathan Gardner. CC BY 4.0	169
9.1	Plan of the 'Science Road' (in orange) and the new tramway of Lund 2019. Source: City Office, Lund Municipality	202
9.2	Scale model of Science Village, with MAX IV in the upper left corner and part of ESS in the lower right. The model was publicly exhibited at a venue in Lund city centre, 2018. Photo: M. Kärrholm	202
9.3	Universitetsplatsen, with Kungshuset (1580s) to the left and Helgo Zettervall's new main university building from 1882 to the right – with four sphinxes on top. Photo: M. Kärrholm, 2020	206
9.4	The Lund University area. University buildings are in black and planned new buildings are in red. The urban layers of different building ages are divided by the dotted lines. Map: M. Kärrholm	207
9.5	Moves of departments and research facilities since the year 2000. The figure includes the planned but not yet realised move of the Physics department to the Science	

	Village, and the move of MAX IV, from the former MAX-lab location. Diagram: M. Kärrholm	210
9.6	The windmill and old farm of Odarslöv, now renovated and transformed into a visitor centre for the ESS. Photo: M. Kärrholm, 2018	212
10.1	Partial view of Ostiense from the Tiber. Photo: Ola Wetterberg, 2019	221
10.2	Engineering school under construction on the grounds of the old ship shute, Vasca Navale. Architect Professor Andrea Vidotto. Photo: Ola Wetterberg, 2010	227
10.3	View of the Mattatoio complex. Photo: Ola Wetterberg, 2019	228
10.4	Città della scienza al mattatoio, Roma. Paolo Portoghesi, 1983. © Accademia Nazionale di San Luca, Roma	234
10.5	Various groups inhabiting the Campo Boario during the 1990s. Nyström, 2015	238
10.6	Art exhibitions outside the MACRO. Photo: Maria Nyström, 2015	239
10.7	Overview of the various actors in Mattatoio 2015. Nyström, 2015	241
10.8	The garden in Campo Boario overlooking the fence to the art school. Photo: Ola Wetterberg, 2018	244
11.1	The artistic installation/performance Recycling a Shell gave people a chance to visit and experience the Khalidy House, a beautiful deserted 1932 heritage building in the neighbourhood. © AUB Neighborhood Initiative	259
11.2	The Van Dyck Stairs packed with people during the theatrical performance 'Jogging' that brought back to life this almost forgotten part of the neighborhood's urban heritage. © AUB Neighborhood Initiative	260
11.3	The acoustic installation Le Souffleur transformed the Ain Mreisseh public stairs into a vertical playground. The sound of the sea, now totally blocked by recent high-rise construction, is transmitted continuously from the fishermen's port nearby. © AUB Neighborhood Initiative	261
11.4	The legendary thyme mana'ish at the Al Jar Lil Jar farmers' market, held every Friday on Jeanne d'Arc Street, giving people a social gathering space, introducing local producers, farmers and artisans and offering homemade dishes that revive local culinary traditions. © AUB Neighborhood Initiative	263

11.5 A Hakawati storytelling performance by Dar Onboz captures the attention of people from all ages, weaving neighbourhood memories into timeless fairy tales and celebrating our intangible heritage. © AUB Neighborhood Initiative   264

11.6 A father teaching his son how to play backgammon on the sidewalk in Jeanne d'Arc Street, where a concrete *Public Tawleh* board was installed on the existing benches to revive this traditional game in the public space. © AUB Neighborhood Initiative   265

12.1a and 12.1b: Paulista School of Medicine in the 1940s. This first townhouse that housed the medical school, which still exists today as its historic headquarters, became the basis for the new university logo. Reproduced with the permission of Federal University of São Paulo, CEFHI collection.   272

12.2 The old campuses of public universities and their expansion in new locations in São Paulo Metropolitan Region after 2005. Source: Author using income distribution map by São Paulo Subway Company Origin-Destiny research   277

12.3 Flyer inviting the public to a meeting with Paulo Freire to debate the worker's university in the East End, 1986. The meeting place was the hall in the basement of Father Ticão's St Francis Church, in which a room was inaugurated for the education movement. Source: CEDI, 1987   278

12.4 Cover of the East End movement's newspaper ('Lack of Education') announcing the worker's university proposal: 'at first it was a dream …', 1987. In the dialogue between boss and worker, while the worker thinks about the worker's university, the boss replies: 'Are you daydreaming?' and 'What I want is production!' Source: CEDI, 1987   280

12.5 Struggles for the East End Unifesp campus plot. Leaflet calling for an act in defence of the expropriation of the Gazarra factory, on 24 March, 2012. Source: Juliana Cardoso, councillor mandate   283

12.6 One of the activities carried out at the East End Unifesp Campus since 2016. Field study on environmental sanitation problems in the Jardim Helian community,

	accompanied by grassroots leader Rodrigo Reis (in the centre, tragically deceased in 2019). Photo: the author, 2017	287
12.7	Plaque at the entrance to the campus with the words: 'This campus …' Photo: the author, 2016	288
12.8	Leaflet inviting candidates to the University-Society Strategic Council in 2018. Design by the author with illustration by Mariana Zanetti	290
12.9	Unifesp students demonstrating against the cuts imposed by the government in August 2019. On the posters, the students of Unifesp Campus Guarulhos (of Humanities) tell the passers-by of the inclusion and outreach actions of the university, all free of charge: a theatre course offered by the Caminho Velho group; music and percussion with the Mala Guetta Drums; 'arteoke', art and singing activities; math course with elementary school children; Portuguese course for immigrants; internship and partnership with public schools; the acquisition of more bus lines to serve the campus surroundings. Photo: Samara Akemi Saraiva	291

List of Contributors

Clare Melhuish is Principal Research Fellow in the Bartlett Faculty of the Built Environment at UCL and Director of the UCL Urban Laboratory, where she has been working on the role of university spatial development projects in urban regeneration and the production of cosmopolitan urbanism and imaginaries in the UK and abroad. She is a coordinator of the Curating the City research cluster in the Centre for Critical Heritage Studies. Her background lies in architectural history and criticism, anthropology, and cultural geography, drawing on ethnographic and visual research methods to interpret and understand architecture and the built environment as social and cultural setting.

Henric Benesch is an architect, educator and researcher with a PhD in Design, based in Gothenburg, Sweden, with a particular interest in critical spatial practice, situated knowledge production, and critical heritage. He currently works as a Senior Lecturer in Design at The Academy of Art and Design, since 2013 as research cocoordinator of the research cluster Curating the city at the Centre for Critical Heritage Studies, and since 2019, as Deputy Dean at the Faculty of Fine, Applied and Performing Arts, all within University of Gothenburg.

Ingrid Martins Holmberg is a senior lecturer and researcher in the Department of Conservation at University of Gothenburg. Since 2013, she is research co-coordinator of the research cluster Curating the City, at the Centre for Critical Heritage Studies, University of Gothenburg and UCL, London.

Her current research interests concern: participatory planning in heritage management; history of landscapes and built environments; Rome's historical places and the official heritage institutions; everyday ethics of maintenance and repair; uses of the past in urban transformations.

Dean Sully is Associate Professor in Conservation at UCL, Institute of Archaeology where he coordinates the MSc in Conservation for Archaeology and Museums, as well as co-coordinator for the Curating the City research cluster within the Centre for Critical Heritage Studies (CCHS). He studied conservation and gained his PhD at UCL and has worked as a practising conservator for the National Heritage Board (Singapore), The Museum of London, The British Museum, and Monmouthshire District Council Museum's Service.

Adam Brown is Senior Lecturer in Photography at LSBU, and is a member of LSBU's Centre for the Study of the Networked Image. He formerly led the BA(Hons) Photography and Media Arts at UCA Maidstone, and taught on the Bachelor of New Media Arts at James Cook University, Townsville, Australia. He has published work on the politics of the networked architectural image in the journals *Philosophy of Photography*, the *Journal of Media Practice*, *E-Tropic* and *Leonardo Electronic Almanac* as well contributing to the volume *On the Verge of Photography: Imaging Beyond Representation* (2013).

Claes Caldenby is Professor Emeritus, Architecture and Civil Engineering, Architectural Theory and Methods, Chalmers University of Technology, Gothenburg. Claes Caldenby has an interest in the history of ideas of architecture but also in its wider social and cultural context. His ambition is that his research should be relevant and readable to practising architects as well as to a broader public, not only to the research community. His field of research has been mainly twentieth-century architecture, starting with studies of Soviet 1920s architecture and later on focusing on Swedish post-war architecture, including both building design and urban design.

Phil Cohen is Senior Visiting Research Fellow at the Institute of Advanced Studies UCL 2018–9, Professor Emeritus at the University of East London, and a Research Fellow at the Young Foundation. He is the founder/research director of the LivingMaps Network and the editor-in-chief of its online journal *Livingmaps Review*. His ethnographic fieldwork and publications over the last 35 years have dealt with issues of racism and multiculturalism, public safety and danger, the role of the cultural economy in urban regeneration, and popular participation in planning, with a focus on East London and more recently the impact of the London 2012 Olympics.

Jonathan Gardner is an archaeologist and heritage researcher based at Edinburgh College of Art. He has a strong interest in how the materials of the past influence the worlds of the present. He is currently investigating the creative potential of 'waste landscapes' – places literally constructed from trash, industrial by-products and rubble. The research that informs his contribution in this volume was undertaken during his PhD at the UCL Institute of Archaeology between 2012 and 2016. Previously, he worked as a commercial archaeologist on construction sites in London, including on the Stratford site of the 2012 Olympic and Paralympic Games.

Mattias Kärrholm is a Professor in Architectural Theory at Lund University, Sweden. His research deals with territoriality, public space, building types, space and culture, and everyday life. He has written the book *Retailising Space* (2012), and edited the books *Urban Squares* (2015) and, together with Andrea Mubi Brighenti, *Urban Walls* (2018).

Albena Yaneva is Professor of Architectural Theory at the University of Manchester, UK. She is the author of several books, including *Crafting History: Archiving and the quest for architectural legacy* (Cornell University Press, 2020) and *The New Architecture of Science: Learning from graphene* (World Scientific Publishing, 2020), co-authored with Sir Kostya S. Novoselov. Her work has been translated into nine different languages. Yaneva is the recipient of the RIBA President's Award for Outstanding Research.

Ola Wetterberg is Professor and Chair in Conservation of Built Heritage and Director of the Centre for Critical Heritage Studies, engaged in the development of cross disciplinary and cross professional education and research. Ola conducts research in religious heritage, urban development and history and theory of conservation.

Maria Nyström holds a PhD in Conservation from University of Gothenburg. Her thesis *Managing Ecclesiastical Heritage – Transformation of Discourses, Roles and Policy* in Sweden deals with the contemporary management of religious heritage. Her research interests include urban heritage and development, and professional roles and expertise within the heritage field.

Cynthia Myntti currently holds a visiting faculty position at New York University Abu Dhabi and is conducting life history research in Beirut. She received her PhD in anthropology from the LSE (1983), an MPH from

Johns Hopkins University (1986), and an M Arch from Yale (2004). From 2007–16 she served as the founding director of the AUB Neighborhood Initiative, which encourages research and outreach by faculty and students in the Ras Beirut area of the city.

Mona El Hallak is a Beirut-based architect and heritage preservation activist, and Director of the AUB Neighbourhood Initiative since 2017. She is a graduate of the American University of Beirut (AUB) and Syracuse University – Florence Program. She led several heritage preservation campaigns in Beirut and is a member of ICOMOS (International Council on Monuments and Sites), and APSAD (Association pour la Protection des Sites et Anciens Demeures au Liban). In 2013, she received the Ordre National du Mérite au grade de Chevalier from the President of the French Republic.

Pedro Fiori Arantes is an architect and associate professor in contemporary art, architecture and cities at the Federal University of São Paulo (Unifesp). From 2013–21, he was the Vice Provost for Planning, and coordinator of the Public Projects Office at Unifesp. During this time, he oversaw the implementation of Unifesp's Zona Leste Campus and its Instituto das Cidades. His most recent book, *The Rent of Form: Architecture and labor in the digital age*, was published by Minnesota University Press in 2019. His areas of interest include architecture, public policy, culture, cities and politics, and he is a long-standing member of Usina, a non-profit organisation that provides technical assistance to popular movements in housing and urban reform.

Acknowledgements

This book grew out of a series of workshops and activities organised by Curating the City urban heritage research cluster in the UCL/University of Gothenburg Centre for Critical Heritage Studies launched in 2016 with funding from the University of Gothenburg. We are indebted to this six-year programme, and the stimulating interaction with our colleagues between Gothenburg and London, for enabling us to develop our research interests, networks and outputs, including this volume. We would like to thank all the contributing authors for their patience and commitment to the process of realising this publication, particularly in view of the disruption to everyone's lives brought by the COVID-19 pandemic; and also Clemency Gibbs, for invaluable last-minute editorial assistance during the manuscript submission process.

We also acknowledge the support of:

UCL Urban Laboratory, which funded Clare Melhuish's original research and outputs on universities as actors in urban development (2013–6), among which parts and early versions of Chapter 1 of this volume were developed and presented in the report case studies in University-led Urban Regeneration (UCL Urban Laboratory, 2015), the conference 'Universities: space, place and community' organised by the Research Group on University History, Manchester University 13 September 2017, and the journal *National Identities* 22: 4 (2020), pp. 423–40 (special issue 'Architecture, Nation, Difference', ed. Samir Pandya; www.tandfonline.com); University of Gothenburg Department of Conservation and UCL Global Engagement Cities Partnerships Programme Rome hub, which co-funded workshops in Rome (Conflicting Heritage in the Timeline: Representations, Misrepresentations and Ways Forward, hosted by Roma Tre University) and London (Evaluating the impact of university development on urban areas, hosted by UCL Urban Laboratory), 2017; and Unifesp (Federal University of São Paulo) which co-funded with UCL Urban Laboratory a research visit by Clare Melhuish to São Paulo in November 2019.

Introduction
Clare Melhuish, Henric Benesch, Ingrid Martins Holmberg and Dean Sully

A transdisciplinary approach to critical heritage

The aim of this book is to expand the field of critical heritage studies in the urban domain, by examining the role of civic institutions – in this case urban universities – in the construction of urban heritage discourses, and in the influence those discourses have on urban planning decisions or how they become instrumentalised as mechanisms for urban change and regeneration (Pendlebury and Porfyriou, 2017). It proposes that universities engage in these processes in a number of ways: as institutional producers of academic *urban knowledge,* through research, teaching and curriculum design, which directly shapes heritage and planning expertise in development contexts; as producers of 'heritage practices' that are implemented in heritage management and development contexts in the urban realm; and as 'developers engaged in campus construction' projects that both reference heritage discourses as a mechanism for promoting support and approval by planners and the public, and capitalise on heritage assets as a resource.

The book presents multiple examples of universities engaging with participatory processes that position them as significant institutions in the development of urban heritage narratives, while also, through its collection of contributions by academics from different institutions, demonstrating the critical role that universities have as observers and critics of the processes in which they are implicated. The case studies included in the volume investigate how many universities, as mixed and heterogenous communities of interest dispersed across urban sites in diverse city contexts, are adopting strategies of engagement with local people and city neighbourhoods linked to conceptualisations of shared urban heritage, and ask how these are contributing to a re-shaping of ideas, narratives and lived experience of urban heritage that are distinctively linked to university input, as well as to the re-shaping of universities themselves and their own institutional heritage, embedded in evolving urban contexts. The contributions cross disciplinary and cultural boundaries, and bridge academia and practice.

The collection was born out of an Anglo-Swedish research collaboration, Curating the City, a research cluster within the UCL– University of Gothenburg Centre for Critical Heritage Studies, and a corresponding focus on two specific case study sites: University of Gothenburg's Näckrosen Campus (Gothenburg) and UCL East (London), both under development at the time the collaboration was initiated in 2016, with funding from the University of Gothenburg. This initial focus allowed us to examine questions of scale, vision, pedagogical intent and heritage context within a directly comparative framework through two transdisciplinary workshops hosted in London and Gothenburg, which drew together a wide range of speakers from different disciplinary backgrounds and practices, including most of the contributors to this volume. We subsequently expanded the scope of the investigation beyond the core cities, to include university developments in Lund, Rome, Beirut and São Paolo, in order to demonstrate the circulation of ideas and practices linking universities, heritage and urban policy and development within an extended geographical and socio-political framework.

Curating the City was formed to develop transdisciplinary, academic research perspectives on our future cities that, through engagement with participatory practice, can help to transform the regulated places that characterise our urban centres into spaces open to a multitude of co-existing initiatives, ranging from bottom-up to institutional, and allowing for a temporally rich and heterogeneous fabric of urban material and social life. Within this framing, it takes a view, counter to the prevailing status quo, of heritage conservation and management as innovation rather than as a regulatory constraint on the development of our cities, and calls for a rethinking and reconsideration of the inbuilt tension between innovative systems and restrictive institutions. It recognises creative activities as being key to challenging and un-making the ways in which certain places, such as heritage places, have become legitimised sites for permissible behaviour, and argues that a reformulation of established heritage practice can support the relevant and resilient development of historic cities. Furthermore, it recognises universities as laboratories of creative, critical and experimental thought and practice that depends on effective translation across academic boundaries into the world beyond, through partnerships, collaborations, participation and the formation of new generations of professionals, in order to make a contribution to such processes of resilient development, healthy change and urban wellbeing.

Led by researchers from UCL Urban Laboratory and Institute of Archaeology (Melhuish and Sully), and University of Gothenburg Academy of Design and Craft and Department of Conservation (Benesch and Holmberg), Curating the City's transdisciplinary research lens is a triangulation between the overlapping research fields of architecture, urban studies, conservation, craft, design, literature, cultural studies, planning and archaeology, supported by the educational platforms at University of Gothenburg and UCL. The idea of curating and the curatorial in relation to the urban condition as heritage has established the overall framework for the research agenda from 2016–21, enabling cross-cutting and experimental perspectives on urban heritage in a globalised, post-industrial and postcolonial world, ranging across a number themes – including a critical inquiry into the relationship between universities as actors in discourses around urban heritage, both as producers of knowledge and as civic institutions and developers in urban neighbourhoods. The transdisciplinary collaborative participatory process of assembly (selecting, organising and presenting) is presented as a valid response to uncertainty and defunct ideas of deterministic management of outcomes.

The university theme was shaped in part through an initial process of mapping the common interests of the cluster leaders, which became layered in the problems faced by universities today, resulting largely from the marketisation and internationalisation of higher education. At UCL, Clare Melhuish and Dean Sully were involved in curriculum and spatial planning dimensions of UCL East's development plans, and Melhuish had previously undertaken research on universities as actors in urban regeneration for UCL Urban Laboratory, which linked to the major development projects underway at UCL and University of Gothenburg. In addition, both University of Gothenburg researchers, Ingrid Martins Holmberg and Henric Benesch, had previously worked in the role of the university as knowledge broker in relation to the city. There was a shared interest in understanding universities not only as mechanisms within larger financial, political and regional systems, but as actual sites entangled in all sorts of temporalities, materialities and socialities. The consolidation of research interests within the cluster opened up the possibility of critical discussion detached from actual projects.

The university as urban heritage, or more so a critical take on university heritage beyond the somewhat canonical lament with regard to the decline of universities, emerged as an important but also somewhat forgotten question to pick up. The transdisciplinary setting of the centre offered a real possibility to address this question, not only from one, but multiple disciplinary and theoretical perspectives. In fact, this particular unruliness is something that we have always embraced. Moreover, it is something that we recognise as being not only welcome among many scholars and practitioners across our field who have grown weary of their institutional and disciplinary confinements, but also quite urgent since the question that we address does not sit within one discipline alone and demands a more holistic approach.

Many urban universities are engaged in processes of expanding and opening their physical and institutional borders to facilitate greater engagement with the cities in which they are situated, for a variety of reasons that are described in *University and community-led urban regeneration* (Melhuish, 2016) and chapter 1 of this volume (Melhuish). University cities in turn are home to increasingly mixed, multicultural populations striving to redefine identities and cultural heritage in the context of shifting physical locations. We set out to produce a volume from our transdisciplinary conversations and analyses that would provide insights, grounded in comparative case studies, into how local and global bodies of knowledge, embodied in different but interconnected university and urban communities and initiatives, intersect to shape new understandings of urban heritage as a framework for diverse urban lives. Structured by critical understandings of co-curated, decolonising heritage, it examines the local, diasporic and global dimensions of heritage-making through the lens of the university as urban institution and university development implicated in urban and social renewal, exploring how universities and citizens participate in a shared urban heritage.

The two workshops organised by Curating the City in 2016 and 2017 utilised the prism of 'curating' to assemble research and researchers to address the affordance of urban heritage as a resource at the crossroads of different lived experiences and expert knowledges (inhabitants, stakeholders, practices, subject-matters, audiences and/or conceptualisations). The research theme, 'Universities, heritage institutions and communities shaping postcolonial urban heritage narratives and lived experience for the future', was developed via two site-based, invitation-only workshops focused on the two university campus development initiatives led by UCL and University of Gothenburg, which have actively sought to engage with local people and neighbourhoods, and participate in a re-shaping of ideas, narratives and lived experience of urban heritage for the future. The workshops explored how universities, as mixed communities of interest dispersed across urban sites, were re-evaluating and re-constructing their institutional identities and heritage in the context of place-based spatial development, and at the same time, through their interventions, participating in shaping the heritage of local populations in contrasting cosmopolitan city contexts. They further considered the close parallels between universities and museums (such as London's Victoria and Albert East) as civic institutions engaged in the development of new urban imaginaries in postcolonial cities through collaborative processes of co-production with local populations.

The disciplinary structures of universities, and the way they are actualised, spatialised, socialised and economised (see chapters 3, 5, 6, 9 and 12), can be thought of as strategies of entanglement and/or disentanglement in relation to other sites and contexts of knowledge production that have profound implications for the urban contexts and histories in which they are embedded. This poses some fundamental questions – what kind of place is the university?; where is it?; and who is it for?; or perhaps, *where* is it for? – that emphasise the situated, multimodal and intersectional character of knowledge production, and engages with the university as host as well as neighbour and guest. It addresses the little-explored role of universities in urban neighbourhoods in co-constructing ideas and practices of heritage as a fusion of places/things, memories/narratives, local knowledge/global expertise.

Building understanding from comparative case studies

The chapters generated by the workshop discussions address a series of key and cross-cutting questions, starting in London and Gothenburg, and spreading out across Lund, Rome, Beirut and São Paulo, drawing in the work and insights of our international collaborators across those sites and conditions. How does the university define its own heritage, and how is that played out both within the site of the university institution itself, and within the wider urban location in which it is embedded; how are the traces of the city embedded, in turn, in the university? What does heritage mean to urban dwellers in adjacent neighbourhoods, and how is it defined in different city/university contexts and embodied in the layers of the city through time, and through processes of urban development? How can universities work in collaboration with different people at material sites to curate the urban environment and produce the cities – and universities – of the future, co-producing new urban imaginaries?

The Olympic Park, the site of UCL's campus project in Stratford, East London, is an exemplary starting-point for exploration of these questions, as an area notable for its rich mix of multiple ethnicities born out of successive waves of migration over time, and also its high levels of urban deprivation, which the Olympics regeneration legacy promised to address and resolve through the development of a new knowledge-based economy in which educational and cultural anchor institutions would have a key role to play as catalysts. The Olympic Park itself exemplifies the ongoing transformation of East London's industrial and manufacturing heritage into new urban forms and patterns of life through the promotion of the knowledge economy, including the opening of new museums, universities and cultural projects.

Melhuish, Sully, Gardner and Cohen (chapters 1, 2, 7 and 8) investigate how it changes UCL's identity and heritage as an institution to be located away from Bloomsbury, in central London, to the city's eastern edges, and critique how the industrial heritage of Stratford and its multi-ethnic communities is being re-shaped by the arrival of the university as part of an Olympics legacy regeneration driven by the knowledge economy. They engage with the physical terrain, archaeology and social history of the site to investigate the layers of the city's heritage and identity, the intentions and impacts of the university's presence as it materialises through new construction, and speculate creatively around the future heritage of East London and UCL.

The UCL East initiative, which plays an important part in this ongoing regeneration, or displacement, of existing cultural infrastructures and understandings of urban heritage, is compared and contrasted with the University of Gothenburg's Campus Näckrosen project on a key site in central Gothenburg – a city also known as 'Little London', with a dynamic mercantile history and a population also strongly shaped by flows of migration over time. Melhuish, Holmberg, Caldenby and Benesch (chapters 1, 3, 5 and 6) present aspects of University of Gothenburg's institutional and spatial development, through histories of disciplinary restructuring, curriculum development and premises acquisition, up to and including its new consolidation of arts and humanities at a prime historic city site much opposed by the city's bourgeoisie. They reveal the intimate interconnection between the university's evolving narrative of heritage and institutional identity and the physical and social landscape of this historic Scandinavian mercantile city, culminating in the challenge of creating and materialising new narratives of heritage and identity at the heart of the city capable of integrating the stories and aspirations of its most recent migrant newcomers.

The first section, 'Critical perspectives' (chapters 1–4) ranges across these sites, from different disciplinary positions, within the context of broader framing questions for the discussions staged by the book, providing pointers to themes that emerge in the case study-based chapters of section 2, parts 1 and 2. Firstly, Melhuish (Architectural and Urban Anthropology) provides a critical overview of the conditions that have catalysed university activity as development actors, responsible for building 'place-based' knowledge capital in cities from the USA, UK and internationally over several decades, and forwards an argument for recognition of their engagement in narratives of shared urban identity and heritage to support development in urban regeneration contexts strongly defined by heritage-orientated policies and practices. The chapter invites consideration of heritage as a tool to bring together 'centre' and 'periphery' in unequal cities across global north and south, understood both spatially and as a representation of elite and marginal interests in cities, represented by universities on the one hand and underprivileged peripheral neighbourhoods on the other, concluding with an introduction to the heritage framing of the UCL East and University of Gothenburg development schemes.

Sully (Archaeology/Conservation) leads the way into a more focused interrogation of the conceptualisation of heritage itself (chapter 2), critiquing the role of universities, as producers of cutting-edge heritage knowledge across academic boundaries, in shifting the focus of urban heritage preservation and management away from nostalgia and regret for the past, and towards a concern for the historic city as an affordance for creative reinterpretation, speculation and bringing-into-being of more inclusive and diverse urban futures. It illustrates this argument with an account of a UCL archaeology-led participatory heritage project on the edge of the Olympic Park, explicitly contrasted with the official UCL East narrative of the future city it will bring into being, that treats the historic traces of the area's industrial past as a 'wasteland' rather than as a site for creative and participatory reinterpretation. In so doing, it also highlights the 'multi-headed' character of university institutions in their relationships with urban heritage in the development context.

In chapter 3, Holmberg (Conservation) develops the thread of analysis more deeply within the university's disciplinary structures, positioning urban heritage practice directly in relationship to the role of universities as producers of a particular kind of knowledge – knowledge of 'urban historic buildings' – through curriculum development and transmission into professional policy and practice. This chapter reveals how shifts in institutional, disciplinary discourses connect and construct urban places and heritage sites in relation to each other. It focuses on the re-shaping of an old and under-valued central and derelict area of Gothenburg as a heritage asset, demonstrating the significance of the university for changes in historic perceptions of urban qualities and values.

Brown (Fine Art and Photography) concludes this section (chapter 4) by exploring a future-orientated framing of the ways in which universities engage with urban heritage through visual imagery. This chapter interrogates projections of future institutional and place-based identity through realistic architectural renderings as a tool to bring into being conceptualisations of the future city forwarded by its knowledge institutions. It underlines the global scope of these developments within an international circulation of ideas and capitalist values that transcends place and physical site, and yet at the same time privileges concepts of identity based in establishment and longevity, or heritage, in order to reinforce the claims of institutional stature that undergird universities' positioning as makers of the new urban knowledge economies in which our future heritage is being invested.

In the second section, 'Sites and historical contexts, past and future', part 1 focuses on University of Gothenburg and UCL East, providing detailed accounts of the development trajectories of the two universities in their urban contexts, in order to critically evaluate their entanglements with conceptualisations of shared and contested university/urban heritage in Gothenburg and London. Caldenby (chapter 5) offers a historian's perspective that tracks the physical development of the University of Gothenburg since its foundation, to understand the place of its material infrastructure in the city's urban heritage, and the implications of its development and growth as a university for the city's urban infrastructure and identity, culminating in the Campus Näckrosen project. It points to the importance of the 'material apparatus' of the university, as much as its cycles of knowledge production, in shaping universities, and in turn, underpinning the symbiosis that occurs between the university and the physical fabric and heritage of the city.

In chapter 6, Benesch (Design) focuses on the development of design education within the institutional and spatial development of the University of Gothenburg, arguing for the importance of understanding the particular heritages of institutions and disciplines and the sites in which they are located, in order to come to terms with what role they may or may not play in relation to the development of our cities, to the shaping of urban relations within a heritage continuum, and in turn, to the future of design education itself within the city. It approaches this discussion through the lens of 'orientations', as defined by Ahmed, which points to the relevance of such a 'microhistory' for understandings of the relationship between universities and heritage as a distributed phenomenon, both geographically and temporally.

Gardner takes an archaeological perspective (in chapter 7), which excavates the histories and sites of other urban mega-events and their legacies in London prior to the 2012 London Olympics, such as the Great Exhibition of 1851, and positions the development of UCL East in a historical trajectory of such events. The chapter argues that while they have both been seen as key signifiers of its modern urban development, re-shaping urban realities in localised areas and projecting future-orientated visions, they are also increasingly framed as part of London's heritage. Its archaeological investigation disrupts established narratives of the past through the detail of its inquiry into the university's ambitions to re-shape London's urban heritage in the Olympic context, working alongside other culture and education partners on the Queen Elizabeth Olympic Park (QEOP) site.

In chapter 8, Cohen (Anthropology) builds on these insights, drawing on ethnographic research and perspectives to question the heritage narrative mobilised by UCL East in the development of its presence in East London, and frames university intervention as a 'civilising mission' that pits traditional working-class heritage, based on manual labourism and systems of informal apprenticeship, against the future heritage of the new urban knowledge economy: globalised culture and creative industry, in a post-pandemic city. It examines the mechanisms that the new UCL campus and the V&A Museum are putting in place to work with local partners to generate new forms of cultural inheritance for those whose life trajectories will never involve higher education, and consider how these might shape new forms of participatory urban heritage discourse.

In part 2 of this section, our case studies range further afield to highlight the nature of these concerns as 'distributed phenomena' that extend beyond our Anglo-Swedish research axis, cultures of university development and understandings of urban heritage, to inform similar processes in distinct but networked cities and their university systems, embedded in different historical and geopolitical contexts: medieval and high-tech Lund in the south of post-welfare Sweden; classical and post-industrial Rome in southern, Mediterranean Europe; cosmopolitan and reconstructed Beirut on the eastern Mediterranean Levantine seaboard; and megacity São Paulo, strongly shaped by colonial European heritage and systemic legacies at its urban heart while the ever-expanding peripheries seed new urban futures. In each of these city contexts, and many others, patterns of university development can be identified that demonstrate the agency of university institutions in the re-shaping of urban morphologies and social infrastructures, through interventions in the thinking, positioning and practice of urban heritage, as these case studies reveal.

In chapter 9, Kärrholm and Yaneva (Architecture) highlight the impact that evolving typologies of university facility have had historically on the physical fabric and identity of cities through a focus on the agency of the University of Lund in the development of a whole new city district. It demonstrates the implications of unprecedented increases in building scale generated by developments in scientific research that is directly tied to urban economic development. The chapter charts the procurement of highly specialised new facilities for scientific research in megastructures that completely alter both the physical scale of the historic city and its distinctive medieval urban fabric and heritage, and the discourses of urban planning, politics and urban identity that have governed its development to date. It highlights how university spatial expansion ignites new processes of re-heritagisation and de-heritagisation where the value of both old and future heritage sites is being rewritten.

Conversely, in chapter 10, Wetterburg and Nyström (Conservation) describe the involvement of Roma Tre University as a principal player in the restructuring of Ostiense and Testaccio, the old industrial areas of Rome, through the transformative appropriation and re-occupation of existing buildings contained within the urban fabric and infrastructure. It analyses how a formal partnership with the municipal authority on the one hand, independent academic initiatives located within the disciplines of architecture, planning, art history and others, and participatory and activist engagement with local communities provided by students and graduates on the other, contributes to a re-evaluation of industrial heritage for a diversifying population shaped by migrant flows, in a city where heritage has historically been enshrined by the archaeological remains of classical civilisation.

In chapter 11, Myntti and El Hallak (Anthropology and Architecture) examine in further detail university agency in leading participatory approaches to urban heritage as a response to the consequences of 'urbicide' in a city destroyed by civil war. The chapter interrogates the ways in which city leaders' recognition of urban heritage as a source of comparative advantage can be monetised through regeneration, presenting the work of AUB (American University of Beirut) in Beirut, a historic institution located on the edge of the city centre, to counter the destructive effects on local populations and ways of life resulting from such processes. The chapter analyses AUB's investment in social, rather than spatial, outreach and engagement to rebuild its own connections with a historic neighbourhood and draw on its own heritage to protect and promote neighbourhood identity and wellbeing.

By way of comparison, both in scale and approach, Arantes (Architectural and Urban History and Design) describes (in chapter 12) the institutional origins and spatial vision for the new, fledgling, East Zone Campus of UNIFESP (São Paulo), which literally embodies the urban heritage of Paolo Freire's radical educational philosophy, invested in the identity and aspirations of São Paulo's Workers Movements. In this case study, the material and social history of the impoverished local area is invested in an East Zone Memory and Heritage Centre and Centre for Peripheral Studies dedicated to participatory research with its surrounding working-class communities. It presents an emerging vision of how a university can engage with and actively participate in re-imagining its urban context and future through engagement with a distinctive urban heritage defined from the bottom up.

Engaging with conceptual and empirical diversity

In history, the university has often been conceptualised as a city in itself, a zone where different values and different rules, even different legislation, applied. The historical autonomy of the university was, however, replaced – or at least marginalised – in the Early modern period, when universities were turned into important assets in nation building. Consequently, the separation between university and city was also gradually erased. The seamless interaction and integration between university and society, between 'town and gown', leading to a role for universities in post-industrial urban renewal, forms a starting point for this book. Exploring the questions posed for universities, cities and city dwellers, by the intersection of academic heritage and urban heritage across a range of urban contexts and scales – from London to Gothenburg, and thence to Lund, Rome, Beirut and São Paulo – and through a range of conceptual and methodological approaches, clearly privileges an acceptance of urban and institutional diversity and underlines an embrace of transdisciplinarity in our approach to this field of critical heritage research to us, as editors. Indeed, we acknowledge the inherent challenge posed by the ambition to turn a rich and productive series of workshops and conversations into a publication, driven not by a single, fundamental organising principle, but rather by a series of overlapping and entangled interests and concerns – relations rather than structures – that have given the book its particular shape and coherence.

Furthermore, the dramatic intervention of the COVID-19 pandemic in what was a work near completion at its start, has created a significant shift in urban and institutional landscapes and narratives of heritage and identity, past and future, which we as authors have barely had time to grapple with, plunging much that we know – or thought we knew – about universities and cities into doubt and deep uncertainty. We address this seismic change in a brief postscript reflecting on our recent experience of a year, 2020–1, spent largely working from our homes, in physical isolation from each other, and embedded in digital networks which have kept us apart but simultaneously facilitated surprising new connections to collaborators and conversations internationally. But what still remains solid and shared between the contributions to this volume is a will to navigate beyond the grand narratives of the university and the city, and to reflect upon more nuanced and situated perspectives emerging in the intersection of everyday experiences and various development processes within a university context, which are still ongoing. In this sense, the book might best be understood as a matrix – departing from the notion of critical heritage – that offers overlapping situated perspectives, not only from a geographical point of view, from which in particular the two original sites of the workshop series – London and Gothenburg – are revisited; but also from a disciplinary point of view, from which multiple sites are travelled, experienced and read through different disciplinary lenses.

References

Melhuish, C. (2016) *University and Community-led Urban Regeneration*. London: UCL Urban Laboratory.
Pendlebury, J. and Porfyriou, H. (2017) 'Heritage, urban regeneration and place-making'. *Journal of Urban Design*, 22 (4), 429–32.

I. Critical perspectives

1
The evolving role of universities in framing critical urban heritage discourse in regeneration contexts

Clare Melhuish

Introduction

This chapter provides a critical overview of the conditions that have catalysed university engagement in urban development, arguing that, in counterpoint to critics of university campus redevelopment and expansion in cities as a manifestation of neoliberal urban forces (Bose, 2015), many universities are engaging with an inclusive politics of development that is often framed by a discourse of shared urban heritage. This discourse, tying together institutional histories, place identity and participatory neighbourhood-based social initiatives, invites a critical interrogation of 'heritage' as a tool to shape a discursive and material space bringing together 'centre' (powerful, elite institutions) and 'periphery' (marginal, under-privileged neighbourhoods) in unequal postcolonial cities across global north and south. Such an interrogation moves beyond the limits of the 'heritage boom' of the late twentieth century – a system mobilised and dominated by elite actors, and critiqued by Winter for its 'conservatism, nostalgic politics, bogus histories and so forth' (Winter, 2012: 532) – to engage with difficult conversations about representation, cultural pluralism, disadvantage and inequality, embedded in the reproduction of the social and spatial fabric of cities from one generation to the next.

In their increasingly recognisable role as actors in urban development, urban universities are attributed a responsibility for building place-based 'knowledge capital' in metropolitan areas in need of 'regeneration' and attracting further financial investment into so-called 'innovation clusters' through hybrid private–public partnerships. This chapter will firstly explain how national heritage discourses have evolved and been instrumentalised to support urban regeneration and place-making initiatives, then turn to the shift in universities' institutional identities away from elite, nation-building heritage discourses towards more localised and democratised narratives of shared urban identity and heritage, which also spring from university development initiatives linked to the regeneration of urban landscapes. It will then explain the reasons for universities' increased involvement in urban regeneration, in its social and material dimensions, and illustrate how institutional and urban heritage narratives are combined and mobilised to support these initiatives in two specific cases: UCL East, and University of Gothenburg. It will finally propose that, as centres of critical urban research and practice, as well as significant urban landowners and developers, universities can – and should – develop critical heritage perspectives that actively engage in widening access to urban space and resources as well as education, and promote a 'right to the city' (Lefebvre, 1968) anchored in concepts of democratic representation and collective, plural urban identity.

Heritage and universities in nation-building and urban place-making

The Western conceptualisation of heritage, and the technical apparatus to support it, is rooted in the creation of secular nation states and narratives of national identity during the nineteenth century (Pendlebury, 2015; Winter, 2012), as is the modern university (Bender, 1998; Kwiek, 2000), rooted in the same period. Material and immaterial 'heritage' has served to represent and reinforce these narratives selectively, identifying particular stories and characteristics for inclusion or exclusion in the 'national story' (Hall, 1999), controlled by the governing classes: 'heritage sites are fundamental (albeit contested) resources for both established and emerging national elites' (Shore, 2002). Universities, resulting from 'a tacit deal made between power and knowledge' (Kwiek, 2000: 76) have naturally played an important role in the construction of those national heritage discourses, through their educative function and curricula, as well as their symbolic significance in the built environment, and in this they share much with museums and the national collections they hold (Hall, 1999).

The perceived value of national heritage and the need to put measures in place to preserve it was heightened dramatically after the destruction of cities, museums and historic sites wrought by the two world wars, and led to the creation of new policy frameworks to ensure this could be achieved. State power and public policy were mobilised to protect 'national heritage', through bodies like the National Buildings Record (1940, becoming National Monuments Record in 1963 and English Heritage Archive 2012) and English Heritage (1983) in the UK; while international conventions were also created to intervene in processes of cultural heritage at a universal level (Venice Charter for Conservation and Restoration of Monuments and Sites, and creation of ICOMOS, 1964; UNESCO World Heritage Convention for the Protection of World Cultural and Natural Heritage, 1972; European Architectural Heritage Year, 1975). Government cultural policy assumed responsibility for establishing and maintaining consensus in respect of the representation of national identity, and town planning policy (certainly in the UK) became increasingly focused on issues around conservation and preservation of the historic built landscape over subsequent decades: the 'heritage boom' referenced by Winter (2012). Indeed, 'by the 1990s, conservation had become a significant objective embedded at the heart of the land-use planning system, with a near-unchallenged consensus that the protection of the historic environment was a fundamental purpose of planning policy' (Pendlebury, 2015: 430).

For several decades previously, the heritage conservation lobby, including the UK's amenity societies and campaigning organisations such as Save Britain's Heritage, had pitted itself against urban development and renewal programmes, to save historic buildings and monuments in the name of national heritage. Over time, however, property developers, urban designers and architects have come to embrace heritage discourses to promote narratives of historic continuity, place-based regeneration (or place-making), and urban branding, through redevelopment. Heritage has become part of the 'experience economy' (Klingmann, 2007; Böhme 2003), and a feature of the new landscapes of leisure and consumption (Smith, 2002) emerging through processes of city centre (downtown) redevelopment around the world (Melhuish, Degen and Rose, 2016), shaped by the international circulation and assemblage of urban policy and expertise from one site to another (McCann, Ward and Roy, 2013). Under Conservative, Labour and coalition governmental regimes in the UK, heritage has notably been instrumentalised beyond historic national identity building discourses, to facilitate a range of policy purposes, particularly urban regeneration strategies aimed at both producing profit from property and promoting social inclusion and citizenship (Pendlebury, 2015: 433-6), particularly in troubled inner-city areas during the New Labour years (Lees and Melhuish, 2013).

The increased public emphasis on the significance of heritage in the urban context is one in which universities are also implicated. In many cases, universities represent historic institutions in the urban landscape that occupy and are identified with architecturally and historically significant buildings protected from significant modification or destruction by national legislation and local planning frameworks. As such, university buildings and university quarters are frequently (though not always) recognised as desirable heritage features, which increase the attractiveness of historic urban centres and enhance the image of a city. Such buildings often typify the focus of the policy and legal frameworks that comprise the Authorised Heritage Discourse (AHD) defined and critiqued by Laurajane Smith in 2006 as a self-referential heritage narrative that 'privileges monumentality and grand scale, innate artefact/site significance tied to time depth, scientific/aesthetic expert judgement, social consensus and nation building' (Smith, 2006: 11; cited by Pendlebury, 2015: 431). Universities and their buildings generally privilege a historic elite perspective on representations of national heritage, 'belonging' and cultural homogeneity, defined by highly educated 'cultural insiders' (Shore and Nugent, 2002; Gilroy, 1993), and excluding the contribution to nation-building and evolving, plural national identities made by working-class and immigrant (usually urban) communities (Hall, 1999; Gilroy, 1993) which historically have not had access to the university system of higher education. Nevertheless, the contribution they make as monuments within the material and symbolic infrastructure of historic civic architecture in city centres is publicly endorsed for its representation of a collective urban – as well as national – heritage, through the heritage policy framework implemented at local metropolitan level.

The social, material and symbolic significance of universities in urban contexts has been discussed by Bender, who describes the shift that has occurred from universities' historic Enlightenment alliance with the nation and national identity, to a closer engagement with the city and urban identities that characterised universities in the medieval period: 'The modern academic disciplines were born in alliance with the rising nation state, not the city ... for its first century the modern university and nation have been more closely tied than the university and the city' (Bender, 1998: 24). As such, universities were also often closely implicated in empire-building and colonising initiatives, providing training grounds for the public service cadres who would build and run the state in far-flung overseas territories, as well as the intellectual structures to support and legitimise those interventions. In the new postcolonial independent states, universities again played a significant role in forming, building and representing national identities and common heritage.

In more recent years, urban universities in the former imperial nation states have increasingly moved away from an identification with the nation, and towards a more globalised identity on the one hand, coupled with an urban and metropolitan affiliation on the other: 'A place for the unexpected, integrated into the city structure', as the University of Gothenburg describes its new Project Näckrosen campus development – where 'people from different places and with different backgrounds will meet and work together.'[1] In another example, the UCL 2034 vision embodies this shift with its re-branding of UCL as 'London's Global University', jumping from the urban to the global with no reference to the nation in between. New York's major universities, such as Columbia and New York University, also promote a strong focus on the role of the university in the city's economic strategy: the 'NYU in NYC' (NYU Framework 2031) brand sets out to position the institution as a globally networked university shaping the evolution of the city as an 'ideas capital' and hub of the knowledge economy. Urban universities in the younger postcolonial nation states of the global south, east and west are also focusing increasingly on internationalisation, 'world-class' status and contribution to global development on the one hand, while promoting place-based community outreach and engagement with a variety of urban stakeholders on the other, including direct participation in urban development initiatives – for example, UTech Jamaica's Papine University Town initiative[2], and Unifesp's East Zone campus programme in São Paulo[3].

Indeed, Bender explicitly compares the sociology of the university to that of the city (Bender, 1998). He argues that one of the most distinctive features of major university institutions is the way in which they ground complex, transnational, cosmopolitan communities and identities in local place – much like 'contemporary immigrant neighborhoods where residents live in local urban neighborhoods and diasporic networks' (Bender, 2002: 162). He argues that 'teachers and students in a university, much like the new metropolitans, live at once in the past and the present, in a local place and a trans-local culture of international scholarship. They must constantly bring together in fruitful ways the past and present, the local and the trans-local' (Bender, 2002: 162–3). This perspective provides a starting-point from which to consider the impact of the university intervention, materialised in built form and space, on the wider spatial and social landscape of big cosmopolitan cities, made up of many diverse, mobile, cultural and ethnic communities; and, from there, to interrogate how critical understandings of shared heritage can be engaged by universities to address issues of under-representation and inequality in urban regeneration projects in which they have a role as actors.

Universities as urban developers in the globalised neoliberal city

In addition to their primary function of delivering higher education, universities around the world are becoming catalysts for city-based economic growth, particularly in relation to the knowledge economy: 'The urban location and centrality of universities to the nature and well-being of cities means that cities and countries can be expected to turn to their universities as part of strategies to respond to the new challenges and opportunities that global economic competition poses for urban regions' (Wiewel, Wim and Perry, 2008: 304; see also Perry and Wiewel, 2005). Universities are increasingly receptive to these expectations, partly because they are also subject to the pressures of an aggressive, globalising, neoliberal higher education regime, linked to public funding cuts and a globalised marketised economy driven by metropolitan hubs of investment, development and profit (Addie, Keil and Olds, 2015). Indeed, Harvey points out that universities have also had a responsibility for promoting neoliberal models globally:

> the business schools that arose in prestigious universities such as Stanford and Harvard, generously funded by corporations and foundations, became centres of neoliberal orthodoxy from the very moment they opened … by 1990 or so most economics departments in the major research universities as well as the business schools were dominated by neoliberal modes of thought. … The US research universities were and are training grounds for many foreigners who take what they learn back to their countries of origin as well as into international institutions such as the IMF, the World Bank, and the UN. (Harvey, 2005: 54)

Today, universities in the USA, Europe and other geopolitical regions around the world, influenced by a global circulation of higher education and urban policy and practice, are increasingly expected by governments, city authorities and other urban actors to perform as drivers of this competitive, globalised, city-based knowledge economy, from which national public funding streams are steadily being withdrawn. Not only must they compete among each other for the best staff, students and revenue streams, they must also demonstrate localised impact in urban regeneration within a global network of cities, particularly through science and technology innovation and translation, medical research and partnerships, and job creation. These processes have been well-documented by economic geographers (for example, Cochrane, 2013, 2015). McCann, Ward and Roy further underline the international and translocal context of these practices 'of actors who assemble policies from close by and elsewhere (Allen and Cochrane, 2007) ... engaging with various policy networks and communities, stretched across the globe, in order to learn, teach, and share knowledge about best practice models' (McCann, Ward and Roy, 2013: 583). As referenced in the previous section, urban heritage policies and practices are themselves part of this global circulation and assemblage of global urban models in which universities are implicated as urban actors.

Driven by competition (for reputation, staff and students) in an international marketplace, universities engage in intense scrutiny of what their peers are doing, in order to produce locally embedded variants of global higher education models. These assume physical and spatial form within the parameters of distinct, but increasingly similar, city planning and urban regeneration contexts. Cochrane points to 'the surprising alignment of regional/local priorities and university priorities, despite different drivers' (Cochrane, 2015) and to the circulation of a shared language and imagery in the promotion of these common interests. Alan Harding has also emphasised the role of universities as anchor institutions in the transition from an industrial to a knowledge economy, increasingly operating in collaboration with local authorities within a framework of 'growth coalitions and urban regimes' such as Local Enterprise Partnerships. As he says, they are in this sense beginning to catch up with American institutions, which have been players in development strategies for a long time, positioned as businesses, deliverers of services and attractors for new investment (Harding, Scott, Laske and Burthscher, 2007; Harding, 2013) – as well as drivers of urban renewal.

Goddard and Vallance have explored the social and civic implications of this shift, pinpointing the question 'is the university *in* the city or *part of* the city? ... we make the case for the civic university working with others in the leadership of the city in order to ensure that its universities are both globally competitive and locally engaged' (Goddard and Vallance, 2011:1). Indeed, they argue that 'all publicly-funded universities in the UK have a civic duty to engage with wider society on the local, national and global scales, and to do so in a manner which links the social to the economic spheres' (Goddard, 2009:4), building on established concepts of public service or civic mission, particularly as developed in US universities from the late nineteenth century (Bromley, 2006). Responding to this context, many universities are engaging in facilities, expansion, spatial development and commercial research translation initiatives, which also encompass community outreach and widening participation programmes. Addie explains that 'as universities pursue diverse modes of organizational restructuring and roll out highly variegated spatial and institutional strategies they have a tremendous capacity to catalyze local economic growth and inform broader debates on responsive, adaptive, and sustainable urbanism through their research, teaching and outreach. For their part, policy makers (from the local to supranational) have embraced calls for universities to take on greater responsibility for their urban environments' (Addie, 2018). Thus, we increasingly see universities becoming implicated in hybrid, public–private models of urban development as 'anchor institutions' (Maurasse, 2007; Work Foundation, 2010) 'place-makers' and 'planning animateurs' (Benneworth and Hospers, 2007), both through their own initiatives (for example, UCL in the Olympic Park in East London) and at the invitation of commercial developers (as in the case of University of the Arts in London at Kings Cross and Elephant and Castle).

However, as higher education institutions increase their capital investment in urban campuses and partnerships, and correspondingly expand their influence on the shape of urban landscapes, there is a surprising lack of documentation or analysis of university spatial development projects (van Heur, 2010), or of their effects on neighbouring communities. University-led urban transformations are embedded in larger processes of global, capital-led urbanisation, exemplified by the landscapes of consumption, production, leisure and capital accumulation in city centres (Smith, 2002; Swyngedouw, Moulaert and Rodriguez, 2002). More often than not, these large-scale urban developments result in the displacement of weaker and more vulnerable urban communities, especially ethnic minorities, and the establishment of elite, often securitised enclaves (Bridge, 2006; Caldeira, 2000). But, as centres of critical thinking, teaching and research, universities are not conventional developers and clients, nor are they perceived as such in the public domain.

Increasingly, we see higher education institutions promoting a rhetoric of urban regeneration, community participation and inclusion (Bromley, 2006), which counters the neoliberal orthodoxies of the market-driven city, and shifts the focus from an urban-/civic-scale to neighbourhood-scale of engagement. Access to a broad range of funding sources and strong credit profiles further empower universities to promote such agendas, and to model alternative ideas about a more progressive and responsive urbanism and architectural practice in the postcolonial, cosmopolitan context. A significant number of institutions internationally are critically re-evaluating their relationship with the cities and neighbourhoods in which they are located, drawing on a development rhetoric of permeability, inclusivity and opportunity, which acknowledges conditions of heightened mobility and intercultural contact – but also rising levels of inequality – in contemporary urban life, and the need for universities to address these problems (Melhuish, 2015; Choueiri and Myntti, 2012; Rodin, 2007; Maurasse, 2001). The next section will examine how universities are evolving institutionally and spatially in the context of complex, pluralist, postcolonial urban settings, and consider the implications for their relationship with national heritage discourses.

Universities and the spatial democratisation of urban heritage

While universities, especially older institutions, are characteristically located in the civic and symbolic, heritage-rich, historic centres of cities, many are expanding their estates on cheaper land situated in the former industrial fringes of those areas and beyond, as anchors for regeneration in, for example, London's 'special opportunity' areas, or New York's West Harlem district, site of Columbia University's new Manhattanville campus. The 'race for space' in land-scarce city centres is the key driver for these moves, but the geographical shift to 'off-centre', peripheral areas of the city has also gone hand-in-hand with an increasing emphasis on widening access to higher education, particularly to students from local working-class and immigrant backgrounds and mature students with families, alongside other forms of university outreach aimed at under-privileged, marginalised and ethnically diverse social groups, including the provision of new accessible spaces and services on university campus sites.

The idea that universities can challenge the unequal distribution of cultural, social and financial capital that defines the divided city, both through their own institutional re-structuring to accommodate widening participation, and through the modelling of inclusive urban and public spaces, such as parks, community centres, life-learning and healthcare facilities, constitutes a shift away from historic models of the university as a project of elite universal knowledge production, represented by utopian and exclusionary architectural projects such as the University of Virginia. Here, Jefferson's Academical Village, dominated by the Rotunda symbolising knowledge and hierarchy, was described as 'incomparably the most ambitious and monumental architectural project ... conceived in this century' by the *New York Times* in 1895. Now a UNESCO World Heritage site, and founded by the third President of the newly created USA, it is a prime example of university heritage embedded in a history of national ideology, which nurtured an elite governing class. Such ideals underwent a significant change with the creation of land-grant universities in the USA in the mid- to late-nineteenth century, to teach practical skills in agriculture, engineering and science, and the 'red brick' or civic universities founded in the major manufacturing cities of the UK during the same period to foster expertise for local industry, which in both cases shifted the emphasis of the universities' mission to a more localised context, albeit within the wider framing of national development. With the massification of higher education from the 1960s onwards, following the Robbins Report (1963) in the UK, and the progressive opening up of the university system to students across the class divide, universities that formerly provided a training ground for the governing classes, and contributed to the construction of exclusive narratives of national identity, have undergone a significant process of democratisation that is today reflected in the focus on widening participation and civic mission, with implications for the diversification of national heritage discourses.

This process is further reflected in the emerging typologies and character of university approaches to spatial expansion away from segregated, introverted campus models of the past, and towards new hybrid forms of development, often embedded in complex urban contexts, with a focus on translation of knowledge into the real world and 'impact', rather than universal principles. Alternative typologies are being evoked to describe this approach to university integration in the urban context that depends on building relationships among different communities and urban stakeholders, and blurs the boundaries between formal and informal development. In the UK, for example, the terms 'non-campus campus' (Durham Queen's Campus), 'living laboratory' (Newcastle University at Science Central), 'urban extension' (Cambridge University), 'communiversity' (Sheffield University) and 'collaboratory' (Bristol

University) have entered circulation via university vision statements, development plans and outreach initiatives, to indicate an evolution of institutional identity and modus operandi away from the so-called 'ivory tower' model of the past (Melhuish, 2015), which we so often see enshrined as national heritage.

It is interesting to consider this evolution of the university as an aspect of what Nalbantoglu and Wong (1997) have defined as 'postcolonial practice' – being one which intervenes in and disrupts models of architecture and urbanism 'that parade under a universalist guise and either exclude or repress different spatialities of often disadvantaged ethnicities, communities or people'. These include the imposing, classically-inspired civic monuments, including historic government, university and museum buildings of European, American, and colonial cities, which constitute a significant part of the identified national heritage and 'story' of different countries, referencing Greco-Roman roots, and suppressing diverse identities. Nalbantoglu and Wong foreground vernacular and informal types of architectural production at the margins of formalised urban spaces as having an important role in the disruptive, postcolonialising process, modelling alternative ideas about urban space, inclusivity and diverse identities in relation to the centres of power. By example (and drawing to the centre urban theory 'from the periphery'), Letchimy analysed the self-built shanty towns (bidonvilles) encircling the colonial French-built city centre of Fort-de-France, Martinique, as 'laboratories of the urban mangrove' working in symbiotic relation with the formal city. He proposed that this symbiosis could form the basis of a progressive and responsive Caribbean contemporary urbanism, embedded in a new culture of democracy and ingenious approach to development, which would also offer a universally-applicable model of shared, postcolonial urbanity (Letchimy, 2011; Melhuish, 2017).

Lefebvre explicitly critiqued the (French) university as a monumental and oppressive institution, colonising space around it (Lefebvre, 1968); but he also explored its emancipatory potential as site of social struggle. As part of Ambasz's 'Universitas Project' of 1966, convened to examine how universities could become more responsive to the urban environment and affairs, Lefebvre identified the problem with the production of space under capitalism as being the necessity for 'comparability', as a basis for its commercial valuation and exchange across a global scale, resulting in a 'homogenization of fragments of commercialised space' (Ambasz, 1966: 466–7) across the world. Universities are entrenched in this game of commercial comparison and evaluation more than ever before – both institutional and spatial. But many are also recognising the necessity of representing and building distinctive, grounded visions of themselves in relation to their urban neighbours, embedded in local situations, embodied in less rigid, more permeable forms of spatial development, and mediated by architects and communities (Melhuish, 2015).

This suggests a shift towards a more embedded, processual and fluid conceptualisation of institutional and architectural identity, which hints at the 'concept of the possible' located by Holston (1996) in 'spaces of insurgent citizenship', defined by informal practices of architecture, urbanism and 'bricolage' (as, for example, in the bidonvilles of Fort-de-France, cited above). Holston clarifies the distinction between these kinds of spaces and 'the fundamentally different idea of alternative futures inherent in modernist planning and architectural doctrine'. While the first are fluid, adaptable and formative of an open and participatory concept of citizenship based on 'right to the city', rather than national identity, the latter are fixed, closed and implemented by the nation state, through its armies of technicians and engineers (as by contrast France's Opération Million in 1945). As Holston explains, 'both express the basic paradigm of modernity which emphasises that alternative futures are indeed possible. But the insurgent and the modernist are competing expressions, which I will distinguish as ethnographic and utopian, respectively' (Holston, 1996: 54).

I suggest that we can identify an 'ethnographic', rather than 'utopian', approach to space and its occupation driving an emerging inclusive – as opposed to monolithic – vision of university identity defined in relation to urban neighbours, and its materialisation through built and lived space in the postcolonial context, which is mobilised by shared discourses of urban heritage working in counterpoint to those of national identity, homogeneity and insiderism. While the first is people-centred, observant of existing practices of everyday life in urban settings, responsive to detail and open-ended, the second is imposed as an ideal, universal, technical and finished schema, regardless of physical or social context. Embracing the reality of the postcolonial city as a 'laboratory of the urban mangrove' involves challenging the technocratic control of urban space and creating space for 'ingenious development' (Letchimy, 2011) that resists the temptation to cast universities as the crucible for cultural, and national, formation. It recognises that spatial dynamics stabilise social problems, leading to their reproduction (Dikeç, 2001), while re-framing notions of citizenship as a 'cosmopolitan project'– 'the world as both a single place and one comprised of multiple differences'

(Binnie, Holloway, Millington and Young, 2006: 5) – through inclusive spatial development capable of accommodating both formal and informal practices. The next section, then, considers the way in which two universities are using heritage discourse as a tool to promote a vision of university and urban identity that might be framed as ethnographic and inclusive in the context of the charged spatial politics of the postcolonial city.

Urban heritage discourse as a tool in university development: University of Gothenburg and UCL East

As this chapter has asserted, universities have assumed an increasingly important role in the control and production of urban space, linked to the development of hybrid (public/private) models of urban development and funding structures, and become deeply implicated in the contemporary politics of urban space and spatial justice, often to their detriment. Bose, for example, with reference to Ohio State University in the USA, draws critical attention to 'universities as important actants in the neoliberal city, specifically through their engagement of development activities … [which] typically means destruction of existing living and workplaces'. She attributes their behaviour as 'entrepreneurial subjects', after Foucault, to the 'pressures coming out of the accumulation process' (Bose, 2015: 2617). In a wider context, Jaffe (2013) has also highlighted the implications of the diversification of multiple governmental actors (among which we can include universities and other public institutions) sharing control of urban space, for the spatial politics of urban inequality and understandings of citizenship under neoliberalism.

    The distinctive feature of university development that seems to set it apart from typical accumulative forms of corporate or commercial property development is an underpinning narrative of identity and purpose that extends beyond the maths around student numbers and income from teaching and research, and varies from institution to institution – shaped by its own founding charter and heritage, and increasingly embedded in the wider discourse of local urban place-making in which universities are both positioning themselves and being positioned by external forces. The development and communication of this narrative in both verbal and visual form performs a vital function, not simply in representing or projecting a future identity for the university, but also in building social relationships and alliances among the different actors implicated in it and negotiating dissent within the free-thinking academic community. Thus, in order to mobilise support both internally and externally for their spatial and material expansion projects in the city, universities are drawing on historical narratives of institutional and urban heritage, rather than national identity or discourses of nation-building.

This reflects shifts in the conceptualisation of shared heritage at a grander scale. Stuart Hall indicates two key factors at work in the UK in changing received understandings of 'the National Heritage' as the material embodiment of 'a shared national identity ... deeply embedded in specific "ethnic" or cultural meanings ... a collective social memory'. They are, firstly, 'the democratisation process', and secondly, 'the critique of the Enlightenment ideal of dispassionate universal knowledge ... coupled with a rising cultural relativism which is part of the growing de-centring of the West and western-oriented or Eurocentric grand-narratives' (Hall, 1999). Both of these have had a significant influence on the ways in which universities frame their institutional identities and missions, and their relationships with other communities in postcolonial, multi-ethnic cities with whom they seek to engage in the construction of a shared urban heritage.

Here, I will focus on two contrasting case studies for critical analysis of the ways in which notions of participation and engagement, permeability, inclusivity, urban encounter and opportunity are being referenced by universities as part of a discourse of shared urban and cosmopolitan heritage, side-stepping national identity, in order to build support and alliances among local and citywide stakeholders for their development projects in the city, and to mediate the spatial politics of these interventions. I will suggest that these processes contribute to the creation of a discursive and material space in which to challenge the inequalities and spatial injustices of the postcolonial city, and position the university as agent of place-based inclusive urbanism, drawing together diverse communities.

UCL East in London and University of Gothenburg's Project Näckrosen, both due to open in 2022, are two significant university development projects of different scales, which nevertheless exhibit a number of relevant comparable features. Both are sited at locations of historic significance in their respective cities' histories – the Olympic Park in Stratford, East London, home of the London 2012 Olympic Games (notwithstanding the national significance of the event) and currently undergoing redevelopment as part of the Olympic legacy scheme for the regeneration of the area; and the site of the Gothenburg Exposition of 1923, which was subsequently redeveloped as the Liseberg Amusement Park at Korsvägen, and the city's cultural centre – including the art museum, library and concert hall at Götaplatsen and, later, several university buildings including the publicly-accessible university library behind it at Näckrosen. Both projects have aroused considerable controversy, both within the university and in the local neighbourhoods in which they will be built. They have also implicated the universities in new kinds of engagements with the relevant urban planning authorities, design consultants, community organisations and their own student and faculty bodies, which have brought city-centred discourses of heritage, identity and belonging to the fore.

University visions of development comprise two dimensions: the institutional – embracing the structure and organisation of the university as an educational institution – and the physical – the university as a particular kind of place where research and teaching are carried out. But often there is a disjunction between the two. Academics and administrators may not consciously visualise universities as physical places, but rather as a complex organisation of teaching and research programmes that need to be accommodated. Estates teams may only see universities as spatial and operational entities that pose particular issues around maintenance and running costs. Communication between the two is often fraught with tensions, and further complicates the process of communication between the university as a unified entity with the heterogeneous communities outside it which have an interest in its plans. Thus, when spatial development projects come onto the horizon, masterplanners, architects and engagement consultants are often brought in to develop a three-way mediation process. Then, that vision needs to be communicated to wider audiences beyond the university, to build support for the project, through both statutory consultation exercises and other types of research and outreach initiatives shaped by that ambition. At this stage, concepts of shared, place-based heritage and participation are often evoked to mediate the spatial politics in which universities are entangled as powerful and influential institutions.

Both UCL and University of Gothenburg have framed their vision for new development around the need for innovation, openness, integration with city neighbours, and a regeneration of urban culture in two cities that are home to significant ethnic minority communities. London's multi-ethnic population is well-established, since mass migration began in the postcolonial period, but tends to be concentrated in the city's poorer neighbourhoods and is disproportionately affected by social and spatial inequalities. Gothenburg has been a host city for incoming migrants and refugees, particularly from Eastern Europe, the Middle East and Africa, since the 1990s, with a dramatic increase in recent years that

Figure 1.1 Aerial view of Olympic Park from south, with UCL East site lying between the Olympic Stadium and Aquatics Centre on South Lawn. Courtesy of UCL East

has led to heightened political tensions around issues of integration, segregation and conflict in the city's suburbs. In both of these university case studies, there is an underlying sub-text around widening access and the role or responsibility of the university in 'making space' for diverse communities of different ethnic and cultural heritage in a common urban context.

The underlying driver for expansion and redevelopment in UCL's case was a lack of space in Central London (at its historic Bloomsbury site), and a desire to promote more effective cross-disciplinary collaboration supported by larger, more flexible facilities. The university's Estates team led on the project from the start, and selected the Olympic Park site from a number of sites around London primarily because of its connectivity to transport infrastructure via the Stratford local and international hub (see Figure 1.1), and because of the offer of a significant government subsidy to develop the site as part of the Olympic legacy regeneration scheme (see Gardner and Cohen, this volume).

For the University of Gothenburg, the primary rationale for the project to build a new Faculty of the Arts and Humanities and a library, along with the conversion of the adjacent county court building into university facilities, was the desire to consolidate university facilities at one site and foster better cooperation between departments, creating a new 'knowledge park for humanities and arts' linking Götaplatsen (culture district) and Korsvägen (events district) in the city centre (see Caldenby and Benesch, this volume).

UCL has worked in partnership with the London Legacy Development Corporation to develop its new site, called UCL East, to signpost not only its geographical location but also its areas of academic focus – Experiment, Arts, Society and Technology (EAST) – and its 'commitment to creating a vibrant, diverse and accessible campus in, of and for East London … [which is] open and highly collaborative with external organisations' (UCL East Vision[4]).

University of Gothenburg has been working with Akademika Hus (a government property subsidiary that owns and manages university buildings nationally) and the City of Gothenburg to create a 'cornerstone of the University', which will also be part of a general development process creating 'a new attraction for Gothenburg as a city of culture and knowledge' (Vision 2020), celebrating its four hundredth anniversary.

Both universities have developed vision statements and strategies over the last five years that have involved complex negotiations and conversations with many different stakeholders within and outside the institutions, and generated a range of narrative and visual imageries to

Figure 1.2 View of existing Faculty of Humanities and Library (to left of image), University of Gothenburg, with Näckrosen construction site and hoarding to right. Photo: C. Melhuish, 2017

support their respective projects. But these processes have also generated controversy, opposition and some uncomfortable self-interrogation as a result of the real urban encounters and spatial politics implicated in development on the ground, in two very different social contexts: in Gothenburg, an elite bourgeois neighbourhood around an exclusive city centre park; in London, a socially-deprived, multi-ethnic peripheral area of blighted opportunity, desperately in need of employment and affordable housing. In response, both universities have used heritage discourses to link their own institutional ambitions to wider urban and community interests around their particular sites – the Olympic Park, and the Gothenburg Exposition site.

The Gothenburg Exposition was a 'mega event' of its time, produced to mark the city's three hundredth anniversary and showcase its strengths as an industrial and mercantile centre. It was dominated by the vertical centrepiece of the Memorial Hall, which stood on an elevated site at the end of the extended axis formed by the Avenue (Avenyn) linking to the historical centre of the city. This building had no function other than to hold a book in which visitors to the expo signed their names. It was

Figure 1.3 Site hoarding showing visualisation of new four-storey faculty building and formal façade, Näckrosen development, University of Gothenburg. Photo: C. Melhuish, 2017

demolished after the event. It was on this site that the horizontal redbrick buildings of the university's Arts and Humanities Faculty and adjacent library were constructed in the 1960s (see Figure 1.2).

Under the current plans, these buildings will be replaced with modern, vertically-oriented facilities, linked to a major new transport interchange at Korsvägen to the east, and a commercial redevelopment of the whole Avenyn axis (by a private developer) running north to the historic city centre. The university proposals evoke a rediscovery of the expo area, symbolised by the new four-storey faculty building and its formal pillared façade (see Figure 1.3). It has been described by a member of the university project team as 'a sort of neurotic repetition of the Gothenburg Exhibition in 1923; the same rhetoric is employed in order that we are granted permission ... That we will renew the city with the help of art and humanities and industry: it's exactly the same discourse'[5].

The university's own heritage is encapsulated in its institutional motto: 'to innovate tradition and traditionalise innovation' (*tradita innovare innovata tradere*). It grew out of the need to meet the demands of the city's emerging professional life, in contrast to the traditional elite universities of Lund and Stockholm. Its leaders were prominent people in business, and it was informed by the ideals of a modern university engaged with society. Its physical infrastructure is widely distributed across the city centre, but institutionally it is characterised by a lack of cooperation between those departments scattered throughout the urban fabric, leading to the current concern for consolidation. The preliminary architectural visualisations for the Project Näckrosen site showed a 'closed-off campus area', made up of 'heavy buildings in a park landscape' (quoting a project team member). The suggested loss of existing green space created a lot of tension with the small population of wealthy, well-educated citizens who live around the area, some of whom had studied conservation. They constructed an argument around the heritage value of the county court building in order to defend against the intrusion of the University on the park, framed as a space of contested heritage in which the court building became the focus of a 'fight about the past'. Meanwhile, left-leaning academics also opposed the project on the basis that the university should be planning to locate any expansion 'outside the city centre, in precarious areas … in a segregated Gothenburg suburb' – comparable to East London.

As Project Director, Johan Oberg worked to build a sense of collective interest around the project 'in the name of a better shared future for all interested parties' and as a 'negotiated University agenda'. This was achieved by getting rid of the early visualisations and organising a series of seminars, in which the 'strong administrative real estate agenda could be articulated with internal academic critique', and then communicated to different groups of resistance in the area with a focus on the symbolic value of the Exposition site in the city's history, re-presented in the university's development plans. This involved a careful framing of the development itself as a 'pure academic project', keeping its distance from city planning politics and any perceived complicity with the transformation of the traditional working-class city into 'a new globalised entity dominated by intellectual production', which would not fit with the idea of a common mercantile urban heritage. At the same time, it developed a focus around the planning of the new library to engage with heritage issues around books and digitisation, and the problems posed by 'migrants in need of an intellectual shelter in the big city', a key issue in relation to Gothenburg's status as the most segregated city in Sweden.

Like Näckrosen, the Olympic Park has emerged as a highly contested heritage space both since and pre-dating the London 2012 Olympic Games, in which UCL's intervention has brought existing tensions with poor, multi-ethnic local communities in the surrounding boroughs to the fore. As a significant site in London's industrial history, which supported around 600 businesses and 1,000 residents before they were evicted to make way for the games, it became a tabula rasa for the construction of new narratives of sporting excellence and national identity in the run-up to 2012. Now the park is infused with a heritage of sport, represented by the numerous Olympic monuments that remain: 'architectural icons that are dotted around' (as described by UCL East's former project director) within the perimeter of the park, symbolising the disconnect that exists between what goes on inside and outside its boundaries. UCL East is part of a wider initiative to bring a number of high profile cultural and educational institutions into the park as an anchor for urban regeneration in East London, and to mitigate the overspend on the Olympic games by securing long-term benefits for the area in the form of jobs, training and housing. In return for its government subsidy, UCL has positioned itself at the centre of a transformative urban heritage discourse which holds up the future of East London at the centre of the new, inclusive knowledge economy as a logical outcome of its former industrial past, and promises to deliver positive changes at local level in parallel with its remit for global engagement and recognition: 'UCL is very much upholding the LLDC's [London Legacy Development Corporation] objectives in terms of delivering regeneration, being sustainable, being interactive, open, welcoming and not being an elite centre but something that welcomes the local people in' (UCL East's former project director).

This positioning also taps into UCL's own institutional history and heritage, as evoked by a former UCL East project director: 'UCL was quite a leading progressive liberal [institution], it had an aspiration to open up to a range of students [as a non-religious foundation], though women still weren't allowed until the late 19th century'. UCL's non-conformist, 'effortlessly radical' and egalitarian origins are emphasised in its academic vision statement for the new campus as a guarantee of its intent to 'discover, co-create and share new knowledge for the benefit of all'[6]. It is echoed in its promise to deliver a physical development that will connect UCL East to its surroundings and 'invite people in', with a 'vibrant public space' at its heart. Whereas UCL's Bloomsbury campus architecture 'really comes from a root of privilege, authority', UCL East, 'both physically and … culturally, … has this challenge of creating these new, almost stand-alone 21st century buildings and trying to make itself part of East London'.[7] In contrast to University of Gothenburg, UCL's approach to this problem was to separate its community engagement activities from the academic sphere, investing them in a specialised 'public engagement unit', and impose a moratorium on architectural visualisations in the early stages of concept development and masterplanning in order to avoid miscommunication, while also creating a vacuum of information. In parallel, many of UCL's academics also developed relationships with local groups through different kinds of community-based research activities, and the university's Urban Laboratory, comprising a network of urbanists, spearheaded a consistent campaign to establish and implement an ethical, inclusive and participatory framework for university-led urban regeneration in the area. But the direct impact of both the public engagement and the academic work on the masterplanning, design and development of new buildings emerging on the site has been constrained by project management objectives and a tight timeframe for realisation. From the project team perspective, 'the poor quality of [neighbouring] housing from the 1960s' suggested that 'there's very little long-term heritage there' from which to develop an appropriate design proposal, integrated with the pre-Olympics urban context. In response, the masterplanners developed a 'fluid concept' for the new campus, 'trying to develop a ground-plan which is open and accessible across the entire piece' (see Figure 1.4), emphasising permeability and public accessibility, while preserving a more cloistered academic privacy at the upper levels (see Figure 1.5). But it was acknowledged that this would potentially reinforce a disconnect 'between the kinds of buildings that are happening in the park, the sorts of places we are creating there, and the historic fabric that we see to the south' (quotations all from a former project team member).

Many in those surrounding local communities have objected to LLDC's and UCL's re-writing of the area's urban heritage, the erasure of its industrial past and the effects of gentrification that they anticipate will define its future identity and lead to their own exclusion (Melhuish and Campkin, 2017; see Gardner and Cohen in this volume). But ultimately, the UCL East project makes little reference either to its historic (industrial) or more recent (Olympic) past and social identity, in favour of a focus on a projected shared 'future' heritage, embodied in the buildings of the new campus (see Figure 1.6) and the activities they will host, as a new powerhouse for London.

Both the UCL and Gothenburg developments disclose a highly city-based rhetoric around integration with the urban fabric, and the creation of new kinds of university spaces that are permeable, inclusive and afford new kinds of social interactions between the university community, its urban neighbours and newcomers to university sites as a kind of 'shelter' in the city. At UCL, these will include outward-facing facilities intended

Figure 1.4 UCL East Final draft masterplan section. Courtesy of UCL East

Figure 1.5 UCL East illustrative masterplan. Courtesy of UCL East

Figure 1.6 UCL East, visualisation of Phase 1 (Pool St West, left, and Marshgate, right, either side of Waterworks River), looking south towards Stratford. Courtesy of UCL East

for public engagement, notably a new Urban Room and Memory Workshop (based on the recommendations by the Farrell Review 2014; see also Tewdwr-Jones, Sookhoo and Freestone, 2019), forwarded by UCL Urban Laboratory and School for Cultural and Creative Industries; and open spaces within the campus area which are accessible to the public, although early plans for a library and learning centre available for public use will not be realised. At Gothenburg, the library is also a focus of attention, and although the café in the faculty building that is currently open to the public will no longer exist, proposals to turn the old courthouse building into a creative hub for university interactions with the public are under discussion.

Conclusion

In both these cases, the rhetoric of development draws on existing narratives of university heritage and identity, projected into symbolic and contested urban heritage contexts. It provides a framework for critical engagement and the construction of social relationships and alliances around the development, through a variety of tactics, which engages with issues of urban diversity and exclusion – even through the processes of confrontation, opposition, and dissent which it generates – and endeavours to create a discourse of shared, place-based urban heritage.

However when it comes to the objectification of such discourses as built form, there is always a high risk of failure. The complexity of claims for access to space and representation in the city, especially ethnically diverse, postcolonial, neoliberal cities beset by inequalities, poses enormous challenges to the fixity and pace of conventional project management and delivery structures, which is further complicated by the relationship between academics, estates professionals, and other actors within the university setting.

This chapter has outlined the evolution of universities from their origins within national heritage discourses and practices, and as training grounds for the national elites who have historically defined and implemented those discourses, into democratised institutions and urban developers involved in regeneration initiatives mobilised by place-based urban heritage narratives, in the context of the neoliberal, postcolonial city. It underlines the ways in which this evolution has been defined by a transformation of university building typologies, from the monumental and formal architectural statements common to historic city centres, to more open-ended, permeable and hybrid models of development conceived as a 'shelter' in the city and place of encounter for diverse communities, framed by a notion of shared urban, future heritage. But, as centres of critical thinking, research and teaching, universities need to mobilise their resources further to address and engage more explicitly with the issues outlined in the section above, if they are to fulfil their role and responsibilities with regard to the construction of more fluid and 'ethnographic' urban heritage narratives, embracing a range of different voices. Somewhere between enclaved and exclusionary urban complexes of privatised, 'smooth' space designed to sustain elite circuits of cosmopolitan cultural capital on the one hand (Bridge, 2006; Caldeira, 2000), and left-over segregated spaces occupied by the (often racialised) marginal and dispossessed on the other (Elsheshtawy, 2011; Kelly, 1993), universities have the knowledge and expertise to shape new, hybrid and accessible urban spaces to accommodate democratic representations of diverse heritage and transnational citizenship, transcending nationalist discourses. As cosmopolitan communities of practice, property owners and institutional developers, they are well placed to facilitate that shared 'civic culture from the interactions of multiple publics' that Sandercock called for in the cosmopolis (Sandercock, 1998: 186–7), grounded in a critical heritage perspective on urban identity and belonging.

Notes

1. University of Gothenburg Project Vision, Project Campus Näckrosen 5 March 2013.
2. Archer et al., in *Sustainability in Urban Planning and Design* 2020, [Working title] Dr Amjad Zaki Almusaed, Associate Prof. Asaad Almssad and Dr Linh Truong-Hong.
3. see Arantes, this volume.
4. http://www.ucl.ac.uk/ucl-east/at-a-glance/vision.
5. All quotes taken from presentations made by project team members at universities and urban heritage: two closed workshops organised by Curating the City research cluster in the UCL/UGOT Centre for Critical Heritage Studies, London November 2016, and Gothenburg April 2017; and from interviews with project team members conducted in April 2017.
6. http://www.ucl.ac.uk/ucl-east/at-a-glance/vision.
7. Quotes from interviews with former UCL East project director April 2017.

References

Addie, J-P., Keil, R. and Olds, T. (2015) 'Beyond town and gown: Universities, territoriality, and the mobilisation of new urban structures in Canada'. *Territory, Politics, Governance*, 3 (1), 27–50.

Addie, J-P. (2018) 'Urban(izing) university strategic planning: An analysis of London and New York City'. *Urban Affairs Review*, published online before print 2018, 1.

Ambasz, E. (1966) *The Universitas Project: Solutions for a post-technological society*. NY: MOMA, 466–7.

Archer, C., Cunningham-Myrie, C., Freeman-Prince, N., Reid, M., Williams, B. and Royal Thomas, T. (2020) 'Jamaican universities aiding the design of an urban public space'. In A. Almusaed, A. Almssad and L. Truong-Hong (eds), *Sustainability in Urban Planning and Design*. London: IntechOpen, 428–89.

Bender, T. (1998) 'Scholarship, local life, and the necessity of worldliness'. In H. van der Wusten (ed.), *The Urban University and its Identity: Roots, location, roles*. Dordrecht, Boston, London: Kluwer Academic Publishers, 17–28.

Bender, T. (2002) *The Unfinished City: New York and the metropolitan idea*. NY: The New York Press.

Benneworth, P. and Hospers, G. J. (2007) 'Urban competitiveness in the knowledge economy: Universities as new planning animateurs'. *Progress in Planning*, (67), 2.

Binnie, J., Holloway, J., Millington, S. and Young, C. (2006) *Cosmopolitan Urbanism*. Abingdon: Routledge.

Böhme, G. (2003) 'Contribution to the critique of the aesthetic economy'. *Thesis Eleven*, 73 (1), 71–82.

Bose, S. (2015) 'Universities and the redevelopment politics of the neoliberal city'. *Urban Studies*, 52 (14), 2616–32.

Bridge, G. (2006) 'The paradox of cosmopolitan urbanism: Rationality, difference and the circuits of cultural capital'. In J. Binnie, J. Holloway, S. Millington and C. Young (eds), *Cosmopolitan Urbanism*. Abingdon: Routledge, 53–69.

Bromley, R. (2006) 'On and off campus: Colleges and universities as local stakeholders'. *Planning, Practice, and Research*, 21 (1), 1–24.

Caldeira, T. (2000) *City of Walls: Crime, segregation, and citizenship in São Paulo*. Berkeley: University of California Press.

Choueiri, T. and Myntti, C. (2012) 'The AUB Neighborhood Initiative: Social responsibility in a university's backyard'. In D. Jamali and Y. Sidani (eds), *CSR [Corporate Social Responsibility] in the Middle East: Fresh perspectives*. London: Palgrave Macmillan, 158–75.

Cochrane, A., speaking at 'Universities 1: Space: universities, cities and globalisation', UCL Urban Laboratory, 9 May 2013; and at 'The Urban University: universities as place-makers and agents of civic success in medium-sized towns and cities', University Town Northampton project, Northampton 2–3 July 2015.

Dikeç, M. (2001) 'Justice and the spatial imagination'. *Environment and Planning A*, 33, 1785–805.

Elsheshtawy, Y. (2011) 'Urban (Im)mobility: Public encounters in Dubai'. In T. Edensor and M. Jayne (eds), *Urban Theory Beyond the West: A world of cities*. London: Routledge, 219–36.
Farrell Review (2014) Accessed 15 July 2020. http://www.farrellreview.co.uk/download.
Gilroy, P. (1993) *The Black Atlantic: Modernity and double consciousness*. Cambridge: Harvard University Press.
Goddard, J. (2009) 'Reinventing the civic university'. Provocation 12, London: https://www.nesta.org.uk/report/re-inventing-the-civic-university/ (accessed 18th February 2022).
Goddard, J. and Vallance, P. (2011) 'The civic university and the leadership of place'. CURDS Newcastle University. https://www.researchgate.net/publication/266471508_The_civic_university_and_the_leadership_of_place.
Hall, S. (1999) 'Un-settling the heritage, re-imagining the post-nation. Whose heritage?' *Third Text*, 13 (49), 3–13.
Harding, A. (2013) Speaking at 'Universities 1' seminar, UCL, May 2013.
Harding, A., Scott, A., Laske, S. and Burthscher, C. (eds) (2007) *Bright Satanic Mills: Universities, regional development and the knowledge economy*. London: Routledge.
Harvey, D. (2005) *A Brief History of Neoliberalism*. Oxford: OUP.
Holston, J. (1996) 'Spaces of insurgent citizenship'. In C. Melhuish (ed.), *Architecture and Anthropology*, AD Profile 24. London: Academy Editions.
Jaffe, R. (2013) 'The hybrid state: Crime and citizenship in urban Jamaica'. *American Ethnologist*, (40) 4, 734–48.
Kelly, M. F. P. (1993) *Rethinking citizenship in the global village: Reflections on immigrants and the underclass*. New York: Russell Sage Foundation. Working Paper 38.
Klingmann, A. (2010) *Brandscapes: Architecture in the experience economy*. Cambridge, MA: MIT Press.
Kwiek, M. (2000) 'The nation-state, globalisation and the modern institution of the university'. *Theoria: A Journal of Social and Political Theory*, 96, 74–98.
Lees, L. and Melhuish, C. (2013) 'Arts-led regeneration in the UK: The rhetoric and the evidence on urban social inclusion'. *European Urban and Regional Studies*. https://doi.org/10.1177/0969776412467474.
Lefebvre, H. (1968) *Le Droit a la Ville*. Paris: Editions Anthropos.
Letchimy, S. (2011) L'urbanisme d'hier à demain, ou l'art de la transmission (extract), *Lyann Karayib*, Cahier Ville Caraibe, No. 1, Fort-de-France: Centre de ressources Ville caraibe. http://www.villecaraibe.com/docs/Lyann%20Karayib01BonDeCommande.pdf.
Maurasse, D. (2001) *Beyond the Campus: How colleges and universities build partnerships with their communities*. New York, London: Routledge.
Maurasse, D. (2007) *City Anchors: Leveraging anchor institutions for urban success*. Chicago, IL: CEOs for Cities.
McCann, E., Ward, K. and Roy, A. (2013) 'Urban pulse – assembling/worlding cities'. *Urban Geography*, 34 (5), 581–89.
Melhuish, C. (2015) *Case Studies in University-led Urban regeneration*. London: UCL Urban Laboratory.
Melhuish, C., Degen, M. and Rose, G. (2016) 'The real modernity that is here: Understanding the role of digital visualisations in the production of a new urban imaginary at Msheireb Downtown, Doha'. *City and Society*, (28).
Melhuish, C. (2017) 'Aesthetics of social identity: Re-framing and evaluating modernist architecture and planning as cultural heritage in Martinique'. *Planning Perspectives*, DOI: 10.1080/02665433.2017.1389659.
Melhuish, C. and Campkin, B. (2017) *Cultural infrastructure around the Queen Elizabeth Olympic Park*. London: UCL Urban Laboratory (report).
Nalbantoglu, G. B. and Wong, C. T. (1997) *Postcolonial Space(s)*. New York: Princeton Architectural Press.
New York Times (1895, January–March). Architectural Record, 4, 351–53.
Pendlebury, J. (2015) 'Heritage and policy'. In E. Waterton and S. Watson (eds), *The Palgrave Handbook of Contemporary Heritage Research*. London: Palgrave 2015.
Perry, D. C. and Wiewel, W. (eds) (2005) *The University as Urban Developer: Case studies and analysis*. Armonk NY: M. E. Sharpe.
Rodin, J. (2007) *The University and Urban Revival: Out of the ivory tower and into the streets*. Philadelphia: University of Pennsylvania, 182–3.
Sandercock, L. (1997) *Towards Cosmopolis: Planning for multicultural cities*. Chichester: Wiley.

Shore, C. (2002) 'Introduction'. In S. Nugent and C. Shore (eds), *Elite Cultures: Anthropological perspectives*. London: Routledge.

Smith, N. (2002) 'New globalism, new urbanism: gentrification as global urban strategy'. In N. Brenner and N. Theodore (eds), *Spaces of Neoliberalism: Urban restructuring in North America and western Europe*. Oxford: Blackwell, 80–103.

Swyngedouw, E., Moulaert, F. and Rodriguez, A. (2002) 'Neoliberal urbanization in Europe: Large-scale urban development projects and the new urban policy'. In N. Brenner and N. Theodore (eds), *Spaces of Neoliberalism: Urban restructuring in North America and western Europe*. Oxford: Blackwell, 80–103.

Tewdwr-Jones, M., Sookhoo, D. and Freestone, R. (2019) 'From Geddes' city museum to Farrell's urban room: Past, present, and future at the Newcastle City Futures exhibition.' *Planning Perspectives,* (35).

Heur, B van (2010) 'The built environment of higher education and research: Architecture and the expectation of innovation'. *Geography Compass,* 4 (12), 1713–24.

Wiewel, W. and Perry, D. C. (eds) (2008) *Global Universities and Urban Development*. Armonk, NY: M. E. Sharpe.

Winter, T. (2012) 'Clarifying the critical in critical heritage studies'. *International Journal of Heritage Studies,* 19 (6), 532–45.

The Work Foundation (2010) 'Anchoring growth: The role of anchor institutions in the regeneration of UK cities'. Research paper 2 in *Regeneration Momentum, The Northern Way*.

2
Universities curating change at heritage places in urban spaces

Dean Sully

Introduction

This chapter investigates the role of universities in forwarding heritage practices that aim to co-curate the legacy of past cities with the human communities who inhabit them, radically shifting the conceptualisation of heritage towards that of a dialogue between different kinds of being in the world and instituting a new framework for action. In the re-making of peripheral, 'latent' heritage places as dynamic urban spaces, new possibilities emerge – for universities to become good neighbours in response to unrestrained gentrification and studentification, and for university-led interventions at heritage places to contribute to the imagining of new future trajectories for these neighbourhoods. The impact of universities on heritage places will be considered in the transitional experience of the House Mill Trust, Bromley-by-Bow, as the coming into being of a complex place (see Figure 2.1). House Mill, 'the largest surviving tidal mill in the world', now endures as an island of relative temporal continuity in a landscape in perpetual flux half a mile south of the Queen Elizabeth Park and UCL East campus development (see Figure 2.2) (Sully, 2019).

> Queen Elizabeth Olympic Park and its surroundings are significant areas of change in one of the most exciting and fastest-growing areas in London. (UCL, 2016: 78)

Figure 2.1 Island of Continuity: House Mill on Three Mills Island (2017). Source: Dean Sully

Figure 2.2 Urban landscape in flux: View from House Mill toward the Queen Elizabeth Park (2017). Source: Dean Sully

The chapter draws on the experience of 'Out of site out of mind'[1], a Critical Heritage Studies workshop exploring the tension between creative artistic practice and authorised heritage practice in order to address how heritage *places* can be transformed into urban *spaces*. It will provide an intellectual framing for discussion of ways in which latent heritage places can be activated as spaces hosting a constellation of encounters between people and the city.

Situating critical heritage in the city

Our historic cities are encountered as a thin veneer of contemporary experience, with the past lying in wait beneath the streets and around the corners. It exists in the imbricated infrastructures of past lives, invisible in plain sight, waiting to be experienced. Episodes of redundancy and utility, latency and activity, decline and renewal, abandonment and development, overlay our contemporary relationships with the city and shape our expectations for the future, even though the physical remains of a city's past are often hidden and inaccessible, with limited obvious impact on inhabitants' everyday lives today (Sully, 2019). In London, we can touch the preserved archaeological remains of the Roman City across a span of two thousand years and speculate on the lives lived in Londinium, on which the present city is built; however, it is more difficult to imagine a future London, two thousand years in the future (Sully, 2019). The enduring fabric of urban places remain as an event in the formation of the world that constitutes a reservoir of memory and past practice (Massey, 2005: 140). As the location of the presence of diverse absences, at times incomprehensible, a matter of no-concern, unattuned, not-noticed, beyond our attention, invisible in plain sight, the left-behind places of the redundant past, of relocated communities, these elements of the city can have recursive effects in unpredictable ways (Haraway, 2016; Tsing, 2015; Harrison, 2013). They are seamlessly experienced in the operative functioning of the familiar, and may only become revealed in the transition from ready-at-hand to conscious-at-hand, from use as functional tools, to an intentional act and objectification of our conscious gaze (Heidegger, 1927). Thus, the affordance of the past city is created in our own experience of it, as a fractured chain of events that connects material remains of past worlds to our present coming into being. The enduring nature of a human-built environment means it offers itself to multiple readings in altered times and places. Rather than having a pre-endowed signification to be disclosed, it is an open site of signification that establishes its active role in different temporal moments and cultures, repeatedly created and lost through the historical act of re-reading (Olsen, 2010: 40).

> We expect to develop a new model for a university campus – one that we hope will inspire UCL, our partners, our neighbours and other universities across the globe. (Arthur, 2014)

UCL's role in the legacy of the 2012 London Olympic Games lies within the development of the East Bank education and cultural quarter on the Queen Elizabeth Park, along with other protagonists including V&A, Sadler's Wells and London College of Fashion. Its role is framed aspirationally as a centre for knowledge production, agent of social change, centre of soft power and its potential to act as a good neighbour:

> UCL East will be an outstanding and dynamic environment for learning, breaking down the conventional barriers between research, education, innovation, public engagement and collaboration. (Arthur, 2014)

But these claims contrast with their implication in the gentrification processes triggered by such large-scale development projects, and their adverse impacts on people already living in the area (Sanz and Bergan, 2002: 9; Anderson, 2006; UCL, 2016). Large urban development projects have routinely utilised a 'wasteland' metaphor to justify appropriations of urban spaces and their transformation into imagined future places. This can be seen in the 'terra nullius' descriptions of East London, prior to the development of the London 2012 Olympic Park, which erased the past histories of urban neighbourhoods earmarked for substantial redevelopment (Gardner, this volume). Counter to this desire to remove what was there before in a frenzied renewal of the imagined city, is the creation of 'heritage' through a process of accumulating conservation inventories, listing buildings, and designating neighbourhoods as conservation areas. This process of documentation and inscription creates things to be valued as heritage, in need of protection by identifying their risk of loss, but at the same time destroys its presence within the everyday realm of peoples' lives. Built Heritage Conservation practice thus responds to the desire to protect, save and stabilise vulnerabilities by the act of separating (constraining, limiting, making accountable for) urban spaces into preserved heritage places. These heritage places can provide a reference point from which to investigate how cities change over time and how future cities will incorporate the legacies of our own lives. This poses the challenge of how to develop effective more-than-human living places and less damaging ways of living, within the conservative constraints of preserving what is already there (Sauer, Elsen, Garzillo, 2016).

Redefining heritage

Heritage in the twentieth century can best be understood as a 'salvage paradigm' that sought to gather together the remains of the past to provide evidence of what has been lost (Butler, 2006) (see Figure 2.3), and reflected the absences created in the progress towards a new optimistic future. In the early twenty-first century, an understanding of heritage has evolved as a vehicle for sustainable development towards 'The future we want' (UN, 2012), in order to maintain sufficient resources to sustain human happiness and wellbeing in our present, and into the future. Heritage conservation is positioned as a means of shaping a preferable future, within a field of cultural adaptation to continuous changes in the world premised on the expectation that the anticipated future will evolve seamlessly from the familiar present. Haraway describes this as 'the great dithering (2000–2050)', a time of ineffective anxiety about environmental destruction and continuing 'business-as-usual' response, despite unmistakable evidence of accelerating mass extinction, violent climate change, population increase, mass migrations and social disintegration (Haraway, 2016: 143).

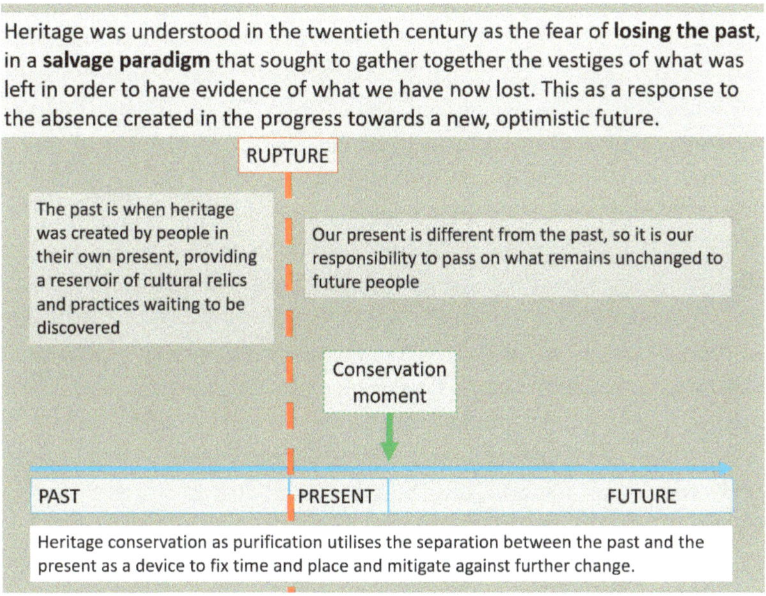

Heritage was understood in the twentieth century as the fear of **losing the past**, in a **salvage paradigm** that sought to gather together the vestiges of what was left in order to have evidence of what we have now lost. This as a response to the absence created in the progress towards a new, optimistic future.

RUPTURE

The past is when heritage was created by people in their own present, providing a reservoir of cultural relics and practices waiting to be discovered

Our present is different from the past, so it is our responsibility to pass on what remains unchanged to future people

Conservation moment

PAST | PRESENT | FUTURE

Heritage conservation as purification utilises the separation between the past and the present as a device to fix time and place and mitigate against further change.

Figure 2.3 Heritage as understood in twentieth century. Source: Dean Sully

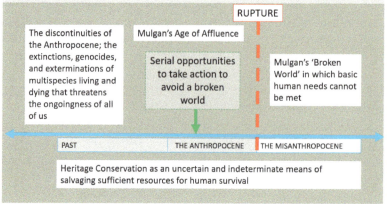

Figure 2.4 Heritage as understood in the early twenty-first century. Source: Dean Sully

In situating the heritage of the twenty-first century within the Anthropocene (see Figure 2.4), the sense of loss about the past is replaced by a fear of losing the future and a view on the past as a source of regret, missed opportunity and guilt (Lewis and Maslin, 2015). The new heritage paradigm frames the past as contaminated, and heritage conservation practice as an uncertain and indeterminate action to salvage sufficient resources for human survival and avoid a broken world (Mulgan, 2011, 2014, 2018). We should resist the temptation to look at the present moment and see it as permanent condition. If we colonise the future with our current ideas of business-as-usual solutions to living in the Anthropocene, we will look for the problems of the present to be fixed by the technologies of the future. If we see the future differently, we can alter our view on the present and engage more effective action. Instead of being afraid of change and uncertainty, we can celebrate them in our understanding of the generosity and diversity of the world, expressed in radically different ways (Haraway, 2016).

The twentieth-century heritage response of redemptive and restorative material-based conservation to the conflicts and destruction of two Western world wars relates to Haraway's concept of 'autopoietic' systems made up of autonomous, individuated, centrally-controlled, predictable and completed objects that militate against evolution, change and adaptation. By contrast, a more appropriate twenty-first-century heritage response of peoples-based conservation (or preferably, a post-humanist conservation response to more-than-human worlds), relates to Haraway's 'sympoietic' collective systems that are without self-defined spatial and temporal boundaries, unpredictable, dynamic, non-equilibrated, uncertain and 'chaotic' worlds (Sully, 2015; Haraway, 2016: 34). This might provide a key framing for *living* heritage concepts that highlight capacity for growth, ageing and death of heritage, in line with biological concepts of inheritance based on the re-creation of entities through time by reproduction and replacement, rather than preservation of specific entities through retention and mitigation (Wijesuriya, 2007; Poulios 2014). So, our buildings can be allowed to age, become lonely and in need of the warmth and joy of living, and then the need to retire, and eventually to die, to be remembered, to be memorialised, and also to be forgotten. In some cases, they will live on through the legacy of enduring entanglements of the made world at certain times and particular places (Haraway, 2016). The real object of heritage, then, is 'temporality', the continuous changes that translate things from the past into newly fabricated places in the present (Olivier, 2011: 63). In order to understand what liveable places are, we need to comprehend polyphonic assemblages of pluri-agent, multi-species attunements, as gatherings of impermanence and emergence that coalesce and dissolve in phased rhythms (Tsing, 2015: 157).

Heritage conservation shifts its focus onto 'change' as the solution rather than the problem, recognising the flux and decay of a place being an essential part of its transition through time. Heritage creates a temporal schema linking the past, present and future, in which the historiographic teleology of time is embedded within ideas of evolutionary cause and effect (De Certeau, 1984: 87). The place-events of the past endure as material sediments of our experience of the present, accumulated in cities and their buildings, which act as a binding mechanism for communal experience of a consensus reality (Massey, 2005). Temporal events have a series of durations that can interact to replicate and replace themselves at different times and places, imbricated unpredictably in our experience of their impact on our lives (Olivier, 2011: 109). This undermines attempts to reveal an authentic past understandable in its own present, rather than in our own present (Olivier, 2011: 170). The pluritemporality of any given moment, from which any sense of typological evolution can only be seen in the wake of time passing, becomes a narrative constructed in retrospect, and the past and the future are equally created in the imaginings of the polychronic present (Olivier, 2011). Our pasts are fixed in retrospect in order to provide certainty in the ineffable uncertainty of the formation of the world (Olsen, 2010: 122).

> Past and future are not physical realities distinct from our own, but dimensions that contribute to shaping different human experiences and social practices in the present. (Holtorf, 2009: 35)

Given that the past is only created in retrospect from the present, as a separated, conscious recovering of a time that has gone forever, then we can understand our predictions of the future to be based on a past that has yet to be created (Connolly, 2011: 8). This points to a tautology in our ability to control/manage the present and predict the future. Heritagisation (the designation of heritage) converts the open-ended dynamic flux of the present into a fixed historic state, a process of closure, selection and statement (Wright, 2012) that exists only in the past tense, rather than in the present (see Brown, this volume).

Heritage places

The designated heritage place thus emerges as a distilled product from all the multipotentiality of that world in formation (Conolly, 2011). The application of the Authorised Heritage Discourse (AHD) to the spaces of the human world transforms them into heritage places within a particular disciplinary discourse (Smith, 2006: 4), and where people and practices can be disciplined and/or privileged (Said, 1978: 202; Agamben, 2009: xviii). The AHD provides an operating framework that justifies and constrains the actions of heritage practitioners that become manifest in strategic choices, intervention events and management control processes. Heritage professionals who work with traces of past cities effectively assemble emergent future worlds that are enacted by our categorisation of them (Sully, 2007). The declaration of heritage phenomena in the heritagification process hardens up the difference that is drawn between heritage and non-heritage places (Latour, 1993; Barad, 2007). The essentialising procedure requires a sacrifice, which is reinforced with the selective removal of physical traces of past events through interventive conservation practice (Nancy, 2000: 24; Sully and Cardoso, 2014), determined by simplified stories or purified heritage ideas relating to a place. The place in question is not only separated from its pre-heritage use, but also continually refreshed to exclude the impact of the passage of time on it as a heritage place (Pink, 2012). However, if we bring those boundaries into stark relief, we can create a refractive surface from which we are able to experiment with alterations, in order to understand how the world might look different. Perturbation, the friction at these boundaries and the chafing from contact, can ferment change in the heritage world. Understood as permeable thresholds, boundaries can generate respect for difference and egalitarianism, in contrast to compartmentalisation and separation of different worlds and ways of being (Agamben, 2002; Augé, 2008: ix).

Defining heritage conservation as the 'careful management of change' suggests that there are some enduring values that can be brought into play to inform decisions about how the present becomes the future (Staniforth, 2000, 2006: 35). Heritage conservation selects some aspects of the present that will be made accessible in the making of the future, in its efforts to mitigate the effects of unrestricted change on human cultural environments. However, there is not a priori reason why a future imagined by heritage professionals will have any credibility with the people whose heritage they conserve (Durie, 1998; Sully, 2015). Heritage conservation must therefore be understood as a fundamentally local act, intensely subjective and political, engaged in privileging certain ideas and erasing others; excluding and defining difference; preventing rather than managing change (Avrami, Mason and de la Torre, 2000; Avrami, 2009). But it can also mediate between the actors in the process, give voice to multiple narratives, empower communities and negotiate change. It can play a role in community building by reinforcing shared histories, cultivating collective identities and providing a sense of belonging. Heritage professionals, as the authorised interpreters of these places and objects, can no longer be considered able to represent a 'proper' reading of the 'true' meaning as an orthodox account from which heretical or insignificant plural readings can be measured and controlled. These merely create boundaries around the proper, which invite transgression (Olsen, 2010: 48). It is necessary to acknowledge that the conservation of heritage is the answer to a question of its own making, a tautological process that creates the problem to which it is the only acceptable solution (Pink, 2012: 16).

Co-curating change

Rather than *managing change* being a constraint on the way the future world emerges from our present, heritage practice should be seen as an opportunity for political action to influence the making of a less damaging, more-than-human future. Critical Conservation Practice, positioned as innovation, is an open and creative process that seeks to respond to the unfolding becoming of the world in new adaptive ways. It is not a reactionary or conservative process, aimed at maintaining established hierarchies by emphasising stability and tradition; rather it is a way of challenging the becoming of the world, that reflects the desires of those involved in the making of our present world (Nancy, 2007; Agamben, 2009). It understands change in heritage places as not being simply something to be managed, but as a necessary innovation to generate more resilient, sustainable, diverse, participatory, bottom-up, community-led, self-organising, experimental responses to contemporary challenges, for a prosperous and humane future. Curating, rather than managing, change in cities, as open, complex systems of dispersed agency and multi-temporality, engages with issues of uncertainty and affordance (Amin and Thrift, 2017: 22). The instability of heritage places as fixed points for rehearsed encounters between people is revealed in the ways in which the city's inhabitants dwell and move differently from their places.

By adopting a perspective based around the broad ontology of connectivity (relationality) between humans and other inhabitants of the world, we can radically re-shape heritage practice (Latour, 1988, 1996, 2005) as a dialogue between different kinds of beings (humans, non-humans, non-animate agents of spaces, things, places and objects), and institute a new framework for action (Connolly, 2011: 30). Appropriating the term 'curating' places conservation actions within acts of caring for the multi-plurality and temporal flows of agents that inhabit the world and that shape the way the future world comes into being (DeSilvey, 2017). Heritage professionals have a responsibility to challenge the internal rationales of their institutions and seek to instigate reform, transforming the institution as a 'site of authority' to a 'site of inspiration', in order that the 'future we want' can become attainable (Butler, 2003: 357).

The authority of the 'curator', in making proper places out of the coming together of things, can be dissolved into a participation with people in caring for the things that they value and consider necessary to stake a claim in the present, as well as recording those claims for those that come after. Acknowledging that decisions to protect endangered heritage come at the cost of other, unprotected heritages means that heritage professionals need to be able to curate stories about a place as official storytellers, building bridges between dominant narratives and alternative stories that may lie hidden, rather than producing traditional, discipline-specific 'statements of significance'. By imagining new stories, new interactions and new pasts, we are forced to speculate on other possible, plausible future worlds; reality may become more malleable, and preferable futures more achievable (Dunne and Raby, 2013). This is to suggest an *insurgent* heritage practice that highlights exclusions, silences and violences evident in designation of heritage that 'stays with the trouble' of deciding what heritage worlds are being cared for at the expense of which others. This provides a speculative exploration of heritage care for living as-well-as-possible in more-than-human worlds, which move beyond concepts that continue to privilege human agency and sustain inequalities, towards a diversity of affective ecosociological potentialities of (post-) human and non-human matter (Haraway, 2016).

The shift away from formalised authoritative accounts of the past shifts our focus to things that *occur* in the world (as assemblages, networks, meshworks), rather than *exist* like objects in the material world (Latour, 1993; Ingold, 2013; Morton, 2013; Harrison, 2013). This enables us to embrace change as the dynamic movement that is the making of the world, and Critical Heritage Practice provides a framework to address these broad questions about how the world comes into being by recognising the making of heritage as a creative act in the present moment (Menon, 2003). It positions heritage as a co-product of material-discursive practices in everyday life, which constitutes an ongoing reconfiguring of the world (Barad, 2007; Höppner and Urban, 2018). This allows a search for innovative improvisational heritage practices as an effective response to inhabiting uncertain more-than-human worlds (Haraway, 2016: 102).

Urban spaces and heritage places

> Place is security, space is freedom, we are attached to one and long for the other. (Tuan, 1977: 3)

The transition between fluid 'space' and fixed 'place' provides a way of understanding the heritagisation of historic cities. A human cultural space differs from a heritage place. The first is produced from the coming together of things at this cross-section of space-time (Connolly, 2011). By contrast, a heritage place is constructed in retrospect: it is the view with hindsight upon an object that is complete, that seeks to fix a state within the place as something secure, as a certain reference point in the ineffable complexity of the world in formation (de Certeau, 1984).

Spaces

A space is a locality-situated act in the present as part of the becoming of the world (de Certeau, 1984: 129). Spaces form open, infinite, unrestricted, relational, qualitative, fluid, dynamic and plural locations for the entanglement of networks of relationships that operate over varying spatial and temporal scales (Lefebvre, 1991: 42). A constellation of encounters and a flow of things, persons and discourses intersect and occur in a space (Massey, 2005: 140; Ingold, 2008: 1808). Space has none of the stability of the proper, the inbetweenness of everyday life; like spoken words, the loss of stories equates with the loss of spaces (de Certeau, 1984: 117; Massey, 2005: 140). As fundamental concepts, spaces form a prerequisite for the reality of our experience of the world (Pink, 2012: 128). The world is created in the space in-between one another, in relation to the exchanges and reference points that we create in being-in-common (Nancy, 2000: 35). Spaces can be stabilised and familiarised through recognition of significant reference points, locations and landmarks, into enduring places (Tuan, 1977: 18).

Places

A place is bordered, stabilised, enclosed, restrictive and self-contained, with a defined geometric personality in which we can dwell. Flows of things, persons and discourses of a place intersect and become interwoven in relation to its administrative boundaries. Places are how things come together and stay together, to reconstitute other constellations as bounded regulated space (Augé, 2008: 18). Place is the context for practice and the product of it, shaped by action produced by discourses of elite power and expert ideologies (Lefebvre, 1991; Pink, 2012: 83). Engaging with place and practice as interconnecting concepts constructs a particular constellation of social relations (Massey, 2005: 154; Augé, 2008: 64). This creates a dynamism in understanding physical location as constituted in the activation of cultural practice (Pink, 2012: 25). Rather than merely a place to go to and be in (actual material locality), places are regulated 'zones of entanglement' or stabilised 'meshworks of interwoven lines' composed of locality, movements, flows, agencies and transformations (Ingold, 2008: 1797; Pink, 2012: 129).

Spaces becoming places

To convert a fluid space into a fixed place (for example, as a monument), as something right and proper, occurs by transposing a terrain of fluid networks into a defined order of things in their distinct locations, a stabilised topography disciplined by the law of 'proper' rules (de Certeau, 1984: 117; Armstrong 2009: 168). Spaces are constantly transformed into places and vice versa; for example, the spoken word (space) and the written text (place), the city street (place) and the act of walking (space) (de Certeau, 1984: 96; Pink 2012: 93). The complexity of space is reduced when control is exerted in making places. Massey considers spaces as 'open and plural, a simultaneity of stories so far', whereas 'places are collections of these stories, articulations of the wider power geometries of space' (Massey, 2005: 130). When boundaries are set between spaces, then limits can be set and transgressed (Heidegger, 1971). De Certeau identifies different approaches adopted by the weak and the powerful: the powerful use 'strategies' that signify ownership over and management of place as the basis of power. The weak apply 'tactics' in the absence of power over the place. Played out in space and of the other, they act to subvert the structures of power in ways that may be less visible and non-confrontational, as tactics in a guerrilla war (de Certeau, 1984; Pink 2012: 18). Tactics represent a non-specialised response, or the perturbation of norms of practice through mechanisms, such as micronarratives, micropolitical action and reflexive/critical practice (Connolly, 2011: 17).

Strategies utilise the establishment of place as a constraint to opportunity, to retain power and resist the erosion of time. This occurs by separating the present from the past, which creates a privileged place from which it claims a clear and proper view. From this privileged place, facts can be manufactured and turned into truths (de Certeau, 1984: 10). The tangible presence of monumental heritage provides the appearance of intergenerational continuity that prevents the past being a mere illusion (Augé, 2008: 63). The constitution of a 'proper place' is made possible through the regulation of time and space through dominant discourses (de Certeau, 1984: 89; Ingold, 2007; 2008). The authority of the proper creates the ideas (theoretical places) that compose a physical place in which a system of control is operative (practised places). The order is given greater power by the fact it is considered 'natural', despite the restrictions necessary to retain the familiarity of the place. This includes foundation narratives that have utility as threats, and cohesive forces that enable groups to look back from the present to the illusory stability of the past events. This historical place confirms stability as a recursive evocation of a living past 'happening' in the present (Augé, 2008: 44). Places and spaces are in a continuous state of becoming, which means that a sense of place is not a monolithic entirety but is polysemic, in flux and formed from multi-centred agency. People create and experience a sense of place in relation to geographic locality (Pink, 2012: 3). Human experience of place is expressed in concepts such as *genius loci* that are established in heritage practice in 'a sense of place' that are developed through 'place-making', 'place-keeping' and 'place-caring' (Feld and Basso, 1996; Rodwell, 2007; Pink, 2012: 24).

The sense of place relates to 'being in the place', as an experience of empirical realities (things, sites, buildings, villages, neighbourhoods, landscapes) that have particular qualities (Augé, 2008; Pink, 2012: 23). New forms of heritage are as much about forgetting as they may be about remembering (Ashworth, Graham and Tunbridge, 2007: 5). Only by not making things into a conscious object can we ensure that this past lives on in our present; it is a paradox of heritage that, in the act of salvage, the past is lost and cannot be reclaimed in the act of memorialising, only reworked and appropriated for its use in our present (Olsen, 2010: 114). Heritage is implicated as a 'proper place' for political legitimation of social engineering, commodification, understanding and control of places as resources. The inevitable conflicts of interest exist in political campaigns of identity construction and management of public and personal agendas (Ashworth, Graham and Tunbridge, 2007: 3). The power to make places out of spaces is largely a consequence of hierarchical agency (Pink, 2012: 37). Heritage places, therefore, are transformed spaces in which heritage practices are enforced through legal, institutional and disciplinary procedures. There is therefore a distinction to be made between the proper heritage place that is actualised by professionalised, authorised heritage practice, and the heritage space that is operative within the practices that transform the locality into an active social space (de Certeau, 1984: 108). House Mill has become a research site for a broader critique of authorised heritage practice, the application of the Authorised Heritage Discourse to the spaces and things of the human world.

The heritage place, House Mill: 'one of the best kept secrets in London'

The House Mill is a Grade 1 listed tidal mill and 'one of the best kept secrets in London', according to its own website. It is located on a fabricated island (known as Three Mills), half a mile south of the Olympic

Park development site on the River Lea, Bromley-by-Bow, in East London. It is hidden in plain sight, beyond a busy urban six-lane freeway, past a large supermarket, cut off by surrounding water, across a bridge blocked by a road barrier. It sits between the boroughs of Newham and Tower Hamlets, in an area of intense ethnic diversity and high economic disadvantage. This heritage place is managed by a volunteer run charitable trust, The House Mill Trust.

The earliest known mills on this site were recorded in the Domesday Book in 1086. The current House Mill building dates from 1776, built on foundations that date back to 1380. Its complex coming into being as a place involves destruction by fire in 1802 and its rebuilding into what is now the world's largest surviving tidal mill (see Figure 2.2). The second mill, the Clock Mill, was rebuilt in 1817, and continued as a working mill until 1952. The third mill, a windmill, survived until about 1840. The mills provided flour for the local bakers of Stratford-atte-Bow, who sold bread in the City of London. In the eighteenth century, the mill was used for gin production as the Three Mills Distillery, supplying the Royal Navy and the London craze for gin drinking. The House Mill stopped production during the Second World War, following significant bomb damage to surrounding buildings (including the destruction of the adjacent Miller's House) and was used as a storage warehouse. House Mill faced demolition in the 1970s, when the House Mill was proposed as the site for a supermarket car park. The Mill buildings were saved by a local conservation campaign, which has now evolved into the House Mill Trust. The Trust has received significant financial support from English Heritage (among others) for the partial restoration of the House Mill. The neighbouring Miller's House was reconstructed in 1995 with funding from the European Union. The Miller's House now provides a visitor, information, and education centre, meeting rooms for hire, and a small café. The House Mill Trust arranges heritage tours, concerts, art exhibitions, training classes and so on. The Trustees aspire to restore House Mill to its former glory, to reinstate the heritage machinery to working order, to develop the education, arts, and visitor experience, and generate hydroelectricity at the site. They have developed detailed plans for each part of the restoration project, and have been seeking support for their project (for example, from the National Lottery Fund and private sector funding).

The Trust has faced over a decade of disruption to its activities, caused by the 2012 Olympic Park development, and is currently subject to a 30-year development plan that will see its surrounding neighbourhood transformed as part of the legacy developments of the Queen Elizabeth

Park (Beverley Charters, 2018). The geography of the neighbourhood will be completely transformed with few fixed reference points in the urban landscape. This affords a critical role for House Mill, as an island of temporal continuity that can provide a sense of identity for local residents beyond the commercial place branding of urban developers. This may be as a form that links people's memory and place in a sense of belonging in the face of rapid urban change. This is a pragmatic approach to making heritage as productive nostalgia in partnership with those that are undergoing transition, and those engaged in inhabiting the emerging reality of the world (along with the ability to account for uncomfortable and contested pasts). Such continuity offers an experience of place that can be translated to local groups as the creative practice in the everyday experience of informal learning about place. The everyday encounters with the life of neighbourhoods in place-keeping and place-making become tools in an activist toolbox. For example, the creation of informal in-between spaces provides an opportunity for the inclusion of new residents from which to build social networks, a sense of community and to perpetuate ideas of familiarity in changing urban neighbourhoods. The heritage place in this way becomes a space for the mutual encounter of us and them, in order to merge these categories. This aims to support the process of becoming included, a sense of being at home, belonging in some place, one of our own. This helps to contextualise the development of local identities and social formation in a place for those not from that place, and holds the possibility of including new people as insiders, rather than being excluded as peripheral. Those brought in by the process of gentrification can become welcomed into the struggle and become allies in a common cause to retain the identity of neighbourhoods in the face of gentrification. Unfolding untold stories allows heritage to be a locus for bringing people together, new future possibilities result, with the past providing a source of new stories in the world.

 A partnership was initiated between The House Mill Trust and UCL Institute of Archaeology (IoA) to develop heritage practice at House Mill. The partnership started in 2017, in advance of UCL establishing heritage programmes at the new UCL East campus and part of the commitment of UCL as a 'good neighbour'. So far, this partnership has been the focus for site-based student learning and research projects for IoA MA Managing Archaeological Sites (Applied Heritage Management, 2017–19), MA Cultural Heritage Studies (Placement and Dissertation Research) and MSc Conservation of Archaeology and Museums (Conservation Studies site projects). Since 2017, an annual MA student conservation management project has worked with the Trustees of House Mill to apply authorised heritage practice to the site management of House Mill. The Managing Archaeological Sites approach provides a 'best practice' reference point for conventional values-based conservation management that is taught and practised at UCL IoA. This offers conventional conservation parameters (that might otherwise be seen as an impediment by others) as creative opportunity for generating new narratives about place-making and place-keeping. This intersection seeks to compare the role of creative practice to that of heritage management in activating heritage places.

House Mill was the site of the first CCHS Curating the City Hidden Sites Research Workshop, 'Out of site out of mind', in 2018. 'Hidden Sites of Heritage' is a research theme in the University of Gothenburg/UCL Centre for Critical Heritage Studies, Curating the City research cluster activities for 2018–22. This theme interrogates the slow and still-to-be-disclosed value, or 'latency', of the physical remains of the past, exploring the implementation of diverse mechanisms for its activation in the present (Olsen, 2010: 118). This traces the entanglements between the projected past and the preferred future, as an act of speculative imagination (Sully, 2019). It blurs the heritage lines drawn between the infrastructures of past and contemporary cities in the buried spaces and uncovered places of vulnerable, minority and marginalised inhabitants of cities. This considers latency as a significant element in the enduring survival of heritage places, where the *tactics* of invisibility of physically and socially hidden sites become *strategies* of disclosure in shaping the world coming into being. Often hidden in plain sight, the concealed spaces of vulnerability can be transformed in their disclosure within activist claims about attachments to places (Amin and Thrift, 2017: 5). This unveiling of shared identities reveals the vulnerabilities and resilience of those people and their places. Such public exposure, in response to change and at a moment of threat, has social agency that may be more potent than the proper histories valorised by the authorised heritage processes.

Hidden sites of heritage: out of site out of mind

The 'Out of site out of mind' workshop in 2018 focused on the role of creative practice in the making of urban spaces out of heritage places. The workshop, co-curated with Artist-in-Residence, Cecilie Gravesen, compared the methods used in authorised heritage practice with the potential of creative activation to engage contemporary city dwellers with heritage places. By reflecting on the language of heritage management, the taxonomy of heritage places and heritage practices of recording space (collections, text, drawing, photography, drones and so on), creative practice can perturb the boundaries across which the living present becomes the detached past. In juxtaposing a tension between creative artistic practice and authorised heritage practice, we are able to activate a field of dynamic encounters between contemporary and past city dwellers, from which to imagine future urban lives. This offers the opportunity for heritage practitioners to look in on themselves, and for artists to gaze across the boundaries of the heritage world that is created. In doing this, we are able to realise the inherent assumptions of heritage practice and the stories it tells about itself, to reveal the edges of the heritage worlds that have been fabricated. This transdisciplinary project involved researchers, students, artists, volunteers and audiences drawing on the triangulated heritage perspectives of heritage, art and architecture. Through participatory speculation, experimental playfulness, insouciant choreographies, alchemic assemblages, lingering and looking in order to see differently, in order to see clearly. In so doing we can understand heritage truths, more as parables in flux between an objectified reality and inter-subjective fictions.

The research site at House Mill was curated in order to mobilise the agency of creative practice in the interrogation of the heritage work conducted on site. Recognising that heritage methodologies are not fixed, and are themselves subject to many interpretations, artists and designers speculated on the value of heritage management practices and examined the palimpsest qualities of the site through artistic and spatial outputs. Sometimes conclusive and sometimes open ended, the results of these explorations become a valid outcome of the heritage conservation process itself. A series of creative dialogues between heritage practitioners and creative practitioners included mindful time travel activities, a '1000-year drawing' communal artwork that transcended temporally laden storytelling and helped to reveal the flux of authorising narratives accumulated in the layers of recording that act as heritage interpretation. A product of this process was the *Pattern Language* exhibition by Cecile Gravesen and Robin Stein at the House Mill in June 2019 (Gravesen and Stein, 2019). Cecilie Gravesen invited people from the neighbourhood to curate a selection of objects from the Mill's stored collections of wooden patterns. Despite the national significance of this collection, stored in a secluded part of the Mill, the objects remained largely unknown to local residents and visitors, as traces of past lives hidden in plain sight. The volunteer curators included residents from surrounding housing, key workers from a local supermarket, the adjacent film studios, and a local pensioner group. The conversations that developed when the objects were selected, handled and assembled were documented as part of the finished artwork, reflecting on regeneration and social care in this neighbourhood. The exhibition was a response to ideas of heritage places and objects as assembled realities, enacting new realities by assembling things in new ways. The collections were made by people's actions (named individuals) and reified (categorised, inventoried, recorded, described, documented) through creative and heritage practice as objects in the world. These curated collections become a means to navigate people's relationships with each other and the Mill, as its neighbourhood undergoes the rapid changes of redevelopment. This transformed the House Mill, as a heritage place, into a portal on the reciprocal making of the world, people and places. The Mill as experienced, the informed Mill, the Mill inside us, the Mill on the peripheries, in the border lands, the Mill as an island, standing alone as slow dwelling in a turbulent swirl of change (Gravesen and Stein, 2019).

Conclusion

Authorised Heritage Discourse creates the proper place for heritage practice, as an administrative boundary around a terrain of authority that governs the rules of operation and knowledge production (de Certeau, 1984: 117; Smith, 2006). These boundaries create the threshold across which the living present becomes the detached past. This is the disciplining of the disposition of the world to reflect what is proper about these places through a system of defined meanings and values (Ingold, 2008: 1797; Harrison, 2013: 13). Authorised heritage practice provides a system that allows the disciplined transformation of 'improper' human spaces into 'proper' heritage places. This transforms spaces and things of the human world into heritage places and objects, and creates the approved ways to manage the heritage world of museums, historic buildings and heritage places. This results in heritage being essentialised in the divide between the present and the past, separated from its embedded state in the complex human systems of everyday life, replaced with relationships that are proper for heritage. This world within-a-bubble creates meaning to itself and of itself. It allows for problems to be created, in which heritage practice is the only proper solution. Inside this tautological bubble, assumptions become normalised and justifications for action remain uncontested.

Critical Heritage Practice requires practitioners to notice their assumptions, and to engage with others who may be able to reveal them, such as working with creative practice artists, makers, performers, hackers, repairers, healers and carers (Puig de la Bellacasa, 2017). Through creative activities that challenge places as legitimised sites for permissible behaviour, we can un-make and de-stabilise heritage places. This allows us to reform established heritage practices to better support the relevant and resilient development of historic cities. Conserving historic and archaeological sites as real *spaces* and heritage *places*, requires flexibility to encourage creative innovative practice, while sustaining heritage processes that allow for *space* and *place* transition. This requires heritage professionals to question how we develop effective living places by creating something new within the conservative constraints of preserving what is there before. This acknowledges the permanently provisional regenerative stages of heritage interventions, preservation and decay in the constant churn of urban spaces. Engaging in forms of maintenance, repair and renewal provides a speculative trajectory for decisions made about interventions in our urban places. This has important implications for the creative process of new developments and the prognosis for their role in future cities. Speculative imagination at point of origin can be calibrated by retrospective imaginings of past assumed futures, every new future shines a new light on its past. It also has implications for heritage processes that no longer imagine their role in recovering a lost past, but are engaged in designing the future city. Curating the city becomes an act of design in which the specifications are constructed within competing modes of practice. Heritage industry (in the administration/operation/actualisation of listed buildings, conservation zones and so on) operate within a specific discourse that will continue to be asserted in debates around the legacy of past cities in contemporary place-making. Rather than an act of wonder with its multivocal fleshy mysteries revealed, the heritage place is more often a dismembered carcass struck dumb with the butchery of heritage professionals.

It is necessary to look beyond human-centred heritage practice and seek to engage with more destabilised ideas of temporality and the more-than-human. How do we engage in pluri temporalities and multi-species relationships in order to inhabit an equitable world (Yusoff, 2018)? How do we re-situate heritage practice, from maintaining the metastable authenticity of heritage places, towards co-curating ecosociologically constituted multispecies worlds (Tsing, 2015)? What does it mean to be a 'good neighbour' within the human-centred world of the city, and our attempts to decentre the human through post-humanist environmentalism that aims to make visible the invisibility of non-human, non-animate inhabitants in claims of mastery and agency in the making of our worlds? This requires a move beyond concepts that continue to privilege human agencies that sustain inequalities, towards a pluriversity of affective ecosociological potentialities of (post) human and non-human matter. This can be addressed via transarticulating sympoietic framing that brings creative practice and heritage processes into flux through experimental science–art worldings. The deep timeframes of the Anthropocene potentially help to free us from a human-centred focus and allow us to step outside of current constraints in comprehending problems and taking action. Some methodological tools for a heritage response to the Anthropocene have been recently applied in the Speculative Design Project: 'Objects of the Misanthropocene'. Temporality, time travel, projected pasts, retrospective futures, broken worlds, truth and insouciance, and perturbations, have been utilised in this project involving a time travelling exhibition of objects from the Illegal Museum of Beyond.[2] These are methods for future making/world building, which can be deployed in order to move beyond the *plausible* future and shape *preferable* futures. This project forms part of an ongoing conversation between heritage and creative practice within the research theme of Curating a Certain Reality (dispersing uncertain fictions, assembling ambiguous worlds). This seeks to embrace inter-agential concatenation, conflict and friction as a starting point for creative responses in heritage, rather than as problems that need to be avoided, that becomes a means of realigning truth between dominant predatory narratives and less powerful stories that lie hidden (Connolly, 2011: 27). In the resulting flux of authorising narratives, multiple ambiguous readings of heritage discourses can emerge. This provides a speculative exploration of heritage care for living as-well-as-possible in more-than-human worlds (Haraway, 2016).

Notes

1   A UCL/UGOT CCHS, Curating the City Research Cluster project, January–September 2018 at House Mill (Sully 2019).
2   https://misanthropocene.wixsite.com/museumofbeyond.

References

Agamben, G. (2002) *Remnants of Auschwitz: The Witness and the archive*. New York: Zone Books.
Agamben, G. (2009) *The Coming Community*. *Theory Out of Bounds, Volume 1*. Minneapolis: University of Minnesota Press.
Amin, A. and Thrift, N. (2017) *Seeing Like a City*. Cambridge: Polity Press.

Anderson, R. (2006) *British Universities Past and Present*. London: Hambledon Continuum.
Armstrong, P. (2009) *Reticulations: Jean-Luc Nancy and the networks of the political*. Minneapolis: University of Minnesota Press.
Arthur, M. (2014) *UCL President and Provost*. https://www.ucl.ac.uk/news/2014/nov/provosts-perspective-why-we-want-your-feedback
Ashworth, G. J., Graham, B. and Tunbridge, J. E. (2007) *Pluralising Pasts: Heritage, identity and place in multicultural societies*. London: Pluto Press.
Augé, M. (2008) *Non-Places: An introduction to supermodernity*. London & New York: Verso.
Avrami, E., Mason, R. and de la Torre, M. (2000) *Values and Heritage Conservation: Research report*. Los Angeles: The Getty Conservation Institute.
Avrami, E. (2009) 'Heritage values and sustainability'. In A. Richmond and A. Bracker (eds), *Conservation Principles, Dilemmas and Uncomfortable Truths*. Oxford: Butterworth-Heinemann, 177–83.
Barad, K. (2007) *Meeting the Universe Halfway*. Durham, NC: Duke University Press.
Butler, B. (2003) *Return to Alexandria: Cultural revivalism and the Alexandria Project*. Unpublished UCL PhD thesis.
Butler, B. (2006). 'Heritage and the past present'. In C. Tilley, W. Keane, S. Kuechler, M. Rowlands and P. Spyer (eds), *Handbook of Material Culture*. London: Sage Publications Ltd, 463–79.
Connolly, W. E. (2011) *A world of Becoming*. Durham and London: Duke University Press.
de Certeau, M. (1984) *The Practice of Everyday Life*. Berkeley: University of California Press.
DeSilvey, C. (2017) *Curated Decay Heritage Beyond Saving*. Minneapolis: University of Minnesota Press.
Dunne, A. and Raby, F. (2013) *Speculative Everything: Design, fiction and social dreaming*. Cambridge, MA: The MIT Press.
Durie, M. (1998) *Te Mana Te Kawanatanga: The Politics of Maori self-determination*. Auckland: Oxford University Press.
Feld, S. and Basso, K. H. (1996) 'Introduction'. In S. Feld and K. H. Basso (eds), *Senses of Place*. Santa Fe: School of American Research Advanced Seminar Series.
Gravesen, C. and Stein, R. (2019) *Pattern Language*. New York: Circadian Press, Brooklyn.
Haraway, D. (2016) *Staying with the Trouble: Making kin in the chthulucene*. Durham: Duke University Press.
Harrison, R. (2013) 'Assembling and governing "cultures at risk" centres of collection and calculation, from the museum to world heritage'. In R. Harrison, S. Byrne, and A. Clarke (eds), *Reassembling the Collection, Ethnographic Museums, and Indigenous Agency*. Santa Fe: School for Advanced Research Press, 89.
Heidegger, M. (1927) [1962]. *Being and Time*. London: SCM Press.
Heidegger, M. (1971) *Poetry, Language, Thought*. New York: Harpers and Row.
Holtorf, C. (2009) 'On the possibility of time travel'. *Lund Archaeological Review*, 31–41.
Höppner, G. and Urban M. (2018) 'Where and how do aging processes take place in everyday life? Answers from a new materialist perspective'. *Frontiers in Sociology*, 3 (7).
Ingold, T. (2007) *Lines: A brief history*. Oxon: Routledge.
Ingold, T. (2008) 'Bindings against Boundaries: Entanglements of life in an open world'. *Environment and Planning A*, 40 (8), 1796–810.
Ingold, T. (2013) *Making Anthropology, Archaeology, Art, and Architecture*. London: Routledge.
Latour, B. (1988) *Science in Action: How to follow scientists and engineers through society*. Cambridge: Harvard University Press.
Latour, B. (1993) *We Have Never Been Modern*. Cambridge: Harvard University Press.
Latour, B. (1996) *Aramis or the Love of Technology*. Cambridge: Harvard University Press.
Latour, B. (2005) *Reassembling the Social: An introduction to actor-network-theory*. Oxford: Oxford University Press.
Lefebvre, H. (1991) *Critique of Everyday Life*. London: Verso Books.
Lewis, S. L. and Maslin, M. A. (2015) 'Defining the anthropocene'. *Nature*, 519, 171–80.
Massey, D. (2005) *For Space*. London: Sage Publications.
Menon, A. G. K. (2003) 'Conservation as a critical activity'. In E. Theophile and N. Gutschow (eds), *The Sulima Pagoda: East meets West in the restoration of a Nepalese temple*. Weatherhill, New York: The Kathmandu Valley Preservation Trust, 106.
Morton, T. (2013) *Hyperobjects: Philosophy and ecology after the end of the world*. Minneapolis: University of Minnesota Press.

Mulgan, T. (2011) *Ethics for a Broken World: Imagining philosophy after catastrophe*. Durham: Acumen.
Mulgan, T. (2014) 'Ethics for possible futures'. *The Aristotelian Society Proceedings of The Aristotelian Society*, (cxiv), part 1.
Mulgan, T. (2018) 'Answering to future people: Responsibility for climate change in a breaking world'. *Journal of Applied Philosophy*, 35 (3).
Nancy, J-L. (2000) *Being Singular Plural*. California: Stanford University Press.
Nancy, J-L. (2007) *The Creation of the World or Globalization*. Albany: State University of New York Press.
Olivier, L. (2011) *The Dark Abyss of Time, Archaeology and Memory*. Plymouth, UK: Altimira Press.
Olsen, B. (2010) *In Defence of Things Archaeology and the Ontology of Objects*. Lanham: Alta Mira Press.
Pink, S. (2012) *Everyday Life, Practices and Places*. Los Angeles: Sage.
Poulios, I. (2014) *The Past in the Present: A living heritage approach – Meteora Greece*. London: Ubiquity Press.
Puig de la Bellacasa, M. (2017) *Matters of Care: Speculative ethics in more than human worlds*. Minneapolis London: University Minnesota Press.
Rodwell, D. (2007) *Conservation and Sustainability in Historic Cities*. Oxford: Blackwell Publishing.
Said, W. E. (1978) *Orientalism*. London: Routledge.
Sanz, N. and Bergan, S. (2002) 'The Cultural heritage of European universities'. In N. Sanz and S. Bergan (eds), *The Heritage of European Universities, Volume 548*. Council of Europe Publishing: 49–63.
Sauer, T., Elsen, S. and Garzillo, C. (eds) (2016) *Cities in Transition: Social innovation for Europe's urban sustainability*. London: Routledge.
Smith, L. (2006) *Uses of Heritage*. Oxon and New York: Routledge.
Staniforth, S. (2000) Advances in Conservation: Significance, relevance and sustainability, inaugural speech. In *Tradition and Innovation*. The IIC Melbourne Congress 2000. Accessed 2 April 2019. http://www.iiconservation.org/.
Staniforth, S. (2006) Conservation: Principles, practice and ethics. In *National Trust Manual of Housekeeping: The care of collections in historic houses open to the public*. Amsterdam: Elsevier.
Sully, D. (ed.) (2007) *Decolonising Conservation: Caring for Maori meeting houses outside New Zealand*. Walnut Creek: Left Coast Press.
Sully, D. and Cardoso, I. P. (2014) 'Painting Hinemihi by numbers: People's-based conservation and the paint analysis of Hinemihi's carvings'. *Studies in Conservation*, 59 (3), 180–93.
Sully, D. (2015) 'Conservation theory and practice: Materials, values, and people in heritage conservation'. In C. McCarthy (ed.), *Volume 4: Museum Practice: Critical debates in the museum sector. International Handbook of Museum Studies*. Sydney: John Wiley and Sons, 1–23.
Sully, D. (2019) 'Unheritaging hidden sites of heritage'. In C. Gravesen and R. Stein (eds), *Pattern Language*. New York: Circadian Press, Brooklyn, 13–15.
Tuan, Y-F. (1977) *Space and Place: the perspective of experience*. Minneapolis; University of Minnesota Press.
Tsing, A. L. (2015) *The Mushroom at the End of the World: On the possibility of life in capitalist ruins*. Princeton: Princeton University Press.
UCL (2016) 'UCL East at Queen Elizabeth Olympic Park, Stage 2 Consultation Report: Soundings.' July 2016. http://www.queenelizabetholympicpark.co.uk/-/media/lldc/cultural-and-education-district-documents/2175-ucle-stage-2-report-appendices.ashx?la=en.
UN (2012) 'The future we want: Outcome documents of the United Nations Conference on Sustainable Development, Rio de Janeiro, Brazil, 20–22 June 2012.' https://sustainabledevelopment.un.org/content/documents/733FutureWeWant.pdf.
Wright, P. (2012) 'Afterword: Dialogue in the space between ethnography and heritage'. In E. Giaccardi (ed.), *Heritage and Social Media: Understanding heritage in a participatory culture*. Abingdon and New York: Routledge, 239–43.
Wijesuriya, G. (2007) 'Conserving Living Taonga: The concept of continuity'. In D. Sully (ed.), *Decolonising Conservation: Caring for Maori meeting houses outside New Zealand*. Walnut Creek, CA: Left Coast Press, 59–70.
Yusoff, K. (2018) *A Billion Black Anthropocenes or None*. University of Minnesota: Minneapolis.

3
Historic urban buildings in the university curriculum: the re-evaluation of Haga, Gothenburg, as urban heritage

Ingrid Martins Holmberg

Introduction

Universities are key actors when it comes to producing knowledge about the city itself, and in taking on this role they are providers but also organisers of the imaginary realms in which cities come into being. This chapter encircles the role of universities as producers of a particular kind knowledge – knowledge of 'urban old buildings' – in order to understand particular relationships of knowledge-and-actions and their implications for urban heritage.

The case used for illustrating the argument is located in Gothenburg, Sweden, where the historic urban settlement Haga, erected just outside the city walls during the same century as the city, was the object for complete re-evaluation in the early 1970s, from 'old-and-ugly' to 'old-and-nice'. This re-evaluation brought about a new narrative: the narrative about Haga as the city's oldest workers' area (Holmberg, 2002; 2006). The new narrative provided input for the articulation of so-called 'historical values', necessary for designation of Haga's old buildings as officially listed cultural heritage. This heritage designation was successful and saved the area from the established political plans for complete erasure through the means of demolition and clearance. Subsequently, Haga's re-evaluation has often been understood as the tipping point when

Sweden's modernist urban planning came to an end and was replaced with preservation-oriented planning, so-called 'urban renaissance'.

Previous research on this case has focused on the different groups of actors – public institutions such as the Gothenburg Historical Museum and cultural heritage institutions acting at regional and national level (Andersson, Ejderoth-Linden, Lönnroth, Nilsson, and Tengnér, 2009), or groups of activists, such as young squatters (Thörn, 2013) – as driving agents behind the process. This chapter investigates the case of re-evaluation from another perspective: it aims to show how different academic disciplines and university curricula have provided the 'knowledge of old buildings' necessary for the re-evaluation and how this knowledge production is deeply intertwined in actions, or lack of actions, taken in different situations. This focus helps to explain the emergence of the new and converted place-identity of Haga as 'old-and-nice'.

The chapter begins with an introduction to the perspective employed in the study and situates the case in the context of several parallel contemporary urban discourses, here understood as 'particular imaginary geographies', identified through analysis. The issue of urban re-evaluation will be covered next. Finally, the role of the university as a producer of knowledge is discussed.

Research perspective, methodology and context

Cities are assemblages of material buildings and spaces produced over long time periods, and contain layer upon layer of meanings, echoing both forwards and backwards in time. In the context of cities, meaning-making is an inextricable nestling of imaginations that concerns memory and materiality in combination. Old cities have a palimpsest character, and can be conceived of and conceptualised in different and disparate manners. Nevertheless, not every building or place in the city is considered heritage, neither formally through listing, nor informally in general understanding. Accordingly, it is relevant to ask how these distinctions between heritage and not-heritage are made, but also what they imply.

The designation of buildings into official heritage 'listing' (the closest Swedish equivalent being *byggnadsminnesförklaring*) is often summarised as a practice of 'picking the raisins out of the cake'. The enterprise to designate buildings into cultural heritage objects relies on both expertise and public consensus, or at least public acceptance, which naturally brings a general conformity to the outcome of the process. Different national contexts employ different ways of designating and safeguarding buildings, but the outcomes indicate shared challenges and similar imaginaries (Holmberg, 2002; Phelps, Johansson and Ashworth, 2002). While these practices of heritage designation have their own history, in companion with the continuous urbanistic tradition established by Lewis Mumford (*The Culture of Cities*, 1938), Kevin Lynch (*The Image of the City,* 1960), Jane Jacobs (*The Death and Life of Great American Cities,* 1961) or Christopher Alexander (*A City is Not a Tree*, 1965), to mention but a few, it seems to be a general understanding that the ethos of heritage designation underwent a major conceptual shift just after the mid-twentieth century (Wetterberg, 1992; Engelbrektsson, 2005, 2009; Janssen, Luiten, Renes and Stegmeijer, 2017). The shift is conceived as a move from the concern for individual buildings, so-called monuments, to a concern for entire built environments. The contribution of the research of this chapter is the identification of the conceptual displacements that were necessary for this shift, here called 're-evaluation'. The issue of concern is the semiotic re-evaluation of ordinary urban old buildings from 'old-and-ugly' to 'old-and-nice'.

Within the scholarly field of urban studies, re-evaluations of ordinary urban old buildings are generally understood in terms of rent gaps, that is to say shifting economic real estate values, where semiotic re-evaluation constitutes a surface phenomenon that is played out visually as an effect of a more fundamental underlying urban socioeconomic restructuring within post-industrial society (Smith and Williams, 1986; Zukin, 1989). In the research for this chapter, the understanding of re-evaluation is contrary: the sociocultural or socioeconomic restructuring and reshuffling in the urban core – that is to say gentrification, post-modern urbanism, rent gaps, planning incentives or regulations – are regarded as 'reactive effects' of meaning-making. The reason is simple. The case of concern clearly shows how discursive re-evaluation occurred while the buildings stayed more-or-less the same (old and derelict). The reinvestments – renovation, modernisation, restoration, rebuilding and so on – happened only after the semiotic re-evaluation was settled. The activities of renovation and other heritage concerns came as a response to the identity switch of the area. Accordingly, semiotic re-evaluations of urban old built environments are here understood as the primary instances of a continual socio-spatial and imaginary co-construction of the city as a moral geography. Although this chapter presents research from only one case – Haga in Gothenburg, Sweden – re-evaluation from 'old-and ugly' to 'old-and-nice', and vice versa, is a phenomenon of its own and a possible constituent to any place (Holmberg, 2009, 2015).

The conceptual tools for my research on the semiotic re-evaluation are, for the discursive aspects, the rules of discourses for an archaeology of knowledge (Foucault, 1969) and, for the spatial aspects, the notions of spatial polysemy and resemantisation (Landzelius, 1999, 2001) in combination with the notion of geographical imaginations (Gregory, 1994). The analysis concerned 150 years of representations, textual as well as pictorial, of the City of Gothenburg's historic urban buildings and the urban settlement of Haga. The material comprises topographical literature in its widest sense, but also publicly available presentations and debates, as well as scholarly work. Through a careful analysis of the character and content of these representations, it was possible to identify four different urban imaginary geographies, each of them with its own internal logic. Three of them appeared in parallel, and one of them, the fourth, replaced them all. The break between the first three and the fourth is where re-evaluation could occur.

In the following section, I give an overview of these imaginary geographies and sketch out how each of them, and one in particular, conditions the appearance of Haga and old urban buildings. The focus is on the relationship of each imaginary geography to particular knowledge claims, institutional contexts and university disciplines.

Knowledge contexts and claims of imaginary geographies

The role of universities as producers of knowledge of urban old buildings is here understood as related to the university curriculum per se, that is to say the lectures, readings and specific procedures as well as overarching guidelines through which knowledge is performed and conceived as truths. Moreover, it is also understood as related to the various institutions and institutional frameworks outside the university in which university students are received as experts after their exams, and where they continue to perform their particular segment of academic knowledge. On a general level of understanding, the knowledge, or in Foucauldian terms these 'knowledge claims', align with the academic principles of accuracy. On a more specific level of understanding, they are in line with the rules that guide the production of knowledge within the individual faculties or disciplines.

The knowledge field of interest in this research concerns 'knowledge of historic urban buildings'. Not unexpectedly, this knowledge field appears as dispersed among the spectrum of historical university disciplines, such as art history, national history, archaeology and ethnology/folkloristics, as well as the polytechnical institution of architecture. However, and as revealed through this research, these disciplines of the humanities are accompanied by other and less expected and less obvious disciplines and contexts in the role of knowledge production. In the examination of the details of the connection between the obvious academic knowledge contexts and the different public practices that intervene in the city as socio-material device (in the case of Haga in Gothenburg), it became apparent that, for example, engineers, healthcare experts, jurists, political scientists, writers, artists and journalists have also made important contributions to the field 'knowledge of historic urban buildings'. In the following section, the specific features and character of academic 'knowledge of historic urban buildings' within the four different imaginary geographies will be outlined.

The imaginary geography of attraction

The imaginary geography of attraction for the city of Gothenburg is delineated in time by the appearance of travel guides for Gothenburg in the 1860s, which is the historical context of a growing bourgeoisie and an increased inter-urban mobility through the inauguration of the railway connection between the capital, Stockholm, and Gothenburg, and the publication of guidebooks in the 1980s of the city of Gothenburg that create a different geography. Research into these texts, published over the course of a century, reveals that they, while making up crucial instances for canonisation of urban attraction, not only had an astounding permanence up until recently but also established a role model for the ways in which the historical knowledge concerning the city of Gothenburg (that appeared somewhat later) should be geographically structured. It is a remarkable find that texts that explicitly address the history of the city of Gothenburg, published a few decades later, construct a geography that seems almost modelled from the travel guides. In the imaginary geography of attraction, guidebooks and history texts present the identical topography.

This imaginary geography comprised a network of buildings, places and routes that were all related to the urban dwelling of the late nineteenth-century bourgeoisie. It contained an astonishingly small number of historic urban buildings. Except for some eighteenth-century architectural masterpieces in the core (which were conceptualised in terms of 'artistic values', not 'historical'), old urban buildings are largely absent during the entire period of c.1860 to 1980. Instead, this imaginary

Figure 3.1 The invisibility of historic urban buildings in the imaginary geography of attraction. This postcard of the early 1900s clearly illustrates how the imaginary geography of attraction set its entire focus upon the monumental features of the city. Accordingly, the postcard shows monumental buildings at the edge of Haga together with the historical fortlet from the seventeenth century in the background. This imaginary geography consequently omitted the city's heterogenous vernacular historic building-stock. To take this shot of Haga, one must keep at the outside from where none of these buildings can appear. Note that not even the name of the area is mentioned: 'The Caponnière street with the public library, the Renström's Public Bath and the fortlet "The Crown" in the fund' [*Kapuniergatan med folkbiblioteket, Renströmska Badanstalten och Skansen "Kronan" i fonden*]. Photo: City Museum, Gothenburg

geography consequently situates 'old buildings' in the urban periphery and literally in terms of 'picturesque' . Not surprisingly, the old buildings of contemporary Haga remain largely absent in the geography of attraction. Exceptions are the traces of an early historical caponnière (part of the city's seventeenth-century defence facility and as such a souvenir of its founding era) and some bourgeoisie milieux (charity-funded institutions situated at the outer edge). When mentioned at all, Haga appears as 'bad' as well as 'ugly' , but *nota bene* not as 'old' .

The imaginary geography of attraction appears to originate among writers and intellectuals competing to sell their work to an emerging squad of publishers, and is published from the mid-nineteenth century onwards in the format of guidebooks containing both texts and illustrations. The early guidebooks can be considered the founding texts of the imaginary geography of attraction, since their topography was taken up in the somewhat later history publications authored by prominent university scholars. The texts presenting Gothenburg history (mainly published in the 1930s and onwards) covered the city from its founding in 1621 and up until the 1920s (shortly before publication). The university here appears through the work of individuals – academics – that perform their knowledge claims while combining the duties that come from the university contract with services in public institutions outside university.

An example is the historian, Professor Helge Almqvist (1880–1944), editor of the many historical volumes of the city's anniversary series, and author of several parts (see Almqvist, 1929, 1935). In this work, the administrative and political history of the city is in focus, which also includes municipal plans and constructions over the centuries. Although the area of Haga in contemporary times has a very distinct feature, originates from the seventeenth century (and as sole suburb has a plan designed in the 1660s) and is thus of the same age as the city inside the walls (officially established by the king in 1621), Almqvist does not give it a section of its own in the historical volumes he is editing.

A more direct focus on the city of Gothenburg as an aesthetic and cultural edifice comes with the numerous texts by art historians. The university professor in art history, as well as head of the renowned design museum Röhsska Museet, Axel Romdahl (1880–1951), authored numerous texts on Gothenburg's architecture and architectural history, which reinforced the imaginary geography of 'monuments' (see Figure 3.1). Even more so, his adept Licentiate of Philosophy, Maja Kjellin (1898–1971), contributed with a mapping of the earliest historical layers of Gothenburg's urban buildings. In her final work, published in 1971 by the commercial real estate company Göta Lejon (established by the municipality for the purpose of clearance of old urban buildings), she actually paid special attention to Haga. The text contains the first ever survey of all original properties and their successive owners and dwellers. In the text, however, the area appears as a distant place of the past. The text represents the historical Haga as completely disconnected from contemporality and the existing old buildings (some of which were actually of substantial age).

The imaginary geography of commemoration

The imaginary geography of attraction is constructed through several unrelated and un-orchestrated publications over more than one hundred years, and established the monumental features, whether old or new, as primary representations of the city. This created a persistent invisibility of the historic urban buildings in general and the old settlement of Haga in particular. The 'imaginary geography of commemoration', existing in parallel during a century-long period, instead works under the logics of memory, and is played out in spatial practices of identification and preservation of individual objects. This imaginary geography commenced in the 1860s with the inauguration of the local historical museum, the

Figure 3.2 The monumentalisation of vernacular buildings of the urban fringe in the imaginary geography of commemoration. This photo is taken at a public debate on the future of the fringe settlement Green Street in 1955. In front of a model of some of the buildings stands, at the far left, the museum director Dr Stig Roth (promoting maintenance) in company of the city's planning manager (promoting demolition) and other prominent men. Shortly after, the area was demolished after thoroughgoing historical documentation by the museum, and transplant of some buildings to a reserve. Photo: City Museum, Gothenburg

Gothenburg Historical Museum (a common phenomenon in the wake of industrial mass-production) and continued up until the publication in 1967 of Gothenburg Historical Museum's inventory of the city's buildings of historical value.

While the main authors of the imaginary geography of commemoration were qualified experts with university education in historical disciplines, mainly but not only art history, and employed by the official city museum – that is to say, built heritage experts – this imaginary geography is also constructed by writers and actors without a strong academic connection. Also, the broader public was concerned about commemoration in terms of identification and selection of urban old buildings, through listing or other, in the ongoing dramatic urban transformations during the twentieth century.

The research reveals that the imaginary geography of commemoration shares the basic assumptions of the imaginary geography of attraction – the monuments and the monumental features are unquestioned as objects of concern – but adds on to it a focus on 'vernacular buildings from the pre-industrial period (before the 1860s) used for dwelling' and situated in the urban outskirts, far from the dense urban core. The pre-industrial era and its vernacular architecture were included also in the imaginary geography of attraction but did not appear with any particular identity or historical significance. The commemorative identity of such buildings was constructed through particular scientific practices: in the 1950s and before new high-rise buildings were erected in their place, the old suburban building complexes of Gröna gatan and Majnabbe were the object of scientific documentation, and then either saved in the format of models (see Figure 3.2) or carefully taken down and re-erected on another site, so-called reserves. These two projects were both based upon the notion of the importance of buildings that were 'vernacular, preindustrial and situated in the outskirts', but run and fueled by different funders: Gröna gatan was in the realms of the Gothenburg Historical Museum, while Majnabbe, the birthplace of the nationally renowned artist Evert Taube, became the object of concern for Majnabbe and, through massive mobilisation, also for the general public.

By and large, the imaginary geography of commemoration only put another layer on top of the chronologically parallel geography of attraction, comprising the monuments (that is to say, buildings often considered as being of high artistic quality). The difference was the addition of buildings that could relate to 'the vernacular dwelling-house'. This means that the imaginary geography of commemoration on a local spatial scale reiterated what on the national scale became a main vehicle for Swedish-ness: the red wooden rural cottage. In that sense, the buildings of concern for commemoration did not have any connections to the contemporary city and its old quarters, but were treated as isolated objects that could even be moved without losing any historical values.

No surprise, then, that the area of Haga was largely absent in the imaginary geography of commemoration, similar to its absence in the imaginary geography of attraction. Also, here in this imaginary geography we find some notable exceptions: Haga's mid-seventeenth-century street pattern plan; a few late nineteenth-century charity-funded dwelling houses, designed by a prominent architect; the street-view with extraordinarily lavish, well-maintained, 1890s dwelling houses (Västra Skansgatan with its so-called *landshövdingehus*, a local wooden housing type, see below). Having remained tacit for a century about urban old buildings that were different from 'vernacular buildings from the pre-industrial period in the urban outskirts', these three exceptions occur in the Gothenburg Historical Museum's inventory of the city's buildings of historical value in 1967, mentioned above and below.

The textual representations that together construct the imaginary geography of commemoration emerge from authors such as the Gothenburg Historical Museum and intellectuals, as well as the local community association. The most prominent texts stem from the built heritage experts, who all had their disciplinary training in the historical disciplines, and most predominately in art history. Dr Stig Roth (1900–72) is a clear example. He became the director of the Gothenburg Historical Museum in 1955 and had his disciplinary schooling in art history. As the director of the museum, Roth was in charge of the listing of buildings that would be considered as heritage. The listing, ordered by the City Council in order to prepare for clearance, was then executed by Dr Harald Widéen (1912–2001), who had defended his thesis in archeology, and was later to succeed Roth as director. The inventory was presented for the City Council in 1967, and the result was an urban geography of commemoration consisting of dots. As for Haga, the minimal selection of buildings included meant that the museum experts, in their knowledge claims, did not gainsay or question the planned urban renewal of Haga. However, the dot that marked Haga's entire street-pattern perhaps indicates an intention to counteract Haga's complete erasure.

The imaginary geography of sanitisation

In parallel with the imaginary geographies presented above, the imaginary geography of sanitisation was present for over a century. This

Figure 3.3 The stigmatisation of the urban vernacular historic buildings in the imaginary geography of sanitisation. The idea of urban sanitisation gradually radicalises when, during the mid-twentieth century, the claims on renewal gain political power. The imaginary geography of sanitisation builds upon the two parallel imaginary geographies (focus on monuments and/or historical buildings in the urban periphery) and develops it into making Haga appear as the epitome of 'old-and-ugly'. The city's planning manager, Tage William-Olsson, in a 1943 daily newspaper interview states that 'Haga lacks the idyll found in for example Majorna [that is, Gröna Gatan] where there are several preservation-worthy buildings. From a cultural-historic point of view I cannot find any reason to keep away from sanitisation of Haga […] The proper and rational thing to do is to demolish the old hovels and build new.' [*Haga saknar sådana idyller som exempelvis Majorna där det finns åtskilligt man vill bevara. Ur kulturhistorisk synpunkt kan jag inte finna att det finns något som hindrar en sanering av Haga. […] Det enda man kan göra i Haga är att rationellt riva ned de gamla rucklena och bygga nytt.* (Stadsplanechef Tage William-Olsson, in *Göteborgs-Posten* 1943, "Sanering av Haga ...."] Photo: Lars Mongs

was established in the mid-nineteenth century with the emergence of investigations – public as well as private – of the population's health in relation to their dwelling conditions, which in Sweden served as a propagator for better dwelling conditions for the many (that is to say, urban renewal) up until the early 1970s. But in contrast to the other imaginary geographies, the imaginary geography of sanitisation comprised substantial and comprehensive representations of both Haga and old buildings – however, only with regard to their prospective renewal and/or replacement with modern equivalents. In this imaginary geography, urban old buildings do appear constantly, but exclusively in terms of 'old' in combination with 'ugly' and 'bad'. The representations are, in fact, statements that support the argument for the erasure of old buildings in general (see Figure 3.3).

This imaginary geography of sanitisation is in fact, as it appears for the city of Gothenburg, born out of notions within national and municipal politics in the housing sphere. In this context, 'the home' appeared as the site of potential social progress, practically as well as symbolically, and therefore as the site where material improvement in terms of modernisation becomes the most urgent. In the beginning, this imaginary geography was established through mere overviews and mappings of the shortcomings of the physical features of old buildings, but successively it transformed into a practical politics of sanitisation of urban homes, that is to say massive urban renewal. The latter was locally played out with particular regard to the central old area of Haga in Gothenburg, that was presented as the city's 'number one area ripe for clearance'. However, and similar to the case in the parallel imaginary geographies above, old buildings situated in the urban outskirts – where they originated from the pre-industrial era and could be considered as picturesque – could appear as 'old-and-nice' but never an affirmative mode: their appearance was always connected with a distinct nostalgic dismissal.

The research not only revealed that this imaginary geography was capable of conceptualising both Haga and urban old buildings in general, it also became clear that for the first time the historical dimension of the contemporary Haga, Haga's history of (the existing) built environments, was put forth and conceptualised. In a series of texts – some of them with an extraordinarily extensive dissemination within national politics – the history of Haga's wooden low-rise and dense nineteenth-century housing stock was explored. One important example is the national public investigation, *Bostadssociala utredningen,* of 1949 that as its main case presented Haga's housing stock. The part that reported on Haga mapped out various technical and social variables on the scale of each individual building, and ended with the laconic conclusion that – since these buildings were erected in the second half of the nineteenth century and hence an outcome of speculation (in contrast to being 'crafted' as in the pre-industrial era) – they were all ripe and ready for clearance.

Symptomatically, the conclusion was based upon studies of only some quarters of the eastern, poorest and most miserable part of the area, but presented as if concerning the entire building stock of the area. Haga's other buildings – some of eighteenth- and early nineteenth-century origin, some erected for the bourgeoisie in the second half of the nineteenth century, some multifunctional buildings combining consumption or workshops with dwellings, some public buildings like schools and a bath, some huge factories (Haga was at that time an extremely heterogeneous space, with deep history) – were all left out from the imaginary geography of sanitisation.

The knowledge field of 'historic urban buildings', in terms of an exploration of the history and origins of the ordinary wooden housing stock of Haga, here appears for the first time. It is surprisingly not related to the historical university disciplines, rather it stems from public institutions that put their knowledge into practice, and that operate through knowledge claims that are based in the rules of the faculty of social sciences. We here meet contributions from sociologists, engineers, healthcare experts and jurists accompanied by journalists, making use of quantitative approaches to present Haga's old buildings. The representations are of various kinds. The mappings (above) on individual buildings, were accompanied by statistical surveys of the inhabitants' attitudes towards clearance (Karsten-Wiberg, 1949).

This survey can serve to illustrate an aspect of the knowledge claims in the imaginary geography of sanitisation. Established for the purpose of serving national politics and governance in overviews and analyses of different fields of interest, the faculty of social sciences in this case contributed with knowledge based on quantitative methods. It is precise and logical. However, here are several examples of friction between the research result produced according to the disciplinary rules, and the imaginary geography of concern. The report of 1949 by sociologist Karsten-Wiberg, for example, offers astounding generalisations in the interpretation of the inhabitants' answers: when the answers diverge from the expected 'yes, I long for a prompt clearance of Haga and a new modern apartment in the suburbs' and instead indicates that the inhabitants are content with Haga, the impulse to explain this fact as an exception to the rule gets too strong. In a similar vein, the surveys of the city's dwelling conditions, reported in quantitative manner, show that Haga is *one* of the areas with deficient dwelling conditions, but that the standard significantly varies between Haga's different quarters (some without complaints). Nevertheless, the summary puts Haga at the top, as number one on the list of areas with deficient dwelling conditions. In these cases, the imaginary geography of concern appears as more powerful than the disciplinary rules for knowledge.

Re-evaluation of urban old buildings as empirical phenomenon

The city of Gothenburg's urban renewal programme was launched in 1962 with the start of the business of the clearance company Göta Lejon (see above), and ran for an entire decade. It has become renowned as Sweden's most comprehensive project in this field. The decision to start up the municipal urban renewal programme was taken univocally by all parties and without questions, and since it needed the support from private enterprises, due to economic-jurisdictional conditions, it was documented that all external parties – local industry, such as SKF, Volvo and shipping agencies, together with the various insurance companies, the many different banks, the merchants' association, but also the NGOs such as the tenants' association and the labour union – unanimously supported the urban renewal programme. No diverging opinions were expressed in relation to the careless erasure and renewal of the historic urban areas of Gothenburg. Not surprisingly, none of the different areas on the map for renewal were part of any of the imaginary geographies of attraction or commemoration.

The imaginary geographies described above were played out as knowledge claims in the urban landscape and, as such, borne by art historians, planners, architects, archaeologists, sociologists, engineers and other experts in official public institutional service, inside and outside the university, as well as by private writers, locals, journalists or amateurs. Their acceptance, therefore, appears as widespread, unquestioned and well established among the general public, but also among the political parties and major economic actors. These three urban imaginary geographies existed in parallel for over one hundred years, and while each individual representation had a scope and means of its own, they were unanimous in their mode of conceptualising historic urban buildings and Haga.

This overview does not answer how re-evaluation could take place. Accordingly, the aim of this research has been to reveal also the instance of 'ambivalence': how within each individual imaginary geography, there are representations that, while presenting the urban landscape in accordance with the established rules, also hesitate. This kind of ambivalence is thus 'internal to each established imaginary geography'. In Foucauldian terms – and related to full discursive formulations – ambivalence, or 'contradictions', are instances of reflection understood as the very points of instability that may enable a discursive shift. The instances of ambivalence – where the knowledge rules are explicitly or implicitly contradicted from within – are thus where re-evaluation could emerge: they are hesitations about how and which is the most appropriate way to let the object appear. In the case of the parallel imaginary geographies, the urban old buildings and Haga were not really objects, they were 'abjects': although existent, they remained invisible; and the research was set out to map out the character of invisibility. Re-evaluation could happen only when new representations, that were building upon other and different knowledge claims, came to undermine the established ones. The details of the ambivalence and contradictions, specific to each imaginary geography as well as their functions and effects, have been explored and discussed in Holmberg (2006, 2011) and are here mentioned merely as fact.

In the following section, I will turn to the next imaginary geography, and it must be stated immediately: it replaced the former three but still draws its concepts and terms from them, and at the same time it turned the meaning of content upside down. This is an 'imaginary geography of maintenance', with the new object: 'old-and-nice Haga'. Through the lens provided by the archaeology of knowledge (Foucault, 1969), it becomes clear that this new imaginary geography of maintenance could amount to an entire new 'discursive formation' with a complete object ('old-and-nice Haga') at its centre of discourse. According to Foucault, a discursive formation occurs when many voices/actors in different positions, and with different rationales, make competing knowledge claims upon the same discursive object. This is what happened from the early 1970s regarding Haga and urban old buildings: there was a massive increase in all kinds of representations, and several positions were being mobilised. This means that the new discourse was not only in opposition to earlier knowledge claims, it in fact comprised an entire conceptual reconstruction of the appearance of Haga and of urban old buildings. Haga and urban old buildings became re-evaluated from 'old-and-ugly' into 'old-and-nice'. The new discourse thus indicated a paradigmatic shift.

The imaginary geography of maintenance

The basic assumption of the new imaginary geography was based in the notion of maintenance, meaning 'caring for', 'saving', 'supporting'. This imaginary appeared rather suddenly and with substantial influence around 1970, and consisted of representations that extensively as well as exclusively addressed urban old buildings in general, and Haga in

Figure 3.4 The imaginary geography of maintenance brought a conversion of Haga's moral geography from the former 'nice-new-outer', to the 'nice-old-inner'. The previously invisible as well as despised inner part of Haga, with low-rise wooden construction and mainly of dwelling function, now became the main bearer of identity, through the means of the narrative of 'the city's oldest workers' area. This narrative was the guideline for the preservation project. Photo: Lars Mongs

particular. These new representations were, thus, distinctly different from the previous ones. Here, the area of Haga constantly appeared as essentially attractive (despite its derelict shape), as being of substantial historical importance (although framed by a 'history from below'), and its physical structure as a role model for town-planning (in the tradition of urbanism). Urban old buildings appeared as repairable and as embodying values of a kind that could not be designed, but that needed long periods of time in order to develop: 'old buildings were not merely of historical interest … they were an asset and a resource, and they embodied many values that couldn't be reproduced in the massive urban renewal project of the 1969s and 1970s' (Åman, 2000: 212, 220). Overall, the new representations exhibited a sense of empathy with the old buildings, their patina and their non-rectilinear material features.

From a retrospective point of view, it is obvious that the new imaginary geography of maintenance for Haga incorporated and built upon several forerunners whose representations of old buildings had hitherto remained unnoticed. In doing so, it immediately could draw together the already existing, but dispersed, knowledge into a coherent imaginary of 'old and nice Haga'. The most important part of this knowledge originated from the realms of the university, and had been produced already during the preceding decades. There are examples of research, publications and even courses, in several disciplines and academic contexts. The focus was on 'the late nineteenth-century housing and culture' (for example, Paulsson, 1950; Gejvall-Seger, 1954; both in art history); or on 'the history of wooden urban buildings' (for example, Rentzhog, 1967, in art history; Norberg, 1937/61, in architecture); or on 'the urban vernacular architecture' (for example, Liedgren, 1961, in art history). These were set pieces, foundation works, all authored by academics or university scholars, that came to make substantial contributions to the establishment of the new knowledge object. At the time they were published, however, these works had generally passed quite unnoticed outside their individual disciplinary contexts in academia.

In addition, more instantly applicable academic works on Haga were revisited. At the schools of architecture, the critical debate – about contemporary urban planning, about the politics of urban renewal, as well as about urban qualities – had been alive and kicking for over a decade, delivering notable critique towards modernist and reductionist spatial planning. From the early 1960s onwards, Professor Göran Lindahl (in duty 1961–91) at the Royal Academy of Arts in Stockholm, wrote numerous debate articles on current public politics and practices in the urban centres. His agenda for academic research, as well as education, pointed in the same direction: '[we] can no longer stay with [addressing a set of] individual objects. The question does not at all concern any particular kinds of buildings or collections of buildings; *the issue is how we are able to address the transformation processes as such*' (Lindahl, 1968, my italics). This academic context continued to deliver important works on the dramatic effects of generalist urban renewal for decades to come. Professor Lindahl was also responsible for the ground-breaking panNordic ICOMOS research project of 1971, *The Nordic wooden town* [*Den nordiska trästaden*], through which the extensive series of 23 publications on small cities with wooden architecture was published. At the Department of Architecture at the Chalmers University of Technology in Gothenburg, the 1968 national conference Preservation–Sanitisation [*Bevarande–sanering*] served as the very mobilising starting-point for an intensive public debate on the local urban renewal project. In this university context, Professor Elias Cornell (1916–2008) had already (in

1963: 46) claimed that the current planning approach to Haga was too narrow-minded, and that at least the more recent examples of Haga's buildings '… are very well suited for conversion into modern housing'. His overt critique of urban renewal set the agenda for the entire department for more than two decades. Cornell emphasised that the studies in the history of architecture must cover the humanistic perspectives on art history, but 'with the aim to turn them into productive tools for addressing contemporary problems' (Werne, 1982: 6). History, or the long-term perspective, was here conceived as an enabling power that could change the future.

With the help of forerunners such as these, all of a sudden Haga's existence was inscribed in the historical contexts of its origin, and it became comprehensible and visible. From that moment on, all kinds of studies of Haga began. In the ongoing combat about the future of Haga (erasure or preservation) that continued for another decade, the construction of Haga's identity *through* a historical narrative was the main controversy.

The main combatants were, on the one side, the established parties that were formally as well as informally responsible for the establishment of the urban renewal programme – the city's planning department, the labour movement and also, as shown above, the intelligentsia of the cultural heritage sector – all contributing to the invisibility, marginalisation and stigmatisation of Haga. On the other side was a set-up of loud, young academics (students as well as academic staff), locals and writers in different constellations, together with a new generation of intelligentsia in the cultural heritage sector. Notably, some individuals were academics, locals, writers and staff at heritage institutions at the same time. The latter party's imaginary geography will be delineated in the following.

The knowledge claims of the imaginary geography of maintenance for Haga concerned neither the particularly old buildings, nor the particularly prominent, nor the particularly poor buildings, it instead encircled the *entire* area of Haga. No dots or aspects, but a clear line that on the map encircled the entire area and thus included all its heterogeneous social and material content. This map, established by the Gothenburg Historical Museum in 1971, is what brings the new object into being. However, Haga's new visibility also came with a new narrative: the entirety had to be made meaningful *as a whole* instead of in its individual components and gems. In the enterprise to save the entire area of Haga from clearance, the representations from now on labelled Haga as 'the oldest working-class district of Gothenburg' (Haga, 1979). This new identity was based upon a realistic account of *some* parts of Haga, of a *section* of its long history, and of a *segment* of its (contemporary as well as historical) population. There are in fact numerous accounts over time of Haga's genuinely socio-spatial heterogeneity, as is also clearly apparent upon making a visit (Holmberg, 2006).

However, this biased identity became the hegemonic understanding of Haga in the imaginary geography of maintenance. Moreover, it was materialised through the endless compromises that followed in the process of turning Haga into heritage (successive steps were taken over a period of 10 years). The narrative of 'Haga as the oldest working-class district of Gothenburg' influenced every step and measure: 'which buildings to focus upon and which to let go', 'which historical features to be transferred to the new buildings and quarters', 'which colour-scheme to apply', 'which street furniture to add', 'how the prescriptions for renovation should be designed' and so on. This narrative appeared to constantly, in all steps and measures, favour particular aspects of Haga's space: the 'innermost', the 'wooden' construction, the 'housing'-function, the 'turn-of-the-century period'. The previously despised wooden inner part of Haga was brought to the fore as the main bearer of identity (see Figure 3.4). On an overarching level, this brought about a consequent conversion of Haga's moral geography: from the former 'nice-new-outer', to 'nice-old-inner'.

The university's role in this new imaginary geography is delineated by the successive appearance of several research works on Haga from the early 1970s. From this time on, the number of publications on Haga increased rapidly, and particularly active was the Department of Architecture at Chalmers University. Almost every event discussed Haga; there were theses on all levels that focused on one or another aspect of Haga; there were research conferences and reports, as well as academic journals with special issues that step-by-step covered what happened in Haga, all with the aim to change the long-established demolition plans. From the Department of Architecture alone, some 10 works on all academic levels covered the case of Haga. Contributions to the focus on Haga also stem from other disciplinary contexts at the University of Gothenburg, such as ethnology, with works of the theme 'working-class culture', art history, with a series of publications on Haga's buildings and other urban vernacular buildings, sociology, as well as psychology theses on life in old urban quarters. With the help of this work, Haga's identity became consolidated in terms of 'old-and-nice'.

The contributions from academia to the imaginary geography of maintenance are substantial and stem from many disciplines, although the work at the architectural departments is outstanding in quantitative terms. Before concluding the chapter, I will turn to the issue of how the connections between academia and public institutions outside the university were played out in this imaginary geography.

An illustrative example is the 1972 publication of the book *Landshövdingehus och trähus i Göteborg*, co-authored by Ursula Larsson, PhD, student at Chalmers University of Technology, and Gudrun Lönnroth, architect and ethnologist employed at the Gothenburg Historical Museum. The work consisted of a comprehensive up-to-date cover of the typical and unique housing type of Gothenburg, the *landshövdingehus*, constructed out of a two-storey, wooden-part-on-top-of-a-brick-basement structure. The type, as such, had been debated heavily among the intelligentsia since its origin in the 1870s, but was nevertheless common in all parts of the city, including in Haga. This publication became one of the cornerstones in the argument to save the entire area of Haga. In the combination of different disciplines, Larsson and Lönnroth's cooperation is symptomatic of the imaginary geography of maintenance. The expertise of both authors was in architecture, and Lönnroth could moreover also draw on her doctoral thesis in ethnology – a reconstruction of the socio-spatiality of 1875 in Haga's eastern and poorest quarters – that was considerably biased towards a proletarian understanding of the findings (Holmberg, 2006). Haga was undoubtedly a workers' area in this knowledge-context.

Another notable aspect of the role of the university knowledge production in this imaginary geography is the extraordinarily blurred line between the university, the public institutions and the activists. The university appeared as a Hydra: many of the individuals that can be identified as knowledge-producers in the re-evaluation process, appeared in several groups. Academics could take part in different contexts at the same time, but they could also shift position. Lönnroth, mentioned above, an architect by training, was employed by the Gothenburg Historical Museum shortly after the museum's new master plan was taken in 1967, and could from this position work for an establishment of the museum's new preservation programme for Haga, while at the same time staying connected with the activities at the Department of Architecture. One of the professors in architecture, Lars Ågren, acted as researcher while in parallel being a member of the city's board for culture, the Swedish National Heritage Board, and as the driving force behind the founding of an independent Centre for Building Culture at Chalmers. Another example is the lively – as well as robust – local residents' association, *Hagagruppen*, consisting of students in architecture, journalism, art, sociology, political economy and so on, together with more established Haga inhabitants with academic training, and non-academics of all ages.

Conclusion

This chapter encompasses the role of universities as producers of a particular kind of knowledge – knowledge of 'urban old buildings' – in order to develop an understanding of the relationship of knowledge-and-actions that came with the complete re-evaluation of the area of Haga in the early 1970s, from 'old-and-ugly' to 'old-and-nice'. While the entire area of Haga, with its seventeenth-century street pattern and derelict and heterogeneous old building-stock, was the number one on the list of the municipal clearance programme of 1962 (decided upon in complete political consensus), the area had some 60 buildings considered as fit for designation into official cultural heritage. Earlier research and understandings have focused upon the influence of power-shifts between various (groups of) actors, in combination with successive re-orientation in public governance. The argument in this chapter is that the re-evaluation cannot be fully understood without considering also how semiotic re-conceptualisations predating the new urban politics, were essential for this comprehensive shift.

With the help of the tools for discourse analysis in combination with spatial semiotics, and on the basis of an analysis of all publicly available representations of Gothenburg's 'urban old buildings' and 'Haga', four imaginary geographies of this urban landscape have been revealed: the imaginary geographies of attraction, commemoration, sanitisation and maintenance. They are connected and show distinctive similarities, but each of them conditions the appearance of the object in very particular ways. It can be argued, however, that while being separate, they nevertheless presuppose each other: the complete absence of Haga in the imaginary geographies of attraction and commemoration (both anchored in notions of monumentality), enable the complete stigmatisation of Haga in the imaginary geography of sanitisation.

The first three (attraction, commemoration, sanitisation) existed in parallel (between approximately 1850–1970) and the fourth (maintenance) replaced them in the early 1970s. The analysis proposes that the university, through its academic knowledge produced according to the rules of accuracy as well as the individual disciplines, played an irreducible role in providing a set of different 'frames' – disciplines and/ or faculties – for conceptualising the urban landscape. However, from this analysis it also becomes clear that the different imaginary geographies had their basis in different 'knowledge claims', not disciplines, and that each imaginary geography could gather contributions from various academic disciplines and contexts, both inside and outside the university. It also became clear that there was a dialectic power-relation between 'the imaginary geography' and 'the disciplinary rules'. While some imaginary geographies (for example, attraction and commemoration) to a large extent could comprise and accommodate the specific disciplinary knowledge claims, others (for example, the imaginary geography of sanitisation) were instead in powerplay and would disrupt the hegemony of the disciplinary knowledge claims. In this case, the principle of accuracy could be set aside in order to align with the basic assumption of the imaginary geography.

The chapter also argues that the key to a better understanding of the controversy (settled once the new imaginary geography of maintenance was established – alive and kicking – in the early 1970s) is to consider it as being a clash between different knowledge claims regarding the most correct representation of Haga's past. Among the propagators of maintenance, all opportunities available to shed light on Haga's poor and marginalised past were used to construct a new imaginary geography based upon the notion of working-class history. Numerous representations of different aspects of its past were produced in different university contexts, and for the first time ever Haga appeared as an integral part of the urban landscape. On the other side, the propagators of clearance persistently held on to the imaginary geography of sanitisation, with Haga as the most 'classical' of urban renewal areas, and insisting that the workers' (past and present) substandard deficient dwelling conditions must be erased. As shown in this chapter, this 'emptification', denial and drainage of Haga's content and meaning was well established for over one hundred years and on the political agenda for several decades. In numerous debates it was explicit that the core controversy was played out on an ideological level – the proper way to address the workers' place in history – while supported by various technical investigations, economic calculations and jurisdictional-administrative re-orientations.

The particular kind of knowledge – knowledge of 'historic urban buildings' – was identified as present over long periods of time. For a long time, its character didn't primarily shift, but between the different parallel conceptualisations (absent in two, stigmatised in the third). The fourth, the imaginary geography maintenance, appears at a certain point in time, the early 1970s, but draws upon a series of forerunners, previously published but relatively unnoticed academic contributions to the knowledge field of 'historic urban buildings'. The new imaginary geography of maintenance quickly proliferates with numerous new contributions to the knowledge field 'historic urban buildings'. It is characterised by multi-disciplinary, problem-based approaches, and by its outreach activities both inside and outside academia. The role of universities as producers of this knowledge, whether of a more basic or a more proactive kind, has been proven to enable dramatic shifts in the conceptualisation of the city. The new questions to be raised at this point concern the many contemporary challenges for knowledge production in times where the university's role is questioned, and the knowledge field of 'historic urban buildings' can be easily dismissed as completely innocent.

References

Alexander, C. (1965) 'A City is Not a Tree'. *Architectural Forum*, 122 (1), 58–62.
Almquist, H. (1929) *Göteborgs historia: Grundläggningen och de första hundra åren, Del 1, Från grundläggningen till enväldet (1619–1680)*, Skrifter utgivna till Göteborgs stads trehundraårsjubileum genom jubileumsutställningens publikationskommitté, 1. Gothenburg: Göteborgs stad.
Almquist, H. (1935) *Göteborgs historia: Grundläggningen och de första hundra åren, Del 2, Enväldet och det stora nordiska krigets skede (1680–1718)*, Skrifter utgivna till Göteborgs stads trehundraårsjubileum genom jubileumsutställningens publikationskommitté, 1, Gothenburg: Göteborgs stad.
Åman, A. (2000) 'Före och efter 1970 – från konsthistoria till konstvetenskap'. In B-I. Johansson and H. Pettersson (eds), *8 kapitel om konsthistoriens historia i Sverige*. Stockholm: Raster, 203–23.
Andersson, H., Ejderoth-Linden, S., Lönnroth, G., Nilsson, L. and Tengnér, L. (2009) *Varför revs inte hela Haga? Om bevarande av en stadsdel i Göteborg*, Rapport 2009:64. Gothenburg: Länsstyrelsen i Västra Götalands län, Kulturmiljöenheten.
Bostadssociala utredningen (1949), SOU 1949:26. Slutbetänkande, Del 2: Saneringen av stadssamhällenas bebyggelse, organisationen av låne- och bidragsverksamheten för bostadsändamål. Stockholm.
Cornell, E. (1963) 'Arkitekturpromenad'. In K. Hjern (ed.), *En bok om Göteborg*. Stockholm: Gebers Förlag.
Engelbrektsson, N. (2005) 'Tendencies to a shift in attitudes to cultural heritage: A survey'. Paper presented at the International Seminar 'Cultural Heritage: Use, maintenance and long-term development' November 2005, University of Gothenburg and Chalmers University of Technology. Publ.: see Engelbrektsson (2009).
Engelbrektsson, N. (2009) 'Il Patrimonio Culturale: Verso un Cambiamento degli Approcci: una Analisi'. In: L. Morrica (ed.) *Conservazione Integrata del Patrimonio Architettonico Urbano ed Ambientale*. Neapel: Università degli Studi di Napoli Federico II, 103–16.
Foucault, M. (1969) *L'archéologie du Savoir*. Paris: Gallimard.
Gejvall-Seger, B. (1954) *1800-talets Stockholmsbostad: En studie över den borgerliga bostadens planlösning i hyreshusen*, diss. Stockholm: Stockholms högskola.
Gregory, D. (1994) *Geographical Imaginations*. Cambridge, MA.: Blackwell.
GUS [signature] (1943) 'Sanering av Haga får börja vid vackraste torget i Nordeuropa?', *Göteborgsposten* 1943-11-07.
Haga: Göteborgs första förstad och första arbetarestadsdel (1979). Göteborg: Göteborgs Museer.
Holmberg, I. (2002) '"Where the Past is Still Alive": Variation over the identity of Haga in Göteborg'. In A. Phelps, B. Johansson and G. J. Ashworth (eds), *The Construction of Built Heritage: A north European perspective on policies, practices and outcomes*. Aldershot: Ashgate.

Holmberg, I. M. (2006) *På stadens yta: Om historiseringen av Haga*, diss. Institutionen för kulturvård, Göteborgs universitet, Göteborg: Makadam förlag; Göteborgs stadsmuseums förlag.

Holmberg, I. M. (2009) 'Historicisation of Malmberget'. In B. Svensson and O. Wetterberg (eds), *Malmberget. Structural change and cultural heritage processes – a case study*. Stockholm: Riksantikvarieämbetet, 42–54. https://www.raa.se/app/uploads/2012/06/Malmberget-structural-change-and-cultural-Heritage-processes.pdf.

Holmberg, I. M. (2011) 'ed bebyggelsehistoria som medel. Om relationer mellan kunskapsbildning och uppvärdering av äldre stadsbebyggelse', *Bebyggelsehistorisk Tidskrift* 2010:60. http://media.bebyggelsehistoria.org/pdf/BHT60_2010_78-93.pdf.

Holmberg, I. M. (2015) 'Historisering in situ? Om Gamlestadens kulturmiljö och kulturarvet som text'. In S. Andersson, K. Olsson and O. Wetterberg (eds), *Gamlestaden. Strukturella förändringar och kulturarvsprocesser: En fallstudie*, Curating the City Series. University of Gothenburg.

Jacobs, J. (1961) *The Death and Life of Great American Cities*. New York: Random House.

Janssen, J., Luiten, E., Renes, H. and Stegmeijer, E. (2017) 'Heritage as sector, factor and vector: Conceptualizing the shifting relationship between heritage management and spatial planning'. *European Planning Studies*, 25 (9), 1654–1672. https://doi.org/10.1080/09654313.2017.13 29410.

Karsten-Wiberg, E. (1949) *Sociologisk undersökning i Haga våren 1949: Redogörelse utarbetad i Göteborgs stads statistiska byrå*. Gothenburg.

Kjellin, M. (1971) *Haga i Göteborg*. Gothenburg: Fastighetsaktiebolaget Göta Lejon.

Landzelius, M. (1999) *Dis[re]membering Spaces: Swedish modernism in law courts controversy*, diss. Gothenburg: Dept. of Conservation, University of Gothenburg.

Landzelius, M. (2001) 'Contested representations: Signification in the built environment'. *American Journal of Semiotics*, 17:2, 139–99.

Liedgren, R. (1961) *Så bodde vi*, 2nd ed. [1961]. Stockholm: Nordiska museet.

Lindahl G. (1968) 'Konstakademins byggnadsskola'. In K. Lindegren, G. Söderström and R. Söderberg (eds), *De sköna konsternas akademi: Konstakademin 250 år*. Stockholm: Allmänna förlaget.

Lynch, K. (1960) *The Image of the City*. Cambridge, MA. and London: The M.I.T. Press.

Mumford, L. (1938) *The Culture of Cities*. New York City: Harcourt, Brace and Company.

Nordberg, B. (1961) 'Landshövdingehusen: Ett stycke Göteborgsk bebyggelsehistoria'. In *Årstryck*, Göteborgs historiska museums årsbok, årgång 1961. Gothenburg: Göteborgs historiska museum.

Paulsson, G. (1950) *Svensk Stad: Liv och stil i svenska städer under 1800-talet, del 1*. Stockholm: Bonniers.

Phelps, A., Johansson, B. and Ashworth, G. (eds) (2002) *The Construction of Built Heritage: A north European perspective on policies, practices and outcomes*. Aldershot: Ashgate.

Rentzhog, S. (1967) *Stad i trä: Ett skede i den svenska småstadens byggnadshistoria*, diss. Stockholm: Nordiska museet.

Smith, N. and Williams, P. (eds) (1986) *Gentrification of the City*. Boston: Allen and Unwin.

Thörn, H. (2013) *Stad i rörelse: Stadsomvandlingen och striderna om Haga och Christiania*. Stockholm: Atlas.

Werne, F. (ed.) (1982) *Människan står i tur: Sjutton uppsatser, en dikt och en bibliografi tillägnade Elias Cornell*. Gothenburg: Sektionen för arkitektur, Chalmers tekniska högskola.

Wetterberg, O. (1992) *Monument och miljö: Perspektiv på det tidiga 1900-talets byggnadsvård i Sverige*, diss. Gothenburg: Institutionen för arkitekturhistoria, Chalmers tekniska högskola.

Zukin, S. (1989) *Loft Living: Culture and capital in urban change*. New Brunswick, NJ.: Rutgers University Press.

4
Deferred heritage: digital renderings of sites of future knowledge production

Adam Brown

Introduction

The future university is a work in progress, via the operations of a convergent network of language, media and technology that is itself a work in progress. The proliferation of images of future university campus developments represents the visible corollary of a global construction boom that has accelerated innovations in construction and imaging technologies. UK universities alone have sunk £27.6 billion into capital projects since 2006 and were forecast to have spent another £19.4 billion in the period 2016–20 (Taylor, Roberts and Coulson, 2018). Taylor et al identify the global boom in campus development as driven by a drive to reimagine the university as part of a productive economy built on innovation and economic growth, 'driven by the international focus on scientific and commercial innovation' (Taylor, Roberts and Coulson, 2018). In this context, the image of the future university plays a functional role in the production of a particular notion of the future itself.

In relation to university developments, images of an institution undergoing rapid change as if the future has already arrived produce the university in the present as already primarily a space of innovation and perpetual economic productivity, reifying particular modes and practices of representation and production, based on ideas of what a 'future' is, was or might be. The resulting synergy of productive technology and discourse represents a complex and perplexing landscape in which discourse, image and function are folded into one another. An institution with long-standing cultural capital is projected into a space in which it disrupts itself: attempting to imagine, or image, the 'university of the future' is to model a temporal hybrid that derives a large part of its identity from establishment and longevity – heritage – as it comes to depend on disruptive change for its perpetuation. It is possible to observe a significant paradox in the race to create future pasts of sufficient potential gravitas to undergird institutional stature, as if the heft of a large and complex institution is something that can potentially be visualised into being, and in doing so, ensure the generation of sustaining capital. The institution (in this chapter treated as form, image or location) thereby becomes a by-product of the mechanisms put in play to produce it. The projected endless construction of architectural form – in the case of an institution representing an embodiment of discursive power – produces what may be termed 'deferred heritage'. If, as Betancourt elucidates, debt is the promise of future labour (in this instance, student debt), then the contemporary university sits at a particular juncture of two kinds of economic risk management, individual and institutional – each to a degree premised upon future institutional status (Betancourt, 2010).

The 'speculative' university would appear to play on paradoxes of this nature, of which there are many. However, rather than observing a divergence from a formerly stable, functional state of affairs, it is necessary to see the binary opposition in each as produced and productive – the relationship between disruption and heritage is not a succession, but a contemporaneous relationship: if the institution lacks the promise of stability, it will have nothing to trade. Simultaneously, unless the established institution participates in disruption – attacking the very notion of establishment and permanence – it becomes itself impermanent, subject to the disruption of the market. This paradox is more than incidental: it pervades and undergirds the institution as representation, as an element in the contemporary discourse that serves to construct it, to produce the ideal of the institution that will be reified in architectural form. This chapter is a way of drawing out this binary opposition in order to speculate on its production, downstream effects and impact in the present, via encounters with images of the contemporary university under these conditions.

I have structured this chapter in the form of a series of 'routes' representing negotiations between solid and immaterial, image and form, following a cue from McKenzie Wark. In Wark's formulation of 'vectorial' capitalism, established forms of labour relationships, resource extraction or commodity exchange co-exist with what he terms 'vectorialism', characterised by digitally accelerated negotiation and speculation relating to value and information (Wark, 2015). As 'vectorialists' trade in such immaterial commodities as intellectual property, future value, risk and debt-bound obligation, the persistence of the commodity mode and the means of material extraction are necessary – not that one supersedes the other, but the relationship between the two is produced, mutually co-dependent and productive. Such divergence of image and form appears to produce the discourse of disruption as a kind of mask, concealing the true relationship between speculation and the commodity, between labour and the trade in labour, by placing emphasis on one of the terms. In this chapter, I will speculate on the formulation of the 'knowledge economy' as one such mask, dependent on a relationship between resource extraction and its exploitation, yet concealing one of its key terms: the domain of 'knowledge' has come to encompass the redaction of certain relations of exploitation or the operations of the market, as knowledge itself becomes commodified. Such a development has been termed 'agnotological' capitalism by theorists such as Betancourt and others (Betancourt, 2010).

Movement along these routes is bidirectional. We might see it as an oscillation. Each pair of co-dependent poles (for example, 'future' and 'past') spin out centrifugally from the immanence of this oscillation, produced as representations. The immanence of the oscillation – the trade in potentialities and negotiation of value – generates capital not in the future, but in the present. It could be argued that the future is not the point at all: the aim of all this furious speculation on futurity is to generate sufficient suspension of disbelief to enable continuous gambling, speculation and renegotiation in the present, so as to accelerate the generation and flow of capital – as Benjamin's gambler, in Convolute O of *the Arcades project*, works to make the future present now, regardless of what might happen when the die is cast.

> Well, what is gambling … but the art of producing in a second the changes that Destiny ordinarily effects only in the course of many hours or even many years, the art of collecting into a single instant the emotions dispersed throughout the slow-moving existence of ordinary men, the secret of living a whole lifetime in a few minutes – in a word, the genie's ball of thread? Gambling is a hand-to-hand encounter with Fate … The stake is money – in other words, immediate, infinite possibilities. (Benjamin, in Rosenthal, 2012)

We can observe the digital architectural rendering as a similar irruption of the future – one of infinite productive possibility – into the immanence of the present. In this chapter, I shall explore the paradoxes presented by images of future institutions, the role of which would appear to be both to embody the past and produce the future, sustained by an economic system that depends increasingly on speculation, chance and the management of risk.

Route 1: between disruption and permanence

The university under production is a space in which decisions relating to pedagogic functions, research focus and funding are hotly contested, in the context of major global challenges to long-established notions of the institution's public function. Integration with industry and innovation – specifically that of a disruptive nature – are key drivers of change. In a recent report by auditors Ernst and Young on the future of Australian universities, following up on their white paper of 2012, a survey of the sector's opinions of the future are observed to reflect those of the authors:

> Participating university leaders noted a tension between the dual strategy needed to continue to reposition and optimise the core business of their universities, while also investing in future disruption for tomorrow. This echoes our own view that … commercial and the disruptor university scenarios are the most likely to become reality. Both will require leaders to simultaneously reposition their institutions by converging with industry, while also exploring disruptive new business models that can fend off new market entrants. (Ernst and Young, 2018)

The production of future reality would appear to be the core purpose of this document: speculative, yet based on accumulated data from Ernst and Young's consultations since 2012, in which I participated as an academic in an Australian higher education institution from 2010 to 2013. The report is a flag driven into a battlefield, which deploys the outcome of six years of consultation as evidence of a common desire for the convergence of university, industry and the financial sector. Crucially, rather than expansion of the knowledge sector encouraging the free exchange of information, Ernst and Young frame the 'disruptive' as itself an exclusive construct that includes 'fending off' as much as expansion and growth. This implies a system that includes efforts to police access to knowledge, and that growth in the knowledge sector simultaneously requires strategies of exclusion and inclusion.

This policing can be seen to be linked to an education system under financialisation that is dependent on the production of students as a standing reserve of consumer debt (McLanahan, 2016). The economics of educational funding have become linked to the contrary production of educational 'non-knowledge' – signifying that those not in possession of the stamp of institutional advancement – a degree – will not 'contribute', 'innovate' or engage in entrepreneurial activity, and will risk poverty. Two possible conditions present themselves to the player in this market, be they aspiring student or academic: that of the precarious worker or the salaried graduate. However, this needs to be seen as a constructed opposition, carried through representation. Professionalism is marketed and semiotically conferred by the institution represented – as much sign as reality, especially considering that the future graduate will almost certainly emerge under obligation of debt to achieve their promised economic potential.

Under these conditions, CGI renderings of campus redevelopments produce the university as a site symbolic of a system that will successfully produce agents with the ability, driven by debt obligation, to continue contributing to the economic system that generates the image: promises upon promises, speculation upon speculation. The image of the university itself possesses the status of a guarantee of the production of more speculative activity, rather than formerly secure, but now semiotic commodities such as 'students' or 'new knowledge' or even 'form'.

The production of the subject is indeed a political function, but it is possible to see this translating rapidly into a technological one – in the sense that the extraction of higher-level functions from certain jobs become a prelude to automation: 'smartness' implies participation in the generation of new machines, 'dumbness' defines jobs that can be done by machines. Astra Taylor uses the term 'fauxtomation' to describe the rhetorical positioning of a mechanised, projected future driven by automation and the replacement of human labour by the mechanical:

> Since the dawn of market society, owners and bosses have revelled in telling workers they were replaceable. Robots lend this centuries-old dynamic a troubling new twist: employers threaten employees with the specter of machine competition, shirking responsibility for their avaricious disposition through opportunistic appeals to tech determinism. (Taylor, 2018)

The notion that networks, data or machines can be as intelligent or more intelligent than humans is mythological: its purpose is to redefine 'knowledge.' On an epistemological level, this serves to generate a polarisation between knowledge that is 'useful' to that which is 'useless,' or to use contemporary phraseology, 'smart' to 'dumb.' 'Smart' in this sense is teleological, defining that which contributes to the production of capital.

The visible signs of agnotology are huge gleaming universities contained within smart structures – thereby delineating where and what constitutes smartness (a paradox in itself), but crucially places where smartness is absent, defining 'smartness' as what can be communicated by such tropes. One can observe an agnotological function in the dual operation of image and building, the production of ignorance of any kind of knowledge that cannot be framed in these terms.

Route 2: between photograph and data

The digital rendering, published ahead of the building's construction, has to be considered in absolute ignorance of what the rendering-as-artefact might signify after topping out, to fully grasp its significance. Suspending disbelief, the viewer will contribute to the coming into being of an institutional embodiment of progress and knowledge production along certain defined lines, notwithstanding the theatrical deployment of glitch or palimpsest, such as found in Hadid's structures or those of campus developments described later in this chapter. A knowing reader will take the disruption of the building's form not as an actual error in the code, but a sign that has had to be produced in order to make it absolutely clear to all onlookers that this is not a pyramid or a Boulée mausoleum, but something defiantly contemporary. Bridle, in his formulation of the New Aesthetic, is acutely aware of the fact that digital production is now so advanced in its ability to produce analogues of pre-digital form that, in order to produce the 'sign' of digitality that is so 'contemporary', signs from the technological past need to be deployed: pixilation, low resolution, interlacing, badly registered colour separations (Bridle, 2011).

The institution is subject to a contest of representation, which attempts to locate it discursively in space and time. The formal resemblance of the architectural rendering to photographic imagery produces a loaded question: paradoxically, it appears to represent a view of an already extant state in advance of its material production. However, as a networked element in a productive technology, the rendering operates both as 'proof of concept' to potential investors, and a fully realisable model embedded in construction technologies: in many ways, the digital rendering could be described as already 'built,' in that within current construction technologies, visual data is mapped on to economic calculations and structural decisions within the platform. Within emerging developments in digital planning and construction, political, planning and consultative insights are converted into 'data' (Future Cities Catapult, 2018). The rendering takes on the form of material fact as a result of its integration into networks in which phenomena are either convertible into data or else lack agency within productive networks. Siegel (in Kitchin, 2014) remarks on two significant characteristics of data: that, as opposed to 'knowledge', it functions to produce change via prediction, as opposed to understanding, with respect to predictive analytics: 'we usually don't know about causation, and we often don't necessarily care … the objective is more to predict than it is to understand the world … It just needs to work; prediction trumps explanation' (Siegel, in Kitchin, 2014).

Furthermore – and here, the visual metaphor is telling – it provides 'oligoptic views of the world', defined as:

> … views from certain vantage points, using particular tools, rather than an all-seeing, infallible God's eye view (Amin and Thrift, 2002; Haraway, 1991). As such, data are not simply natural and essential elements that are abstracted from the world in neutral and objective ways and can be accepted at face value; data are created within a complex assemblage that actively shapes its constitution. (Kitchin, 2014)

The production and analysis of data would appear to be one of the key functions of the new university, depicted in predictive images produced by data environments informed by oligoptic perspectives, with the intention of producing reality by means of strong-arming it into being.

In Nassim Taleb's prescient and widely read analysis of economic catastrophe *The Black Swan*, the author uses the metaphor of a 'fire in the casino' (Taleb, 2007) to describe devastating unforeseen contingencies disrupting the otherwise routine play of speculation and trading within capitalist economies. Benjamin also uses the very same architectural metaphor on multiple occasions to describe such economies (Benjamin, in Rosenthal, 2012). Speculative activity – circumscribed by the parameters of the market (which excludes, of course, any black swans) – is formed from associations, commodities, value systems and mutually negotiated behaviours. To render it as a thing, such a dispersed, networked

Figure 4.1 Zaha Hadid, rendering of HKPU Jockey Club Innovation Tower, 2012. © Zaha Hadid Architects

and performative organism can be framed by an image of a building. Indeed, this would appear to be an increasingly pressing societal and economic imperative.

Maybe the university is beginning to look a little like a casino, and vice versa. Examining renderings from 2012 of Zaha Hadid's Jockey Club Innovation Tower, for Hong Kong Polytechnic University, completed in 2014, we encounter images of a future university building funded by philanthropic donations from the proceeds of gambling activity, represented as if it has already been built (see Figure 4.1). Representations of this building in advance of its construction may offer a way of exploring how contemporary notions of two kinds of speculation – academic and economic – relate together in a functional way under what Betancourt (2010) terms 'digital capitalism', which itself is based on trade in the spectacular.

> The digital is a symptom of a larger shift from considerations and valuations based in physical processes towards immaterial processes; hence, 'digital capitalism' refers to the transfer of this immateriality to the larger capitalist superstructure. Because the digital is a semiotic realm where the meaning present in a work is separated from the physical representation of that work, the 'aura

of the digital' describes an ideology that claims a transformation of objects into … semiotically-based immateriality. (Betancourt, 2010)

Semiotic activity, in the context of neoliberal economic networks based on speculation, produces capital in the present, not the future. One might recall Debord's famous description of the 'spectacle' as 'capital accumulated to the point where it becomes image' (Debord, 1994) and describe the rendering as an example of a functional element of an emerging means of production, masquerading as a spectacular image that represents an extant – and itself spectacular – structure. Significantly, such image-objects can be seen to relate to divergent understandings of temporality and process in relation to markets in property and commodities, but also to knowledge and research. Despite their projection, their ability to generate capital is immanent. What is happening now, in relation to these images of the future, is the marshalling of productive force that will secure their coming into being: a powerbase solidifies; reification is under way.

Route 3: between knowledge and location

We can regard such structures as the Innovation Tower – and its renderings – as salient examples of the kind of architecture proper to what has been termed the knowledge economy. James et al, in exploring the significance of this concept to global education, trace its roots in the work of management theorist Peter Drucker (1959) and sociologist David Bell from 1979, and outline how 'the term "knowledge economy", and its synonym, the "knowledge-based economy" [KBE], did not emerge until the early 1990s. The development of a KBE has since become the guiding principle for economic development policy across the world, although it remains a poorly (often tautologically) defined and contested concept' (James, Guile and Unwin, 2011).

What unites its divergent definitions is a notion of knowledge as commodity in space: in effect, metaphors of commodity exchange – flows, inequalities, temporal and causal models and market-like systems – underpin a territorialising concept that sutures epistemology to the generation of capital via the medium of accelerated technological networks of information exchange and control in physical space. For James and her co-authors, considering the educational spaces of the KBE, such networks are distinctly topological:

We identify three important insights: a) that learning is interactive, involving both individual and institutional actors, and therefore territorially embedded; b) that learning is a collective process that can be conceptualised at the scale of the firm and region, as well as the individual; and c) that learning should be seen not only as the acquisition of specific technical (or 'component') knowledge but also in terms of routines and informal institutions ('architectural knowledge'). (James, Guile and Unwin, 2011; 3–4)

Though the idea of the KBE has become dominant since the 1990s, the trade in 'knowledge' requires the existence of an attendant market in manufacturing and labour. A great deal of work goes into asserting the inevitability, futurity and destiny of this new model of economic progress, while also concealing its relationship to labour and the dirty business of resource extraction and exchange (Berardi, 2011). The KBE could be said to be itself 'work in progress'. In which case, the idea gives rise to the generation of spatial representations that could be claimed to be promotional, propagandistic, but also engaged in a project to rapidly reify an ideological project based on disruption and deregulation, which divides the world into those participating in it and those subjected to it, and which polices the borders between the two. In interrogating these image-objects, it is possible to identify two categories of viewer: those participating in the financialised economy – the world of investments, futures speculation, and so on, in which value is derived from a set of representations of conditions and commodities – and a 'naïve' position characterised by the perception of the image as an analogue of a 'reality', in relation to which the market is an abstraction.

Renderings such as those of the Innovation Tower possess a programmed ability to migrate and operate across and between contexts of production and speculation, bridging material and speculative commodity forms. For a KBE under production, they represent fragments of a possible world, credibly rendered, which open onto a totalising landscape. It is also possible to observe the space between the image considered as a representation (built form) and an object in its own right (an 'image-object') as a field in which something is produced. If the photograph demands of the viewer a certain practice of viewing, based on extrapolation beyond the frame, and a conviction of the believability of the presented scenario, then the presentation of data in the form of the photographic can be argued to function as a rhetorical device that retrospectively guarantees the empirical truth of its prior assumptions, through the accultured behaviour of the subject in the act of viewing. In a sense, a critical viewer needs to unlearn how to view these images – they are no longer anything as graspable as representations, but have come to exist as elements of a productive network. However, this duality – at once a discrete, framed and migratory image and a networked artefact – is not incidental but, I shall argue, precisely keyed into the mechanisms of agnotological capitalism. The mode of viewing that sees such images as previously understood – models, projections, drawings – draws the viewer away from an understanding of precisely what kind of abstraction they are.

Route 4: between representation and production

Digital images of future development projects are increasingly materially integrated into technological networks of accelerated production, playing a functional and networked role in relation to material changes in the built environment. If in 1967 the architectural historian Manfredo Tafuri argued that architecture was becoming a 'moment in the chain of technological production' (Tafuri, 1969), this condition is now itself undergoing a process of prototyping and production as a mechanised, and not merely a linguistic or discursive, network. Emerging technologies such as Building Information Management (BIM) are characterised by innovative approaches to building design represented by the integration of processes of visualisation, calculation and construction via a common platform. Autodesk, producers of popular BIM suite Revit, claim that within such data environments:

> … computation is applied to represent built artifacts as three dimensional, behaviourally simulative predecessors of their physical counterparts. It provides a critical foundation to help designers, builders, and owners gain a competitive advantage with the ability to access, share, and make use of enormous amounts of information throughout the lifecycle of buildings and infrastructure. (Autodesk, 2018)

BIM and its attendant innovations produce the image itself as 'graphical information'. Within such networks, the image is considered to be part of a 'common data environment', which also includes engineering, surveying, legal, economic and consultative data. A fully realised simulation, in the form of an articulated and networked model including images and predictive data, precedes construction of the building itself.

The image is conceived as a distinct category and form of such data, with the power to be framed, portable and to migrate across a range of contexts. This ability is dependent upon the persistence of historical codes of representation – single point perspective, framing, formal continuity – and established tropes. In both data and image form, it is still possible to subject it to critical exploration of its function as linguistic or discursive signifier, according to methodologies derived from critical theory. The rendering is still 'encoded' and 'decoded', to apply Hall's useful framework, which locates the image as one element in a discursive chain of production and reception (Hall, 1980).

Considering the database, Lev Manovitch makes some broad generalisations:

> During the 1980s and 1990s all image making technologies became computer-based thus turning all images into composites. In parallel, a Renaissance of montage took place in visual culture, in print, broadcast design and new media. This is not unexpected – after all, this is the visual language dictated by the composite organization. What needs to be explained is why photorealist images continue to occupy such a significant space in our computer-based visual culture. (Manovitch, 1999)

The persistence of representational schema that consider the image as a framed and bounded object allow such 'data' to coalesce into useful form, and by doing so gain the ability to migrate across a range of discursive contexts not limited to productive technologies: the image retains its established function: affective, prophetic, documentary, or in the case of the photographic, clinging to the legacy of its truth function.

Route 5: between function and sign

In Hadid's structure, traces of the processes of image production – glitch, imperfection, translation – have been integrated into its design. One might term this an 'ironic' reading, in which the architect anticipates Debord's critique.

The external form of the Innovation Tower plays on the symbolic registers of modernist dynamics: extended by use of cantilevered structures and top-heavy geometry, it represents an embodied abstraction, a glitched-up Brancusi rendered in whichever software has currently captured the market. However, the top-heavy form of the structure is a cunning synthesis of an economic imperative – the progressive increase in floor space above ground level giving rise to greater square footage – with the semiotics of speed and productive instability, consistent with modernist stylistic tropes (in this case possibly derived more from the realm of graphics than architecture – there are no right-angles to be seen). The dynamics of the building recall Baudrillard's reading of aerodynamic form in 1950s automobile design, which reveals a division between the mechanics of production and the operation of the aerodynamic as sign:

> The car's fins became the sign of victory over space ... yet they were purely a sign, because they bore no direct relationship to that victory [and] indeed if anything they ran counter to it, tending as they did to make vehicles both heavier and more cumbersome. (Baudrillard, 1968)

The rendering presages the coming into being of a building resembling the inverted and distorted tail fins of a vehicle driving so fast that its structure begins to deteriorate while it still powers forward. Of course, 'riding so fast ones hat blows off' is a performative imperative known to anyone brought up under capitalism and its collective unconscious, screen media. Furthermore, what for the moderns should properly have been a coherent and legible form is disrupted by numerous cuts, striations and linear deformations. Glitched, the building clearly signals the intervention of networked technologies in its production by the inclusion of signs of digital imperfection. The construction promotes a plenitude of signifiers conforming to James Bridle's definition of the New Aesthetic from 2010 (Bridle, 2011), in which signs of digital production are foregrounded: it screams its digital origins from its seemingly unstable rooftops.

In another reading of the 'glitch' by which Hadid disrupts this aerodynamic form, the building may be 'intact but fast': the glitch is generated by imaging technology failing to properly capture the speeding structure, especially from the neighbouring freeway. The rendering depicts, in detail, a future form derived from legible traces of the failure of imaging technology to capture form in motion – blur, striation, yesterday's interlaced video signals played on the latest progressive monitors. The building itself appears to be trying to escape the possibility of its own representation: the rendering produces the reality it depicts so convincingly by virtue of its status as a wager on a future in which imaging technologies are incapable of representing the rapid flow of resources

– commodities, form, knowledge. It takes its form from the visual traces of past innovations, or obsolescence. As a networked image tied to productive technologies in the context of speculative economics, it makes capital from a spectacular paradox. The rendering functions to produce capital in the present – and secure the inevitability of the coming into being of the building – by defining progress as the simultaneous existence of 'things moving too fast to see' and 'imaging technologies that fail'. It is a metaphor of technological failure and success, in a single form.

It is important to acknowledge the difference, but also the convergence, of these two readings of the glitch in the rendering. If the *building* is pre-ruined, this is nothing like Speer's ruin value, which proposed the construction of buildings in anticipation of their eventual impact as ruins (Speer, in Holtorf, 2002). This is decay at the point of origin – if anything, it resembles the pre-constructed ruins of the eighteenth-century 'picturesque'. Furthermore, of course, any such glitch at the level of construction would compromise the intricately calculated structural integrity of the building. Ruins in the age of BIM look nothing like this, but rather take the form of the 'non-existence of form' coinciding with a legacy of representations which look like photographs of completed buildings, which never decay.

Here are two readings of Hadid's digital modernistics: one proclaims that everything that the twentieth-century avant-gardes promised – machine aesthetics, disruption, acceleration and the endless now – has reached its apotheosis in a machine for the production of new disruptions, new knowledges, within economies that produce knowledge and capital from its flows and territorialisations. The sign of digitality is here essentially theatrical, invoked as sophisticated marketing and promotion: the architectural sign as rearguard action or insurance against any attempt to disrupt the intended relationship between commodity, form, future and heritage. Betancourt's framing of the 'digital' as essentially a semiotic regime is hereby rendered into style. Following Baudrillard, both the building and its imagery conceal the divergence of function and sign. The actual facts of its construction – the effort and labour involved in the production and maintenance of such a structure – are in direct and stage-managed opposition to the semiotic play of its design. The suspension of belief necessary to consume its symbolism of acceleration and disruption is mobilised to obscure the processes by which it comes into being, and by which it will be maintained – it is necessary to consider the structure after weathering, adaptation, montage and change of use. One can scarcely imagine Hadid's structure enhanced by the addition of Styrofoam neoclassical columns – the kind of violence that was inflicted by the nationalist government of Macedonia (now North Macedonia) on Kenzo Tange's brutalist masterpieces in Skopje in 2014 (Brown, 2013). But I would claim that this is the exact kind of violence that needs to be imagined to envisage the character of disruption that would represent a true contest of knowledge – a sufficiently ambitious epistemological challenge for a university environment. The heretical possibility of thinking – or imaging – this violence delineates the limits of market-driven disruption and its representations – it violates or exceeds a temporality defined by the maintenance of the intact form, or its legibility.

Route 6: between fragment and world

Boyer, in *The City of Collective Memory* (Boyer, 1994), explores the city as historically productive of, and produced from, representations, tracing a history of the ways in which spectacle and representation parenthesise each other: for Boyer, visual forms – the panorama, the photograph – frame the city in divergent ways that reflect shared conceptions of spatial and social organisation. Drawing on Foucault and Benjamin, and deep archival research into city developments, Boyer links form, representation and frame in order to draw out their evolving interdependency and trace a line from the origins of the planned city to the hyper-capitalist, spectacular city presaged by Debord and Baudrillard. In this narrative, the photograph emerges in the nineteenth century as a museological form: its frame – the bounding limit, container and locator of the image artefact – fragments the city as it 'slices' it into discrete scenes, while simultaneously hinting at topographical and stylistic coherence beyond. Boyer describes how just as the photograph isolates fragments of the city, it suggests, via a subtle twist, a homogeneous chronological domain – a consistency where there once was heterogeneity. Beyond the frame, numerous Parises stretch out, Hausmannised in the imagination or desire of the viewer. Photography – as other critics have noted from different perspectives, social in the case of Hall, or economic in the case of Tagg – demands extrapolation from the contents of the frame to a coherent and consistent topography beyond. Boyer's historical narrative is derived from Benjamin's forensic excavation of nineteenth-century epistemologies and forms:

> [In the nineteenth century], abetted by photography, the concept of an organic city totality – one that gave rise to involuntary memory – died and in its place arose a new visual perception, an archival

consciousness that focussed on details, on the recollection of past images, on the comparison and contrast of similarities and differences. The photograph was an excellent recorder of the past; it offered greater control over what could be termed 'historic'. But simultaneously, it was a destroyer of tradition. From the camera's viewpoint, the past was a pile of rubble and the present a chaos of information; both offered a thousand views to be appropriated and recorded. (Boyer, 1994)

However, in the contemporary city under late capitalism, this fragmentary landscape is itself taken for coherent design, as it is the notion of a city in pieces, each piece representing a totality, remapping the city as a hoard or future museum of potential cities visible from the fragments. The museological merges with the spectacular city, the production of endless synecdoche becoming naturalised under laissez-faire planning as a free-for-all in which developers construct endless permutations of spaces which, though framed by topographical location and spatial boundaries, open onto further totalising visions. Extrapolating from Boyer, it would seem that the overarching totalising vision is one in which the production of totalising visions is sustained indefinitely: let a million Haussmanns bloom, for 15 minutes each! Increasingly mechanised and encouraged by professional hubris, for the industries attendant on the production of space the past is itself repurposed as only productive of the future. The 'cut' Boyer describes, in which the fragment is isolated and removed from the realm of 'involuntary memory', is a wrenching of the past into the future. Photography itself – and here it may be helpful to place a delimiting frame around architectural photography as a category – offers up a store of possible worlds to fragment and re-order. For photography itself, even in advance of the development of rendering technologies or BIM, the networked reimagining of photography as productive rather than documentary necessitates a re-evaluation of the rhetorical function of the image. Boyer, in meshing image and construction, articulates a viewpoint from which the photographic image is observed reversing its direction of transit – facing forwards, not backwards.

Considering the photographer Edward Weston's claims to universality, Hollis Frampton remarks:

> The photographer's print, prodigy of craft though it may be, is a potentially indestructible *scenario* whose paramount quality is its legibility. Thus the photograph is made to resemble the word, whose perpetuation is guaranteed by the mind of a whole culture, safe

from moth or rust; and the photographer's art becomes the exercise of a *logos*, bringing into the world by *fiat*, things that can never escape. (Frampton, 1983: 157)

The persistence of photographic modes of representation in architectural rendering is therefore more than incidental: photography as an act of framing or sampling carries the promise of extrapolation of the contents of the frame to the world beyond. In the rendering, the photographic stands as a key signifier of the viewing of a pre-existing reality, but also the practice of viewing attendant on the photographic image: it is meant to be decoded as real, it is produced as real by virtue of what the viewer is instructed to do by the coincidence of frame and seeming verisimilitude: it produces the possible real as extant and unproblematic.

Route 7: between future and past

If Hadid constructs a historical narrative that incorporates a meshwork of references that appear to be futuristic, yet originate in past process and practice, it is also revealing to explore images of projects that construct what could be termed 'planned palimpsests'. If Boyer presents a critique of the 'City as spectacle', and the nineteenth-century construction of 'memory', then renderings of future museological montages – Radford University, Swansea University's Bay Campus, or Gothenburg's Campus Näckrosen development – collide the contemporary with heritage styles, digitally rendered and framed. Boyer's outline of the relationship between fragment and totality sheds a critical light on images framed in such a way as to predetermine the coming into being of museological and fragmented campus-scapes. It is also necessary to understand these images not as 'mere' representations (a redundant definition) but as functional and productive elements of mechanised systems, or in another potential reading, proofs-of-concept of mechanised systems coming into being: the trade brochure of BIM, or other convergent techno-semiotic systems.

In 2012, Swansea University received planning permission for its £450 million Bay Campus, designed by Porphyrios Associates and Hopkins Architects, in collaboration with developer St Modwen. A blend of classicism, contemporary industrial and British post-war civic modernism, construction involved 'cutting-edge construction programming and prefabrication technologies' (Latham, 2016). The seafront development occupies a site gifted to the university as part of energy giant BP's regional exit strategy.

Figure 4.2 Swansea University Bay Campus, Hopkins and Porphyrios (Architects), St Modwen (Developers), screenshot from flythough, 2014. Reproduced with permission of Swansea University

Figure 4.3 Swansea University Bay Campus, Hopkins and Porphyrios (Architects), St Modwen (Developers), screenshot from flythough, 2014. Reproduced with permission of Swansea University

A CGI flythrough, released in 2012, takes the viewer on an annotated glide through a campus that feels established – careful attention to building typology and sensitivity to the beachfront site result in coherence, choreographing distinct temporalities. Reviewing the semi-completed development in 2016, Ian Latham remarked: 'there is no small achievement in imbuing the Swansea Bay campus with a sense that it has evolved over some decades' (Latham, 2016) (see Figures 4.2 and 4.3).

The appearance of heterogeneous chronologies in images purported to depict (and produce) the future space of knowledge production offers up a range of paradoxical positions: fragments within a fragment, and to extrapolate Boyer's argument, a landscape of stylistic totalising visions contained within a totalising vision. If a typology of contemporary digital architectures might seem to predominantly include a range of futuristic styles, here contemporary imaging and construction technologies are deployed to create facsimiles of past styles – even the creation of a chronological narrative through planned simultaneous superimposition or 'palimpsestification'. Exploring the content of the representation, it is possible to drill down into the meaning of the totalising vision itself, its layers, juxtaposition, and what such a 'palimpsest' says about the way in which it artificially constructs a narrative of temporal succession on campus, a kind of 'Disneyland' effect, to echo Baudrillard (1994). However, treating the rendering itself as spectacular, it is possible to trace the digital framing of these fragmentary images as constitutive of the message 'this technology can produce heritage, as much as it can produce the future'. Another possible reading may be that 'this technology has the power to produce the past, in the future'.

The use of heterogeneous temporal codes is, of course, deeply significant: a space emerges that embodies values of institutional heritage, civic urbanism and industrial production – in form, it could not be more strikingly divergent from the bold disruptive coding of Hadid's Hong Kong Polytechnic University (HKPU) project. Considering the visual dissimilarities between the two projects, it is difficult to say which 'skin' would be more productive of an intangible asset such as 'disruptive production'. There is an argument to be made that the underlying conception of the Bay Campus is possibly more consistent with the imperative of the digital as a permanently malleable archive – both mobilisation and destabilisation of the notion of heritage. At its heart is exactly the disruptive intention that Hadid's development loudly declares. If both projects aim for the same goal, it is possible to claim them as stylistically coherent with regard to an aesthetics of process, as opposed to form – a performative landscape of visualisation, prefabrication, time compression and financialisation. Collage them both together, and the consistency is evident. Diller and Schofido's recent proposal for the University of Toronto, slamming decadent gold sheen against Victorian brick, attempts just such a tear in the matrix. Again Baudrillard's framing comes to mind: any apparent stylistic conflict between Swansea and HKPU 'never happened, in the future'.

Route 8: from now to when

The appearance of the photographic in renderings of Radford, Gothenburg or Swansea is deceptive: these are not images in the conventional sense, but functional elements in a mechanised web that includes economic, affective and productive domains. It is possible to claim that, based on the immediate productive potential built into the networked image, such images are not so much derived from previous phenomena, as much as the present reality of the university's existing faculty and students, the conditions of knowledge production, *are derived from it*. In a very real sense, this is a mechanism by which predetermined conceptions of the future are mobilised to produce the present: if the represented structure is to come into being, then decisions made at the present moment are carried that, if this were not the case, would be differently formulated or resolved. The definition of university functions by Ernst and Young's report, for example, is a claim for an inevitable set of conditions demanding a revision of focus which renders certain other functions obsolete, not to be carried forward, 'futureless'.

Epistemologically, the kinds of gathering, association or institution it frames reify that which is seen as 'proper' now, and have an impact on activities that could take many forms, but which are now in the shadow of a long future: certain options are hereby redundant, while work is to be done to reify that which is to come. The image is a kind of heritage in reverse: it is an image of a reality in relation to which the present university is the past – but which past? The image leapfrogs the present in that its existence as a rendering – or the immanent event of the rendering – does not belong to the category of 'thing' that will be commemorated. In the future, memory will take this form: whatever obtains now will not endure. When this is built, other pasts and futures will be commemorated, but never now; never this immanence. Following construction and topping-out, the rendering itself gradually disappears from collective memory: the file degrades, the software on which it is constructed is deprecated, the networked links to productive mechanisms are severed. The rendering will not be heritage, it will be forgotten. If anything, this chapter is part of ongoing work to remember, and productively archive, what has occurred, and what was productive, in this condition of deferred completion.

References

Autodesk (2018) *Connected BIM For Building Design: Improved project insight with the cloud.* Accessed 15 September 2021. https://www.seiler-ds.com/wp-content/uploads/sites/11/2021/01/Autodesk-report-2018-print.pdf.
Baudrillard, J. (1968) *The System of Objects.* Paris: Editions Gallimard.
Baudrillard, J. (1994) *Simulacra and Simulation.* Ann Arbor: University of Michigan Press.
Berardi, F. (2011) *After the Future.* Thoburn, London: AK Press.
Betancourt, M. (2010) 'Immaterial value and scarcity in digital capitalism'. *ctheory.net,* 6/10/2010. Accessed 15 September 2021. https://journals.uvic.ca/index.php/ctheory/article/view/14982/5883.
Boyer, M. C. (1994) *The City of Collective Memory: Its historical imagery and architectural entertainments.* Cambridge, MA: MIT Press.
Bridle, J. (2011) 'The New Aesthetic'. Accessed 15 September 2021. https://jamesbridle.com/works/the-new-aesthetic.
Brown, A. (2013) *Stills from a Monster Movie: Populism and escapism in digital architecture,* paper to the conference 'On the verge of photography: Imaging, mobile art, humans and computers', 24–25 May 2013, Birmingham School of Art.
Debord, G. (1994) *The Society of the Spectacle.* New York: Zone Books.
Ernst and Young (2018) *Can the Universities of Today Lead Learning for Tomorrow?* Sydney: EYGM Ltd.
Frampton, H. (1983) 'Impromptus on Edward Weston'. In *Circles of Confusion: Film, photography, video.* Rochester, N.Y.: Visual Studies Workshop.
Future Cities Catapult (2018) *City Data Sharing Toolkit.* Accessed 15 September 2021. 15/09/2021 at https://futurecities.catapult.org.uk/project/city-data-sharing-toolkit/ .
Hall, S. ([1973] 1980) 'Encoding/decoding.' In *Centre for Contemporary Cultural Studies: Culture, media, language: Working papers in cultural studies, 1972–79.* London: Hutchinson, 128–38.
Holtorf, C. (2002) 'A Theory of Ruin Value: The word in stone'. In *Monumental Past: The life-histories of megalithic monuments in Mecklenburg-Vorpommern (Germany).* Electronic monograph. University of Toronto at Scarborough: Centre for Instructional Technology Development.
James, L., Guile, D. and Unwin, L. (2011) *From learning for the knowledge-based economy to learning for growth: Re-examining clusters, innovation and qualifications.* Published by the Centre for Learning and Life Chances in Knowledge Economies and Societies at: http://www.llakes.org.
Kitchin, R. (2014) 'Big data, new epistemologies and paradigm shifts', *Big Data and Society,* April–June 2014, Sage Publications.
Latham, I. (2016) 'University Challenges: Porphyrios Associates at Swansea Bay', *Architecture Today* (271).
Manovitch, L. (1999) 'Database as a symbolic form', *Millennium Film Journal,* 34.
McClanahan, A. (2016) *Dead Pledges; Debt, crisis and 21st century culture.* Stanford: Stanford University Press.
Rosenthal, M. A. (2012) 'Benjamin's Wager on Modernity: Gambling and the arcades project ', *The Germanic Review: Literature, culture, theory,* 87 (3), 261–78.
Tafuri, M. (1969) 'Toward a Critique of Architectural Ideology' [Per una critica dell'ideologia architettonica], *Contropiano 1,* January–April 1969; trans. Stephen Sartarelli.
Taleb, N. N. (2007) *The Black Swan: The Impact of the highly improbable.* New York, Random House.
Taylor, A. (2018), 'The Automation Charade', *Logic Magazine* (5): August 2018. Accessed 15 September 2021. https://logicmag.io/failure/the-automation-charade/.
Taylor, I., Roberts, P. and Coulson, J. (2018) *University Building Boom is Reshaping our Cities,* THES 17 March 2018. Accessed 15 September 2021. https://www.timeshighereducation.com/blog/university-building-boom-reshaping-our-cities.
Wark, M. (2015) 'The Vectoralist Class', *E-Flux SuperCommunity,* 29 August 2015. Accessed 15 September 2021. http://supercommunity.e-flux.com/texts/the-vectoralist-class/.

II. Sites and historical contexts, past and future

Part 1: University of Gothenburg
and UCL East (London)

5
From dispersed multi-site to cluster and campus: understanding the material infrastructure of University of Gothenburg as urban heritage

Claes Caldenby

Introduction

The evolution of University of Gothenburg over the last century presents a spectrum of university location models, from concentration in one single building to being a dispersed multi-site university, followed by attempts to gather its buildings in clusters or campus-like structures. This chapter will argue that the development of these location models is important for understanding the 'material apparatus' of universities, which in turn frames the way in which universities contribute to the shaping of urban heritage discourses in any given city.

This approach builds on the conceptualisation of university institutions by the historians of ideas, Liedman and Olausson (1988: 11–13), in relation to three types of cycles. The first one is that of the students who come from different backgrounds, pass through the universities and find their roles in society. Some of them stay as teachers and influence new generations of students. The second one is the cycle within the universities of teachers and researchers who are formed by the universities and contribute to forming them. The third cycle is the relation of the knowledge developed in universities to the surrounding society and its expectations on the usefulness of universities. Liedman and Olausson are interested in understanding the ideologies – or systems of ideas – and the institutions – or 'material apparatus' and norms – that have shaped universities. The material apparatus is understood as offices, lecture halls and administration, but its significance is dismissed in a single sentence: 'whether the university is concentrated in a few common buildings or dispersed on different facilities in different parts of the city or district where the university is located, [material apparatus] has a certain role to play'.[1]

By contrast, this chapter proposes that the 'material apparatus' should be considered as a fourth cycle, which is formative in shaping universities. Through the construction and reuse of buildings, the university as a developer is actively involved in 'reworking of the past in the present', to paraphrase the definition of cultural heritage in the 2013 strategic plan for the Centre for Critical Heritage Studies at University of Gothenburg. The Centre asks critical questions about how our interpretation of the past shapes the present, at an ideological level.

But reworking also has a practical side. Buildings are constantly adapted to suit changed or new uses. This can be made easier or more difficult by the design of the buildings, but also by their relation to, and heritage significance in, the surrounding city – whether on the grounds of architectural quality or of historical importance in the collective memory, or both. Here, a hypothesis will be presented and tested in the case of University of Gothenburg: a building with a strong ideological identity is more difficult to change, at least as long as the ideology is still valid. A building that is well-integrated in its urban surrounding is easier to change, while large 'insulated' campus-like areas resist more radical reworking.

Early history: a bourgeois 'building in a park'

The start of University of Gothenburg can be dated back to 1891, when a university college (*högskola*) was founded. It was the fourth Swedish university, after the two old ones in Uppsala and Lund, dating back to the fifteenth and seventeenth centuries, and Stockholm, opened in 1878, also as a university college. Gothenburg started with only 15 students and a profile fitting a mercantile city, with modern languages and open lectures for the city bourgeoisie. In the beginning, the location was in rented facilities in a former college, Schillerska gymnasiet, in the very centre of the city, at the northern end of Kungsportsavenyn. In 1901, a newly built combined city and university college library was opened, and in 1907, a new main building, both on Vasagatan in the late nineteenth-century extension of the city.[2]

Figure 5.1 Main building from 1907, the only protected building of University of Gothenburg. Withdrawn from the street, in a park and reached by stairs. Photo: Krister Engström

Figure 5.2 City and university library from 1901, reopened as university library in the 1990s after a period as city archive. In a park but not withdrawn from the street. Photo: Krister Engström

The main building (see Figure 5.1) and the library (see Figure 5.2) are both typical, purpose-built public buildings, but with a difference in their location in relation to the city. The library is at the eastern end of Vasagatan, near the workers' district of Haga and the first purpose-built public library in Sweden, the Dickson library from 1897. Both these libraries stand directly on the street, with only a few steps up from the pavement. They are free-standing buildings but with a close interface with the city. The main building of the university, on the other hand, is located in a park, with a distance from the street and several steps to climb to get into the building. It is clearly a 'building in a park', considered to be a modernist type of planning, but rather initiated by the wish to give a certain status to nineteenth-century bourgeois institutions like operas, theatres and schools. Before the nineteenth century, only palaces and churches were free-standing buildings in the city, and often not even they were. For further discussion below, we can also note that both the libraries have had other uses over time, while the main building has remained the symbolic hub of the university. The main building is also the only building of University of Gothenburg that is protected as a designated heritage building, which of course restricts what changes can be made to it.

The president of the university had to fight with the city to get this high and monumental location in what was otherwise a public park. The city gave the site, which was a condition for the donation by one of the leading local merchants, Oscar Ekman, of the money for the building. The architecture follows the typology of the recent main buildings of Uppsala and Lund universities, both opened in the 1880s. They are all buildings in a park with a central entrance reached by several steps, two symmetrical wings of rooms with larger windows to the lecture halls on the second floor and on the backside a large auditorium. The entrance leads to a two-storey hall with auditorium doors in front and open access to the galleries on the second floor. The inscription over the entrance tells the story of the university: *Göteborgs högskola* is cut in stone and under it, metal letters saying *Göteborgs universitet* were added later.

Gothenburg University College became a state-financed university in 1954. The growth during the first half-century was slow. In 1945, the university had 500 students. All the teaching took place in the main building. Like the main buildings in Uppsala and Lund it was planned for teaching humanities in lecture halls and seminar rooms. But as opposed to Uppsala and Lund, there were not yet any institutions built for the sciences. This meant considerable difficulties for the laboratory-based subjects. A professor in oceanography in 1953 described the main building as 'a monumental building of a sad kind conceived as an envelope for strolling philosophers'.[3]

The post-war decades meant a boom in the number of students everywhere. A much higher share of the population continued to academic studies and research was growing. In Gothenburg, existing institutes became incorporated into the university – including medicine, which had started as an independent faculty in 1949 on a location near the main hospital. In 1969, University of Gothenburg had 21,000 students, 42 times the number from 25 years earlier. This caused huge problems with facilities and several improvised solutions. University of Gothenburg was spreading across the city, with its central administrative functions still housed in its main building.

A contrasting model of development: Chalmers' enclave

The dispersed development of University of Gothenburg after the Second World War can be contrasted with that of Chalmers University of Technology (*teknisk högskola*), an older institution with a different, 'enclaved' type of location in the city. As opposed to the Faculty of Medicine or the School of Economics, it was never incorporated into University of Gothenburg. That makes it worth a detour.

Like so many other nineteenth-century institutions in Gothenburg, Chalmers was founded with donation money from one of the many influential merchants or industrialists of the city. William Chalmers worked for the East India Company and bequeathed money for a craft school for boys, started in 1829. This developed into a technical institute and finally became a technical university in 1937. Its first location was in a small building near the river. In the 1860s, it moved to a new building on Storgatan, sharing a block facing Vasagatan on its other side with the arts and crafts school, later to be incorporated with University of Gothenburg. From the 1920s, Chalmers moved to its present location uphill to the south, in what is now called Campus Johanneberg.

The use of the concept 'campus' for university areas is fairly recent in Swedish. It can be dated back to the 1990s and we will come back to that. But the idea of an external location with space enough for future expansion is not that new. The placing of Chalmers on what was then the southern outskirts of Gothenburg in the 1920s would offer space for its growth until the late 1900s. In the 1990s, a new campus, Lindholmen, was opened for parts of Chalmers' education on a former shipyard site north of the river. Campus Lindholmen consciously sought an integration with technology companies and a science centre, in what was then called a 'triple-helix' concept, emphasising the cycle of knowledge and staff between city, business and academia. Campus Johanneberg, on the other hand, to a large extent stayed a world of its own in the city, with its focus on heavy laboratory facilities. It was a separate entity, or an academic enclave, as opposed to the integrated 'city university' of University of Gothenburg. Constant additions were made within the area but its relation to the urban context by and large remained a bit aloof. Only recently, from the 1990s, has Chalmers sought some integration, expanding into the former Vasa hospital area.

The 1960s: an open, dispersed and multi-site university

The rapid growth of University of Gothenburg demanded planning to find sites for an expansion. A building committee in 1945 proposed to build behind the main building in the Vasa park but this was not acceptable for the city, which defended the need of a park in this otherwise densely built nineteenth-century urban grid. At the same time, there was not only a lack of central sites but also of means for financing the expansion. The nineteenth-century philanthropic donation culture was no longer there. The wealthy bourgeoisie of Gothenburg could not continue their conspicuous lifestyle. They even left their large central villas, like in Lorensberg, just behind Götaplatsen. This opened an opportunity for improvised solutions. From the mid-1950s, the university started to buy villas to house university institutions like Art History and History of Literature. A villa of 400 square metres could accommodate a small institution. A similar development happened in London, where UCL purchased terraced Bloomsbury houses.

However, this was only seen as a temporary solution. Several locations for a more congregated expansion were discussed. When the university college was made into a university in 1954, the National Board of Building made a general plan for an expansion around Näckrosdammen, close to the city's cultural centre at Götaplatsen, and the new university library opened in 1954. There was space enough here for the whole planned expansion. The basically rationalist, functionalist ideology of the National Board of Building was in favour of campus-like university areas, preferably with expansion space and no need to adapt to any urban contexts difficult to control. In parallel, the National Board of Building made a proposal for the whole of the University of Stockholm to move to a location far north of the city centre at Frescati, disregarding the wishes of both the city and the university. This initiative for a consolidated and, as a consequence of this, external location in Stockholm seems to have been taken by Gunnar Myrdal, Professor of Economics at the university, inspired by his experiences of American campus universities.

Once again, and even within the larger state budget, there was a lack of financing resources. There was a large expansion of both the Faculty of Medicine and of Chalmers at the same time, and there was simply no more money in the state budget for the building of new university buildings. Only one, 'the language building' (*Språkskrapan*, finished in 1966), was built near Näckrosdammen. The improvised solutions continued and by the end of the 1960s University of Gothenburg was scattered over some 70 addresses in the city, including villas and even large apartments. In comparison with Stockholm, despite all the criticism of the Frescati campus when it was opened around 1970, this was considered by the National Board of Building to be a very unsatisfactory situation.

In 1975, University of Gothenburg hosted an OECD (Organisation for Economic Cooperation and Development) conference on 'dispersed and multi-site universities'. In a publication, the university director Lars Gurmund discussed the pros and cons of the Gothenburg situation in a balanced manner (Gurmund, 1977). Some disadvantages were obvious. The flexibility for each institution is smaller when it is located on its own. It might also contribute to a negative feeling of the university as a more provisory institution. The most important problem for the everyday work is the difficulty to spread information (this is before the internet!) and the lack of economies of scale concerning services like library, cafeteria and cleaning. With rented facilities, there is also a possible exposure to the fluctuations of the real estate market.

But there are also advantages of a dispersed location according to Gurmund. Local politicians appreciate a university that is not a world of its own, but part of the society. For the administration, decentralisation means greater independence and responsibility and easier decisions on schedules as well as economy. For teachers and students, the 'family-like' situation in small institutions means easier informal contacts. Gurmund also points to the transdisciplinary centres organised at University of Gothenburg from the early 1970s as a way of countering a potential isolation.

Some of the disadvantages are, according to Gurmund, connected with the improvised situation. University of Gothenburg was not planned as a dispersed and multi-site university. He looks forward to university 'clusters' that have some economy of scale without losing the integration

Figure 5.3 Map of University of Gothenburg and Chalmers in the early 1990s. A centrally located dispersed university from the 1970s transformed into faculty size 'clusters'. Credit: Claes Caldenby

in the city. One of his arguments for the advantage of a dispersed location is the growing interest from students to choose part-time education and evening courses. Such a 'clustering' into faculty-size units spread out in central parts of the city was to become the development that University of Gothenburg followed during the 1980s and 1990s (see Figure 5.3).

An outsider: a fit-for-all flexible structure

In the 1960s, there was a desperate search for facilities for expanding university institutions. The Teachers' College (*Lärarhögskolan*) was located in a building from 1912, the Annedal seminar, which was by far not sufficient for its needs. In the early 1970s it had rented facilities in 14 different locations around the city. Together with the Institute of Education, the college searched everywhere for a site for a new building. Several external locations within the city of Gothenburg were proposed. Then the neighbouring municipality of Mölndal offered a site for a very advantageous prize on the condition that it should be used for higher education and research at least until the year 2000.[4]

The Faculty of Education, the new building in Mölndal designed for the Institute of Pedagogics and Didactics, was the only part of University of Gothenburg that moved out of the city centre to an external location (see Figure 5.4). It was typical of 1970s structuralist architecture, designed for change. Client and manager of the building was the National Board of Building, at the time in charge of all state building. Based on their maintenance experience, they had developed a 'structural philosophy' in the 1960s aimed at facilitating changes over time. Different

Figure 5.4 Faculty of Education in the 1970s. A flexible structure around interior courtyards in an external location in the neighbour municipality Mölndal. Photo: White architects

Figure 5.5 New faculty of Education, built in 2006 as an addition to an 1850s hospital. The only externally located faculty now became the only one inside the moat of the former fortifications. Photo: Krister Engström

building parts with different life spans should be separated. Thus, interior walls, moved relatively frequently for new uses, were separated from loadbearing structures. Installations were to be accessible, not built in. The low, grid-like structure of the Education building, with small courtyards, was a solution often used in the 1960s for schools as well as hospitals. The two spaces with larger spans, the restaurant and the sports hall, were situated on the periphery of the structure. The Faculty of Education was a general, flexible structure in a low-key architecture. There was even a rumour spread when the building was new that it was designed to be possible to transform into a hospital in case of war. This has no support in documents or memory of an architect involved, but theoretically it would have been possible.

The Education building was opened in 1975. Changes to the building programme had happened already during the design period and could be easily accommodated in the open structure. During its 30 years in use, changes were made continually. The general tendency was that lecture halls were made into offices and new lecture halls were built in the open central spine of the building.

In 1999, one year before the contract with Mölndal municipality expired, the Institute of Pedagogics and Didactics started planning a move back into the very centre of Gothenburg. The former Sahlgrenska hospital, a semi-circular brick building from the 1850s, got an addition in glass and a second building, also with a glass façade, was built on an adjacent block, a former school yard (see Figure 5.5). The Institute moved back to Gothenburg in 2006. The only externally located part of the university now became the only one located within the moat of the former fortified city.

The building left behind in Mölndal was the first purpose-designed building to be left by the ever-expanding university. In the beginning, there were plans to tear it down and build new housing on the site, one of the few uses the flexible structure was not fit for. But in the end, the choice was to reuse it for offices for some 40 companies – now with some pride – called Education Park. The structure was cut into two halves to get more separate entrances for all the small companies, but otherwise the building proved its adaptability. There are also plans to build new housing on the site (Education Park, 2010).

The Institute was purpose-built but small enough to be easily reused for other purposes. It was also relatively anonymous, so as not to be difficult for the university to leave for any ideological reasons. Interestingly enough, the staff had some difficulties accepting the division on two different city blocks coming with the inner-city location. They seem to have brought with them the idea of a large coherent structure from the external location, which also means more-or-less turning your back to the context.

The city university: adapting faculty-size clusters to an existing urban structure

The move back to the city of the Institute of Pedagogics and Didactics can be seen as symbolic for the 1990s idea of a 'city university'. This was an international tendency, possible to connect with ideas about a new economic geography and the rise of a 'creative class'. Cities were seen as creative environments, where universities and student life were an asset. The externally located 'education factories' of the 1960s were now outdated. At the same time, the post-industrial society offered emptied, centrally-located industrial sites and other nineteenth-century facilities. A French project, called Université 2000, tried to relocate universities into city centres. Manufacture de tabac in Lyon was a former tobacco factory, remodelled for the Faculty of Law, an iconic project with a McDonald's restaurant on the corner as a sign of a modern, more urban sort of university. Universities were no longer seen as monumental historic institutions, but as creative hubs, and the reuse of old factory sites became an attractive option.

The same happened in Sweden. In the 1970s, there was a wave of new universities and university colleges founded in smaller towns in Sweden. All of them, except one (Borås), had peripheral locations. In the 1990s, there was a second wave of new, regional universities. Now all the newly founded universities were in relatively central locations, taking over disused former industry buildings or military barracks. One example is Norrköping, where the university, as well as culture and private companies, took over the textile industry landscape along the river, which had closed down in the 1970s.

In a longer perspective, this can be seen as a shift of balance between two important aims of university location, ever since its beginning in medieval times: a search for autonomy, or identity, and a search for integration in the surrounding city. The early *universitas* in cities like Bologna were spread out in a part of the city, using ordinary buildings for their teaching. In contrast to this, Collegio di Spagna, also in Bologna, was built as the first purpose-built university building in the 1360s. The model for the *collegium* was the monastery, an enclosed world where students and teachers spent their life not only studying, but also eating and sleeping. The same model was used in the colleges of Oxford and Cambridge. They were also worlds of their own, based on a separation of 'town and gown', although distributed in a network across the city. The continental European universities, on the other hand, were much more spread out in the city, being what could be called 'institution universities'. The USA took over the English model in their 'campus universities', where the campus was a lawn that filled the same function as the courtyard or quadrangle in the denser medieval English cities. The American campus typically has both student housing and sports facilities, which is usually not the case in European universities. In the late twentieth century, the 'external university' of the 1960s emphasises the autonomy, and identity, of the university, while the 'city university' has integration in the city as an ideal.

These two tracks are followed through the 800 years-long history of universities, with a lot of examples and illustrations, in a book I wrote in the early 1990s (Caldenby, 1994). The reason for writing this book was, somewhat paradoxically, the launching of the concept of 'campus' for Swedish university areas. The background was a change of governance of university building, typical for the marketisation of the late 1980s. The National Board of Building, which had a state budget for all state building including universities, was split up in 1993 into four (later three) separate state-owned companies. One of these was Akademiska hus (Academic Buildings), which was responsible for university building. As opposed to the National Board of Building, it was acting on a market, both for providing universities with facilities and for financing its buildings. Akademiska hus presented themselves as providing 'campuses' for universities. Obviously, they were interested in campuses as congregated university areas, where they had a location monopoly, as opposed to dispersed universities where the university could more freely choose between different real estate providers.

Since 'campus' had not been a very frequently used word in Swedish for university areas, architects designing universities asked what the meaning was when it was now being used by Akademiska hus. I organised a few seminars on the issue and searched for literature. Much to my surprise, very little seemed to have been written by academics about the relationship between the university and the city, as if universities were a world of their own. One of the few books I found was the anthology edited by the New York historian Thomas Bender (Bender, 1988). There, Bender describes the university as a 'semi-cloistered heterogeneity'. By this he wants to underline on the one hand that a university consists of many more-or-less independent parts. To describe this, others have used the word 'multiversity'. On the other hand, 'semi-cloistered' means that it is not an 'open heterogeneity' like the city, but neither a closed world of its own. Universities have a semi-permeable interface with the city. They are involved in cycles with the surrounding world. Bender is critical of the campus model, which he calls an 'academic pastoralism'. He argues for the creativity of the dispersed city university with an analogy to biology. The archipelago is genetically the most creative environment since it offers both a relative autonomy and an exchange with the surrounding environment, Bender claims.

The city university model also involves adaptation to an existing context and an acceptance of what may be a mix of new buildings and reused buildings, partly in separate but nearby city blocks and not all of them purpose-built. In this there is a potential conflict between ideas of integration and identity.

Cluster and campus: integration and identity

In the late 1980s and early 1990s, University of Gothenburg built a number of faculty-size units in central parts of the city, thereby implementing the cluster idea from the 1970s. This development can be seen as belonging to the city university model.

A few words on the broader context of this should be added. Gothenburg in the 1990s was a 'post-industrial' city. From the early 1970s to the mid-1980s, it had been a 'shrinking city', affected by suburbanisation – those who could afford it moved out to houses in the car-based 'sprawl' of surrounding municipalities. Another, more specific, reason was the closing down of the three large shipyards of Gothenburg. Routes towards a more differentiated labour market were sought and universities were considered an asset in such a development. 'The entrepreneurial city' and 'governance' as a more complex form of managing a city in 'public–private partnership' are concepts dating from this period.

One example is a small booklet called *Universitetet i centrum* (*The university in the centre*), published in 1993. It is written by the president of the university together with people from the city. Its aim is to underline

Figure 5.6 'Samvetet', Faculty of Social Sciences, built in the early 1990s in a central location and closely integrated with new housing in an old workers' housing district. Photo: Krister Engström

the importance of a more differentiated economy, a closer collaboration between university (research) and business, and the advantages of having the university and students in the city centre. The booklet points at a centre for social sciences being developed at the western end of Vasagatan (see below) and wants to strengthen this into a 'campus' in collaboration with local business. Somewhat abstractly, it describes three belts (*stråk*) in central Gothenburg: the 'event belt', the 'culture and entertainment belt' and the 'knowledge belt'. To this it adds a 'university ring'. In the crossing point between knowledge belt and university ring, the new centre for social sciences would be located. Nothing seems to have come out of these ideas.

But a few years later, things of a similar kind happened on the other side of the river, on the site of the former Lindholmen shipyard. In 1996, a municipal company called Norra Älvstranden utveckling AB (Northern Riverside Development) was founded with the aim to develop the shipyard area that had been bought by the city. Based on the idea of 'triple helix' to develop university-industry-government collaboration for a 'knowledge-based economy', they very quickly managed to get both Chalmers, Ericsson and Volvo involved in the area. Chalmers established

Figure 5.7 School of Economics from early 1990s in a block of its own next to the faculty of social sciences. On the corner the library with a large 'urban window'. Photo: Krister Engström

its new 'campus Lindholmen', Ericsson moved a large part of its activity here and Lindholmen Science Centre was started.

In the meantime, the first cluster of University of Gothenburg to be established was Humanisten in 1984, the Faculty of Humanities, between the university library, Språkskrapan and Näckrosdammen. The winning entry in the architecture competition had the motto *Pelouse*, pointing at the grass slope, or 'campus' if you will, in front of the building. Spatially, it is more a building in the park with internal streets than a city university. In 1992, Artisten was built nearby for theatre and music educations, as an addition of performing spaces to a former secondary school. It is partly open to the public and has a slightly more urban location than Humanisten. Soon followed Samvetet (an abbreviation of 'Samhällsvetenskapligt centrum', a social sciences centre, but also meaning 'conscience' in Swedish), in 1991. It is a very urban location in two blocks with a bridge between and closely integrated with new and old housing, even sharing courtyards with the houses (see Figure 5.6). Across the street the School of Economics was built in 1995 as an addition to the old School of Economics, with buildings facing the street directly but mainly turned towards an interior courtyard (see Figure 5.7). Parts of the old school have recently been torn down (spring 2020), to be replaced by much bigger buildings in a process of densification going on in many places in central Gothenburg.

A densification is also going on at what has been called 'Campus Näckrosen'. Starting in 2012, there has been planning for a 'Park for Humanities and Arts', that is a cluster of all institutions for humanities and arts, as well as an extended university library, around Näckrosdammen. The idea was also thereby to create a meeting point between academia and cultural institutions in Gothenburg. 'The Näckrosen area will change from a closed backside to, in 2040, a city integrated park for humanities, art and culture – an environment which is unique in the Nordic countries', is how Akademiska hus presents the development plan.[5] The densification met with negative reactions from people living in the neighbourhood, which has generated some institutional self-reflection on the project. One interesting conclusion is that 'the original campus idea of the project has passed into an idea of a city university'. This is described as the university wanting to have openness and to invite people and make them feel welcome.[6] To begin with, the university wanted to have an impressive and 'unique' presence as an institution in a central location, which also meant tearing down an old existing building. During the process, the understanding changed into a wish to be a part of the city, which included preserving the existing building as part of the university.

University of Gothenburg and the heritage discourse

This chapter has discussed the different location models followed by University of Gothenburg over more than a century, and how these models reflect relations between the university and the city. The larger picture is a development from a very concentrated location with the whole (relatively small) university in one monumental building, to a very dispersed university in the 1970s – with some 70 more-or-less improvised addresses in the city centre – and then to a 'dispersed concentration' today in fewer than 10 purpose-built faculty-size units. Despite some attempts to introduce the campus model, University of Gothenburg is more of a city university than many other universities. This was not a self-evident ideological stance in the beginning. Indeed, there was some concern within the university administration in the 1990s that the dispersed location could make the institution's identity unclear, the director asking 'do people know where the university is if it is spread across the city?'[7]

In the beginning, a hypothesis was presented, saying that: (1) a strong ideological identity of a building makes it more difficult to change; (2) a building well integrated in its urban surrounding is easier to change; and (3) large campus-like areas resist more radical reworking and remain more-or-less 'insulated'.[8]

Change of function is a central driving force in buildings. For universities, this might mean a cycle of changes of university buildings into other functions; or the opposite: the changes of other building categories into universities. But changes can also happen within universities, for the simple need of more space, or different space. Such driving forces are then reworked – accepted, adapted or contested – into physical changes.

A starting point to discuss this might be the general remark that universities as a very rapidly expanding institution, especially after the Second World War, seldom have left any buildings empty. That is, of course, unless they have completely changed location from a central one to an external, which is what, for example, Stockholm did in the 1960s. But University of Gothenburg stayed in the city and thus there are no examples of university buildings left to other uses. The only exception, the Faculty of Education, Mölndal, was built for change and could in the end be adapted to ordinary offices. In the future, Campus Näckrosen will lead to the emptying of buildings in the city centre for arts and crafts. This tendency of university buildings to remain university buildings may partly be caused by difficulties of reuse: larger lecture halls and studios can be a challenge for adaptation to other purposes. Less often, it is caused by the high symbolic value they have for the identity of the university, maybe with the exception of the protected main building. The high quality and specific character of university buildings might, however, influence how they are treated as heritage, if the university does vacate them for adaptation to other uses.

The opposite of this, reuse of other building categories for university institutions, is less common in Gothenburg than in smaller, newly established universities from the 1990s. Perhaps the most striking example is Education in its new location in the city centre, which is an addition to an 1850s hospital. Another example is the secondary school that is part of Artisten, just like Education with larger spaces in the addition. Yet another example is the former Court of Appeal, which is a small, free-standing part of Humanisten and that at an early stage was proposed for demolition as part of the Näckrosen campus project. Rethinking this project meant seeing the qualities of an odd older building.

A cluster-like structure of the university can mean a need to give up demand for interior communication when the cluster is so large that it has to be spread over more than one block. This was the case with the new Education building that divided up on two blocks. The faculty wanted a bridge over the street joining the blocks, but this was not accepted by the town planning authorities. And after all, the quality of a city university for city life is students and teachers using the streets to move between buildings. Large units in the city with interior communications tend to 'drain' city life.

The School of Economics has gradually got a location spread over more than one city block and wants to change this. The building of a new station for the underground railway gave the opportunity to considerably increase the exploitation of the main block. This meant recently (spring 2020) tearing down the lower early 1950s lecture halls of the old School of Economics, buildings of high architectural and historical quality. The argument heard from the School of Economics that these buildings were of low quality is not convincing. As always, there is a potential conflict between practical and economical demands and heritage protection. And the question of what happens next time the School of Economics wants to expand remains unanswered. Will they go on tearing down the older parts and increase density? Or could they accept moving in the city between institutions?

The 'semi-cloistered' city university structure bears a promise of a creative urbanity, so much wished for these days. But its circulation of students and teachers through the semi-permeable interface of university and city also means a demand for a sensitive meeting of the university buildings with the built environment of the surrounding city. Any internal practical demands for more or different space maybe cannot be met. They have to be reworked. Maybe students and teachers even have to go out on the street to get to the next lecture. Which is not such a bad thing after all. Both for city life and for heritage.

Notes

1. Liedman and Olausson (1988), 11. My translation, CC. In Swedish: Det spelar en viss roll om universitetet är samlat i några gemensamma byggnader eller är utspritt på olika lokaler i skilda delar av den stad eller det område där universitetet är beläget.
2. For a history of University of Gothenburg see Lindberg and Nilsson (1996). A short summary with a focus on the buildings can be found in Caldenby and Boberg, 1996. Tepfers (1991) gives the architectural history of the main building of the university.
3. Caldenby and Boberg (1996), 18. My translation, CC. In Swedish: en monumentalbyggnad av sorgligt slag tillkommen för att utgöra hylle för promenerande filosofer.
4. The background, as well as an analysis of the changes over time of the building, are given in Roos (2007).
5. *Utvecklingsplan Näckrosen 2018–2040*. My translation, CC. In Swedish: Näckrosenområdet går från sluten baksida till att med sikte på 2040 vara en stadsintegrerad park för humaniora, konst och kultur – en miljö unik i Norden.
6. Öberg and Sjöberg (2017). My translation, CC. In Swedish: Projektets ursprungliga campusidé har övergått i en idé om cityuniversitet.
7. Conversations with university director ('akademidirektör') Gunnar Dahlström.
8. For an in-depth discussion of this see Brand (1994). Brand's discussion of 'Low Road' as easily adaptable buildings and 'High Road' as buildings with strong ideological identity has some similarities to my hypotheses.

References

Bender, T. (1988) *The University and the City: From medieval origins to the present*. New York: Oxford University Press.
Brand, S. (1994) *How Buildings Learn: What happens after they are built*. New York: Viking.
Caldenby, C. (1994) *Universitetet och staden: Inför fältstudier!* Göteborg: White Coordinator Påbygget.
Caldenby, C. and Boberg, E. (1996) *Universitetet i Göteborg: En arkitekturguide*. Göteborg: Chalmers tekniska högskola.
Education Park (2010) www.pedagogenpark.se. (Accessed 18th February 2022)
Gurmund, L. (1977) *Gothenburg University: A dispersed institution*. Göteborg: Universitetet, Informationssekretariatet.
Liedman, S-E. and Olausson, L. (1988) *Ideologi och institution: Om forskning och högre utbildning 1880–2000*. Stockholm: Carlsson.
Lindberg, B. and Nilsson, I. (1996) *Göteborgs universitets historia*. Göteborg: Rektorsämbetet universitetet.
Öberg, J. and Sjöberg, P. (2017) *Slutrapport Projekt Campus Näckrosen*. Göteborg: Göteborgs universitet.
Roos, J. (2007) *Pedagogen i Mölndal: Bebyggelsehistorisk dokumentation*. Göteborg: ARQ.
Tepfers, I. (1991) Universitetsbyggnaden i Vasaparken. Göteborg: Informationsavdelningen universitetet.
Universitetet i centrum (1993) Göteborg: Stadsbyggnadskontoret.
Utvecklingsplan Näckrosen 2018–2040 (2018) Göteborg: Akademiska Hus, Göteborgs universitet.

6
The dis- mis- and re-membering of design education: understanding design education as urban heritage

Henric Benesch

Introduction

This chapter argues that we need to engage with the more particular heritages of institutions and disciplines and the sites in which they are located, in order to come to terms with what role they may or may not play in relation to the development of our cities. In this case, I will focus specifically on the heritage of design education at University of Gothenburg, and how its relation to the city has changed over time. This includes a discussion not only of the officially acknowledged heritage of design education, but also a heritage currently unremembered or disabled. The question being what role these heritages have played and might play for the future of design education and how it is situated, impacts on and relates to the city in which in resides. This is discussed in terms of a set of 'orientations' (Ahmed, 2006), with different relations to and implications for urban heritage and university heritage at large. This is essentially a story of design education in Gothenburg, and therefore likely to be of particular interest to those who are familiar with design education or the particular Gothenburg context. Yet the ambition is that this somewhat granular narrative, as a microhistory of sorts (Ginzburg, Tedeschi and Tedeschi, 1993) may point to a less localised and more distributed phenomena in relation to university heritage and urban heritage at large.

Such a narrative stretches beyond a contemporary and modern understanding of 'design'. As noted by Clive Dilnot, a design conference was not possible two hundred years ago; nor was a design-debate possible a hundred years ago, since 'the concepts of high-level design education and design research waited for another half-century' (Dilnot, 2015b: 115). Still, the roots of design education stretch beyond its disciplinary horizon. This is certainly the case with the design programmes at The Academy of Art and Design at The Faculty of Fine, Applied and Performing Arts at University of Gothenburg, which originated in 1848 with the formation of the Slöjdföreningens skola (School of the Handicraft Association), to provide vocational training to craftsmen and artisans following the abolishment of the guilds (Fabriks- och hantverksförordningen/Factory and Crafts Ordinance, 1846). However, it would take another 129 years for the word 'design' to find its way into the syllabus in 1977, and a further 12 years for it to be included in the school's name – Högskolan för Design och Konsthantverk (School of Design and Crafts), or HDK, in 1989 (Brunius and Mörck, 1998). Today after having merged with Academy Valand in 2020, the school is known as The Academy of Art and Design at The University of Gothenburg.

Regardless of its name, design and design education, together with the rest of the world, are thrown into the historical and cataclysmic event called Anthropocene. And the legacy of designers, among others, as stewards of this momentum, prompts us to question the role of design and design education in the ongoing social, political and environmental crisis. Finding itself at a pivotal moment in time, design education (together with all sorts of societal manifestations) is wavering, and at a loss. And if design, as suggested by Dilnot, is a historical product where 'we never yet had design – only its weak, subaltern industrial-capitalist, version' (Dilnot 2015b: 118), is it time to revisit the emergence of design and design education, and to look beyond its current late-modern formations, to identify alternative futures if possible? Put differently, the current formation of design, and in consequence design education, can be seen as the offspring of one particular version of design, one out of many possible heritages of design; suggesting that there might indeed be other heritages of design, obscured by the current formation.

As suggested by the long history of Slöjdföreningens skola, the heritage of design education stretches beyond the formal emergence of design education as we know it today in the late 1960s. While substantial changes have occurred since then, even more substantial changes forego these later transformations. The ambition of this chapter is thus to look at how the school and its educational programme have changed or not, and how this has changed its relationship to the city in which it resides. Asking questions like *where, for whom, within what forms, under what conditions* and *for what purpose*, gives us a hint of how design education, to use Sara Ahmed's words, is 'oriented'. From a phenomenological perspective, orientation is about 'orientating ourselves toward some objects more than others, including physical objects … , but also objects of thought, feeling, and judgment, and objects in the sense of aims, aspirations, and objectives' (Ahmed, 2006: 553). The location of the school, its premises, its student uptake, the demographic profile of students and staff, the educational model, its financial model, and whether degrees or certificates are involved, are all parameters which are decisive for the way an education is orientated and orients itself in the city in which it resides. Decisive for what parts of design education are considered as 'heritage' and crucial for the identity and continuity of design education, compared to other non-essential parameters or factors.

Tracing changes of orientation in and over time can provide us with an understanding of how and why things have changed and why some things are valued as 'heritage' while others are not. But more importantly, it can also help us to understand how things could have been otherwise. A similar observation is made by Sara Ahmed. She writes: 'Looking back is what keeps open the possibility of going astray. We look back, we go behind; we conjure what is missing from the face. This backward glance also means an openness to the future, as the imperfect translation of what is behind us' (Ahmed, 2006: 569–570).

The particular focus of this chapter will be the school and its design education's orientation vis-à-vis the city in which it resides. Consequently, this will be an exercise in four parts pointing towards the past, present and future of design education, and how different heritages are at play within those processes. In the first part, there will be a more detailed outline of the history of Slöjdföreningens skola, including the emergence and development of design education. This outline primarily draws on four sources, the publications marking the school's 75th (Ericsson, 1924), 100th (Ericsson, 1948) and 150th (Brunius and Mörck, 1998) anniversaries, and *Historien om Göteborgs universitet* (Elmäng, 2012). But for the last 10–15 years, the outline is reconstructed through a combination of my first-hand experiences, having worked at the school for the past 15 years, and various organisational documents. Based on that, in the second part, four distinct yet overlapping periods are identified and characterised in terms of orientation. Eventually, in the third part, changes in orientation of the school vis-à-vis the city are discussed and problematised. Finally, in the fourth part, the different heritages of design education and their implication for the future of design education and its relation to the city as urban heritage is brought forward.

Remembering design education

In this section there will be a more detailed account of Slöjdföreningens skola, and how proto-design and design programmes emerged within its physical setting in the city. The ambition is to point at a set of smaller and consecutive acts that produced more substantial changes over time. This includes changes in the curriculum, building-related issues, organisational changes and policy changes which all, directly or indirectly, have transformed the relationship between design education, its heritage and its relation to the city and its urban heritage. Studied individually, these changes or transformations present different yet clear rationales, but analysed together they point to significant changes and what could be described as particular periods regarding the school's history. These will be discussed in the following section – The transformation of design education, so for those readers who do not have a particular interest in the emergence and transformation of design programmes within what originally was known as Slöjdföreningens skola, I suggest you jump there directly.

Slöjdföreningens skola was born in 1848 out of a national reform effectively abolishing the guilds, as one of many schools that started to provide training and education to a new generation of craftsmen. In Stockholm, this already happened in 1844 with what came to be known as Konstfack (University of Arts, Crafts and Design). As suggested, the initiators of the school were Slöjdföreningen i Göteborg (The Handicraft Association in Gothenburg), an association set up by local intelligentsia and industrialists to promote craft and craftsmanship. In the years to come, it rapidly went from having 20 students the first year to around 1,100 students a year by the turn of the century. At the time, it was a much larger school than Göteborgs Högskola, eventually to become Göteborgs Universitet (University of Gothenburg), founded in 1891 – then with seven professors and 15 students.

Around the turn of the century, Slöjdföreningens skola, after having merged with Göteborgs Hantverksskola (The Gothenburg Craft School), had outgrown its premises at Vasagatan 50. An ever-increasing collection of craft objects used for educational purposes and the lack of proper workshop facilities became the main arguments for a new purpose-built building for the school – financed through a partnership with the city (Slöjdföreningen i Göteborg) in recognition of the school's importance for the growing industry and the local economy – which was inaugurated in 1904 (Slöjdföreningens skola) at Kristinelundsgatan 6–8. By then the school, operated by Slöjdföreningen i Göteborg offered four fee-based programmes. Two day-schools: Skola för lantmaskinister (School of Engineering) and Skola för konstslöjd (School of Handicraft) and two evening-schools scheduled for the weekends as well, enabling the students to keep a day job in parallel with their studies: Teknisk afton och söndagsskola (Technical Evening and Sunday School) and Fackskola för bokindustri (Vocational School for the Book Industry). By comparison, Göteborgs Högskola had grown to 500 students by 1907 (Gurmund, 1977).

Over the years, the school came to align with the arts-and-craft movement inspired by schools primarily in the UK and Germany. In 1915, the attic was refurbished to meet the expanding needs of the programmes. However, evening schools continued to be an essential component in the educational offer well up until the 1950s. And one year later, in 1916, a new purpose-built building for the collection at the other side of the block at Vasagatan 39 (Röhsska Muséet) was completed through substantial donations from a local businessman and power-broker August Röhss (Ericsson, 1924, 1948). While the collections continued to be an important of the curriculum for many years to come, this moment also presents a clear junction point from a heritage point of view. And while Röhsska Muséet can be recognised as part of the educational heritage, the separation into two different institutions paved the way for two significantly different trajectories when it comes to the institution's relation to and position within the city.

In 1948 a total 786 students were enrolled at the school, within: Konstindustriella Dagskolan (The 'Design' Day School) – a one-year day school; Högre Konsthantverksskolan (The Higher Craft School) – a three-year day school with various tracks such as *Dekorativ måleri och grafisk konst* (painting and print), *Heminredning* (interior design), *Textil Konst* (textile), *Dekorativ Skulptur* (sculpture); Dagsskolans textila grundkurs – a two-year day school in textiles; Aftonskolans Konstyrkesavdelning (roughly 50% of the students) – a three-year evening school with specialised tracks with printing, painting, book-binding and so on; Fotografiskolan (a three-year evening and daytime school in photography); Guldsmedsskolan (a four-year evening school in jewellery), Kartritningsskolan (a one-year evening and day school in map drawing); Skolan för Bokbinderi (intensive courses for printers); Aftonskolans Tekniska Avdelning (roughly 20% of the students) – two-year courses in building construction, engineering, shipbuilding and electricity.

By the 1950s, the school had started to become a high-profile day school with a smaller number of students, with programmes such as *Keramik och glas* (ceramics and glass), *Metall och plast* (metal and plastics), *Möbler och inredning* (furniture and interior design), *Reklam och grafisk formgivning* (graphic design), *Textil* (textiles), *Skulptur* (sculpture), (Brunius and Mörck, 1998; 72–73). By 1962, two new wings were built to accommodate more extensive workshops and new production technologies necessary for keeping the education programme up to date, forming an inner courtyard facing the back of Röhsska Muséet. The new orientation of the school, in line with the overall societal, cultural and industrial change, was manifested in the adoption of a new name in 1964 – Konstindustriskolan – which roughly can be translated into the 'Design School'.

During the 1960s, there was an increased concern regarding the general lack of stable funding (for the school) and secure employment conditions (for the staff). Additional funding for investing in new technologies necessary for keeping the education up to date was also lacking. Therefore, in 1967 the school underwent substantial organisational changes, where the state – through Skolöverstyrelsen – was given the economic responsibility for the teaching staff, while the rest of the responsibilities continued to be a municipal concern (Brunius and Mörck, 1998; 72–73). The transition also ensured access to so-called *studielån* (student loans offered by the state) otherwise restricted to university studies (Brunius and Mörck, 1998; 101).

In parallel, the building at Kristinelundsgatan 6–8 came into the custody of HIGAB – a new municipal company set up in 1966 to supply smaller local companies and organisations with premises, but which over time came to have responsibility for buildings of 'cultural value', meaning that many historical buildings that were not of a residential character or owned by the state, such as various schools, libraries, museums, arts and music venues and other buildings of public character, became part of HIGAB's portfolio.[1] While this change did not have any direct implications for the school or its curriculum, the 'local' orientation of HIGAB as compared to the emerging national orientation of the school would later become one key aspect in a development project involving a relocation of the school – Nya Konst, within the new Campus Näckrosen.

With the restructuring of the whole higher education sector at a national level in the late 1950s and 1960s, with the state as principal, entirely or in parts, a more long-term and regular planning, informed by an overall national agenda and supported with regular funding, was created. Thus, the school started to orient itself more towards higher education, with an awakened interest in research and scholarly autonomy, while the previously strong ties to local industry and commercial interests were weakened. The new orientation of the school was settled in 1977 through the integration of the school into University of Gothenburg, as part of *Högskolereformen* (Higher Education Reform). This meant that not only Konstindustriskolan (The 'Design' School), but also Valands Konstskola (Valand Fine Arts School), under the new name of Konsthögskolan Valand (Academy of Fine Arts), Musikhögskolan (Academy of Music) and Scenskolan (School of Theatre), were integrated into University of Gothenburg.

This reform meant a more stable financial situation, improved conditions for students and staff, and better possibilities to interact with the university sector as a whole. The reform also included a definition of *konstnärligt utvecklingsarbete* (artistic development work) as a particular category within the legislation (Germund, 1977: 263), acknowledging the particular character of arts education. However, it also meant a loss of autonomy, being subsumed in a larger organisation (Brunius and Mörck, 1998: 112). In addition, the school's bonds to the city were formally cut, except the lease of the school building, which came to be handled through University of Gothenburg. Again, at the time this change had no significant impact on the school nor the curriculum, but over time University of Gothenburg as 'city university' (Caldenby, 1994), with multiple locations and multiple different landlords, grew to be a challenge, prompting a development into a limited number of campuses and a lesser number of landlords, such as the currently planned Campus Näckrosen of which Nya Konst is a part.

The number of students had dropped to 220 in 1977 and the new educational offer, not too dissimilar from the educational offer in 2020, included three-year-long programmes in *Grafisk Design* (graphic design), *Inredningsarkitektur* (interior design), *Industridesign* (industrial design), *Produktdesign* (product design), *Keramikkonst* (ceramics), *Metallkonst/ Smyckekonst* (jewellery), *Textil Konst* (textiles), *Högre Grafisk Kurs* (print). In principle, all evening schools, as well as the more technical-oriented programmes, ceased. As part of the school's new and more internationally-oriented agenda, the programmes were converted into internationally recognised MFAs in Design and Applied Arts and Crafts, and University Certificates in the case of Graphic Design, in 1978 (Brunius and Mörck, 1998: 117). The exclusive character of the programmes, with a small number of students, remained throughout most of the 1990s. And the school's more academic orientation was eventually manifested in the renaming of the school to Högskolan för Design och Konsthantverk (School of Design and Craft) in 1989.

Through *Högskolereformen* (Higher Education Reform) 1993 – the so-called 'Freedom reform' – the higher education sector as a whole was deregulated. And while the reform brought more autonomy to the universities in most internal matters, it also brought reporting, audits and evaluations on a regular basis. The reform also included the establishment of an artistic doctoral degree.[2] The same year (1993) *Fastighetsreformen* (The Property Reform) deregulated Byggnadsstyrelsen (The National Building Board) with responsibility for all state buildings, into Statens Fastighetsverk (The National Property Board), Vasakronan (Sweden's largest property company) and particularly important in this context, Akademiska Hus with the responsibility for higher education facilities. At the same time, the universities in effect were forbidden to own property (Förordning, 1993).

At Högskolan för Design och Konsthantverk, the inner courtyard of the school was covered over in 1993, producing a new aula – also used as an exhibition space and for other public activities, indirectly making the school less dependent on other public institutions (such as Röhsska Muséet) in the city. In addition, the entrance area was refurbished with a new library and café and new floors facing the new courtyard were built, including new spaces for the textile studios as well as new studio spaces.

In 1995 the seven three-year programmes were changed to five-year programmes, resulting in an increased number of students. In 1998, a total of 261 students were enrolled in: *Grafisk Design* (graphic design); *Inredningsarkitektur* (interior design); *Industridesign* (industrial design); *Produktdesign* (product design); *Keramikkonst* (ceramics); *Metallkonst/ Smyckekonst* (jewellery); *Textil Konst* (textile); while *Högre Grafisk Kurs* (print) had ceased (Brunius and Mörck, 1998).

On an organisational level, there was a significant change when *Konstnärliga Fakulteten* (The Faculty of Fine Applied and Performing Arts) was formed in 2000, comprising Högskolan för Design och Konsthantverk (HDK), Högskolan för Film och Fotografi (HFF), and Konsthögskolan Valand, Musikhögskolan, Teaterhögskolan and Operahögskolan. This meant that the school effectively came under the control of a dean (at faculty level) as opposed to the vice-chancellor (at university level). The same year, *konstnärlig forskning* (artistic research) was included in the Research Bill (Prop. 1999/2000: 81) for the first time. The following year, 2001, *Vetenskapsrådet* (The Swedish Research Council) started allocating funds for *konstnärlig forskning* (artistic research).

By 2001, 647 students were attending Högskolan för Design och Konsthantverk, mostly within programmes (459 students) but also within free-standing courses (184) as well as doctoral students (four). And four years later (2005), there are similar numbers within the programmes (518 students) and the free-standing courses (195 students) while the number of doctoral students almost doubled (seven students) – in total 720 students. The same year *Angeredsateljén*, a post-compulsory design programme in Angered (one of Gothenburg's suburbs) aiming to help long-term unemployed and ethnic minority groups into integration and permanent jobs, was launched. Five years later, in 2006, the Business and Design Lab (BDL) was launched, an interdisciplinary research centre involving scholars primarily from design and economics. In parallel, a new interdisciplinary MA programme in Business and Design was developed.

The well-known Bologna Process was implemented in Sweden through the 2007 *Högskolereform*, aiming at strengthening the quality and bringing more coherence to higher education across Europe, with a first, second and third cycle of higher education. Furthermore, in 2009 (Förordning, 2009: 933) a practice-based doctoral degree – *konstnärlig doktor* (artist doctor) – was established in parallel to the already existing PhD. The same year, 2009, another interdisciplinary MA design programme, Childrens' Culture Design (CCD), was launched at HDK. There would be three further new MA programmes: Design, Business and Design (relaunched as Embedded Design in 2020) and CCD; and a BA programme in Design.

In 2011, Business and Design Lab became a formal centre within the university. In the following years, there was also an increased push for research and increased involvement in university centres on HDK's part, primarily through design, such as the Centre for Consumption Research, Centre for Critical Heritage Studies, Centre for Tourism, Centre on Global Migration and Centre for Ageing and Health.

One year later, the scope of the school was changed significantly as parts of Stenebyskolan, a post-compulsory education institution 160 km north of Gothenburg, was partly integrated in HDK. By then, HDK had also come to include teacher training programmes in crafts and visual arts. The student numbers started to increase for the first time in over a hundred years. On an organisational level there was a push towards forming larger units, where the departments at Faculty of Fine, Applied and Performing Art shrunk from eight to three, through the 2005 merger of Musikhögskolan, Teaterhögskolan and Operahögskolan into Högskolan för Scen och Musik (HSM) and through the 2012 merger of

Konsthögskolan Valand, Högskolan för Fotografi and Filmhögskolan into Akademin Valand.

The same year, *Projekt Campus Näckrosen* was initiated as a development project in dialogue with Akademiska Hus, as part of a new focus on the development of a set of university campuses with different profiles. The purpose of this project was to look at how the area including Humanistiska Fakulteten (The Faculty of Humanities), Universitetsbibliotek (the university library) and parts of Konstnärliga Fakulteten (the Faculty of Fine, Applied and Performing Arts) – all owned by Akademiska Hus – could be developed into a 'Park for Humanities and Arts'. For the Faculty of Fine, Applied and Performing Arts, it presented an opportunity to bring all of its Gothenburg-based programmes under one roof.

By 2015, HDK had almost doubled its number of students since 2005. In total, there were 1,317 students, 215 more than when the school peaked in 1904. One year later, HIGAB, the municipal real estate company responsible for Högskolan för Design och Konsthantverk's building at Kristinelundsgatan 6–8, received a new directive from its proprietor, the city. It stated that the company should prioritise specialised premises that are of strategic importance for the city and not taken care of by the ordinary real estate market. In addition, the directive stated that rental arrangements for the city's tax-based businesses should be based on the production cost. In all other cases, it should be market-based. As Högskolan för Design och Konsthantverk had not been one of the city's tax-based businesses since 1977, a market-rent would be applied in the near future, changing the lease-cost of Kristinelundsgatan 6–8 dramatically. In addition, HIGAB declared that it did not see HDK as a future tenant.

Two years later, the annual Gothenburg Design Festival was launched for the first time: 'an open mobile collaborative laboratory that investigates what design is, if and why it is significant and for whom', signifying an increased will to renegotiate the school's position within the city.[3] While exam-shows, with the primary focus to exhibit student work, had been in practice at least since the 1990s, the festival was informed by the idea that the school should also put itself on display and invite a general audience and prospective students in particular to meet and interact with design and craft education. In addition to the exhibitions (for instance degree shows), the festival offered public workshops (to all ages) and lectures across multiple sites and in partnership with other organisations and elementary schools, during the daytime and evening as well as at the weekend.

In 2019, HDK enrolled 1,131 students, 601 programme students, 493 free-standing-courses students, 19 doctoral students and 18 students on new validation programmes, within four subjects: Craft, Design, Sloyd (teacher training) and Visual Art (teacher training). And one year later, in 2020, Högskolan för Design och Konsthantverk, HDK and Akademin Valand merged into HDK-Valand (Academy of Art and Design) which, together with HSM (Academy of Music and Drama), constitute Konstnärliga Fakulteten (Faculty of Arts) of today (with approximately 420 employees and 3,200 students in total). The same year, the first part of the Campus Näckrosen plan was completed with the opening of the new building for Humanistiska Fakulteten, while the plans for the new building for HDK-Valand and HSM – Nya Konst – are well underway, aiming to be completed in 2026.

The transformation of design education

The period before the completion of the new building for *Slöjdföreningens skola* in 1904, leading up until the 1950s, could be described as a period of local consolidation. While there was indeed a restructuring and re-orienting of the curriculum and the staff, the school remained local and independent, managed by Slöjdföreningen i Göteborg with support from the municipality. It had a vocational orientation, with a local intake of students, and offered both a general as well as specialised education, with the purpose of providing the expanding local industry with skilled artisans and craftsmen. Classes were given all week, in both daytime and evenings, since most students had a working-class background and had to work in parallel in order to make a living and cover the tuition fees. The links to the city, through Slöjdföreningen i Göteborg and the city's financial commitment to the school, were strong. Also, not insignificant for the school's relation to the city at large, statistically, 1 in 150 inhabitants in Gothenburg were students at the school. Slöjdföreningen i Göteborg and Slöjdföreningens skola were firmly placed in the local economic and political landscape, providing a skilled workforce to the local industries, in many cases owned by the families that supported the school and the foundation financially. The school was clearly, *of* the city, and in all aspects a local school. And the impact of the school, through its students exercising the knowledge and skills acquired at the school in the growing industrial sector was substantial.

The following period, the 1950s to the 1970s, could be described as a period of increased stabilisation. While the school remained independent, though supported by the municipality, some of the school's priorities had shifted to a national level by the end of the 1960s, and to a more international orientation by the 1970s. In parallel, it became more specialised, no longer offering any general education programmes, and primarily giving classes during daytime and regular work days (weekdays). This change was enabled through the provision of more extensive and improved national student loans schemes. Although the students were often still drawn from a working-class background, they were also increasingly from a lower-middle or middle-class demographic. They were also increasingly recruited from a more national base. The vocational character remained, as well as the strong focus on industry as the primary context for the graduated students, but increased specialisation was also mirrored by the diminishing number of students.

The period of the late 1970s, 1980s and 1990s was highly formative, characterised by the school's integration into the national framework for higher education and University of Gothenburg. While the school building continued to be supported by the municipality through HIGAB, the school itself could no longer be said to be 'of the city', but indeed only located within it. It started orientating itself towards academia, away from the industry, and specialisation, from having been driven by a purely vocational agenda, started to become an academic concern, informed by the aspiration to develop research on an equal footing with the rest of the university. The number of students continued to decrease, and became increasingly middle-and upper-middle-class in character. Many of them had already completed at least two years of post-compulsory art education, also eligible for the national student loan programme. Throughout this period, although integrated into the university, the school to some degree can be said to have remained a school in its own right, sitting directly under the vice-chancellor.

From 2000 onwards, there was a period of further integration and growth. The forming of a new faculty consolidated the position of arts education within the university, while at the same time moving the school one step down the organisational ladder – a rationale that since then has characterised the development of the school (and the university). During this period, the school changed from being a school organised directly under the vice-chancellor, to being a department within a faculty, to being units at a department. A section of the Stenebyskolan was integrated into HDK; also, teachers' programmes in visual arts and crafts were added, broadening the scope of the school. Moreover, while the repertoire and number of students in the school, mostly from a middle-and upper-middle-class background, started to grow, the design programmes started to move away from the disciplinary frames of product design, interior design and graphic design. The implementation of research and research education, partly on top of existing profiles, and involving the contracting of new staff with PhDs from other neighbouring fields, as well as increased collaboration across the university through different research centres, added to this momentum but also caused friction. The new orientation towards a more international and interdisciplinary horizon, within highly specialised full-time programmes, also included a growing interest in the public and cultural sector with a clear social agenda. The vision of Nya Konst, while driven at a pragmatic level by HIGAB's lack of interest in having the university as a tenant, also foregrounded interdisciplinarity and the ambition to establish a more open and dynamic relationship between the school, the surrounding city, and its inhabitants.

Design education and the city

But now let us return to the question of design education's 'orientation' (Ahmed, 2006) vis-à-vis the city in which it resides. What are the particular 'objects' that the education is oriented towards? What are its 'aims, aspirations and objectives'? Being orientated *towards* something (new) also means that you at the same time turn *away* from other things (old). I will now have a closer look at such changes in orientation, or 'turns', in design education. There are, in particular, three distinct yet related domains – the 'educational', the 'organisational' and the 'demographic' – in which a change in orientation has occurred, directly or indirectly impacting the relations with the city in which the education is located, which I will highlight.

While the 'educational orientation' of programmes at Slöjdföreningens skola throughout all its iterations have kept a focus on materiality and making, the formats and the profile of the programmes, individually as well as a whole have changed drastically, as this chapter has described. For example, the previous strong connections to industry, such as Volvo, originally a Gothenburg company, were more-or-less gone by the 2010s. From the mid-2000s there was a clear turn towards interdisciplinarity – within sub-disciplines within design at bachelor level – and in relation to other disciplines at master-level. In addition, the programmes became increasingly international (or European) and by the 2010s there was a growing interest in the socio-political role of design, expressed as an interest in critical practice, social sustainability and the public sphere more broadly. A turn that led strong lobbying organisations, such as the Swedish Architects' Association, to question the relevance of the programmes, and represented a radically different situation to that of 1904. Yet the exclusive and specialised programmes, attractive within the international and lucrative fee-based market, remain.

The 'organisational orientation' of the school up until the 1960s was that of a local independent and nimble organisation with a constant focus on keeping its business running. The more stable conditions following the 1977 reform, with the state as principal, was a relief but also meant significant changes over time. While longer planning horizons as well as more opportunities for intra-academic exchange were an obvious benefit, the school's autonomy in all sorts of issues gradually decreased. As such the school was increasingly orientated toward a national and international horizon, but also subordinated to the organisational logic and regulations of the new mother organisation – University of Gothenburg – gradually and increasingly detaching itself from its local context. A development, once and for all manifested in HIGAB's uninterest in having the school as a future tenant. In parallel, new partnership and exchange programmes with other schools, primarily but exclusively in Europe, are built. A strong European orientation is eventually established through the Bologna-reform. But over the last decades, after decades of disinvestment with regard to the city, there is a turn towards non-academic cooperation and outreach – *samverkan*. The bonds with the surrounding society and the city are revisited and new sorts of cross-sectoral and international projects within increasingly competitive regional, national and international markets are cultivated.[4]

Thirdly, the 'demographic orientation' of the school has changed substantially between the early and late twentieth century. Since the turn of the century, there is also an increased number of international students from comparable middle-class backgrounds, such that the narrow demographic profile of staff and students is becoming a concern. At a national level, the main reasons for this are identified as the weak position of artistic subjects within primary education, the cost and extent of arts education (including years at post-compulsory level), and limited career possibilities (in the absence of good social networks) (Nykvist, Blomberg, Eineborg, Eriksson, and Larsson, 2018). There is a renewed interest in the city from the university as well as on the school's part, and a more socially engaged orientation of the design programmes has gained ground. But the conditions for working as a designer have become increasingly precarious, and the programmes are kept exclusive in order to avoid the risk of educating students into unemployment, perpetuating the demographic pattern.

In short, the orientation of 'design' education in Gothenburg and in relation to Gothenburg in the latter half of the twentieth century can on all accounts, educationally, organisationally and demographically, be characterised as a gradual withdrawal from the local, with an increased focus on the national, international and intra-academic horizons provided, generated and supported by the higher education frameworks and organisation(s). Educational programmes become increasingly competitive, specialised and exclusive in their uptake and profile. From having been (a product) *of* the city, the school, more and more, came to be merely *in* the city. A development somewhat in contrast with University of Gothenburg's identity as a city-university (Gurmund, 1977), already questioned by Claes Caldenby (Caldenby, 1994), with regards to the clustering tendency (into campuses) at the time.

Nevertheless, by the turn of the century, it is as if the decoupling of the school and the university from its surroundings has gone too far. What was once a refuge is now understood as 'not real', artificial and secluded. Within the design programmes there is an increased interest in conducting education in relation to its surroundings and making use of other settings as sites of education, framed as participatory design and co-design, including more outreach and collaborative initiatives with traditional public institutions in the city (Lenskjold, Olander and Halse, 2015), as well as smaller citizen-initiatives or professional entities (DiSalvo, Clement and Pipek, 2012).

Yet, there is a paradox here. While design (in a broader sense and more than ever) can be found almost anywhere, the sites where the will and capacity to design is cultivated are only accessed by a few and the already privileged. And while the orientation of the programmes has started to change, and various measures to attract a broader range of students are increasingly made, the structural conditions, with small and exclusive programmes, remain. It is as if the historical momentum of the past 50 years of development, driving design education into increasingly more specialised and exclusive educational and professional models, is finally biting its tail. Has the current model reached its end? Are we indeed at a point, to quote Tony Fry, where the current model of 'design education (and most other forms of higher education) serves to extend the status quo rather than address the problems they have created' (Fry, 2015: 417)?

Design education oriented otherwise

The development of Slöjdföreningens skola into its current manifestation within The Academy of Art and Design is in no way unique, at least from an Anglo-European perspective. As stated by Michael W. Meyer and Don Norman in 'Changing Design Education for the 21st Century':

> Contemporary design education has several origins. The Royal College of Art in London began in 1837 as the Government School of Design. The Glasgow School of Art began in 1845 as the Glasgow Government School of Design. The Rhode Island School of Design (RISD, United States) began in 1877. Konstfack (Stockholm) began in 1844. The National Academy of Craft and Art Industry (Norway) began in 1818, surviving today as the design faculty of the Oslo National College of Art. Much of the curriculum developed over the years at these schools and several of the European academies survives in design education today. (Meyer and Norman, 2020: 20).

But suppose the current model of design education has reached a dead end. In that case, the proper question might not concern the parts of the curriculum of these historical design programmes that have survived in higher design education today, but rather what parts have survived outside these academies? And how indeed may the rich history of Slöjdföreningens skola, in all its iterations and transformations, help us to think otherwise of design education? From such a perspective the history of Slöjdföreningens skola and the 'design' education within is not a linear path pointing towards today's particular manifestation of design education, but a tree, reaching into the future in multiple ways. More so, it is a tree that shares its roots with other entities which have branched into other settings and sectors. For instance, the educational profile of the school up until the second half of the twentieth century is closer to the profile of the design-related post-compulsory educations of today, than the current ones within higher design education – not only in terms of offering both general and specialised education, but also classes every day of the week, daytime as well as in evenings. A rough estimate – based on the number of students in higher arts education more broadly and compared to the number of students attending post-compulsory education in the arts – would be that for every design student within higher education, there would be three within post-compulsory education. More so, Röhsska Muséet, growing out of the collections used for pedagogical purposes at Slöjdföreningens skola, has continued to be an educational site. Not only as an exhibition venue for design students but more importantly, a site where basic education, as well as citizens more broadly, are engaged in issues of design. In 2019 Röhsska Muséet had 104,366 visitors. It is therefore possible to imagine a much broader base of 'design students' and broader forms of 'design education', not limited to prospective design professionals and higher education only (Benesch, 2017), and to further consider in which way the very notion of 'students' and 'education' enables as well as disables diverse modalities of learning.

Such a broader narrative of design education stands in stark contrast to the one envisioned in Michael Meyer's and Don Norman's article 'Changing Design Education for the 21st Century', clearly centred around the design professional. Out of 37 pages, there is only one paragraph addressing design as a subject for students who do not foresee a professional career as designers. In this case, within an American context:

> The minor in design – or for that matter, single courses designed for those not majoring in design – can also be of great value for those who do not wish to become designers. Courses and minors have the virtue of educating non-designers in the power, methods, and various disciplines of design, which means that when they embark upon their career, they are better equipped to work together with design teams, or if they move into managerial roles in industry, to recommend the hiring of designers and the use of design firms' (Meyer and Norman 2020: 37—38).

Is this not an example of how 'we never yet had design – only its weak, subaltern industrial-capitalist, version …', where '… designers, as well as struggling to exemplify the capabilities of design, also, in some ways, "got in the way" of design' (Dilnot 2015b: 118)?

This brings us to the central argument of this chapter: namely, that change of orientation, of 'design education', from its less disciplined and more varied forms in the first half of the twentieth century, to its increasingly disciplined forms by the end of the twentieth century, also in effect meant a withdrawal from the city in which it resides. This shift in orientation can be said to be the combined effect of the development of increasingly specialised and scholarly-oriented programmes functional within a large university context, and the integration of the school into a large organisation (the university). From having been an actor directly involved in local urban development, based on the local needs of the school, the school has increasingly become an integral part in other and larger schemes. Although the 1993 real estate reform (*Förordning*, 1993: 527) had little effect at the school at the time since the school already was in a lease agreement, it effectively closed down any possibility for the school to act more directly with regard to its spatial needs, as manifested in the case of 1904 building at Kristinelundsgatan 6–8. And on a broader basis, universities which by themselves develop, build, manage and own facilities, would need quite a different organisation and competence, than universities who merely lease. From that perspective, the decisive question in regard to the relationship between university heritage and urban heritage is whether the university is a lease or landlord organisation or not (or both). It is also a question of scale. In 2016, University of Gothenburg had 130 rental agreements with around 30 landlords, regarding 73 buildings, in total 383,363 square metres. As a reference, the building at Kristinelundsgatan 6–8 is around 10,000 square metres – about 2.5% of the total lease. 57% of the premises are leased from Akademiska Hus, and 20% is leased from HIGAB.[5] In turn, Akademiska Hus, with its portfolio of 3.3 million square metres of real estate, controls 61% of the market.[6]

The outcome of an alternate historical development, where the school and the university retained its right to develop facilities for their use beyond 1993, is, of course, hard to speculate on. Still, it is likely to have had an important impact on the development of the school and the design education, being able to act as an organisation that actively *designs* its premises, rather than responding to a development as a tenant. With regard to *'orientation'*, the shift from a landlord organisation to a tenant organisation is a substantial one, being a question not only of relations but also of competence and skills, which includes ideas about the role and responsibilities of the organisation, and in this case a shift from a more 'worldly' interpretation on what this entails to a more 'academic' one. In effect, the school became a school that was not allowed to design its own premises, and consequently we must understand the urban heritage of the school and its 'design' programmes beyond 1904 as an 'un-heritage': one that has not developed in its own right past the second half of the twentieth century, disabled in effect by 1993 real estate reform.

The withdrawal from the city is also apparent on a sheer numerical base. In between 1900 and 2019 the city of Gothenburg has grown from 150,000 to 1,050,000 inhabitants. In 1904, Slöjdföreningens skola had 1,105 students and in 2019, Högskolan för Design och Konsthantverk, just before merging with Akademin Valand, had 1,131 students. And while the building at Kristinelundsgatan 6–8 has been refurbished and extended numerous times, the school has essentially retained its actual size. At the same time, its relative size vis-à-vis the city has decreased seven-fold, while University of Gothenburg as a whole has essentially grown with the city (49,150 students in 2019). What is inherited from the first of the half of the twentieth century are the size of the school and the individual programmes, but what was large-scale then is small-scale today. The same goes for the organisation. The downgrading of the school on the organisational ladder (within a growing organisation and including an addition of managerial and administrative layers and staffing), is indeed an indication of a change of relative scale. Similarly, on a demographic register, retaining the size of the programmes (being able to stay within the premises) within a growing population (and expanding international recruitment base), produces even more exclusive programmes. This pattern is shared with other Swedish design educations, for instance Konstfack, in many regards sharing the same past as Slöjdföreningens skola, can be considered to be connected to the particular Swedish model of higher education: free-of-charge, with national student loan schemes, where the financing is connected to the throughputs of students. Other admission and fee-based educations, for instance in the UK, display a much more expansive pattern.

And while it can be argued that there are broader societal, political and economic shifts behind this development, it is also true that there is very little evidence that a different kind of development has been sought. While there has indeed been increased interest, on all sorts of levels, in changing the relation vis-à-vis the city and its inhabitants more broadly, as a community as well as future students, more substantive structural developments have not surfaced. It is as if the building itself has restrained the school, enabling it not to change. Here the questions around the shift in orientation from an *active* landlord to a *passive* tenant once again emerges. Once again, this can be considered a question of an un-heritage.

The Gothenburg Design Festival was a first attempt to think and act differently on this relation between the school and the building, and the school's relation vis-à-vis the city in which it resides: an attempt structured around a process of reciprocity and interdependence, as compared to a process structured around autonomy. Here earlier attempts such as *Angeredsateljén* can be considered a precursor in considering the school as not bound by the building but a relational site. And let us look further back, beyond the late 1960s. There is, in fact, a resemblance between these 'new' relational, educational models – *Angeredsateljén* and the Gothenburg Design Festival, with a broader address and scope and conducted outside regular work hours – and the educational models of the first half of the twentieth century. In this, in some capacity, a heritage (of design education), is yet unacknowledged, constituting a latent 'memory' we no longer know. A heritage, as it seems, hidden under decades of disciplining exercises and reformations.

And when the school and its design programmes project itself into the future, as actualised in the Nya Konst process, the relationship between these two pasts is still to come to terms with. On the one hand, the immediate past, riding on a wave of extensive structural changes which has built its momentum over half a century – disciplined, autonomous yet somehow closed, as expressed in the commitment to a particular size and orientation of education that has been cultivated at the school for the past decades; and on the other hand, a more distant, precarious and more unruly yet open past – that has gone sideways finding its home in other settings and at other locations outside the school, but now returns through 'new' and interdependent and reciprocal educational models, anchoring design education at particular sites once again.

And as it seems that its due time to question where the current wave is bringing us, Sara Ahmed's reminder (quoted in the first section) can indeed be helpful:

> Looking back is what keeps open the possibility of going astray. We look back, we go behind; we conjure what is missing from the face. This backward glance also means an openness to the future, as the imperfect translation of what is behind us. (Ahmed, 2006: 569–570)

We actively engage in acts of dis-, mis- and re-membering design education as it was and as it could have been, in order to come to terms with what it can and possibly should be. This includes remembering heritages dis-re-membered or mis-remembered, such as the educational orientation, as well heritages not only dis-membered but disabled, such as the change from landlord to tenant. To paraphrase Clive Dilnot:

> The question of design education in relation to history and the future is therefore the question of design education thought within the processes of re-establishing a flow between the causative and consequential past, the present as the site through which we test, with anticipation, the relation of the actual and the possible, and the future as that which we must now cultivate into being. (Dilnot, 2005a: 134)

Through such a dis-, mis- and re-membering in new ways, it might be possible again to revisit the question 'what are the wheres, whens and whoms of design education?' when writing a new chapter of design education, enabled through the process of Nya Konst at Campus Näckrosen.

Furthermore, the case of Kristinelundsgatan 6–8 displays how the complex interplay between the building, its user and the way they are entangled in all sorts of external relations over time, obscures both past and futures; where a building, an urban heritage un-reflected upon, risks consolidating and projecting (into the future) only what is remembered, rather than prompting us to engage critically in what seems to have been dis- or mis-remembered or simply forgotten, while placing ourselves within more extensive timeframes. Such a 'backward glance' could indeed change the perception of urban heritage as something linear and possibly teleological, to something more open; a resource allowing us to look at other versions of the past, and through that peer into the future from multiple and less hegemonic perspectives. It is through such a glance we can come to terms with how things have, and therefore could, be oriented otherwise. From such a perspective the concept of orientation as developed by Sara Ahmed may indeed be helpful in framing what we understand as urban heritage and what role it can play in a near and distant future.

Notes

1   https://www.higab.se/om-higab/historik/ retrieved 20201023
2   https://www.lagboken.se/Lagboken/sfs/sfs/2009/900-999/d_591561-sfs-2009_933-forordning-om-andring-i-hogskoleforordningen-1993_100
3   https://gothenburgdesignfestival.se/en/about-the-festival/ retrieved 20201120
4   https://www.gu.se/en/about-the-university/vision-and-values retrieved 20201101
5   The University of Gothenburg (2016) Strategisk lokalförsörjningsplan 2016–40.
6   https://www.akademiskahus.se/globalassets/dokument/ekonomi/ekonomiska-rapporter/arsredovisning_2019.pdf retrieved 210108

References

Ahmed, S. (2006) 'Orientations: Toward a queer phenomenology'. *GLQ: A Journal of Lesbian and Gay Studies*, 12 (4), 543–74.
Benesch, H. (2017) 'To be a student of design'. In D. Hamers, N. Bueno de Mesquita and A. Vaneycken and J. Schoffelen, J. (eds), *Trading Places*. Barcelona: DPR.
Brunius, J. and Mörck, N-H. (eds) (1998) *HDK 150 år: 1848–1998: Slöjdföreningens skola, Konstindustriskolan, Högskolan för design och konsthantverk vid Göteborgs universitet*. Göteborg: Göteborgs slöjdfören.

Caldenby, C. (1994) *Universitetet och staden: inför fältstudier!*. Göteborg: Påbygget, White Coordinator [White arkitekter].

Dilnot, C. (2015a) 'History, Design, Futures: Contending with what we have made'. In T. Fry, C. Dilnot and S. Stewart (eds), *Design and the Question of History*. London: Bloomsbury.

Dilnot, C. (2015b) 'The matter of design'. *Design Philosophy Papers*, 13 (2), 115–23, DOI: 10.1080/14487136.2015.1133137.

DiSalvo, C., Clement, A. and Pipek. V. (2012) 'Participatory design for, with, and by communities'. In J. Simonsen and T. Robertsen (eds), *Routledge International Handbook of Participatory Design*. New York: Routledge, 182–209.

Elmäng, C. (ed.) (2012) *Historien om Göteborgs universitet*. Göteborg: Göteborgs universitet.

Ericsson, S. (ed.) (1924) *Slöjdföreningens skola på jubileumsutställningen i Göteborg 1923: skrift till 75-årsminnet av skolans stiftande*. Göteborg: Skolan för bokindustri vid Slöjdföreningens skola.

Ericsson, S. (1948) *Slöjdföreningens skola 1848–1948: Skolans historia genom hundra år*. Göteborg: Skolan för bokindustri.

Fry, T. (2015) 'Design: On the question of "The Imperative"'. *Design and Culture*, 7 (3), 417–22, DOI: 10.1080/17547075.2015.1105713.

Ginzburg, C., Tedeschi, J. and Tedeschi, A. (1993) 'Microhistory: Two or three things that I know about it'. *Critical Inquiry*, 20 (1), 10–35.

Gurmund, L. (1977) *Gothenburg University: A dispersed institution*. Göteborg: Univ., Informationssekretariatet.

Lenskjold, T. U., Olander, S. and Halse, J. (2015) 'Minor Design Activism: Prompting change from within'. *Design Issues*, 31 (4), 66–77, DOI: 10.1162/DESI_a_00352.

Meyer, M. and Norman, D. (2020) 'Changing Design Education for the 21st Century'. *She Ji: The Journal of Design, Economics, and Innovation*, 6 (1), 13–49.

Nykvist, A., Blomberg, G., Eineborg, A., Eriksson, C. and Larsson, H. (2018) '*Konstnär – oavsett villkor?* Stockholm: Norstedts juridik'. Accessed 21 January 2008. http://www.regeringen.se/rattsdokument/statens-offentliga-utredningar/2018/03/sou-201823/.

Swedish Government (1993). *Förordning 1993:527 om förvaltning av statliga fastigheter, m.m.* Accessed 21 January 2008. https://www.riksdagen.se/sv/dokument-lagar/dokument/svensk-forfattningssamling/forordning-1993527-om-forvaltning-av-statliga_sfs-1993-527.

Swedish Government (1999). *Forskning för framtiden – en ny organisation för forskningsfinansiering* Prop. 1999/2000:81. Accessed 21 January 2008. https://www.regeringen.se/rattsligadokument/proposition/2000/03/prop.-1999200081-/.

7
London's mega event heritage and the development of UCL East

Jonathan Gardner

Introduction

This chapter considers the development of UCL East in Queen Elizabeth Olympic Park, Stratford, as a 'legacy' of two of London's previous 'mega events': the 2012 Olympic and Paralympic Games and the Great Exhibition of 1851. Since their emergence in the mid-nineteenth century, mega events – a genre of large-scale international, transitory spectacles including expositions, world's fairs, and sporting events like the Olympic Games – have been recognised as drivers of dramatic urban change (Kassens-Noor, 2016). In the case of UCL East, the 2012 Olympic and Paralympic Games are directly responsible for the existence of its site and the support it has received from central government through the event's legacy development (LLDC, 2019).

In what follows, I provide an overview of how UCL East emerged as a result of these earlier mega events. I suggest that the new campus' development relies upon a selective understanding and use of heritage discourses, pertaining not only to its location in Queen Elizabeth Olympic Park ('the Olympic Park' hereafter), but also its relationship to the Great Exhibition of 1851 and that event's legacy educational institutions at South Kensington (collectively known as 'Albertopolis'). I demonstrate that the comparisons that have been made between these earlier mega events and UCL East (along with East Bank) are based on an over-simplification of their complex geneses and argue that we must be wary in assuming a simple line of travel between these 'ancestor' events and the present.

Heritage discourses

Like other contributors to this volume, I argue that universities and other cultural organisations rely upon constructed heritage discourses to justify their programmes of expansion, appealing to notions of tradition or appropriateness for how that institution 'fits' with its host city and community. Following David Harvey (2001), heritage can be understood as an ever-changing 'process', a social phenomenon that is not fixed or ever fully agreed upon, and whose invocation has great power to influence behaviour and the claims we make about how the world is understood to 'work' and the construction of understandings about the past, present and future (Wu and Hu, 2015: 41). I suggest that we must understand UCL East and East Bank's emergence as being at least in part derived from several competing visions of the past: a genealogy of understandings of both the history of the host site and London's previous mega events, each of which can be 'excavated' to examine the original assumptions and evidence upon which they were founded.

Below, I critically analyse these discourses through examination of texts, media and other materials related to the UCL East, East Bank and Olympic projects for their contents and intertextual relationships, to highlight the value claims they make to effect change or maintain the status quo. I suggest that two interlinked discourses are at play in legitimising and creating the current development of UCL East and East Bank as a whole.

The first of these heritage discourses is the portrayal of both the physical traces of 'the past' (old buildings, archaeology, landscapes, existing populations) within the UCL East and East Bank projects *and* the mechanisms by which these traces have been 'dealt with' – both literally and discursively – in the creation of the Olympic Park, without which no legacy development would be occurring. Given that the current projects have directly benefitted from narratives that often portrayed the pre-Games site as an 'industrial wasteland', I suggest it is critical that we now interrogate how the past has been represented here and to ask how UCL East and its fellow institutions can be true to their desire to become 'rooted' in this 'new piece of city' without reproducing such tropes (UCL 2017a: 4, 20).

The aforementioned ancestor story operates as a second discourse that connects East Bank's planned cultural and educational institutions to London's first mega event, the Great Exhibition of 1851 (also referred to as '1851' hereafter) and the institutions that emerged from its aftermath, particularly the South Kensington Museum (now V&A). The desire to 'learn' from this illustrious ancestor was reflected in the nicknaming of East Bank as 'Olympicopolis' in 2013 by (then) London Mayor Boris Johnson (examined further below). I suggest that a tension exists between this ancestor discourse and that of the wasteland and, at the end of the chapter, I consider how UCL East might act as a useful opportunity for reconciliation of these discourses.

Situating UCL East

UCL East emerged in its current form in 2014 with UCL's '2034 Strategy', which outlined a desire to strengthen the institution's role as a 'global university' situated in London yet accessible to its communities and, more practically, to provide additional teaching space and new degree programmes (UCL, 2014). The 2034 Strategy and East project had an earlier genesis in a 2011 UCL Council 'White Paper' (UCL, 2011a), with major plans for the redevelopment of its existing estate with the 'Bloomsbury Masterplan' (UCL, 2011b), and, a scheme for a Stratford-based campus on the site of the Carpenters Estate (see Figure 7.1), a collection of council housing managed by the London Borough of Newham and located immediately to the south of the Olympic Park (UCL, 2011c).

'UCL Stratford', as this initial eastern campus became known, was opposed by a coalition of local Newham residents and UCL students and staff after its announcement in late 2011 (CARP, 2012; UCLU, 2013). This saw campaigning against plans for a campus that would have entirely demolished the estate and seen its remaining 700 residents rehomed elsewhere (BBC, 2012). The scheme, developed in partnership by UCL and its Provost, Malcolm Grant, along with (then) Mayor of Newham, Robin Wales, eventually collapsed in 2013 due to difficulties agreeing a business case. However, according to Grant's successor, Michael Arthur, the negative publicity received by UCL played a significant part in the university's decision to pull out (UCL, 2013).[1]

From the ruins of UCL Stratford emerged UCL East in 2013, developed in discussion with the Mayoral Development Corporation responsible for developing the Park – the 'London Legacy Development Corporation' (LLDC) – with plans to develop a campus within the Olympic Park itself (UCL, 2013). This campus is now being built in the south of the Olympic Park across two parcels bisected by the Waterworks River, a much-modified channel of the River Lea (sometimes spelt 'Lee'), itself the

Figure 7.1 The Carpenters Arms and housing blocks of the Carpenters Estate, Stratford, East London, January 2016. Site of the now cancelled UCL Stratford scheme. Photo: Jonathan Gardner. CC BY 4.0

largest tributary of the River Thames. The easternmost area of the UCL East site, adjacent to the London Aquatics Centre, is subdivided as 'Pool Street East' and 'Pool Street West', while the westernmost site is known as 'Marshgate', with the first phase projected to open in 2023. As detailed elsewhere in this volume, this campus will be the largest expansion of the university in its 195-year history and will provide a wide range of new degree programmes and research opportunities, as well as laboratory facilities, student accommodation and community engagement programmes.

The history of 'a new piece of city'

Moves towards hosting the 2012 Olympic and Paralympic Games in London emerged from the late 1990s onwards, with the Lea Valley identified as a potential site by 2000 (Lee, 2012: 6). London's eventual bid, launched in 2003, is generally seen to have been successful due to its emphasis on a planned 'legacy' of social and material change to East London and the UK (Gold and Gold, 2017).

The intention to radically rework the urban landscape in this part of East London has had a long gestation, with the Lea Valley and, particularly Stratford, eyed as a place of 'opportunity' since the Second World War (Abercrombie, 1944: 105). Stratford was chosen for the 2012 Games' main venues for a wide range of factors: it had excellent transport links, areas of dereliction and contamination of former industry that was earmarked for regeneration, and cheap land costs (Rose, 2006: 7–8). This dereliction was partly a result of deindustrialisation related to the closure of London's docks, as well as wider structural changes to the UK economy over the second half of the twentieth century.

Following the beginning of dock closures from 1967, docklands-related industrial areas like Stratford saw a long period of disuse and stalled development projects (Hostettler, 2002). In the docks themselves, it was only with a 1980s programme of state investment under the quasi-governmental 'London Docklands Development Corporation' (LDDC) that this began to change. The LDDC was controversially granted full planning controls over the dockland area, the ability to compulsorily purchase sites and, from 1982 onwards, its lands operated as an 'Enterprise Zone', with developers exempted from paying most property taxes (Brownill and O'Hara, 2015). This, alongside government-funded infrastructure improvements (particularly the Docklands Light Railway), led to massive office and residential development that continues to this day and kick-started the ongoing mass redevelopment of the East End more broadly.

It is important to recognise that the development model pioneered by the Docklands Development Corporation now also underpins the Olympic Park's legacy, with the *LLDC* (a Mayoral Development Corporation – but note the similar name to LDDC) having similarly devolved planning responsibility for the former Olympic Park until the 2030s.[2] The wave of deindustrialisation that affected the docks – and the planning model which was developed in response – can therefore be said to have played a significant role in directing development of East Bank and UCL East.

The Olympic Park itself was developed following London's winning Olympic Bid in 2005, with construction starting in 2007. This led to the exit of 5,000 workers from over 280 businesses and over 1,500 residents from the site as a result of a compulsory purchase order enacted by the London Development Agency (Davies, Davis and Rapp, 2017: 1; Rose, 2006). The vast scale of preparations for the Games saw almost all pre-existing structures demolished, the cleaning of the upper layers of the site's contaminated soil, archaeological and ecological 'mitigation', and construction work to build stadia and other facilities for the mega event. In 2012, with the Olympic Park completed (along with other venues across southern England), the Olympic and Paralympic Games were held from 27 July to 9 September.

Following the Games, legacy plans came into place that saw the Olympic Park remodelled to maintain several permanent stadia, the dismantling of temporary venues and construction of new homes, schools and offices. The success of this legacy is still debated, though it has demonstrably delivered a major clean-up of the area's soil and waterways, improved infrastructure, new parklands, led to the creation of permanent sporting facilities and seen the building of thousands of homes. However, there has also been strong criticism of the mega event and its legacy programme as it currently stands. Much of this centres most prominently around a failure to deliver the amount of affordable housing as originally promised and a failure (so far) to provide a similar number of replacement jobs from those lost through the original compulsory purchase (London Assembly, 2017; Cheyne, 2018). I will not add to this here, but clearly UCL East will have to grapple with these concerns as it develops. Instead, I now consider how heritage discourses were employed in the construction of the Olympic Park and how these may have influenced UCL East.

Mitigating the past and creating the wasteland

As part of the Olympic Park's development, large-scale archaeological investigations took place in advance of construction, with the digging of 121 small evaluation trenches, and eight larger excavations, along with the recording of significant historic buildings prior to their demolition. Some of this work provided important discoveries, including a prehistoric settlement at the Aquatic Centre, a rare Neolithic hand-axe, an early nineteenth-century rowing boat and a Second World War anti-aircraft gun emplacement (Powell, 2012). The future site of UCL East itself showed evidence of prehistoric use, including a likely Bronze Age/Iron Age settlement at Pool Street East (AECOM, 2017: para. 6.4.62).

This archaeological work was mandated by UK planning guidance, with the developers – the government-run Olympic Delivery Authority (ODA) – obliged to fund mitigation of damage to archaeology and historic buildings either through preservation or recording and documentation. However, I suggest that a second sense of the word 'mitigation' was also at play here: the use of findings and representations of the ancient past to *mitigate against* negative perceptions of the project.[3] Archaeological investigations provided a 'good news story' for the project and the language used in press releases appears to aim to legitimise the changes the Olympics wrought. An example is found with a 2007 ODA release where the discovery of three prehistoric roundhouses on the banks of the Waterworks River (said to house 'the first Londoners'): 'We are taking this opportunity to tell the fascinating story of the Lower Lea Valley before it is given a new lease of life for the Games and future generations. It is a story of change and transformation dating back centuries' (ODA, 2007a).

The implication here seems to be that the seasonal occupation of a piece of riverbank by a small group of people more than 3,000 years ago was no different from the wholesale re-landscaping and change of the 250 hectare, £9 billion mega project.

While such use of archaeological data by developers as a 'good news story' is perhaps inevitable on construction projects, this and similar examples of where the legitimacy of change and development of the Olympics was situated somewhat awkwardly, showed that the past was, at this point at least, seen as useful to the project (see Gardner, 2020a and 2022 for further examples). However, while I would suggest that this positive view of the Olympic Park's ancient past provided useful PR, in order to complete the area's transformation, another portrayal of the past was required, namely, the denigration of the more recent history of the site.

The pre-Olympic Park area was frequently labelled an 'industrial wasteland' and a 'problem place' by the ODA and much of the national media, with the activities of existing inhabitants often shown in a negative light: for example, a focus on abandoned buildings, rather than the numerous businesses and creative industries that were still operating here until 2007 (Raco and Tunney, 2010: 2070; Farquhar, 2012; Gardner, 2020a). Strohmayer has noted that spaces seen as 'brownfield' or 'underdeveloped' like the pre-Olympic site are often taken to be unproblematic 'mirrors' of their supposed opposite: the dystopian 'industrial wasteland' contrasted with utopian regeneration of promised Olympic 'legacy' (Strohmayer, 2018: 543). The way in which the wasteland narrative operated was therefore to delegitimise the recent past in favour of promising a better future and legacy, often through contrasting images of dereliction and CGI renders of the future Olympic Park (see also Brown, this volume). In this calculus, in contrast to the ancient past, recent history and still operating industrial businesses (not to mention residents) on the site in 2007 were seen as 'underutilising' the area and were required to be made absent in the 'post-industrial' future of the Games and their carefully planned aftermath (ODA, 2011: 33).

A wasteland of a sort was soon made real, however, through the enactment of the compulsory purchase in 2007, with the commensurate exit of workers and residents, and demolition of industrial premises and housing. The only traces of the past recorded (officially) were those heritage 'assets' that were safely archaeological or considered architecturally 'significant' (buried villages, gun emplacements) rather than any pertaining to those recently working or living on the site (for example, businesses and allotment gardeners). Even the older archaeological past that was excavated was barely recognised after 2012: there are currently still no plans to display or provide interpretation of any of this material in Queen Elizabeth Olympic Park (though a site publication was produced – see Powell, 2012).

Most of the traces of this recent past were instead recorded only by photographers, artists and academic researchers in 2005–7 (though on occasion some more unusual work on contemporary structures was ODA-funded – for example, see Dwyer, 2007). These investigations contradicted the idea that the area was entirely 'post-industrial' or empty of inhabitants by interviewing and photographing businesses still in operation, and residents of the Clay's Lane housing estate and users of sites like the Manor Gardens Allotments (Davies, Davis and Rapp, 2017; Hatcher, 2012; Marshall, 2012).

The assertion that this place was a barely inhabited 'wasteland' still seems to pervade legacy planning today, with elements of the Legacy Masterplan Framework describing the pre-Olympic site as an 'industrial backwater' and a 'historically disjointed part of the city' (LLDC, 2013: 146), and, post-Games, almost no traces of these former industries or inhabitants are visible in its landscape today.

Why then was the recent past seen to be unacceptable? Primarily, I would suggest that the presence of contemporary industry and inhabitants acted to contradict the positive or 'redemptive' promise of such a mega project (see Butler, 2007 for a similar example): that is to say that such a project inevitably produces negative effects as well as positive ones. For this area to truly be 'regenerated', anything that was a holdover from the past was potentially seen as a threat to the future. This not only included physical traces such as contamination or old factories, but also the activities of people who still inhabited and used this space in a way that was seen to be incompatible with what was planned. With this in mind, I now turn to how UCL and East Bank are engaging with the history of the site and how far this wasteland discourse can be said to persist today.

UCL East and the Olympic Park

UCL East's own recognition of the history of the Olympic Park currently appears to be only fleetingly articulated, but even at this stage it is worth examining how conceptualisations of the past are presented by the project.

In UCL East documents and webpages, efforts have been made to establish both a local and a London-wide connection to the past. On its 'Location' webpage – first seen from 2017 –for example, a brief 'History of the area' was presented and is worth quoting at length:

> In 1868, the area was largely agricultural. Adjacent uses included a gasworks, a brick field, a spinning mill and nearby railways on the embankment. By 1893, a number of light industrial premises (Victoria Oil and Candle Works, Varnish Works, Oil and Chemical works and Hudson's Bay Fur and Skin works) occupied a vacant area of land to the south including the UCL East site. From the end of the twentieth century until the early 2000s the site was used as a scrap yard.
>
> The wider site was subsequently developed for the London 2012 Olympic and Paralympic Games. The Legacy Communities Scheme (LCS) planning application, which was approved in September 2012, is the overarching scheme developed to guide the long-term development of the Olympic Park and its neighbourhoods after the Games.
>
> Building on East London's reputation as a trailblazer in design and creativity, and inspired by the vision for the legacy of the Great Exhibition that created Exhibition Road in Kensington, the Olympic Park now plans to make its name as a new centre for attracting and nurturing talent and industry. The Cultural and Education District will create a world-class destination, bringing together outstanding organisations to showcase exceptional art, dance, history, craft, science, technology and cutting edge design (UCL, 2017b).

This shows a succinct overview of the site's recent past, including the details of individual businesses.[4] It is notable, however, that nothing prior to 1868 is mentioned or that no history of the wider Olympic Park is included – for example, the prehistoric settlement at the Aquatics Centre and nearby Pool Street mentioned above. That said, a relatively neutral emphasis on more recent industrial uses does stand in contrast to the 'wasteland' narrative discussed previously.

The reference also made here to a 'trailblazer in design' is similar to language used by the LLDC within the overall East Bank project, and which emphasises a non-location specific 'vitality of East London' narrative (LLDC, 2019). This more general sense of being part of a 'vibrant' idea of the East End as a whole suggests that while a wasteland discourse is less overtly in use today, a certain need for distance from the local past lingers, and that an alternative, more acceptable and generic recent past is to be foregrounded.

> Within the wider East Bank project webpages where UCL East is mentioned, we see the LLDC's desire for the project to slot into an existing topography of other 'cultural destinations' in London rather than those pre-existing within Stratford (for example, the Theatre Royal or University of East London):

> The ambition of the project is recognised in the new name – the East Bank – which will complement London's major cultural and education centres, such as the South Bank, the cluster of museums and academic institutions in South Kensington and the Knowledge Quarter around King's Cross and Bloomsbury. (LLDC, 2019)

The overall intention with East Bank therefore appears to be to create a destination within the Olympic Park and East London whereby the area is no longer primarily associated with the Olympic and Paralympic Games (or indeed the supposed previous 'wasteland') or significant local history, but fundamentally, is to be understood as a wholly *new* part of London (Mayor of London, 2018). Arguably, the eye-catching institutions of museums, universities and concert halls are an attempt to make good on promises for legacy, which espoused a wholesale transformation of the area and to create a 'destination' beyond sporting venues or new housing (Gold and Gold 2017: 527). In Graeme Evans' view, East Bank appears to assume that the pre-2012 era was therefore also a 'cultural wasteland' and argues that the project ignores any pre-existing industrial and creative heritage in favour of 'a Guggenheim style import … without a vernacular reference' (Evans, 2020: 67).

Thus, potentially the wasteland heritage discourse lingers but its emphasis shifts from a focus on physical signs of dereliction or contamination to something less tangible, and perhaps an assumption that this place is in need of a 'cultural regeneration' alongside a physical one. With regard to UCL East's efforts at place-making, despite discussion of being 'rooted' in the community, the absence of much discussion of contemporary or ongoing heritage value here seems odd. While at least some of the planned academic departments of UCL East will actively engage with local heritage and history (particularly the 'Urban Room and Memory Workshop' focusing on the 'impact of industry, globalisation and gentrification on the six Olympic Park Boroughs and their people' (see UCL, 2018), those planning the buildings of the new campus itself appear unaware or uninterested in this heritage. For example, Clare Melhuish relates that a member of UCL East's development team suggested their approach to the new campus was based on a belief that 'there's very little long-term heritage' nearby the site, specifically on the basis of the 'poor quality' of the buildings of nearby housing estates like Carpenters (Melhuish, 2019: 15). Not only does this ignore UCL's negative influence on the residents of Carpenters Estate in 2011, given its original expansion plans, but it also highlights a failure to integrate the experience of people living in the area today or those who worked (or lived) in the Olympic Park area previously, not to mention its industrial history and buried archaeological remains.

This lack of short-term institutional memory may be related to UCL's contrasting use of its own 'institutional history and heritage' to justify the East campus (Melhuish, 2019: 14). This includes UCL presenting a generally positive version of its own past, such as the fact it was the first university to accept women and enrolled all students regardless of 'race' or religion. Relatedly, Beverley Butler notes the way 'utopian' origins are often foregrounded in UCL's 'myth-history' particularly around the auto-icon of Jeremy Bentham and his utilitarian belief in 'greatest good for the greatest number' (Peters, Wengrow, Quirke, Butler and Sommer, 2018: 60). This 'myth-history', that the university is more progressive or 'radical' than others, is epitomised by the branding on hoardings around the current UCL East worksite stating the university's 'heritage of disruptive thinking', 'since 1826'. While clearly much of this history is indeed noteworthy, it is obviously valorised over more problematic episodes in the institution's past, including the abortive Carpenters' expansion as UCL Stratford, while the idea that this space was simply empty is not helped by another hoarding slogan claiming to be 'breaking *new* ground in East London' (my emphasis; McLaughlin, 2019).

Above, I have explored how heritage was used in the building of the Olympic Park and in the early stages of UCL East's development. The developers of the Olympic Park, and those now responsible for its legacy plans, appear to have relied on a simultaneous valorisation and denigration of different elements of the past, resulting in what I have called the 'wasteland' discourse. While the ancient past was briefly of interest in supporting landscape changes or useful for positive news stories, this relied on the more recent history of the Olympic Park being castigated as entirely dirty, ruinous and wasteful, despite evidence to the contrary. With the development of UCL East and East Bank, this discourse becomes somewhat modified: the fear or 'threat' of the wasteland appears less directly but the developers of these institutions seem instead to either highlight a more generalised sense of East End history which bypasses Stratford, or their own institutional 'myth-history'. Another ancestor is also at play here, however, that I have not yet discussed, and it is one that lies at the heart of UCL East and East Bank's development: the Great Exhibition of 1851 and its 'legacy' as Albertopolis, to which I now turn.

An educational heritage: 1851 and its legacies

Looking again at UCL East's 'location' webpage (above) we see that the project is said to be, 'inspired by the vision for the legacy of the Great

Figure 7.2 One of the few photographs of the Crystal Palace in Hyde Park in 1851, which hosted the Great Exhibition. Attributed to Claude-Marie Ferrier. Public Domain. Available at: https://commons.wikimedia.org/wiki/File:Crystal_palace_1851.jpg

Exhibition' (UCL, 2017b). UCL here draws on a wider East Bank foundational narrative that makes reference to South Kensington, this first appearing at the district's December 2013 launch by then Mayor of London (and LLDC chair), Boris Johnson. Johnson referred to the planned 'Culture and Education District' (as it was then officially called) as 'Olympicopolis' and noted that '[t]he idea behind [the project] is simple and draws on the extraordinary foresight of our Victorian ancestors', referencing the fact that institutions such as the South Kensington Museum were developed in part from the profits of the Great Exhibition (Mayor of London, 2013). Johnson thus deftly established a connection between the legacy of the London 2012 mega event and that resulting from its Victorian predecessor.

Though described as 'his vision' in UCL East documentation (Soundings, 2016: 17), it seems unlikely that the Mayor's nostalgia for the Victorians was the sole reason for making the link to Albertopolis, given that the district is arguably the world's most successful mega event-led cultural legacy project (albeit one that was originally unplanned – see below). Such evocation of the 'spirit of 1851' is not new or specific to London. Following 1851, many Great Exhibition imitators appeared, ranging from the short-lived and combustible New York Crystal Palace (1853), to the enormous *Expositions Universelles* in Paris (held regularly from 1855 until the Second World War), with many other mega events subsequently hosted around the world from the late nineteenth century up to the present day.

The Great Exhibition (see Figure 7.2) has also been frequently referenced by subsequent UK mega events. For example, the other 'ancestor' most often mentioned by the current East Bank developments, the 1951 Festival of Britain, was held in the Great Exhibition's centenary year, although it only grudgingly acknowledged the date, given its organisers' progressive emphasis (Conekin, 2003: 85–6). Reference to 1851 was also made in support of the ill-fated 'Millennium Experience' and its Dome at North Greenwich (Porter and Stokes, 1999), and this ancestor event is once again now enthusiastically taken up as inspiration for the planned 'Great Brexhibition' of 2022 to celebrate the UK's departure from the EU (Sandbrook, 2018).

Imitations of this original event (and its legacies to some extent) are therefore not uncommon, but to understand how appropriate it is to draw links between UCL East and this 'ancestor', it is important to revisit the context of the original spectacle in 1851 and its legacy developments, given the significant differences between them and East Bank.

The Great Exhibition

The Great Exhibition of the Works of Industry of All Nations was held in Hyde Park in London between May and October of 1851, in a vast temporary structure that became rapidly known as the 'Crystal Palace'. Plans for the Exhibition were led by Henry Cole (Assistant Keeper at the Public Records Office) and by Prince Albert (husband of Queen Victoria) and it was funded through public subscription. The Exhibition housed around 13,000 exhibits (with over 100,000 individual items), encompassing everything from lumps of coal and steam-powered machinery to looted colonial diamonds and elaborate displays of taxidermy. Attracting some six million visitors, the event was primarily intended to display the UK's manufacturing prowess to the world and to stimulate demand for British-made goods (Auerbach, 1999; 12–13).

The Exhibition was considered a great success, with its closure attracting consternation and calls for the Crystal Palace's retention as a 'winter garden' or exhibition hall (Piggott, 2004: 33). Its novelty and this great success led to its almost instant 'heritagisation', with letters calling for the erection for a memorial found as early as October 1851 ('Delta', 1851). Such nostalgia – and a degree of mythos – continues to exert a strong pull on both scholarly and political imaginations of the event to this day.

Despite East Bank and UCL East's emphasis on 1851's educational 'vision', and though famously linked to the origin of modern museums by Tony Bennett (1995), the Great Exhibition was not intentionally created as a museum-like space by its organisers; its educational focus was instead intended primarily to improve the 'taste' of consumers. Similarly, the Exhibition was planned as a one-off spectacle and hosted in a temporary venue with no plans made to leave a legacy in the form of permanent educational institutions or buildings (indeed, the 'temporariness' of its structure was a key condition of securing its site – see Gardner, 2018). As discussed below, the institutions of South Kensington emerged only afterwards with the addition of significant government investment and decades of effort (Gold and Gold, 2005: 70; Physick, 1982; Gardner, 2022: chapter 4). We must therefore be careful in assuming a clear line of travel between 1851's 'legacy' and current day initiatives like East Bank, given that conscious mega event 'legacy planning' is a phenomenon that really only fully appears with much later mega events and particularly the Olympic Games from the 1960s onwards (see Gold and Gold, 2008: 304). Albertopolis and the other cultural/educational ventures that emerged from the Exhibition can be more properly understood as unplanned, albeit fortuitous, legacies, and thus quite different from the detailed plans for the aftermath of London's 2012 Olympics, which were always a part of its original Bid and planning applications (ODA, 2007b).

Albertopolis

The development of Albertopolis was kick-started with the Great Exhibition's profits of £186,000 and the actions of the Royal Commission for the Exhibition of 1851 to distribute these funds. After much discussion, the commissioners decided to use this money, along with match-funding from the government, to purchase 86 acres of land in South Kensington to create 'a Site for Institutions connected with Science and Art', and to 'serve to increase the means of Industrial Education' (HM Government quoted in Physick, 1982: 21). This eventually led to the formation of the South Kensington Museum (renamed the Victoria & Albert Museum (V&A) in 1899), which officially opened in 1857 in several temporary buildings. The Museum and its planned permanent structures were then developed in piecemeal fashion with the building 'finished' (excluding later extensions) in 1909, following more injections of government money and several aborted schemes (Physick, 1982: chapter 3).

Following the South Kensington Museum, numerous other institutions were then developed in Albertopolis, again in stop-start fashion over several decades, with the Natural History Museum opening in 1881, what became the Science Museum emerging in the 1860s, and the Imperial Institute (a precursor to Imperial College London) in 1887. Evans has argued that the Great Exhibition and Albertopolis were a 'Victorian example … of event or culture-led regeneration' just as the Olympics and its legacy schemes are to Stratford and East London (Evans, 2020: 52). He leaves unspecified just what was actually 'regenerated' in 1850s South Kensington, but I would suggest this comparison is misleading given that the original Crystal Palace was built within a Royal Park and Albertopolis was constructed (mostly) over a combination of mansions, paddocks and market gardens and was spatially and socially very different from twenty-first-century Stratford.[5] So while Evans rightly draws attention to other differences between South Kensington and East Bank, his argument is overly simplistic in equating the impact of two very different mega events upon London's landscape. A correction to this is important given that the Olympic Park, despite claims of 'wasteland', was no edgeland or *tabula rasa* prior to the mega event and had considerable density and variety of occupation, and was quite unlike the semi-rural Hyde Park and South Kensington in 1851.

Before concluding, I now want to briefly consider one last and sometimes forgotten legacy of the Great Exhibition, the rebuilt Crystal Palace at Sydenham, South London, and what it might tell us about the long-term fate of post-event educational legacies.

Meet the ancestors

While development of Albertopolis ramped up through the late 1850s, the Crystal Palace building that had housed the Great Exhibition was already in operation from 1854 as a privately operated venture at Sydenham in south London. Its owners, the Crystal Palace Company, sought not only to stay true to the educational ideals of the Great Exhibition but to 'outdo' it and, later on, actively competed with the South Kensington Museum (Piggott, 2004: v, 34). This saw the Palace rebuilt at Sydenham five times larger than the Hyde Park version and filled with educational exhibits. The vast range of these cannot be covered here but included ten 'Fine Art Courts' (reconstructions of rooms and artworks

Figure 7.3 The models of dinosaurs and extinct animals that remain as one of the few surviving traces of the Crystal Palace at Sydenham. Photo: Jonathan Gardner. CC BY 4.0

from ancient civilisations), a 'Tropical Department' complete with palm trees and parrots, exhibits of industrial machinery, and a display of model indigenous people arranged in a racist 'civilisational' hierarchy (Qureshi, 2011). These, along with displays of geology and extinct animal models outside in a vast elaborately landscaped park (see Figure 7.3), supported the Palace Company's vision to 'create a visual encyclopaedia of culture and nature' (Moser, 2012: 5), and to operate as '[a]n institution intended to last for ages, and to widen the scope, and to brighten the path of education throughout the land' (Phillips, 1854: 10).

Unlike Albertopolis, the Palace and its Park also rapidly developed an entertainment component as the finances of the Crystal Palace Company worsened. These leisure uses included fairground rides, sporting events, fireworks displays and many temporary expositions, including the enormous Festival of Empire in 1911 (Piggott, 2011; Gardner, 2018). Following bankruptcy during this last event in 1911, and their purchase 'for the nation' by Lord Plymouth, the Palace and Park operated as a Naval training base during the First World War and then hosted the first iteration of the Imperial War Museum from 1920 to 1924. Under new management from the late 1920s onwards, the Palace began to turn a profit, only for it to accidentally burn to the ground in November 1936, with its loss much mourned (Auerbach, 2001: 93).

To summarise; though the establishment of East Bank and UCL East is said to be inspired by the successes of Albertopolis as a legacy of the Great Exhibition, the Crystal Palace at Sydenham arguably provides a useful 'alternative' ancestor. If nothing else, it illustrates the risk in creating such large-scale educational ventures that may not always benefit from regular injections of government funding. In the case of East Bank, such funding is heavily reliant on development of adjacent residential units (and commensurate growth in the east London housing market), and in UCL's case, its own financial resilience and ability to recruit more students (Viña, 2016), both of which are inevitably subject to uncertainty, particularly in the wake of Brexit and the COVID-19 pandemic. Sydenham also shows that 'legacy' can be a messy business, and its (mis)fortunes confront us with evidence of how such an educational institution can struggle to stay true to the aims of both its backers and 'ancestors' alike (Gardner, 2020b; 2022).

An added complication to this desire to evoke Albertopolis has come with the renaming of Olympicopolis as 'East Bank'. This brings yet another ancestor into play: the Thames-side site of the South Bank Exhibition of the 1951 Festival of Britain and its (originally unplanned) legacy of the 'South Bank' cultural centre. Upon relaunching Olympicopolis in 2018,

Sadiq Khan, the present Mayor of London, said that East Bank was 'inspired' by South Bank's institutions and their 'transforming a location through [providing] world class art and learning opportunities' (Mayor of London, 2018). Thus, just like Johnson, the past of a whole district is to be employed in condensed form for the service of the present. Should a new Mayor be elected in 2024, perhaps yet another mega event forebear will be found.

Much like the long gestation of Albertopolis, following 1951, the South Bank complex took many decades to arrive at anything like the place we see today. The Festival of Britain was hosted by a Labour government who were ousted in a snap election at the end of 1951 – shortly after the South Bank Exhibition's closure – and all of the mega event's structures were razed except the Royal Festival Hall (always intended as a permanent venue). The district then saw no further permanent cultural developments until 1967 with the construction of the Queen Elizabeth Hall, the Hayward Gallery in 1968 and the National Theatre in 1976. No original legacy plan was made for the area beyond the retention of the Festival Hall, except for an intention to construct a large-scale set of government buildings that were never built alongside a vague intention to locate some kind of cultural centre here under the wartime *County of London Plan* (Hutchinson and Williams, 1976; Forshaw and Abercrombie, 1943). It was only with the end of the twentieth century, and further redevelopment, that the area took on its current coherent form. It will be difficult for East Bank and UCL East to replicate such a unique environment quickly, which, like South Kensington, went through a complex series of false starts and, like the Olympic Park, also had a rich history prior to 1951 despite being branded a 'slum' prior to the South Bank Exhibition's construction (*Picture Post*, 1951).

Conclusion: remembering the past at UCL East and East Bank

A complex picture emerges from this survey of how the mega events of 1851 and 2012 have informed the development of UCL East. As part of East Bank, the campus construction now occurring at Queen Elizabeth Olympic Park relies upon a pair of interlinked heritage discourses. Firstly, a particularised understanding of the history of the Olympic Park and Stratford and, secondly, a reification of the (apparent) success of the institutions of South Kensington and, latterly, South Bank. Albertopolis, after a long gestation, has become one of London's most preeminent centres for education and culture and is rightly recognised as a successful and long-lasting legacy of the original event. Its referencing by the institutions of East Bank is therefore easy to comprehend, particularly given the Games' site was in an area which was said to have no prior value under the 'wasteland' narrative, but, as I have argued, this somewhat distant ancestral heritage has come at the expense of an understanding of the broader historical context of both Stratford and these earlier mega events.

A comment from London's Deputy Mayor for Culture and Creative industries, Justine Simons, at the East Bank 2018 (re)launch event shows that there seems to be a confused attitude towards London's past mega event legacies:

> East Bank represents the most significant single investment in London's culture since the legacy of the 1851 Great Exhibition, and will shape the cultural life of the city for the twenty-first-century and beyond. (Mayor of London, 2018)

Thus, we see a complicated movement between 1851, its legacies at Albertopolis, and the Festival of Britain and South Bank (along with an absence of discussion of Stratford's past and the Sydenham Crystal Palace) and between its different partners and developers. Just as mega events and their structures are often conflated (Gardner, 2018), there seems to be a lack of certainty between the use of different events and their legacies (not to mention a certain degree of Mayoral political manoeuvring).

David Lowenthal's concept of 'creative anachronism', our tendency to project our own desires and wishes upon the past, is useful here (Lowenthal, 1985: 363). In this case, both the changes brought by the Great Exhibition and the 2012 Games have become overdetermined as paradigmatic shifts, 'precipice[s] in time' that are alleged to have utterly changed both society and their host city (Johansen, 1996). Therefore, much nuance related to the complexities of these events' geneses, their uneven social impact, institutional history and popularity is lost, along with alternative histories and the story of entire institutions like the Sydenham Crystal Palace and Park.

Melhuish (2019) suggests that UCL East is already moving towards creating its own heritage, one that is mainly based around the activities within the new structures themselves and combined with the history of UCL in Bloomsbury as a 'disruptive' institution. While this may be preferable to misrepresenting or oversimplifying the past, it potentially means that a valuable opportunity to be 'rooted' in the community is lost. While I do not suggest a focus exclusively on the industries or former residents of the Olympic Park should be the only way of engaging with the past here, it would be a bold move for institutions like UCL to make a positive break from the wasteland discourse and the near constant denigration this area has faced for over 15 years. One of Cohen's informants (this volume), a care worker, speaks of their frustration at this misrepresentation and speaks of a desire to be proud of the contribution their family made in working in this area over generations for example. In being silent on such an issue, UCL East risks, like the Games project before it, being seen as an alien or elite presence in the East End and just the latest example of a desire to reimagine the east of the city by those in the west (Newland, 2008).

Funding

This research was funded from 2012–15 by an AHRC Studentship at the UCL Institute of Archaeology (ref. 1159756).

Notes

[1] Carpenters' future still remains uncertain; its few remaining residents will be neighbours to UCL East project (L. B. Newham, 2019).
[2] The Games' site was developed by the quasi-governmental Olympic Delivery Authority which acted as the planning authority, with compulsory purchase handled by the London Assembly-based London Development Agency (LDA). These were not Development Corporations but had similar powers over planning and development, with local London Borough council districts where venues were built unable to overrule decisions – such a planning model has been criticised for its lack of democratic accountability.
[3] The opinions of the author are solely his own and do not reflect the position of any archaeological company he has previously worked for or any other entity or individual involved with the Olympic project, East Bank or UCL/UCL East. All information discussed in this chapter is derived from material in the public domain which can be found by following links in the references.
[4] Shortly after the final version of this chapter was submitted in early 2020, this text disappeared from the web (though an earlier version captured in 2017 remains accessible; see UCL, 2017b). A new webpage now stresses the importance of 'understanding the area's rich history prior to the Olympics, and its diverse local communities' (see https://www.ucl.ac.uk/ucl-east/explore-east-london). Georeferenced mapping of the area can be viewed through the National Library of Scotland: https://maps.nls.uk/geo/explore/#zoom=16.27&lat=51.54073&lon=-0.01558&layers=6&b=1.
[5] For example, consider this map of 1843 (tick 'view' checkbox): http://hgl.harvard.edu:8080/opengeoportal/?ogpids=STANFORD.RT316DV2497&bbox=-0.18091%2C51.485011%2C-0.165932%2C51.503861.

References

Abercrombie, P. (1944) *Greater London Plan*. London: HMSO.
AECOM (2017) *UCL East Environmental Statement, Volume 1: Cultural Heritage*. Accessed 27 February 2020. https://tinyurl.com/rqtvvn7.
Auerbach, J. (1999) *The Great Exhibition of 1851: A nation on display*. Newhaven, CT: Yale University Press.
Auerbach, J. (2001) 'The Great Exhibition and historical memory'. *Journal of Victorian Culture*, 6, 89–112. https://doi.org/10.3366/jvc.2001.6.1.89.
BBC (2012) 'Anger over university campus plans'. *BBC News*, 12 January. Accessed 4 March 2020. www.bbc.co.uk/news/uk-england-london-16531386.
Bennett, T. (1995) *The Birth of the Museum: History, theory, politics*. London and New York: Routledge.
Brownill, S. and O'Hara, G. (2015) 'From planning to opportunism? Re-examining the creation of the London Docklands Development Corporation'. *Planning Perspectives,* 30 (4), 537–70. https://doi.org/10.1080/02665433.2014.989894.
Butler, B. (2007) *Return to Alexandria: An ethnography of cultural heritage revivalism and museum memory*. Walnut Creek, CA: Left Coast Press.
CARP (2012) 'About C.A.R.P.'. *Carpenters Against Regeneration Plans*. Accessed 29 March 2019. https://savecarpenters.wordpress.com/about/.
Cheyne, J. (2018) 'Still no jobs legacy from the London 2012 Olympics'. *Games Monitor*, 29 May. Accessed 4 March 2020. http://www.gamesmonitor.org.uk/node/2347.
Conekin, B. (2003) *'The Autobiography of a Nation': The 1951 Festival of Britain*. Manchester: Manchester University Press.
Davies, M., Davis, J. and Rapp, D. (2017) *Dispersal: picturing urban change in east London*. Swindon: Historic England Publishing.
'Delta' (1851) 'Site of the Crystal Palace'. *Illustrated London News*, 11 October 1931.
Dwyer, E. (2007) *Overhead Power Transmission Lines and Associated Structures, Lower Lea Valley: A built heritage assessment*. Unpublished standing buildings assessment report. http://archaeologydataservice.ac.uk/archives/view/greylit/details.cfm?id=17302.
Evans, G. (2020) 'From Albertopolis to Olympicopolis: Back to the future?'. In G. Evans (ed.), *Mega-Events: Placemaking, regeneration and city-regional development*. London: Routledge, 35–52. https://doi.org/10.4324/9780429466595,
Farquhar, G. (2012) 'London 2012: The long journey from bid to Games'. *BBC Sport*, 30 March. Accessed 4 March 2020. https://www.bbc.co.uk/sport/olympics/17561309.
Forshaw, J. and Abercrombie, P. (1943) *County of London Plan. Prepared for the London County Council*. London: Macmillan and Co.
Gardner, J. (2018) 'Beneath the rubble, the Crystal Palace! The surprising persistence of a temporary mega event'. *World Archaeology* 50 (1), 185–99. https://doi.org/10.1080/00438243.2018.1489734.
Gardner, J. (2020a) 'Competing for the past: the London 2012 Olympics, archaeology, and the "wasteland"'. In V. Apaydin (ed.), *Critical Perspectives on Cultural Memory and Heritage: Construction, transformation and destruction*. London: UCL Press, 4566. https://doi.org/10.14324/111.9781787354845.
Gardner, J. (2020b) 'Recurring Dreams: Mega events and traces of past futures'. *Archaeology International*, 22, 86–99. https://doi.org/10.5334/ai-399.
Gardner, J. (2022) *A Contemporary Archaeology of London's Mega Events: From the Great Exhibition to London 2012*. London: UCL Press. https://www.uclpress.co.uk/collections/archaeology/products/155981
Gold, J. and Gold, M. (2005) *Cities of Culture: Staging international festivals and the urban agenda, 1851–2000*. Aldershot: Ashgate.
Gold, J. and Gold, M. (2008) 'Olympic Cities: Regeneration, City Rebranding and Changing Urban Agendas'. *Geography Compass*, 2 (1), 300–318. https://doi.org/10.1111/j.1749-8198.2007.00080.x.
Gold, J. and Gold, M. (2017) 'Olympic futures and urban imaginings: From Albertopolis to Olympicopolis'. In J. Hannigan and G. Richards (eds), *The Handbook of New Urban Studies*. London: Sage, 514–34.

Harvey, D. (2001) 'Heritage Pasts and Heritage Presents: Temporality, meaning and the scope of heritage studies'. *International Journal of Heritage Studies,* 7 (4), 319–38. http://dx.doi.org/10.1080/13581650120105534.

Hatcher, C. (2012) 'Forced Evictions: Legacies of dislocation on the Clays Lane Estate'. In I. Marrero-Guillamón and H. Powell (eds), *The Art of Dissent: Adventures in London's Olympic State.* London: Myrdle Court Press, 197–206.

Hostettler, E. (2002) *The Isle of Dogs: The twentieth century. A brief history. Volume II.* London: Island History Trust.

Hutchinson, D. and Williams, S. (1976) 'South Bank Saga'. *Architectural Review,* 160, 156–62.

Johansen, S. (1996) 'The Great Exhibition of 1851: A precipice in time?'. *Victorian Review,* 22 (1), 59–64. https://www.jstor.org/stable/27794825. https://doi.org/10.1353/vcr.1996.0032

Kassens-Noor, E. (2016) 'From ephemeral planning to permanent urbanism: An urban planning theory of mega-events'. *Urban Planning,* 1 (1), 41–54. https://doi.org/10.17645/up.v1i1.532.

L. B. Newham (2019) 'The Carpenters Estate, Stratford'. Accessed 4 March 2020. https://www.newham.gov.uk/Pages/ServiceChild/The-Carpenters-Estate-Stratford.aspx.

Newland, P. (2008) *The Cultural Construction of London's East End: Urban iconography, modernity and the spatialisation of Englishness.* Amsterdam: Rodopi.

Lee, M. (2012) *The Race for the 2012 Olympics.* London: Random House.

LLDC (2013) 'A walk around Queen Elizabeth Olympic Park'. London Legacy Development Corporation. Accessed 4 March 2020. https://www.queenelizabetholympicpark.co.uk/~/media/qeop/files/public/a%20walk%20around%20queen%20elizabeth%20olympic%20park.pdf.

LLDC (2019) 'East Bank'. London Legacy Development Corporation. Accessed 17 January 2019. https://www.queenelizabetholympicpark.co.uk/the-park/attractions/east-bank.

London Assembly (2017) 'Relighting the torch: securing the Olympic Legacy'. Accessed 4 March 2020. https://www.london.gov.uk/sites/default/files/convergence_short_report_final.pdf.

Lowenthal, D. (1985) *The Past is a Foreign Country.* Cambridge: Cambridge University Press.

Marshall, P. (2012) *Before the Olympics: The Lea Valley 1981–2010.* Staines: Self-published.

Mayor of London (2013) 'Mayor and Chancellor support developing Queen Elizabeth Olympic Park'. Mayor of London, London Assembly, 4 December. Accessed 4 March 2020. https://www.london.gov.uk//press-releases-5960.

Mayor of London (2018) 'Mayor unveils £1.1bn vision for East Bank'. Mayor of London, London Assembly, 5 June. Accessed 4 March 2020. https://www.london.gov.uk//press-releases/mayoral/mayor-unveils-11bn-vision-for-east-bank.

McLaughlin, A. (2019) 'UCL makes its mark on the disruptor trend in new campaign'. *Creative Review,* 29 November. Accessed 4 March 2020. https://www.creativereview.co.uk/ucl-jumps-on-the-disruptor-bandwagon-in-new-campaign/.

Melhuish, C. (2019) '"A place for the unexpected, integrated into the city structure": universities as agents of cosmopolitan urbanism'. *National Identities,* 22 (4), 423–40. https://doi.org/10.1080/14608944.2018.1498472.

Moser, S. (2012) *Designing Antiquity: Owen Jones, Ancient Egypt and the Crystal Palace.* Newhaven, CT: Yale University Press.

ODA (2007a) 'Archaeological work on Games site finds evidence of the first Londoners and Romans'. Olympic Delivery Authority press release, 28 November. Accessed 4 March 2020. http://webarchive.nationalarchives.gov.uk/20071105013006/http://www.london2012.com/news/media-releases/2007-11/archaeological-work-on-games-site-finds-evidence-of-the-first-londoners-and-.php.

ODA (2007b) '07/90011/FUMODA – Olympic, Paralympic & Legacy Transformation Planning Application'. LLDC Planning Register. Accessed 2 March 2020. https://tinyurl.com/s2ubgzl.

ODA (2011) 'Building the Olympic Park 2005–11'. Olympic Delivery Authority. Accessed 4 March 2020. http://webarchive.nationalarchives.gov.uk/20120403073945/http://www.london2012.com/documents/oda-publications/oda-transform-web-pt1.pdf .

Peters, R., Wengrow, D., Quirke, S., Butler, B. and Sommer, U. (2018) 'Viewpoint: Archaeology of strikes and revolution'. *Archaeology International,* 21, 54–63. https://doi.org/10.5334/ai-389.

Phillips, S. (1854) *Guide to the Crystal Palace and Park.* London: Bradbury & Evans.

Physick, J. (1982) *The Victoria and Albert Museum: The history of its building.* Oxford: Phaidon.

Picture Post (1951) 'From mud to festival'. *Picture Post,* 5 May 1951 (5), 11–15.

Piggott, J. (2004) *Palace of the People: The Crystal Palace at Sydenham 1854–1936.* London: Hurst & Company.

Piggott, J. (2011) 'Reflections of Empire'. *History Today,* 61 (4), 32–39.

Porter, R. and Stokes, M. (1999) 'Mean time?'. *Cultural Values*, 3 (2), 235–43. https://doi.org/10.1080/14797589909367163.

Powell, A. (2012) *By River, Fields and Factories: The making of the Lower Lea Valley. Archaeological and cultural heritage investigations on the site of the London 2012 Olympic and Paralympic Games*. Salisbury: Wessex Archaeology.

Qureshi, S. (2011) 'Robert Gordon Latham, displayed peoples, and the natural history of race, 1854–1866'. *The Historical Journal*, 54 (1), 143–66. https://doi.org/10.1017/S0018246X10000609.

Raco, M. and Tunney, E. (2010) 'Visibilities and invisibilities in urban development: Small business communities and the London Olympics 2012'. *Urban Studies*, 47 (10), 2069–91. https://doi.org/10.1177/0042098009357351.

Rose, D. (2006) *Report to the Secretary of State for Trade and Industry – London Development Agency (Lower Lea Valley, Olympic and Legacy) CPO 2005. Inspector's Report*. Bristol: The Planning Inspectorate.

Sandbrook, D. (2018) 'Let's make it a festival of fun – not another Millennium Dome disaster', *Daily Mail*, 1 October. Accessed 4 March 2020. https://www.dailymail.co.uk/debate/article-6225535/Lets-make-festival-fun-not-Millennium-Dome-disaster-DOMINIC-SANDBROOK-explains.html.

Soundings (2016) *UCL East – Stage 3 Consultation Report*. Accessed 25 February 2020. https://www.ucl.ac.uk/ucl-east/sites/ucl-east/files/2175_ucle_stage_3_report_101116_web.pdf.

Strohmayer, U. (2018) 'Dystopian dynamics at work'. In K. Ward, A. Jonas, B. Miller and D. Wilson (eds), *The Routledge Handbook on Spaces of Urban Politics*. London: Routledge, 542–54. https://doi.org/10.4324/9781315712468.

UCL (2011a) *UCL Council White Paper: 2011–2021*. UCL. Accessed 4 March 2020. https://web.archive.org/web/20160304094344/http://www.ucl.ac.uk/white-paper/provost-white-paper.pdf.

UCL (2011b) 'Bloomsbury Masterplan – Overview'. UCL. Currently unavailable: last accessed 17 January 2019. https://www.ucl.ac.uk/transforming-ucl/bloomsbury-masterplan/overview-4.

UCL (2011c) 'UCL to explore plans for additional campus in London Borough of Newham'. UCL, 23 November. Accessed 4 March 2020. https://www.ucl.ac.uk/news/2011/nov/ucl-explore-plans-additional-campus-london-borough-newham.

UCL (2013) 'Provost's View 14/11/2013: Our position in London'. UCL, 14 November. Accessed 4 March 2020. https://www.ucl.ac.uk/news/2013/nov/provosts-view-14112013-our-position-london.

UCL (2014) 'UCL 2034: The next 20 years'. UCL. Accessed 4 March 2020. https://www.ucl.ac.uk/news/2014/mar/ucl-2034-next-20-years.

UCL (2017a) *UCL East - Design and Access Statement (outline)*. UCL. Accessed 27 February 2020. https://tinyurl.com/vqg47m4.

UCL (2017b) 'UCL East: Location'. UCL. Accessed 3 March 2020. https://web.archive.org/web/20171023211114/http://www.ucl.ac.uk/ucl-east/getting_here/the_olympic_park.

UCL (2018) 'UCL East: Academic vision'. UCL. Accessed 3 March 2020 (original now updated). https://www.ucl.ac.uk/ucl-east/academic-vision.

UCLU (2013) 'Save Carpenters Estate'. UCL Students' Union. Accessed 4 March 2020 (requires UCL login). http://studentsunionucl.org/campaigns/save-carpenters-estate.

Viña, G. (2016) 'Warning over UCL finances after rapid expansion'. *Financial Times*, 9 June. Accessed 18 February 2020. https://www.ft.com/content/c2e5b786-2e53-11e6-a18d-a96ab29e3c95.

Wu, Z. and Hu, S. (2015) 'Heritage and discourse'. In E. Waterton and S. Watson (eds), *The Palgrave Handbook of Contemporary Heritage Research*. London: Palgrave Macmillan, 37–51. http://dx.doi.org/10.1057/9781137293565.

8
Building back better? Hysterical materialism and the role of the university in post-pandemic heritage making: the case of East London[1]

Phil Cohen

Introduction

The removal of World Heritage status from Liverpool's new dockside development in 2021 re-animated a rhetorical divide in urban planning that many people had thought well and truly buried: the conflict between the priorities of heritage conservation (renovation must preserve and enhance, leaving everything as far as possible intact) versus iconoclastic slash and burn regeneration (everything must be demolished to make a new start). In this chapter, I argue that both sides of this bitter binarism share the same conflation of cultural heritage with physical fabric, a conflation that rests, in turn, on a set of highly problematic assumptions about how the urban fabric anchors collective memory and is an example of what I am going to call 'hysterical materialism'. I will explore where the British university, and those who work and study there, figure in all this, asking whether the Academy represents a refuge from the perfect storm of history or a privileged prospect on its unfolding. Is it a place where the traditional values of critical enquiry and scientific rationality are conserved and the heritage of accumulated knowledge passed on as a living legacy of scholarship to successive generations of students? Or has it become just another node in the global information economy, vying with its competitors to maximise its market share of research funding and student fees? Is it a place where we fast forward to the future or backtrack to the past? Or perhaps do both at the same (but different) times, as it participates in the post-pandemic rhetoric of 'building back better'.

Hysterical materialism

Under this rubric, the project of transforming urban fabric through the intervention of material processes (artefacts, instruments, infrastructures, buildings, and technologies of every kind) undergoes a curious process of transubstantiation. Instead of treating these materialities as affordances or hindrances to various projects of human enterprise, they are magically invested with an autonomous power of efficacy or designation, a mysterious performative capacity to condition, compel or change human behaviour on their own account and in their own image.[2]

We have long been familiar with this effect in urban policies and discourses based on environmental and/or technological determinism, from attempts to design out street crime, and the broken window theory of urban decay, to the project of building 'smart cities' whose traffic with the world is regulated by algorithms. Material efficacy and symbolic action are here conflated or actively (hysterically) substituted for one another in order to suppress or disavow their dialectical tension.

The dual impact of the COVID-19 pandemic and the rapid onset of global heating has given new impetus to the vitalist epistemology that often underpins such over-determinisms. The belief that materiality has become an increasingly toxic and active force in human affairs, containing within itself a hidden capacity to destroy the lives of the human subjects who interact with it, has become part of the dominant common sense[3]. This hyper-valorisation of active matter is just the flip side of a pervasive sense of human impotence faced with the overwhelming impact of the pandemic and the Anthropocene[4]. Against this background, conspiracy theories re-introduce human agency in the form of a hidden hand controlling events, with COVID-19 or carbon dioxide emissions as their vehicle.

At the same time, the pandemic – and the series of 'lockdowns' (stay-at-home orders) that were introduced in an attempt to manage it – has transformed the way in which we inhabit, navigate and think about the city, at least in the UK. Spaces of conviviality and congregation became overnight places to avoid 'like the plague', and hitherto benign affordances, like door handles, chairs and shopping baskets became perceived as potential death traps. Equally, the distinction between those working on the 'front line', in hospitals and public services, and those able to hunker down safely in more-or-less luxurious 'backyards' at home, revealed with stark visibility the spatial dimensions of structural health inequalities linked to class, race and generation.[5] For some, like the architect Norman Foster, this particular cloud has a silver lining in stressing the opportunity to build back better, to create cleaner, greener, more equitable cities.[6] For the majority of architects and planners, however, the priority was to return to business as usual as quickly as possible, now that the British planning system has been de-regulated, and the go-ahead given to property developers and realtors to plunder green field sites for lucrative housing developments.

Perhaps less remarked upon has been the way lockdown has brought into sharper focus the relation between what Richard Sennett calls the city of stone and the city of flesh,[7] the city as a material infrastructure, made up of buildings, streets and parks, transport facilities, sewers and networked communications infrastructure; and the city as a place of embodied social encounter and symbolic inhabitation, of shared stories and memoryscapes, the *mise-èn-scene* of public events and intimate personal meanings. The lockdown has shown us just how entangled these two cities are. As the city of flesh melted away, it revealed with brutal clarity the material configurations of power and wealth that created the city of stone; it also showed how fragile were the institutions of the state and how important the networks of civil society for sustaining everyday urban life and, not least, its public services. The rapid depopulation of business districts and the high street, the flight of the affluent to safer, less densely populated and less polluted ex-urban areas points to a possibly permanent shift in the social ecology of city and town centres. In the case of global heating, while its precise local instantiations remain largely unpredictable, the emergent geography of environmental risk is both dependent upon and disrupts the traffic flow of information, commodities and people that connects the circuits of capital with urban infrastructures.

Yet perhaps the most profound change concerns not urban spatiality, but time. In their different ways, both COVID-19 and the climate emergency have altered perceptions of the urban past, present and future. We are used to thinking of cities as complex, constantly changing structures that are busy either expanding or shrinking. Heritage-making is thus simply a matter of recording and representing the traces of these shifts. To view physical fabric suddenly as fragile, as subject to unpredictable and devastating floods, fires and disease as depicted hitherto in dystopian fiction, films and video games, is to experience the present as a chaotic synchronicity dislocated from any leverage on past or future. The city's familiar diurnal rhythms and routines were not just temporarily suspended during lockdown, but are becoming routinely, yet unpredictably, disrupted by extreme weather events, and by sudden localised spikes in infection rates.

If the time of a pandemic is one of chronic repetition, it is also one of suspense: time and again putting plans on hold while waiting for it all to be over, while also never knowing what may be coming next. In contrast, the time signature of the climate emergency is proleptic: it pushes us to fast forward to a tipping point of no return, while retrospectively we travel backwards across the ruined biosphere in search of the genealogy of the crisis. In the age of the Anthropocene, we live suspended between the dreadful that has already happened and the final catastrophe that it is always and already too late to avert. And then, superimposed on this split temporality, there is the urgent tempo of just-in-time production, whether of goods, services, information or the self, coupled with a consumerist culture organised around instant gratification and 24/7 distraction.

This hetero-chronicity, in which the times are always out of joint,[8] is the context in which urban heritage makers now have to operate. It is also part of a wider question that the pandemic has raised about what one generation might expect or reject as an inheritance from another. Against this background, the mainstream heritage industry has mobilised all its resources to support a pervasive nostalgia for the return to a past that is recognisably in and of itself, providing a fixed pattern of meaning, thus future-proofed against possible revision. Inevitably, the maintenance of physical fabric housing historical artefacts remains the main priority here.

In contrast, the heritage of minority communities continues to be defined in terms of cultural identity and to stress the continuities between past, present and future struggles, often framed within a teleological narrative centred on triumph-over-adversity and the quest for a long-promised land of freedom and equality. This is a form of heritage-making based on shared memoryscapes, often anchored to networked oral traditions located primarily in a translocal urban realm where site specific stories converge around common existential themes of diasporic community and belonging.

The university as heritage-maker

In considering these questions, it is important to recognise that university campuses are today promoted as places where dreams of the future – associated with the achievement of social mobility and creative lifestyle – can be materialised; and not only by students, but by their host communities:

'The sky is the limit!'; 'Aspire-achieve!!'; 'You can be whatever you want!!' These exhortatory mantras of neoliberalism still flutter bravely on banners hung around now largely deserted campuses as universities shift gear to online teaching, and wait for travel restrictions to be lifted so that lucrative foreign students can return. Thanks to the pandemic, the university campus has been reduced to a virtual simulacrum of itself, neither a city of flesh nor of stone, but their spectral presence. Meanwhile, off the record, an entirely different drama is playing out.

The role that the corporate university has increasingly claimed for itself as an agency of urban regeneration, with its concomitant, the accelerated embourgeoisement of its immediate locality, increasingly grates against its no less important function in civic place-making. Is it possible to square this circle, to preserve local cultural heritage while erasing its material traces, to decouple the collective memoryscapes of local host communities from the sites in which it is historically embedded and yet still create a platform in which these values are somehow validated?

In critically examining the credibility of this claim, I will draw on my research with communities in East London – from both before and after the 2012 Olympics, work undertaken for most of the time as an academic staff member of the University of East London and more briefly as a visiting academic at Birkbeck College and University College London, all of which have campuses in the vicinity and thus have a stake in its heritage developement. I will focus on how conflicts of interest and priority between the university and its host community activate tensions between two modes of heritage creation (the embodied and the prosthetic) and civic place-making (cities of flesh and stone). I will suggest that, far from transcending these bitter binaries, the re-imagination of East London undertaken by these universities has reproduced them in an even more exaggerated form. In the final section I will describe a new heritage trail in the Queen Elizabeth Olympic Park, in which we have attempted to address some of these problems through an imaginative – but not hysterical – materialism, and which attempts to unearth and make visible a history that has been rendered intangible and invisible through the process of Olympic-led regeneration.

Beyond town and gown

In the referendum about the UK leaving the EU and in subsequent national elections in 2017 and 2019, a new player entered the political stage.

Conurbations with one or more major universities, and/or with a demographic heavily weighted in favour of those with university degrees, voted overwhelmingly to remain, and subsequently refused to vote for the Conservative party. At the same time, but in different places – characterised by an absence of universities and by a population of which the majority had not enjoyed higher education – people voted in equally large numbers to leave the EU and refused to vote Labour. Commentators have made much of this new ideological division, between a university-educated cosmopolitan elite who by and large hold progressive ideas and liberal cultural values and those who lack their cultural and intellectual capital, who often feel patronised or despised by the so called 'creative class', and who have adopted increasingly chauvinistic and reactionary positions on a range of issues, including heritage.

What has been less well observed is what happens when an elite university moves into a hitherto working-class area that has historically had a strong industrial base, but which is struggling to adapt and where very few people have any experience of higher education. Such moves are becoming increasingly frequent, and to understand why – and what its consequences might be – we have to understand some of the context.

Since the 1960s, in order both to implement and justify their expansionist plans, universities had to become active players in place-making. Real estate, the building of bigger and better facilities, was increasingly pushed to the top of the vice-chancellors' agendas; indeed, the construction of iconic campus buildings became a benchmark of their personal success as well as an indicator of the institutions' standing in the world. The cosy, mutually parasitic relation between town and gown as carriers of a common heritage, which was obtained in the older university towns, was replaced by something much more brutal, as the cutting edge of the global knowledge economy sliced through areas designated as 'ripe for change'. Gone was the pastoral vision of the university as a community of scholars set amidst dreaming spires or semi-rural landscapes. New campuses were increasingly being built on brownfield – not greenfield – sites, as part of the reclamation of once-upon-a-time industrial land.

However, to make this happen universities increasingly had to demonstrate that their plans would be of benefit to a wider – but still local and ex-industrial, working-class – community. For this purpose 'community' had to be imagined in a peculiar, and somewhat contradictory way. Firstly, as a locus of lacks: lack of educational qualifications, occupational opportunity, critical knowledge, cultural sophistication and social resource. By no coincidence, these lacks are all something that it is the university's mission to redress. Secondly, as the flip side to this deficit model, the host community is validated as having the capacity to benefit from the university's presence by virtue of possessing an existential authenticity as a source of informants for the purposes of academic research into poverty, health, crime, unemployment and a whole host of other endemic social problems. Thus the building of a new campus is represented both as the implantation of an opportunity structure that is otherwise lacking *and* as the materialisation of a latent – but hitherto frustrated – desire for sponsored educational mobility on the part of local people in the host community. So in this trade off, the structural inequalities in the distribution of cultural and intellectual capital that characterise the real relations between global universities and their local host communities are magically dissolved into a set of imaginary relations of equal exchange taking place on a level playing field.

Enter the heritage wars

The burden of my argument thus far has been that the extraction of locally situated knowledge and its transformation into global intellectual capital is one of the disavowed payoffs for relocating some elite university facilities to the poorer parts of town, as well, of course, as the more readily acknowledged fact that land values are less and it is cheaper to build here. I now want to look at how heritage and civic place-making have got entangled in this extraction process.

I have suggested that heritage can be understood and enacted in a number of different ways. Firstly, as the preservation of physical fabric and real estate where this is entailed in a historical grand narrative.[9] What I have called 'prosthetic heritage' is reserved for iconic buildings or sites in the city of stone. Colchester Castle, for example, dates back to Roman times and houses an archival collection of artefacts that it uses to tell the town's story. War memorials, cemeteries and public statuary are all important features in the manufacture of heritage in and by the city of stone.

Secondly, heritage can be considered as a site-specific memoryscape, sustained through oral traditions by communities who are not largely represented in the first kind of heritage. This kind of heritage-making takes the form of living archives associated with particular communities of memory practice, which can be either virtual or face-to-face, but do not depend on physical fabric to sustain them.

These two kinds of heritage-making have increasingly come into conflict. For example, where campus buildings occupy contested heritage sites, as for example occurs in many parts of Australia, Canada and the USA. Here, the university authorities have taken to making formal acknowledgement of the rights of indigenous peoples before every public event, while subtantively continuing to ignore them. The mission statements of museums and other cultural organisations are today littered by such pseudo-performatives, statements of intent that slide into an assumption that their mere utterance achieves the desired material effect. Not surprisingly, these ritualised affirmations of historic colonial guilt are widely regarded by indigenous communities as a form of virtue signalling or simply bad faith, since they do nothing to alter their actual situation for the better. It is this very substitution of symbolic action for material interventions (such as financial reparations, the legalisation of land claims and measures to end institutionalised discrimination in the education system) that has become the object of their critique.

Heritage has thus become ever more central to the culture wars currently being waged in the West, a war not of fixed position such as the 'liberal left' intelligentsia is accustomed to pursue (its long slow march through the institutions), but a war of manoeuvre, with rapid attacks and counter-attacks led by the right-wing press on one side and direct community action on the other. As a result, conflicts around contested heritage sites and claims are increasingly becoming zero-sum games, where one side's advance is another's instant retreat.

Universities that have become caught up in these situations are often ill-equipped to deal with them. The 'new' universities have a strong investment in being seen as proto-modernist, 'always forward looking', at the cutting-edge of research and pedagogic innovation. They have been caught offguard by the populist upsurge of retro-modernist values, fuelled in part by post-imperial nostalgia, and in part by quasi-tribal allegiances to local prides of place among their host communities. Meanwhile the 'old' universities, strongly positioned on the conservationist side of the heritage debate, find themselves faced with iconoclastic challenges that threaten their priviledged assets and amenities to an unprecedented degree. The furore over the statue of Cecil Rhodes on the façade of Oriel College, Oxford is symptomatic of this conjuncture and its complexities.[10]

The legacy games, university challenge and the reinvention of East Enders

These examples show clearly the conflict between heritage as 'prosthetic entailment' – the holding in trust of fixed material and cultural assets by one generation for its successors – and heritage as 'embodied legacy' – in the Oriel case, a history of colonialism and racism written on the bodies of the generations who have suffered its symbolic and physical violence.

In this section, I want to look at how such conflicts play out on the ground in a situation where elite cultural and educational institutions seek to rebrand their own heritage *and* that of its local host community in a way that legitimates their advent. In the case I am going to discuss, their presence was made possible by the intervention of a mega event, in the shape of the 2012 London Olympics, which succeeded in erasing the material traces of local history while displacing existing populations and their economic activity.

London 2012 branded itself from the beginning as the 'legacy games'. The 2005 bid asserted 'the most enduring legacy of the Olympics will be the regeneration of an entire community, for the direct benefit of everyone who lives there'.[11] Once the Games were won, the Mayor of Newham went on record as claiming that the Olympics would be 'of direct and immediate benefit to the people of Newham'.[12] The Strategic Regeneration Framework published after the Games promised that 'within 20 years the communities who host the 2012 Games will have the same social and economic chances as their neighbours across London'.[13]

So the exisiting host community was being promised a series of bread-and-butter benefits, in terms of affordable housing, decent well-paid jobs, a public health and educational dividend. This is what the Olympic heritage industry calls 'hard' legacy, measurable in quantitative metrics, none of which unfortunately has materialised, at least not on the scale promised.[14] The legacy buildings on the Olympic Park, including the International Business Quarter, have however made a substantial contribution to the 'city of stone'. At the same time, there is a 'soft' legacy operative within the city of flesh that has entailed the creation of an aspirational memoryscape around the event itself and is designed to inspire a generation to 'live the Olympic Dream' – just as posters showed giant athletes jumping over iconic heritage landmarks urging Londoners to 'back the bid'. In this way, the Olympified city of flesh was pressed into service to fly the flag for a rhetorical exercise in building 'faster, higher, stronger'. This message has subsequently been appropriated by the Brexiteers who have retro-fitted London 2012 as a spectacular platform on which this otherwise disunited kingdom could demonstrate its global ambition as a sovereign nation.

The new cultural quarter that is being built on the Olympic Park – which includes the V&A Museum, a new campus for UCL and Sadlers Wells dance venue, all establishing offshoots of their main Central London operations – is an attempt to square the circle by combining hard and soft legacies in a seamless web of material and symbolic benefits. This requires for its local legitimation some acknowledgement and even validation of the fact that East London has its own distinctive identity and history. At the same time, reading between the lines of the internal literature produced for these projects, it is hard not to recognise a set of all too familiar assumptions about local deficit: the gift of high culture and higher education is being brought to communities deprived of these opportunities. It is the very formula of settler colonialism: educational and cultural organisations without enough land for a land without enough educated and cultured people.

Attempts are, however, being made to mitigate (or perhaps mystify?) this message by establishing some principle of cultural homology, if not actual synergy, with local communities. The putative link is being made in terms of histories of 'making', so that the new design and IT companies coming onto the Olympic Park are seen to be continuing a local tradition of manufacturing innovation and enterprise going back to the Victorian age. The term 'making' itself is useful in conflating industrial manufacturing, artisanal and craft workshop production, and the plastic arts, into a seamless web of creative industriousness. This could be considered a somewhat cynical rewriting of Ruskin's orginal project to create organic communities of aesthetic practice in which the moral distinction between the skills of manual and mental labour was dissolved in a mutually enriching way. In reality today, the de-skilling and casualisation of manual work in the gig economy is acclerating at the same rate as the cultural industries are creating a new aristocracy of immaterial labour in the guise of what Richard Florida called a 'creative class'.[15]

We can see this process at work in the mission statement of V&A East, which 'celebrates global creativity and making [it] relevant to today's world'. On its website, we learn that 'the new museum will build on the V&A's long-standing heritage in East London and our founding mission to make the arts accessible to all. V&A East is a new champion of creativity for the 21st century. Through the lens of makers and making, we will focus on how artists and designers work to transform our world for the better. We will platform diverse, global stories addressing the most pressing issues of our time and champion the pioneering and radical visionaries of the past and present to inspire future makers and critical thinkers.'[16]

Given that the V&A was originally established as part of 'Albertopolis', the cultural complex established by Queen Victoria in memory of the Prince Regent and located just down the road from

Harrods department store in one of the most exclusive parts of the West End, we might wonder how its claim to have a 'heritage' located in East London could possibly be substantiated. In fact, the local heritage referred to can only refer to the artefacts held in its collection made by people who once lived or worked in East London but who have made it big 'up West'.

Courtesy of urban imagineering, cultural geographies have thus been floated free from their localised social and economic co-ordinates and now occupy a fluid non-place realm of their own devising. The new cultural quarter was originally named Olympicopolis by Conservative Mayor of London Boris Johnson, to evoke a Victorian imperial precedent, but has now settled for the somewhat more modest 'East Bank' moniker, under Johnson's Labour mayoral successor, Sadiq Khan, evoking the South Bank cultural complex established as part of the legacy of the Festival of Britain in 1951. In both cases, these references serve to generate useful cover stories as the West End 'moves East' to create a habitat in its own image, in a process of accelerated gentrification that involves both the material displacement of lower income families and the symbolic embourgeoisement of the area.

Rhetorically then, prosthetic heritage associated with the city of stone is being actively substituted for an embodied one linked to the city of flesh. But then in a second move, some flesh is to be put on these 'bare bones' through an outreach programme designed to recruit local young people and 'empower' them through their engagement in forms of creative making. The V&A East initiative can perhaps best be regarded as an updated form of the civilising missionary settlements of the late Victorian period, now centred on the arts rather than sports, and concerned not with the social reform of material conditions or the disciplining of youthful bodies but, rather, the cultural reformation of young minds: 'making' as 'making over' an area in its own image.

Universities cannot mobilise the same resources or devices, although, of course, they continue to function as important engines of social mobility for the minority from disadvantaged communities who are awarded places. UCL advertises itself as London's global university and since the 1980s has been pursuing a successful strategy of corporate growth, gobbling up a series of smaller, hitherto independent institutions in the process. It is engaged in leading-edge research in a wide range of disparate fields in the arts, sciences and humanities and attracts high-flying staff and students from around the world. As a result, it has outgrown its historical location in Bloomsbury and is in the process of establishing a new campus in the Queen Elizabeth Olympic Park. So how does this 'multi-versity', which epitomises the intellectual power and cultural wealth of a metropolitan elite located in the heart of the capital, represent itself to its erstwhile 'poor relation'? Is the fact of UCL moving east part of the rich history of cultural slumming?[17] Or is it rather the leading edge of the gentrification of East London, completing the process started by the building of Canary Wharf as London's new financial centre in the 1980s, and accelerated by the 2012 Olympics? Or is something else going on here?

A clue is to be found in one of the internal documents produced by the editors of this book at UCL/University of Gothenburg Centre for Critical Heritage Studies (CCHS), framing the first workshop from which this book emerged. The document cites the historian Thomas Bender:

> The pluralized culture of the university resembles the complex life of contemporary immigrant neighbourhoods, where residents live in local urban neighbourhoods and diasporic networks ... The challenge for us as contemporary metropolitans (and cosmopolitans) is to locate ourselves – both in time and in relation to the places of local knowledge – in such a global perspective'.[18]

This 'paralellism', which conflates elite cosmopolitanism with popular multiculturalism, also has a history. The projective identification of dissident intellectuals with the socially marginalised was a feature of the Romantic movement that carried over into late nineteenth- and early twentieth-century political culture. Fast forward to the 1980s and we find certain members of the globe-trotting glitterati lecturing about the 'post-modern nomadic subject', by which concept they attempted to associate their own 'transgressive' intellectual journeying with the situation of migrants and refugees driven from their homelands by war and famine in search of safety and a better life.[19]

The attempt to synergise the heritage of an elite university and its host community in terms of a shared 'glocality' may gloss a somewhat similar strategy of cultural misrecognition and appropriation, in which the participation of local groups – especially BAME (Black and Minority Ethnic) groups – is exploited for the local authenticity their involvement can confer. At the same time, the multiversity is able to tolerate and even encourage the presence of groupings of dissident academics who challenge this approach, provided that their actions do not seriously impede the main thrust of corporate growth.[20]

In this context, it is interesting to compare the situation of UCL with that of the University of East London (UEL), which has been the area's local provider of higher education since its inception as a polytechnic in

1970. This university has always had a strong student base in East London, especially in Stratford and Barking and Dagenham; its intake has reflected the demographic transformation of these areas with BAME students now far outnumbering all other groups and white working-class students significantly under-represented. The university always struggled to recruit foreign or PhD students and to retain high flying academics; however from the 1970s onwards it did attract a critical mass of radical staff who were committed to a democratic vision of higher education, and who developed a new curriculum based on a pedagogy of critical vocationalism in fields such as journalism, the creative industries, environmental and heritage studies. Despite this, the main thrust of the university's growth was entrepreneurial, and its campus in the Royal Docks is now devoted to knowledge transfer with start-up facilities to support embryonic SMEs. The advent of the 2012 Olympics on its doorstep gave UEL a much needed injection of public funding and resource, with a new sports centre and a campus in Stratford; however, this did little to enhance its academic standing. Its expertise in the field of urban planning was limited, with the result that it failed to make a significant impact on policy thinking around the delivery of the Games and its legacy, despite the publication of some major research studies.[21] This institution's situation is the exact reverse of UCL's, in that it has plenty of 'street credibility' but insufficient academic credentials, and its research culture, always weak, has now been effectively dismantled. UEL simply cannot compete with UCL in the global market place of higher education and research funding, and its senior management have now opted to turn it into a glorified further education college aimed at the students who will never be admitted to UCL. Its History and Heritage Studies programme was one of the early casualties of this re-structuring.[22]

Prides of place: community stakeholding and the post-Olympic legacy in East London

These then are some of the issues raised by and for incoming institutions in East London. I consulted the focus group that I have been running since 2008, and which comprises a representative sample of local residents, to understand how members of the local host community perceive and respond to their arrival. I anticipated that there would be a strong continuation of attitudes between the two contexts – the infamous confirmation bias – but in fact the patterns of transference were often more complex.

In previously reported research, I identified a number of key patterns of civic stakeholding that shaped perceptions and expectations of the 2012 Olympic project as a 'legacy games'.[23] These perspectives were closely linked to Robert Putnam's distinction between what he calls 'bridgers' and 'bonders'[24] and are strongly correlated with the amount and type of social and cultural capital – and hence bargaining power – that a group or individual may have at their disposal. This may be concentrated in efforts to sustain or strengthen specific forms of identity and belonging (Putnam's bonding capital), or on creating platforms for building partnerships with others that may extend local influence into new areas of activity (Putnam's bridging capital). I found that while these positions related to different stories about the East End of London, its past and its immediate prospects, they were also about different kinds of stakes that individuals, groups or organisations may have in its future development. Bridgers tended to see regeneration legacy in terms of a material 'pay-off' or 'dividend':

> Well, the way I look at it, we've had to go through all this kerfuffle, and now it's over I think the community is owed something in return. What we get back should reflect what we've put in, shouldn't it? The legacy is a just reward for all the effort of so many local people to make the games the success they were. (Public service worker)

In contrast, bonders tended to see the Olympics as a windfall, albeit one which is part of a *'gift'* legacy:

> It's like we've been left something by a distant relative, who's very well off. We weren't expecting it, maybe we don't even deserve it, but it's dropped into our lap and we're entitled to it. We've been left this fabulous gift on condition we look after it, and hand it on to our kiddies for their children to enjoy. (Nursery teacher)

Bridgers were more likely to recognise that the Queen Elizabeth Olympc Park had the potential to continue to attract visitors and bring money to the area, and therefore represented an ongoing investment from which they could expect future dividends. In contrast, bonders saw the post-Olympic legacy less as a payback or dividend, but more in terms of a 'public bequest' or 'civic endowment'. From this perspective, East London's history is not so much a shareable asset, a public heritage accessible to all, but a valuable 'heirloom', something that has to be held in trust by one generation for the next and safeguarded as a platform for the assertion of local pride of place.

On re-visiting these positions in relation to the post-Olympic legacy and particular attempts to rebrand the area by incoming institutions, I found that those bonders who had the highest expectations of what 2012 would deliver, as 'their thing', inevitably felt the most disappointed when the legacy promised failed to materialise:

> When 2012 came along I was 19 and I was all up for it – like it was gonna be one big party. I was one of the volunteers and it was really exciting. One night some of us went back to the athletes' village and got well stoned with a couple of guys from the US team, it turned into a bit of an orgy to be honest. But then after it was all over, it was one big let-down. All the stuff they promised just didn't happen, did it? And now the area is full of rich people who swank around as if they own the place, which they probably do. East End kids who have grown up in the area are made to feel they are not wanted and don't belong. (Former Olympic volunteer, currently unemployed)

This attitude found its echo in some of the views of the older generation:

> The way I look at it, the people who built the Olympics didn't know much and cared even less about the area's history. As one of them put it Stratford was 'a pretty terrible place' that needed to be fixed. As far as they were concerned the area was a polluted wasteland and the only heritage that was of any value was the legacy of 2012 itself. But people who have been living in East London for generations see it differently. The area is part of our family history, and we want our kids to know and be proud of what their parents and grandparents struggled to achieve. (Retired care worker)

Bonders who had much lower expectations of what the Games might deliver, and thought the Olympics were 'not for the likes of us', were likely to carry over this scepticism to the post-Olympic context:

> I said at the time the Olympics were a poisoned chalice. They promised us local businesses a bonanza , but the visitors spent their money on the Park itself and then went back to their hotels in the West End. The marathon was even re-routed so it didn't go through the streets of East London as we were promised, because they said no-one would recognise where it was taking place. How is that for

> putting us on the map? Now with the so-called legacy, we get a load more trojan horses, lining up promising us these wonderful golden opportunities for our kids if only we welcome them into our community. I've heard a lot of sweet talk about how valuable an asset we are, how much they want our opinions, but they have already decided what they are going to do and they only want us onside so they can look good. (Market trader)

Yet bonders could also articulate a more positive standpoint:

> What people don't seem to realise is that we have our own culture round here, we don't need big swanky buildings to make our music, to get the shout out. We make our own hits. The vibe is with the Mandem on the streets, it's in the pubs and the clubs, in the estates. We don't need a bunch of well-off folks from up West coming in telling us how 'jolly authentic' we are. (Youth worker and musician)

Those bridgers who had made the most gains from partnership with Olympic delivery agencies were also of course well-disposed towards a second bite of the legacy cake:

> I think it's great we are getting our own version of the South Bank, with a lot of great art and culture right on our own doorstep. A lot of the people round here don't know how lucky they are; thanks to the Olympics, Stratford has become a really buzzy place, people come here from all over. Westfield is a great success. You always get a few moaners saying things ain't what they used to be. It's up to them if they want to live in the past, they only have themselves to blame if they miss out on the new opportunities. (Hospitality events manager)

Those bridgers who had been disappointed or felt betrayed by legacy promises that were not kept, were unsurprisingly much more sceptical of the new offers:

> They promised us local businesses a bonanza, but it never happened. They even re-routed their Marathon. Likewise the legacy is a joke. And the worst thing is the joke is on us, especially all the young people who bought into it. There are all these quotes from local people on the Park benches, and stuff about the local history, but it's tokenism, it costs them nothing, or very little, but it looks good to

> the visitors who know nothing about East London – they look at it and think 'Oh that's nice, the local people are being listened to'. But when push comes to shove, when it's a question of the big decisions, the ones that cost money or make money, then we don't get a look in. It's the commercial interests, the corporates, who call the shots. (Local business owner)

Hostility was often tempered with indifference:

> They call it East Bank, all I can say it's not a bank I would ever put my money in, though I expect they think it's going to pay its way with those who are into that sort of thing and can afford it. Most of the people round here are just not interested, they have their own stuff to get on with. To be honest the only time they go to the Park is to watch the Hammers play. (Retired bus driver and West Ham supporter)

This sense of resentment, of being cheated out of an entitlement – whether of a birthright or legacy – feeds all too easily into a populist backlash against groups and institutions that are perceived as being 'not from round here'. This is a difficult political climate for global universities and other elite cultural organisations who want to move into such areas. They have a lot of local pride and prejudice to contend with and in some cases their failure to take account of local sensitivities has compounded the problem.

The groundbreakers

These considerations have been paramount in the development of a new multimedia heritage trail for visitors to the Olympic Park; it is designed to tell the backstory of the site, from its ancient archaeology to its recent transformation to host the 2012 Games, focusing on its rich environmental, industrial and social history.[25] Our starting point was the notion that heritage is a form of living archive, and as such must have traction on the present and point to possible futures.[26] Today, with the exception of some surviving buildings such as the Bryant and May match factory and Three Mills, most of the industries and traces of the communities that served them are entirely invisible; much of what was left of that material culture, plus the few surviving workshops and small businesses, were destroyed during the 'Dig, design and demolish' phase of site construction.[27]

The landscape design of the park is an interesting experiment in what might be called simulated environmental place-making. The South Park, where the UCL East campus is located, is supposedly modelled on the urban pleasure grounds of the late Victorian city, although it entirely lacks the combination of intimate spaces and density of congregation that made these sites so exciting to visit. Meanwhile, the North Park is meant to reproduce the pastoral features of the traditional English country park, but unfortunately its carefully controlled topography lacks the biodiversity of the urban wilderness it has replaced. What both sides of the park share is the absence of any 'dead ground' – there is nowhere in the park where visitors are not being monitored by the ubiquitous CCTV cameras.

There was no possibility, then, of literally re-materialising the history of the site, for instance by constructing replicas or markers of objects and artefacts that had once been there. That would only have further contributed to a sense of fake heritage and the hysterical materialism that underpins it. Instead, we opted to construct ten history 'hot-spots' around the park and at each site visitors can experience an immersive VR re-creation of an important activity, building or event once located there. This is supplemented with an online guide organised around four themes: *Fluid histories, in and against the flow* traces the entangled flows of people, goods, water, electricity and waste that have shaped the landscape; *Encampments and other dwellings* documents patterns of human habitation and home making from the Bronze Age to the digital age and the impact they have had on the local environment; *Edgelands remade* looks at the many ways in which the site and its inhabitants both human and non-human, have been transformed as it is excavated, engineered, polluted, demolished and re-built; and *A level playing field?* examines changing patterns of local labour and leisure in the nineteenth and twentieth centuries as communities struggle to improve their conditions of life, including through sport.

A connecting thread is provided by the theme of groundbreaking, considered as both a disruptive material process in which capital, labour and technology interact with the non-human environment to transform the landscape, whether positively or negatively, *and* as a metaphoric statement about the collective hopes and dreams invested in that enterprise.

One of the aims of the project is to challenge the dominant heritage narrative in East London that is currently organised around four assertions or assumptions about its recent history: that there is a more-or-less frictionless transition between East London's industrial past and its present development as a post-industrial economy; that East London is and always has been a 'melting pot' of cultural and ethnic differences and its diversity is frictionless; that the Olympic Park site was a tabula rasa awaiting the imprint of an Olympic legacy; and that the change now taking place in East London is no different from previous changes. In contrast, the trail and guide explore the hetero-chronicities and spatial dislocations that make the history of this site so richly interesting, and so relevant for understanding the wider forces of transformation that have shaped not only this area but London as a whole, and which will continue to do so in the future.

One of the most significant aspects of the Groundbreakers project is that it has been developed by people who have a long track record of work with communities in East London and at UEL, going back in some cases over four decades. It has a high degree of input from local groups, including children and senior citizens, and involves partnerships with a consortium of community arts organisations and schools. There has also been encouragement and support from UCL Urban Laboratory, and the London Legacy Development Corporation, but the point is that their role has been facilitative *not* directive and that surely must be the model for how such organisations should operate in relation to community-based heritage place-making in the future.

In terms of the conceptual framework developed here, the support role of universities for heritage-based place-making must clearly be delivered in the form of an endowment *not* as an investment in expectation of some future divident or pay-off to the institution itself. Equally, the strategy of community capacity-building must be genuinely redistributive of intellectual and cultural capital, not the impression management of 'community participation'. Finally, instead of cherry-picking community partners from groups and organisations who are already well-established bridgers (and who consequently already have considerable social and cultural capital), the priority must be to reach out to those who may be initially hostile and defensive, and pursuade them of the collective benefit of transforming their prized cultural heirlooms into a shareable public heritage. Such an approach calls for the exercise of tact and a recognition that hard-pressed communities who find themselves on the front lines of the pandemic and its long aftermath have much to teach academics about the processes of urban transformation that universities are so busily implementing.

Notes

1. This is a revised version of a talk given to the UCL/University of Gothenburg Centre for Critical Heritage Studies workshop Co-Curating the City: universities and urban heritage past and future, 2016. Many thanks to Clare Melhuish for her editorial skill and persistence in helping me revise the text for publication.
2. For a further discussion, see Cohen, P. 'A Place beyond belief? Hysterical materialism and the making of East 20' in Cohen, P. and Watt, P. (2017).
3. For a statement of the vitalist impulse in 'new materialism' see Bennett, J. (2010). For a critical discussion of this development see Eagleton, T. (2017).
4. See Latour, B. (2018).
5. See Cohen P. (2020).
6. Interview in *The Guardian* 16 May 2020.
7. See Sennett, R. (1996) and for an application of this distinction to contemporary urbanism see Sennett, R. (2019).
8. See Gumbrecht, H. (2014).
9. Often in Britain, this is a narrative constructed around the disavowal of slavery, Empire and the capitalocene. Visit almost any stately home run the by the National Trust and you will be able to trace the close meshing of styles in landscape gardening and painting, portraiture, furniture and architecture with aristocratic values and lifestyles sustained through the hyper-exploitation of land, labour and learning, both at home and in the colonies abroad.
10. This case is discussed in the fuller version of this text to be found on my website: www.philcohenworks.com.
11. See London 2012 Candidate City Statement 2007.
12. Quoted in the Newham Recorder November 2008.
13. London 2012, the Legacy Games 2013.
14. See for example Bernstock, P. (2016) and the contributions to Cohen, P. and Watt, P. (eds) (2017).
15. See Florida, R. (2012 and 2018).
16. Extract from V&A East Mission Statement www.vam.ac.uk.
17. In the late Victorian and Edwardan period, well-to-do bohemians were noted for their expeditions to see how the other half lived in Whitechapel and the Mile End Road, and for their sexual dalliances with the 'rough trade' they found in docklands. See Koven, S. (2004).
18. See 'The University and the City' in Bender, T. (2002).
19. For a critique of the hubristic stances of some postmodern intellectuals, see Thomson, M. J. (ed.) (2015) and for a wider angled view, see Lilla, M. (2018) and Piketty, T. (2018).
20. In the case of UCL, outfits such as Just Space, the Urban Lab and the Critical Heritage group have succeeded in challenging or mitigating some of the negative impact of corporate expansion strategies on host communities. For example, when the UCL authorities proposed to demolish social housing to build their new campus on the edge of the Queen Elizabeth Olympic Park, UCL urbanists mobilised internally to challenge and ultimately reverse the decision and also worked with local tenants to develop an alternative regeneration strategy for the area.
21. See for example Cohen and Rustin (eds) (2016) and Poynter, G. (ed.) (2015).
22. For an account of the University of East London's recent history, see Poynter, G. and Rustin, M. (eds) (2020).
23. This research took place between 2007 and 2016. The final phase of the research was part funded by a grant from the London Legacy Development Corporation. Much of this work is reported in Cohen (2013) and Cohen and Watt (eds) (2017). Further material is to be found at www.livingmaps.org.uk.
24. See Putnam, R. (2001). Although Putnam confines his analysis to social capital, the distinction he makes between bridging and bonding as different strategies of trust building can be usefully extended to cultural and intellectual capital, that is to say to social networks of production and exchange that accumulate resources of symbolic and knowledge power.
25. The Groundbreakers is funded by a grant from the Heritage Lottery Fund and the Foundation for Future London. It was carried out by the Livingmaps Network in partnership with Hyperactive Productions, who developed the VR app. We are also grateful for the support of the Urban Lab in the initial phase of the project. The online guide and trail app can be accessed at www.livingmaps.org.uk.

26 For a discussion of contemporary memory politics and its relations to cultural models of inheritance, see Cohen, P. (2017).
27 For a visual history and analysis of the processes of displacement and erasure set in motion by the construction of the 2012 Olympic Park, see Davis, J. (2017).

References

Bender,. T. (2002) *The Unfinished City*. New York: New York University Press.
Bennett, J. (2010) *Vibrant Matter: The political ecology of things*. London: Harper Collins.
Bernstock, P. (2016) *Olympic Housing : A critical review of the 2012 legacy*. London: Routledge.
Cohen, P. (2013) *On the Wrong Side of the Track?: East London and the Post Olympics*. London: Lawrence and Wishart.
Cohen, P. and Rustin, M. (eds) (2016) *London's Turning: The making of Thames Gateway*. London: Routledge.
Cohen, P. and Watt, P. (eds) (2017) *London 2012 and the Post Olympic City*. London: Palgrave.
Cohen P. (2017) *Archive That, Comrade! Left legacies and the counter culture of Remembrance*. Oakland: PM Press.
Cohen, P. (2020) *There Must Be Some Way Out of Here: Mapping the pandemic from left field*. Portsmouth: Compass.
Davis, J., Davies, M. and Rapp, D. (2017) *Dispersal: Picturing urban change in East London*. London: Historic England.
Eagleton, T. (2017) *Materialism*. New Haben: Yale University Press.
Florida, R. (2012) *The Rise of the Creative Class Revisited*. London: Oneworld Publications.
Florida, R. (2018) *The New Urban Crisis*. London: Oneworld Publications.
Gumbrecht, H. U. (2014) *Our Broad Present*. New York: Columbia University Press.
Koven, S. (2004) *Slumming: sexual and social politics in Victorian London*. Princeton: Princeton University Press.
Latour, B. (2018) *Down to Earth: The politics of the new climatic regime*. Cambridge: Polity Press.
Lilla, M. (2018) *The Reckless Mind: Intellectuals in politics*. New York: Monthly Review Press.
Livingmaps Network www.livingmaps.org.uk. Accessed 04 March 2022.
London Legacy Development Corporation (2013) *Strategic Regeneration Framework* London: LLDC
London Legacy Development Corporation (2013) *The Legacy Games*. London: LLDC
London Organising Committee for the Olympic Games (2005) *London 2012 Candidate City File*. London: LOCOG
Newham Recorder (2008) 12 November 2008.
Piketty, T. (2018) *Brahmin Left vs Merchant Right: Rising inequality & the changing structure of political conflict*. Paris: PSE Working Papers.
Poynter, G. and Rustin, M. (eds) (2020) *Building a Radical University: A history of the University of East London*. London: Lawrence and Wishart.
Poynter, G. (ed.) (2015) *The London Olympics and Urban Development: The mega event city*. London: Routledge.
Putnam, R. (2001) *Bowling Alone*. New York: Simon and Schuster.
Sennett, R. (1996) *Flesh and Stone: The city in western civilisation*. London: Penguin.
Sennett, R. (2019) *Building and Dwelling: Ethics for the city*. London: Penguin.
Thomson, M. J. (ed.) (2015) *Radical Intellectuals and the Subversion of Progressive Politics*. New York: Springer.

Part 2: Elsewhere: Lund, Rome, Beirut and São Paulo

9
Big Science and urban morphogenesis: the case of Lund University

Mattias Kärrholm and Albena Yaneva

Introduction

Universities have always had a large impact on cities, and this impact grew over the late twentieth century. Their physical footprint increased in particular with the introduction of Big Science and the first large synchrotrons during the 1950s (Hallonsten, 2016: 18). The development of nanoscience during the 1980s triggered an unprecedented increase in the construction and use of large-scale facilities since, paradoxically, 'to examine the smallest details of nature, the largest instruments must be used' (Wilson, 1999: 459). Big Science has today become an important part of economic growth and innovation and, as it takes on new scales and dimensions, has led to universities progressively becoming city-builders. In the last couple of decades, we have witnessed the university leaving the single building or even the campus as a model. This strategy of spatial expansion contributes to the development of entire city districts and turns the university into a driver for urban growth, and it has also come at the expense of a disconnect between the university and city life.

What kind of urban spaces does this new kind of university produce? What kind of relation to the city does it sustain? How has this changed over time? Drawing on the case of the Swedish city Lund and its university, this chapter investigates how the changing spatiality of the university (understood as sites of university buildings, positioning and location) affects the city, its heritage and urban futures. As universities grow and their buildings become increasingly specialised, zoning and enclosure into larger territories becomes inevitable. Rather than being incorporated within the city, vast research facilities now accommodate visitor and conference centres, science museums, university shops and so on, to deal with the integration between research and urban public life. As the gap between the university and the city gradually widens, the pedagogical ways of visualising, advertising and branding science have become more important, affecting the ways in which universities are designed, built and subsequently seen as places of heritage. Research is not just done behind closed doors in the city, but also inside large mega structures in the city outskirts, and this has also raised a new demand for outreach and communication. If in the past (and especially in the 1950s and 1960s) many campus buildings turned their back on their neighbours and did not encourage engagement with urban publics, the growing concern that currently drives the design and planning processes of contemporary campus buildings is how to open up the university premises. Design features such as atria, viewing corridors and the like are meant to draw the attention of passers-by and invite them to come and witness 'science in action', to see high-tech equipment and blue-gowned human figures working in a lab, or academics from different disciplines running around a lit and airy atrium. Yet, more importantly, urban publics can witness that 'public money' is being used in a sensible way.[1]

Following how Lund, a city of medieval origin, and its university have co-developed over the centuries, this chapter scrutinises how, far from being a simple offshoot of national or city politics, the university and its specific spatial logic has become a motor for its urban development. The chapter also outlines a new way to deal with the university's history and heritage. A recent development showcases this specific relationship between city Politics (with capital P) and university growth. Between the 2000s and 2010s, Lund University developed new large-scale facilities for nanoscience and particle physics, including a synchrotron light source called MAX IV (fourth generation at Lund University) that was completed in 2016. Additionally, the European Spallation Source (ESS) is currently under construction, the result of a partnership of 17 European countries, and will be the world's most powerful pulsed neutron source when it is put into use in 2023. The ESS stretches over about 1 km of land in the north-east part of Lund. In relation to these research facilities, a new urban development, known as Science Village Scandinavia, is planned as a city for scientists with additional nano labs and departments, dwellings for researchers, restaurants, offices, gyms, a visitor centre and the Lund Science Centre. Aspiring to work as a meeting place between science and society, Science Village Scandinavia is expected to: '… develop into a

Figure 9.1 Plan of the 'Science Road' (in orange) and the new tramway of Lund 2019. Source: City Office, Lund Municipality

Figure 9.2 Scale model of Science Village, with MAX IV in the upper left corner and part of ESS in the lower right. The model was publicly exhibited at a venue in Lund city centre, 2018. Photo: M. Kärrholm

dynamic, creative and sustainable city district that not only stimulates world-class research but also provides a forum for interaction with society' (Science Village Scandinavia, 2020).

Science Village Scandinavia is part of the new urban district of Brunnshög, which is planned to accommodate an additional 40,000 people on top of the city of Lund's existing 92,000 inhabitants (as of 2018). The ESS science facilities and the Science Village are connected to the city centre of Lund through a tramway that traces the 'Science Road' (Kunskapsstråket), a line through the urban tissue of greater Lund (see Figures 9.1 and 9.2).

The ESS was already, before it was even built, widely debated and researched by scholars, who often focused on it as a political project (Hallonsten, 2012), its legitimisation (Kaiserfeld and O'Dell, 2013) and its history and potential use both in research and as an object of research in itself (Rekers and Sandell, 2016; Hallonsten, 2018). Thus, the ESS has often been regarded as a projection of big Politics and decision-making at governmental and European Union level. Our ambition in this chapter is to shift the attention towards the university's way of spatially reorganising the city that has its own political dimension (or, politics with small p). We ask: what kind of spaces do the university claim? Through what kind of morphologies? How does this affect existing urban dynamics and structures? How is this gradually shifting the traditional centre of politics and heritage? By looking closely at the spatial evolution of the university, and its development from medieval times to the most recent developments with the ESS, we trace how the spatial positioning and proliferation of specific university buildings within the city affects urban growth, redefines the existing social and cultural patterns of life in the city of Lund and ultimately generates new connections, new relational politics (Yaneva, 2017).

In addition, the idea of an urban planning focusing around routes (such as the tramway and the Science Road) may also question traditional ideas about Lund's urban development (by focusing on areas rather than routes as the basic object of development). These new ideas not only have an impact on future developments, but also play a part in re-evaluating the heritage of the university. The spatial expansion ignites new processes of re- and de-heritagisation where the value of both old and future heritage sites is being rewritten (Sjöholm, 2016).

The spatial expansion of Lund University

European universities began their existence as a 'child' of the city. From their beginnings in the thirteenth and fourteenth centuries, universities depended on their host cities to get students and supplies, as well as to enable an academic community (Hyde, 1988). But cities also depended on their universities. The city of Bologna, for example, encountered problems with scholars moving to competing universities in other cities during the 1300s, and legislated against it (Ferruolo, 1988: 23). Other universities provide examples of a move towards more anti-urban or more pastoral ideals, especially in the Anglo-American tradition (Bender, 1988a), and even invented new urban morphological patterns in this spirit. In *The City in History*, Lewis Mumford notes that: 'In the original layout of the colleges in Oxford and Cambridge, medieval planning made its most original contributions to civic design: the superblock and the urban precinct divorced from the ancient network of alleys and streets' (Mumford, 1961: 276).

The superblock, so much favoured by the anti-urban modernists, can thus be seen as a descendant of early European university building. The tradition of the anti-urban and even pastoral university grew even more strongly in the USA. The word 'campus' was first used to name the greensward around Nassau Hall at Princeton in the 1700s, and the first properly built campus is said to be the 1817 plan of the University of Virginia in Charlottesville. Soon, the scientific ideal was, as Thomas Bender has suggested, to aim for a denial of place where the academic profession and international relations severed academic life from locality (Bender, 1988a: 3). The role of large cities as attractors for students and teachers has, however, continued to be important, and the struggle between urban and the anti-urban tendencies is an ongoing one.

In Lund, education at university level began in a monastery in the early fifteenth century, but a proper university was not founded until 1666. In contrast to other European countries, Sweden began universities not in relation to central power but in connection to dioceses and their cathedrals in different provinces (Klinge, Knapas, Leikola and Strömberg, 1988: 262). Sweden's first university was founded in Uppsala in 1477, with a second in Dorpat (now Tartu, Estonia) in 1632; the third was Åbo (now Turkku, Finland) in 1640; the fourth was Lund in Scania, a city and region then newly captured from the Danes. The first important building used by Lund University was the cathedral, where lectures were held, but the university also used Kungshuset (The king's house), a building to the north of the cathedral, built as residence for the (then Danish) king in Lund in the sixteenth century. In 1744, the area around Kungshuset was walled and a park was planned by the celebrated architect Carl Hårleman, leaving the city with a small, central and clearly demarcated university area and park, secluded yet positioned in the very centre of the city. A few years later, a botanical garden with an orangery, also designed by Hårleman, was added to the north of Kungshuset (Johansson, 1982: 101–20; Tägil, 2001).

It was only in the nineteenth century that the first purpose-built scientific buildings, identifiable as building types of their own, were built in Lund. Since the early days of the European universities, buildings were used to attract students and to lure quality teachers. In the case of Bologna mentioned above, the problem of migrating professors during the 1300s was first confronted with legislation (including death penalty as a punishment), but it has been argued that what motivated scholars to stay was in fact the university's first building, a chapel exclusively built for scholars in 1322 (Ferruolo, 1988: 23). Similarly, there had always been a competition for students and teachers between Lund and other university cities, especially Uppsala. However, there was also a debate in the 1820s, and again in the 1860s, about centralisation, that suggested closing the old universities in Uppsala and Lund and opening one in Stockholm instead. There was a struggle for power, which Stockholm eventually lost, and the erection of new buildings both in Uppsala and Lund probably had its part to play in this outcome (Lindroth, 1976: 150–57; Kristenson, 1990: 16).

Apart from the old orangery, and the administration building 'Kuggis' built in 1802 (as a wing to Kungshuset), the first purpose built scientific building in Lund was the Department of Zoology, Chemistry and Physics, built in 1842.[2] Following this, a building for Anatomy opened in 1853, a Chemical department in 1863, a new botanical garden was built in 1862–67 and the observatory building in 1867. Lund University thus expanded in the city centre and, by 1882, a new main university building, designed by Helgo Zettervall, was also erected (see Figure 9.3). This building in Lund was different from its contemporaries at several other universities at the time. Whereas main university buildings often faced a square or an important urban space (as the case is with Copenhagen University), Zettervall's building instead looked inwards towards the park-like University Place (*Universitetsplatsen*) and turned its back to the city and its main street, Kyrkogatan (Kristenson 1990; Tägil, 2001). The university consisted of a miniature city (a building and a park) within the city of Lund, and this formed an original urban concept; a concept that has evolved spatially over the years with the development of various campus strategies and science parks.

During the second half of the nineteenth century, Lund University started, for the first time, to build outside the perimeters of the old urban walls. This included the botanical garden and the three new large buildings, the Department of Physics (1886), Physiology (1893) and the

Figure 9.3 Universitetsplatsen, with Kungshuset (1580s) to the left and Helgo Zettervall's new main university building from 1882 to the right – with four sphinxes on top. Photo: M. Kärrholm, 2020

new building for Anatomy (1897) (Kristenson, 1990: 281; Tägil, 2001: 16). The expansion outside the walls happened in a north-east direction, with several further new buildings emerging during the 1920s. A new, large campus area was also built as the Lund Institute of Technology (LTH), which opened in 1961. The campus area, completed in 1968, was soon incorporated as a part of the university. In 1983, a new kind of science park, Ideon, was founded next to the LTH campus as a place where private companies and research could interact. Ideon has today grown even bigger than the LTH campus itself (see Figure 9.1).

We could argue that the further expansion of the university to the north-east follows a direction set already in the nineteenth century. However, whereas previous expansions more-or-less followed the emerging layers of the city, where the north-east part of each layer could be seen as being a segment of the spatial growth of the university, the most recent expansion embraces a fully different shape and scale. With the MAX IV and the ESS, the university, with the helping hand of the Municipality of Lund, takes on the role as a city builder. As city development focused around the Science Road and the partly intersecting new tramway – both cutting through former expansion zones (see Figure 9.4) – what the MAX IV and the ESS add is not simply a new urban layer, but a self-sustained urban entity that substantially stretches the borders

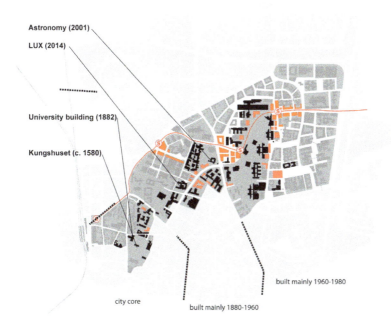

Figure 9.4 The Lund University area. University buildings are in black and planned new buildings are in red. The urban layers of different building ages are divided by the dotted lines. Map: M. Kärrholm

of the city and leads to renegotiations of the boundaries of the existing areas. During the first decade of the 2000s, the university expanded mostly through the densification of existing areas and additions to existing buildings (Tägil, 2001: 97). With the plans of the new tramway line between the Central Railway Station in the city centre and the ESS, the university and the city of Lund have embarked on an expansion that could be considered to be a city of its own. In fact, the new Brunnshög district makes all of Lund's other urban districts look small in comparison. The tramway connects university facilities in the city centre with all buildings along the larger part of the route, from the University Hospital, the LTH Campus and Ideon Science Park, to the MAX IV, the Science Village Scandinavia and the ESS (Figure 9.1).

What can we learn from tracing the spatial expansion of Lund University? Here we would like to point out two observations. Firstly, the development of the university is not only directed by top-down political decisions but is also driven by specific scientific developments, as well as by spatial translations of scientific needs. Looking back at the history, we can see how the development of Physics has driven Lund's university and campus development. At first, Physics was part of the Department of Zoology, Chemistry and Physics, and as such was hosted by one of the very first buildings designed specifically for the university in 1842. However, already by 1886, it needed both its own department and its own building. In the 1950s, a series of connected buildings were built for Physics along Sölvegatan; and today, Physics has become an independent urban unit – a science village with nano labs and the ESS. The development of Physics in Lund showcases how the growing demand for research facilities drives various architectural responses that ultimately lead to urban restructuring. Secondly, the consolidation or clustering of 'the university area' has evolved through different phases, following a line of flight in the north-east direction. The core area around the cathedral was gradually complemented with new departments in other parts of the city core in the mid-nineteenth century; the university buildings located in the old city core were subsequently complemented with a series of new departments constructed outside of the old city walls (1880–1930s). Over the course of the twentieth century, the university area was supplemented not just with single buildings but with entirely new areas, such as the campus area of LTH and the science parks of Ideon and Medicon Village. Finally, the most recent developments, the MAX IV, the ESS and Science Village Scandinavia, are situated even further out, at the very outskirts of the city. Following the line of flight in the north-east direction, these moments of urban expansion, addition and consolidation set a specific rhizomatic pattern of urban growth.

Urban crystallisation and heritage

Since 2000, a number of new university buildings have seen daylight in Lund. The new Astronomy building opened in 2001, the New Design Centre in 2002, the Geocentrum in 2003, and the Language and Literature centre in 2004. The joint departments of the Faculties of Humanities and Theology all moved into the so-called LUX building in 2014. All of these projects were built within the existing university area, and most of them involved additions to existing buildings. What they also have in common is that they were all built along Sölvegatan Street, the main artery of the Science Road, where more similar additions are planned to follow in the years to come (Akademiska hus, 2012).

What we witness here is that the spatial expansion of the university follows a pattern of a (north-east bound) crystal growth. Following Lewis

Mumford, Fontana-Giusti (2011) has described how cities crystallised through citadels and even more through the formation of fortifications and city walls. In a recent article, Brighenti (2020) has taken the notion of crystallisation, and its role in political and urban history, a step further. Discussing the process of crystallisation as an urban phase transition, Brighenti (2020) suggests that it includes individual entities that grow around certain given critical points and that, once started, these resultant 'crystals' often evolve at a quicker pace than their surroundings. Crystallisation entails both an increase of order and a break with existing orders. The process establishes a state of metastability, which allows for certain dynamics while also setting some limits for the change, and for the crystal to evolve through certain 'recurrent features and privileged directions' (Brighenti, 2020: 4).

A similar process of urban crystallisation can be witnessed in the case of Lund. Here, the new spatially expanded city takes form with Sölvegatan Street and the tramway – including their nodes and tramway stops – to form the Science Road as the centre of a series of aligned crystal nucleuses (on urban nucleus, see Conzen, 2004: 252–55). As the new, large facilities align themselves at greater densities, and at an accelerating pace, the urban shift from the city centre to the outskirts may be witnessed. The previously less-ordered urban tissue, consisting of different dispersed morphological patterns, turns into an easily legible and more coherent morphology. This crystallisation has to do with the forming of a specific growth pattern, but also can be perceived to gradually affect the relation between the university and the city. If, previously, the city and the university were always connected, now we witness a shift where a city-university gradually crystallises as a distinct rhizomatic figure of the urban tissue. A new *Gestalt* has come to town, and as such it also becomes an actor of its own, affecting the way in which both the university and the city heritage are perceived (Brighenti and Kärrholm, 2021). If studied over time, the lines between city centre and the different spatial nodes and clusters of university buildings do not come hierarchically from above or in a linear causal relationship, but rather pass through the tissue of associations they produce with other entities, forming a kind of rhizomatic structure (Deleuze and Guattari, 1987). The line of flight that connects central Lund with Brunnshög passes through the 1880s department buildings in the fringe belt outside the old walls, runs energetically through the street of Sölvegatan and shapes a rhizomatic urban formation. As that line of flight runs through the 'veins' of Sölvegatan, a complex, multi-layered urban space emerges, composed of transversal folds and nodes of different scales, now stabilised

Figure 9.5 Moves of departments and research facilities since the year 2000. The figure includes the planned but not yet realised move of the Physics department to the Science Village, and the move of MAX IV, from the former MAX-lab location. Diagram: M. Kärrholm

through the ongoing densification projects around the new tram stops. The connections of Lund with Brunnshög, via Sölvegatan Street, shape an informal diagram of crystallisation running through different lines and nodes of the urban tissue (see Figure 9.5). To grasp the dynamics of these processes, we need to visualise and analyse how the different associations between entities of different scale emerge and gradually shape an urban network, a flexible and transversal one, which stands perpendicularly to all vertical structures.

The urban crystallisation process sheds new light on heritage sites. As the internal network of the university area evolves and transforms, certain buildings and heritage sites suddenly find themselves outside of the centre of attention and risking deterioration, like the old observatory that has been standing empty since 2001. On the other hand, new sites and buildings become the focus of attention, like the old windmill of Odarslöv (dating back from the mid-1600s) situated at the threshold of the new ESS. Rediscovered recently, the windmill was subsequently renovated and turned into a visitor centre (see Figure 9.6). It enacted new forms of relational politics as it connected – in a fresh way – local communities, architects, planners, students, farmers, artists and academics.

Thus, buildings that colonise the Science Road become a focal point of heritage interest, while buildings that fall outside the line of flight are left behind. The urban crystallisation process therefore affects the ways in which the university rethinks its built heritage. A close look into the spatial morphology of old university buildings shows that buildings have come and gone; this is the natural course of history. Hårleman's orangery was partly torn down and partly integrated into the building Palestra et Odeum, built in 1883, while Kuggis was torn down in 1897. Yet, during the last few decades, this process has speeded up. The facility once built as the Department of Zoology, Chemistry and Physics in 1842 is strategically located on the Science Road. It was bought back from the church in 1994 and is now used for academic conferences. The academic activities of the university (research and teaching) have all moved out of the old city centre during the last few decades, thus enlarging the rhizomatic formations. Departments like History, Art History, Archaeology, Astronomy and Philosophy have moved out of the old city centre to new premises along Sölvegatan Street. At the same time, many of the centrally located buildings are now used for administrative functions, meetings and conferences (Kungshuset, the old departmental buildings for Physics, Physiology, Anatomy and others), whereas buildings located less strategically were sold or are rented out. The Chemical department, built in 1863, was sold in 2016 and has now been rebuilt into apartments by a private company. The Anatomy building from 1897 is now the location of a private high school. The School of Social Work left its premises on Bredgatan in 2019.

A closer look at student housing shows a similar pattern of development. Student housing in the east part of Lund has recently been abandoned, a large part of the student housing area Vildanden was sold in 2017, and Blekingska nationen (a student nation with housing) moved their activity in 2019. Large, new student housing areas are now being built in relation to LTH Campus or in the area north of campus (Norra Fäladen). We can thus witness a move from city centre to outskirts and a gradual process of studentification (Smith and Holt, 2007), which is to say a concentration of students that starts to dominate certain parts of the

Figure 9.6 The windmill and old farm of Odarslöv, now renovated and transformed into a visitor centre for the ESS. Photo: M. Kärrholm, 2018

city, following behind the university development described above. The student population thus follows the architectural and urban nodes of the slowly crystallising rhizomatic morphology.

University heritage and public visibility

The university as an institution can be described in its 'semi-cloistered heterogeneity' (Bender, 1988b: 290). It is half-opened, yet half-closed. This is true for Lund University, which was never fully urban but was established in a park from the beginning and walled-in since its beginning (a crystal node). On the other hand, it has never been fully external in its approach (which is to say, located wholly outside the city) but has been integrated into the urban infrastructure as a cohesive entity within the city. Lund University has also slowly increased its visibility in the city over the years and established a recognition relating to individual, personal and categorical – as well as spectacular – aspects of heritage (Brighenti, 2010: 53). Individual recognition includes the possibility of being recognised as a university among others, this is as an individual entity.

Personal recognition comes with time and, for Lund University, this has been clearly established with its park, Lundagård, built between Kungshuset and the cathedral during the eighteenth century. With the first new university buildings during the nineteenth century, personal recognition was probably strengthened further, but it also came with a categorical recognition, which is to say the possibility of recognising a certain *type* of building as a university building. As the first buildings leave the original nucleus, as we witness when following the line of flight, and buildings (and hence part of the university) land in dispersed urban contexts outside of the old university walls, the notion of categorical recognition becomes more important. During the twenty-first century we can also see increasing efforts to establish a kind of spectacular recognition, or the recognition of something beyond the ordinary. Both the university and the city of Lund aspire for the ESS to become an iconic development. As stated in the brief, the buildings should be 'profiling for the ESS and a branding symbol for the science community of Lund' (Kildetoft, 2012: 4). The call for the spectacular becomes clear as Lund University not only has the ambition but also the means to establish and brand itself in a European context.

Architecturally, the ESS is in many ways treated as an architectural icon of Big Science developments. The brief also stipulated the importance for the ESS urban complex not to appear isolated and fenced-off; instead, it was important for the complex to remain visually accessible, even though the actual accessibility is impaired through so called 'ha-ha walls'. In our talks with architects from the Henning Larsen firm, the partner in charge of the ESS, Jacob Kurek, explained that an important question for the designing team was how to 'connect the city to science and to research so that somehow it does not become a barrier, but something that can raise someone's curiosity' (interview on 6 November 2019). To do this, the architects tried different strategies. For example, a specific landscape design was used to invoke curiosity and afford panoramas, whereas security and safety issues required a design that is less noticeable. The concept of 'spallation', as the breaking-up of a bombarded nucleus into several parts, played an important inspiration for the architects to approach the complex spatial design of the ESS. During the conceptual stage, the architects developed ideas about having a moving light along the proton beam corridor to make visible the movement of spallation; yet, these design ideas did not come to fruition. The spallation is, however, noticeable now in its urban dimension. As Jacob Kurek argued, 'one of the places where you are able to understand the scale and the magnitude is actually on the motorway, so how do you understand and read the building, driving by?' (interview on 6 November 2019). Only when one drives for a while, can one fully grasp the scale of a one-kilometre-long building as seen from the motorway, and it is also here that the full scope of the ESS becomes perceivable and observable as part of a longer, urban and moving line of flight. In fact, the entire ESS complex is designed as several buildings, and the location of these were chosen to mimic a spallation process since they are scattered on the premises as if broken up through spallation. Furthermore, the different colour schemes (mostly different shades of grey) of the buildings are designed to enable the passers-by to read the spatial layout and the positioning of these buildings, ensuring that the 'exploded' layout is perceivable also from afar. Thus, the iconography of spallation accompanies the design and urban reading of this new crystal-shaped development.

Following the history of spatial evolution presented above, we can argue that the ESS and its design-mimicking spallation, has triggered a process of 'urban spallation'. This process breaks out of the urban centre of scientific and political authority, related to the traditional urban heritage of the city core, and into several offshoots spreading out of the city nucleus and, consequently, extending the city-university. The ambition of these iconic-to-be science developments, such as the ESS, is not so much to represent a certain Politics with capital P, but to establish live mundane connections with the city, its growing rhizomatic morphology and its urban publics who are the consumers of heritage and research spectacles. And that is how the growth of Lund University generates political effects, understood as relational politics. Echoing the breaking out of the nucleus, urban spallation is an important imitation that transgresses scales and accelerates the urban morphogenesis of Lund.

As research and teaching facilities become more complex, and as they become more distant from everyday urban life, the spatial pedagogic (that is, informing about use through spatial form) of building design becomes increasingly important. This does not only include the way in which research buildings are designed, but also affects the repertoire of different building types that the university needs to mobilise. New and old building types focusing on mediating science are thus built, including science centres and visitor centres (Kärrholm, 2016). Since the research facilities are no longer built as an integrated part of the city, the city has to be brought, in a manner of speaking, into the research facilities. That is why the newly-built science structures incorporate urban and public qualities, including mediating spaces such as plazas and large atriums. As a result, some ambitious public spaces are designed in relation to the new facilities. LUX (hosting the Departments relating to Humanities and Theology), for example, has a proper plaza in front of its main entrance, and received the City of Lund's urban design prize (*Lund Stadsbyggnadspris*) in 2014. In the Science Village, Rydberg's square (named after a professor in Physics from Lund) is planned in relation to the last tram stop, unifying both a series of iconic buildings related to the university and its research, and allowing for a strategic view towards the ESS-facilities. In conjunction with this trend to include new, open public spaces related to university facilities, we also witness the developments of large indoor atriums (Yaneva, 2010), often located together with cafés and libraries and connected to the main entrance. As buildings expand into large complexes, they start to act like small cities with streets and different neighbourhoods (in this case, the departments), where large atriums act as interior public spaces; the LUX is an example in that regard. Thus, the zoning and enclosure of the large science facilities integrate research and public spaces to accommodate wider audiences interested in university heritage and contemporary research.

The idea of solving planning problems through public space has grown increasingly strong over the last decade, especially so in the Nordic Countries, where the influence of urban designers such as Jan Gehl cannot be underestimated (Listerborn, 2017: 21). Also, when it comes to problems of social segregation, researchers, designers and planners are looking at public spaces, as part of the answer (for example, Legeby, 2010; Sarraf, 2015; Sandström, 2019). It is therefore expected that universities and municipalities will use similar strategies to integrate science. However, one could argue that this strategy of re-staging the interaction between research and urban life tends to rewrite the role of urban citizens as tourists who, in their capacity as visitors and spectators, can encounter 'Academia' (with capital A) and 'Science' (with capital S), and engage in experiencing them as objects of, for example, heritage. The process of crystallisation, and the forming of a specific and legible *Gestalt* (the Science Road), goes hand in hand with this development.

Urban heritage and Big Science

The situatedness of science has been systematically ignored or denied by scholars both from the fields of science and technology studies (STS) and geography (Livingstone, 2003). The 1990s saw the advent of the 'localist' or 'geographical' turn in science studies as a great accomplishment of scrutinising science in relationship to site and urban context. This also prompted a dialogue between architects, architectural theorists and science studies scholars interested in the design of university science buildings (Galison and Thompson, 1999; Gieryn, 1999, 2006). Such work is indebted to the growing exchange between STS and the fields of geography, urban studies and architecture, but while representing a considerable achievement, it is still incomplete. Recent studies of the architecture of the new generation of university buildings focused on science lifestyles (Kaji-O'Grady and Smith, 2018), the symbolic imageries of the buildings (Kaji-O'Grady and Smith 2019) and how science architecture matters for research and accelerates the speed of invention (Novoselov and Yaneva, 2020). Yet, the new dynamics between science architecture and urban developments are yet to be explored more thoroughly. Engaging in an analysis of the relationship between university science and urban dynamics, the case study discussed here contributes to advancing knowledge on the urban situatedness of university science in the context of Lund.

By tracing how the spatial positioning and proliferation of specific buildings within the city fabric affects urban growth and redefines the existing social and cultural patterns of city life and heritage, we have reached three conclusions. Firstly, urban morphogenesis is not simply steered by top-down political decisions (Politics with capital P) but rather goes in tandem with specific scientific developments and spatial translations of academic needs, and the resultant architectural responses. Secondly, just like the nucleus spallation, the urban morphogenesis of Lund, as witnessed here, follows a line of flight (a movement of 'urban spallation') from the city centre: as a traditional nucleus of heritage that goes towards the urban periphery, then as a vector running in the north-east direction and gradually adding single buildings, followed by larger science parks and villages, and, recently, by mega structures like the urban complex of the ESS. Thirdly, the spatially expanded and splintered university-city, acquires a new crystal-like nucleus – or rather a route with nucleuses grouped around Sölvegatan and the tramway line – that accelerates further the process of urban crystallisation (of clustering and densification) and thus de-centres both the core of political authority and cultural heritage. As a result, spatially dispersed offshoots of the dense crystal-like urban morphology gain heritage value. The rhizomatic crystallisation of the urban tissue affects the ways in which the university rethinks its built heritage and escalates the processes of de- and re-heritagisation.

Arguing that a shift is taking place in the fabric of capitalism as a result of a change in how the business of invention is understood, Nigel

Thrift (2006) points to the importance of studying the new generation of science buildings as innovation incubators. These 'performative' machines share a number of features in common: they include some forms of public display of science, their design is intended to stimulate interdisciplinarity, they are porous as both scientists and information constantly flow through them, they encourage a 'buzz' of continuous conversation oriented to 'transactional knowledge' that contributes to innovation, and they are meant to be transparent. While Thrift's account captures well the architectural trend in the development of new university facilities, it fails to acknowledge the shift in urban morphogenesis that accompanies the construction of these iconic 'temples of interdisciplinary science', and how the scalar transformation affects urban development and heritage sites. The Lund case shows convincingly how university buildings make a larger impact on the city fabric, and that they take on new dimensions and gradually become 'cities within cities'. The city-university emerges and re-distributes the sites of heritage and the standard patterns of heritage valuation.

Spatial transformations affect the university as a site of heritage. Like many other nations, Sweden is today a society that builds universities. The research facility is on its way to become the paradigmatic building project of our time. Yet it is important to acknowledge how this building type has changed over the years. During the 1960s and the 1970s, Sweden was a society that invested in housing facilities. The huge housing projects from that period required old housing areas to be torn down and the old housing types suddenly became obsolete. Similarly, when a university expands at an unprecedented pace, it also leaves old buildings in its wake. Therefore, heritage valuations and discussions cannot be confined to one single site (or the quality of, or the knowledge about, individual buildings) but need to account instead for the scope of large-scale spatial transformations. It is this awareness of the broader processes of urban morphogenesis that sets the heritage agenda in motion.

The ESS is planned to be up and running for 40 years with the prospect of being dismantled at the end of this period. What will remain on its site will remind the future generations of our great ambitions for Big Science and the urban expansion of Lund. A new site of urban heritage will emerge, and new forms of heritage valuation will be devised. Yet, more importantly, these new forms of heritage will require novel choreographies of human and nonhuman types of expertise to be put together, and new forms of relational politics to be activated. The university of tomorrow will never cease to surprise us in its friendly rally with the ever-expanding rhizomatic silhouette of the city.

Acknowledgment

The research of this chapter was supported by the Swedish Research Council (VR) through project 2018-01663, 'The role of architecture in shaping new scientific cultures: the case of nanoscience'.

Notes

1. A possible comparison with the National Graphene Institute building in Manchester (UK) can be drawn. As one of the first buildings on the University of Manchester campus that 'opens up to the public', its design aims to encourage a relationship with people walking past who may see and wonder: 'Oh, what are they doing? Can I do this? Can I be part of that?' The building design encourages this train of thought and inspires other buildings on campus to follow this trend (Novoselov and Yaneva, 2020).
2. However, the original building for the Department of Zoology, Chemistry and Physics became the bishop's new residence by 1848. The new bishop had refused to live in the residence built for the bishop just next to the cathedral, and the church thus swapped buildings with the university (Tägil, 2001: 12f.).

References

Akademiska hus. (2012) *Lunds Universitets Campusplan*. Lund: Akademiska Hus.
Bender, T. (1988a) 'Introduction'. In T. Bender (ed.), *The University and the City: From medieval origins to the present*. Oxford: Oxford University Press, 3–10.
Bender, T. (1988b) 'Afterword'. In T. Bender (ed.), *The University and the City: From medieval origins to the present*. Oxford: Oxford University Press, 290–97.
Brighenti, A. M. (2010) *Visibility in Social Theory and Social Research*. Basingstoke: Palgrave MacMillan.
Brighenti, A. M. (2020) 'Urban phases: Crystallisation'. *City, Culture and Society,* 20, https://doi.org/10.1016/j.ccs.2019.100327.
Brighenti, A. M. and Kärrholm, M. (2021) 'Urban crystallization and the morphogenesis of urban territories'. *Territory, Politics, Governance*. https://doi.org/10.1080/21622671.2021.1872040.
Conzen, M. R. G. (2004) *Thinking about Urban Form: Papers on urban morphology 1932–1998*. Bern: Peter Lang.
Deleuze, G. and Guattari, F. (1987) *A Thousand Plateaus*. Minneapolis: University of Minnesota Press.
Ferruolo, S. C. (1988) 'Parisius-Paradisus: The city, its schools, and the origins of the University of Paris'. In T. Bender (ed.), *The University and the City: From medieval origins to the present*. Oxford: Oxford University Press, 22–43.
Fontana-Giusti, G. (2011) 'Walling and the City: The effects of walls and walling within the city space'. *The Journal of Architecture,* 16 (3), 309–45.
Galison, P. and Thompson, E. (eds) (1999) *The Architecture of Science*. Cambridge, MA: The MIT Press.
Gieryn, T. (1999) 'Two faces on science: Building identities for molecular biology and biotechnology'. In P. Galison and E. Thompson (eds), *The Architecture of Science*. Cambridge, MA: MIT Press, 423–59.

Gieryn, T. (2006) 'City as truth-spot: Laboratories and field-sites in urban studies'. *Social Studies of Science,* 36, 5–38.
Hallonsten, O. (ed.) (2012) *In Pursuit of a Promise: Perspectives on the political process to establish the European Spallation Source (ESS) in Lund, Sweden*. Lund: Arkiv.
Hallonsten, O. (2016) *Big Science Transformed: Science, politics and organization in Europe and the United States*. Basingstoke: Palgrave Macmillan.
Hallonsten, O. (2018) *Big Science in a Small Town: An introduction to ESS and MAX IV for the humanities, social Ssciences, economics, and legal studies*. Lund: Lund University.
Hyde, J. K. (1988) 'Universities and cities in Medieval Italy'. In T. Bender (ed.), *The University and the City: From medieval origins to the present*. Oxford: Oxford University Press, 13–21.
Johansson, G. (1982) *Lunds Universitets Historia II, 1710–1789*. Lund and Stockholm: Liber.
Kaiserfeld, T. and O'Dell, T. (2013) *Legitimizing ESS: Big Science as a collaboration across boundaries*. Lund: Nordic Academy Press.
Kaji-O'Grady, S. and Hughes, R. (eds) (2018) *Laboratory Lifestyles: The construction of scientific fictions*. Cambridge, MA: MIT Press.
Kaji-O'Grady, S. and Hughes, R. (2019) *LabOratory: Speaking of science and its architecture*. Cambridge, MA: MIT Press.
Kärrholm, M. (2016) 'In Search of Building Types: On visitor centers, thresholds and the territorialisation of entrances', *The Journal of Space Syntax*, 7 (1), 55–70.
Kildetoft, B. (2012) *European Spallation Source, Design Contest Architect, Contest Brief – General Description*. Lund: ESS AB.
Klinge, M., Knapas, R., Leikola, A. and Strömberg, J. (1988) *Kungliga Akademien i Åbo 1640–1808*. Helsingfors: Otava.
Kristenson, H. (1990) *Vetenskapens Byggnader Under 1800-talet: Lund och Europa*. Stockholm: Arkitekturmuseet.
Novoselov, K. S. and Yaneva, A. (2020) *The New Architecture of Science: Learning from graphene*. Singapore and NYC: World Scientific Publishing.
Legeby, A. (2010) *Urban Segregation and Urban Form: From residential segregation to segregation in public space*. Stockholm: KTH.
Lindroth, S. (1976) *A History of Uppsala University 1477–1977*. Stockholm: Almqvist & Wiksell.
Listerborn, C. (2017) 'The Flagship Concept of the "4th urban environment": Branding and visioning in Malmö, Sweden'. *Planning Theory & Practice*, 18 (1), 11–33.
Livingston, D. N. (2003) *Putting Science in its Place: Geographies of scientific knowledge*. Chicago: Chicago University Press.
Mumford, L. (1961) *The City in History, Its Origins, Its Transformations, and Its Prospects*. New York: Harcourt, Brace and World.
Rekers, J. V. and Sandell, K. (eds) (2016) *New Big Science in Focus: Perspectives on ESS and MAX IV*. Lund: Lund University.
Sandström, I. (2019) *Towards a Minor Urbanism: Thinking community without unity in recent makings of public space*. Lund: Lund University.
Sarraf, M. (2015) *Spatiality of Multiculturalism*. Stockholm: KTH.
Science Village Scandinavia (2020) 'Science Village – A Part of Brunnshög'. Accessed 21 January 2020. https://sciencevillage.com/en/science-village-2/science-village-a-part-of-brunnshog/.
Sjöholm, J. (2016) *Heritagisation, Re-heritagisation and De-heritagisation of Built Environments: The urban transformation of Kiruna, Sweden*. Luleå: Luleå tekniska universitet.
Smith, D. P. and Holt, L. (2007) 'Studentification and "apprentice" gentrifiers within Britain's provincial towns and cities: Extending the meaning of gentrification'. *Environment and Planning A*, 39 (1), 142–61.
Tägil, T. (2001) *Universitetsmiljöer i Lund*. Lund: Lunds universitet, Akademiska hus and Statens Fastighetsverk.
Thrift, N. (2006) 'Re-inventing invention: New tendencies in capitalist commodification'. *Economy and Society*, 35, (2), 279–306.
Wilson, R. R. (1999) 'Architecture at Fermilab' In P. Galison and E. Thompson (eds), *The Architecture of Science*. Cambridge, MA: MIT Press, 459–74.
Yaneva, A. (2010) 'Is the atrium more important than the lab? Designer buildings for new cultures of creativity'. In P. Meusburger, D. Livingstone and H. Jöns (eds), *Geographies of Science*. Dordrecht: Springer, 139–150.
Yaneva, A. (2017) *Five Ways to Make Architecture Political: An introduction to the politics of design practice*. London: Bloomsbury Publishing.

10
The university as regeneration strategy in an urban heritage context: the case of Roma Tre

Ola Wetterberg and Maria Nyström

Introduction

Roma Tre University in Rome was founded in 1992 in close collaboration between the Municipality of Rome, the Ministry of Universities and Research, and the first university, La Sapienza. The outspoken intention was to place the new university close to the city centre, utilising the old industrial districts in and around Ostiense (See Figure 10.1). In this way, a derelict area near the city core could find new usage, and the new university would be conveniently located along the already established Metro line. The ambitions were to stretch even further, linking urban regeneration with university development in an integrative manner addressing social, cultural and environmental issues. The existing urban tissue, partly described in terms of heritage, was regarded as an asset in the large-scale redevelopment of the larger metropolitan area (Manacorda, 2001; Ricci, 2001; Marroni, 2017).

The ambitions to regenerate the old industrial and working area into a new centre for culture, creativity and leisure is extensively described in a 2017 book edited by one of the key politicians involved in the Ostiense-Marconi project, Umberto Marroni (Marroni, 2017). The overall impression of the presentation is a story of success, even if the authors underline that the goals of the project are still not fully achieved. The volume can be read as a way in which to prepare or to advocate for the final realisation of the project. It is also clear that the implementation had been filled with obstacles. Other publications and interviews with

Figure 10.1 Partial view of Ostiense from the Tiber. Photo: Ola Wetterberg, 2019

involved parties indicate that the development might be even more complicated. Several authors express a certain degree of disappointment at the outcome of the 25-year expansion of the university in Ostiense. Today, the university has been firmly established in the area. Still, a significant part of the public amenities, transport and green structures has not been implemented in the way that was anticipated (Marroni, 2017; Palazzo, 2017).

Aspects of heritage and conservation were present in the process from the start, and Ostiense was claimed to have 'a high density of collective memories and values' (Garano, 2001: 261). It can be noticed in the conscious use of existing structures, thorough historical analysis, adaptive reuse of historical buildings, integration of archaeological remains, collaboration with heritage authorities and museums, references to film and art, and not least in the discourses surrounding the new university and the urban plans. Looking at the development of Ostiense as processes of heritagisation over a longer period, it is possible to discern several approaches and directions. There are planned and intentional actions spanning different paradigms: preservation, urban development and design. But there have also been more informal actions where the historic fabric and the heritage of the area have been used both for practical reasons and for cultural and political purposes.

In this chapter, we will first outline the relationship between the establishment of the new university and the overall urban planning and the specific project in the Ostiense-Marconi area. We will then centre our attention on the slaughterhouse area and how the university processes were related to a rising and shifting discourse on industrial heritage. We will also test the concept of a permanent provisional state to characterise parts of the urban development process and look at the relationship between planned and official interventions and discourses on heritage in the area.

Three universities of Rome

In the second half of the twentieth century, it became apparent that the first and only university of Rome, La Sapienza, was expanding too massively, reaching more than 150,000 students. Two new universities in Rome were initiated. The first addition was planned already in 1962 and was located on the outskirts of Rome, outside the ring road, in a conventional large-scale campus. It was, because of its location, called Tor Vergata. (Manacorda, 2001) The complicated land ownership of the site, combined with economic and political circumstances, meant that Tor Vergata was not founded until 20 years later, in 1982, and even after this, struggled to establish its facilities on the chosen site.

The establishment of the third university of Rome, Roma Tre, followed a different strategy, with a location close to the city centre in the industrial area of Ostiense. The original idea of placing Roma Tre here seems to have been restricted to practical reasons: proximity to the city, available land and existing transport systems. The location soon came to be part of a culture-led regeneration programme based on the university's idea as an essential driver of change and as an integrated part of the urban setting (Manacorda, 2001; Ottolenghi and Palazzo, 1997; Palazzo, 2017).

Planning the city of Rome

From the city's point of view, the university location was part of a larger development plan. The massive expansion of the urbanised area that had been going on for decades was, to a large extent, uncoordinated, and there were problems with infrastructure, transport and green structures.

The municipality decided in 1992 on a new programme with an overarching strategy to approach these problems. In this programme for the capital of Rome, the new university campus for Roma Tre in Ostiense had a prominent position. Five strategic areas, or structures, were pointed out as being of particular interest. Besides the new university location in Ostiense, we find the archaeological and green spaces of the Appian Way; the park of the two rivers, Tiber and Aniene; a new and improved traffic system in the east (including a Metro line); and the investment in neglected suburbs, providing infrastructure and liveable space.[1]

This way to develop the planning of Rome in strategic structures, different goals and multiple themes in a complex web, eventually led to a master plan for the metropolitan area – Piano Regolatore Generale (PRG) – gradually taking shape. The PRG was first approved in 2000, with subsequent decisions coming to a final step in 2008.

The PRG presented a vision for the urban development, structuring the whole, acknowledging the outward expansion and movement, and at the same time creating new strong centralities (Cecchini, 2001). Areas with expected dense growth were identified and broken by wedges of green and historical structures. Eighteen urban centres were designated as primary nodes in the development; a vision for a complex and integrated urban tissue challenged the customary principle of zoning; the overall vision was supplemented by improved traffic systems and rail lines. The five strategic urban structures that were outlined in 1992 remained in the PRG in a slightly developed form: the two rivers; the city walls; the north-south axis from Flaminio to EUR; and the Parco dell'Appia Antica. These large-scale physical elements gave necessary and historical borders, connections and directions within the larger area, as well as environmental and historic qualities to improve the liveability and attractivity.

Among key themes identified in the metropolitan plan were the role of the three universities in urban development, the transformation of the existing built environment, and the intersection between architecture and archaeology. In short, this was a visionary plan that went beyond physical structures and transport, and it was a plan to meet the demands of the new networked knowledge economy with cultural planning and place branding (*Urbanistica*, 2001; Linde Bjur and Bjur, 2015: 214).

Progetto Urbano Ostiense-Marconi

Parallel to the evolution of the PRG, the municipality of Rome initiated a specific urban development project for the area Ostiense-Marconi in the mid-1990s. 'Progetto Urbano Ostiense-Marconi' included an extensive range of industries and workers habitation, mixed with the conglomerate of historic Rome. The site had become more and more desolate as the development of industry and trade was directed eastward. Ostiense-Marconi consisted of about 800 hectares of land along the Metro line, inhabited by more than 100,000 people in high-density areas. It was easy to reach by bike, and even by foot, from central Rome. And it contained a lot of unused lands merged with housing, shops, services and people, but to a large extent in bad and dilapidated shape.

Ostiense included the same components as the whole city. Four of the five strategic structures of the PRG met in the area: the Aurelian Wall, the Tiber, the rail system and the central axis between Flaminio and EUR and Ostia. The Progetto Urbano aimed to address the restoration and improvement of the industrial heritage in the area, and at the same time enhance the links to the sea. Plans included new green infrastructures, public parks, improvement of transportation and infrastructure, development of public space, streetscapes, and cultural and leisure institutions.

Ostiense-Marconi was the perfect place to situate a new university as a generator of development and to create attractive spaces for students and staff. The university was predicted to need several hundred thousand square metres, more than 30 hectares of land harbouring 30,000 students and the university staff (Ottolenghi and Palazzo, 1997; Università degli Studi Roma Tre, 2004; Palazzo, 2017; Rabazo, 2018).

The university as a city within a city

One of the professors present at La Sapienza, when the first scheme for the new university was presented, recalls the event. In the hallway of La Sapienza was a presentation of a new modernist megastructure to be built over 'the clean slate' of land. This approach was not what he had expected. It was not in line with contemporary thinking about the rehabilitation of urban areas; it was not in line with thinking about the interaction between the university and the surrounding city. And it was not in line with architectural ideas of the time. Instead, the concept of a 'city university' which used the existing urban fabric was developed between the planners of the city and the architects of the new university (interview with Professor Andrea Vidotto).

The newly established university came to be a key actor in this complex web of stakeholders and objectives in Ostiense-Marconi. An intense formal and informal collaboration between the university and the municipality evolved, including analysis, strategies, proposals and projects, and formalised partnerships, including other actors and stakeholders.

Some of the university's ambitions, but also cautions, show in the writings of the university staff of the time (Ottolenghi and Palazzo, 1997). Two professors from the Department of Architecture identified the vision of the university to be a 'city within the city' and to create a strong interrelation with the city on all levels. They also underlined that the challenges were significant and the uncertainties daunting. A project with these dimensions and timescales needed to be fluid and flexible to allow for continuous adaptations. The reliance on public–private partnerships for funding was fundamental and at the same time threatened to let the market set the conditions for cultural and social choices. The ecological requirements, including the Tiber, transport and sewage systems, were substantial, at the same time as the riverside banks and green features supplied opportunities for parks and recreation (Ottolenghi and Palazzo, 1997: 93).

Tensions between the inhabitants' expectations and the university were anticipated. Local citizens would probably value the existing city market much more than expected rise in cultural activities. But most of all, it would be hard for citizens to make an informed comparison between the offer of future cultural structures and disappearing industrial production. All in all, these circumstances demanded a focus on communication and interactions from the municipality administrators and the university community (Ottolenghi and Palazzo, 1997: 96).

In 1999, the Rome municipality commissioned the Department of Design and Architectural Sciences to make a plan with detailed studies of the area Ostiense-Marconi. Under the scientific leadership of Professor Francesco Cellini, and with significant contributions from an extensive number of professors and staff from the university, a strategic implementation plan for the whole area was produced and published in 2004 (Università degli Studi Roma Tre, 2004). This work developed in parallel with the planning and implementation of plans and regulations made by the municipality.

The analytical approach of the university team built on a firm Italian tradition with morphological and historical studies, covering the urban landscape and tissue as well as specific buildings and projects. Proposals incorporated urban parks, river walks, projects for adaptive reuse of industrial buildings, as well as inserts of new architectural projects (see

Figure 10.2). There were plans to place the university in new and old buildings, as well as to convert the megastructures of the abandoned wholesale markets into a complex neighbourhood centre.

The methodology behind the proposal for the wholesale market (Mercati Generali), one of the largest projects, is illustrative. Based on a detailed study – including history, architecture, morphology, geology, infrastructure and traffic systems – three main objectives were identified: (1) to restore the identity of the urban layout; (2) to achieve a clear typological and morphological character of the new university settlements; (3) a clear relationship between the education system and the planned public services. The programme for the public services was grounded in 'numerous neighbourhood workshops' and contained an overwhelming number of functions, such as experimental laboratories for contemporary arts and entertainment, workshops for craft activities, spaces for exhibitions, an internet service, a library, a centre for sports, a nursery and green spaces to mention some (Università degli Studi Roma Tre, 2004). In 2003, there was an architectural competition for the Mercati Generali, with Rem Koolhaas as the winner. The programme and concept were close to the ideas of the university plan, converting the place into a modern civic and entertainment centre called the 'City of the young'.

The planners knew from the start that the possibility to implement and determine a plan for the whole area would take a very long time and probably be impossible to carry out in the end. The different stakeholders and interests were diversified, and the task was enormous. The choice was to prioritise flexibility and determination to work in a step-by-step strategy of transformation, relying on public–private partnerships (Palazzo, 2017). The way forward, and to get things going, was to use the newly decided law (*Accordo di programma*, 1990) in which the implementation of urgent public work could be pursued in collaboration between two or more public institutions and private owners (interview with Guiseppe Manacorda, 2019). The first programme agreement was signed by the City of Rome, the Province of Rome, the Region of Lazio and Roma Tre University in 1993, and concerned the integration of Roma Tre in Ostiense. This agreement was modified, changed and adjusted to new ideas and circumstances in three following agreements between 1998 and 2003.[2]

Today, a large part of the university programme has been realised. Old buildings have been redeveloped, and new ones built. But discontent remains. The university has done its part, but the municipality has not been able to fulfil its. Some infrastructural projects have begun but not

Figure 10.2 Engineering school under construction on the grounds of the old ship shute, Vasca Navale. Architect Professor Andrea Vidotto. Photo: Ola Wetterberg, 2010

finished. Public space and new transportation are not in place, and green space along the rivers is unavailable. Starting with one of Europe's most ambitious urban plans in the late 1990s/early 2000s, for economic and political reasons, quality improvements of the surrounding urban areas have not been realised (Palazzo, 2017).

Anna Palazzo, professor from the Department of Architecture at Roma Tre, has followed the process for several decades. She acknowledges the clear advancement brought by the Progetto Urbano, noting the presence of a 'knowledge city' in Ostiense-Marconi. But she also points to the remaining and substantial challenges. Some of these are traced back to the incremental approach of the *Accordo di programma*, and she calls for a more overarching institutional and political coordination. The problems are connected to the negotiation between different interests and, most of all, the quality of public space and infrastructure, not least the handling of the Tiber River (Palazzo, 2017: 25) In this light, a solid and long-term actor as the university is shown to be even more critical, but at the same time it clearly illustrates the significance of a multilevel collaboration in urban development.

Mattatoio: the old slaughterhouse in Testaccio

Having outlined the overall situation in which Roma Tre was established in the urban setting, we will take a closer look at some specific aspects related to heritage and the involvement of the university. To do this, we will focus on one area within the Progetto Urbano, the old slaughterhouse, Mattatoio, in the urban quarter Testaccio (see Figure 10.3). We will look into the relationship between planned interventions and the more spontaneous processes that took place over the following decades. We will also describe how the area became mentally transformed over time.

Even if Testaccio lies in close connection to Ostiense, it is not formally a part of the area. It is situated inside the Aurelian city wall and was not included in the original project for Ostiense-Marconi in the early 1990s. However, Testaccio soon came to be brought into the planning process. Roma Tre found Mattatoio to be a good location for the Department of Architecture and Planning. This inclusion added to the overall ambition to integrate both sides of the Tiber in the project. The axis from Via Marmorata through Testaccio and Mattatoio to Trastevere on the other side of the river had an existing bridge. It would contribute to physical integration and make a flow of communication possible.

The neighbourhood of Testaccio is situated on the site of the archaeological remains of the old harbour in Rome and was during later times part of the rural outskirts of the city. Testaccio, as we find it today, is mainly defined by the later urban development of Rome dating back from the Risorgimento and the early twentieth century. It is regarded as the first proper industrial and working-class area of Rome and has had a central position in the growth of the modern city. The establishment of the urban quarters was part of the first masterplan for Rome after it

Figure 10.3 View of the Mattatoio complex. Photo: Ola Wetterberg, 2019

became the capital of Italy in 1870. It is closely related to the new and modern slaughterhouse, built by the municipality. Gioacchino Ersoch was responsible for the project carried out between 1888 and 1890.

The complex of the slaughterhouse and the Campo Boario (cattle market) is covering a total area of about 100,000 square metres. The slaughterhouse became famous for its innovative design, combining the decorative ideals of the late nineteenth century with the new demands of function and hygiene. The most creative ideas of Ersoch's plan were the use of new materials in the building. Travertine, brick and cast iron are the primary materials used in the pavilions of the Mattatoio. The extensive use of cast iron was not only new in Rome but was also innovative in this particular category of buildings. Ersoch's reasoning behind his choice of materials was motivated by reasons of hygiene and functionality on one hand and by economic reasons on the other (Pistone, 2007: 65). While active, the slaughterhouse and its surrounding activities employed up to two thousand people (Neri, Pariesella and Racheli, 2000: 88).

Mattatoio was a primary employer and a key feature of the local neighbourhood. But it was also tied to the most modern international industrial development and connected and integrated with the surrounding industrial sites in Rome, not far away from the huge wholesale market (Mercati Generali) in Ostiense. Since the slaughterhouse closed down in the 1970s, the area lost its industrial core and has been awaiting regeneration and new uses.

One counterpoint to the development of planning measures and urban development is the 'heritage history' of the remains of the industrial past, the ways in which the area came to be inscribed in history and as heritage. This inscription of heritage into places can be seen as a driver of change, as a tool for change, and a result of these changes.

The heritagisation of Mattatoio, as well as of Testaccio and the wider industrial landscape, was a long process, going through several different phases. The university took part in a complex web of levels and activities, both as an institution but also through its professors. Visions and projects for the enormous slaughterhouse area took form, some of them incorporating adaptive reuse of the existing buildings. Grand plans for a city of science developed but could not be realised. Testaccio/Mattatoio went into an area in waiting. During this time, opportunities arose to use the buildings in more informal ways, by settlers and migrants, and through more structured initiatives by artists and organisations like the Villagio Globale and the Città del Altra Economia. Artists' residencies were organised, as well as rock concerts, markets and so on. Some of these events were more-or-less legal, some not. The university settlement was in its turn part of the latest stage in the development when a more formalised vision of this area as a *Città delle Arti* took form around 2000.

We can therefore identify at least three different but overlapping periods in the process of heritagisation spanning from the sixties up until today: (1) a contested heritage in the making; (2) an area in waiting; (3) building a *Città delle Arti*.

A contested heritage in the making

The slaughterhouse of Testaccio had not even faced its final closure when its future began to be discussed. During the 1960s, the decision to move the slaughterhouse to a more peripheral location had been taken. The issue arose of how to use the structures that would soon be redundant. This discussion quickly turned into a debate about the value and future of the entire complex. Industrial archaeology had not so far had a strong base in Italy, and during the 1970s many expressed their concern of whether or not the industrial area that the slaughterhouse was part of could be properly regenerated (Ranaldi, 2012: 137).

Engaged in this debate were architects and art historians from the university, as well as politicians and the local community of Testaccio (Rossi, 2007: 61). The *Piano Regolatore Generale* of 1962 suggested demolishing the slaughterhouse and replacing it with a public green area (Rossi, 2007: 61). Among those in favour of demolition were the architects and professors Bruno Zevi and Leonardo Benevolo from the university, La Sapienza. Benevolo made the case against the conservation of the slaughterhouse in 1976, claiming a general lack of quality of the built environment of the Umbertine era that would not merit its future preservation (Perego, 1993: 102).

One of the main protagonists of the conservation and safeguarding of the slaughterhouse was Simonetta Lux, Professor of Art History at La Sapienza. Her emphasis lay on the originality and artistic value of the architectural features and the innovations of Gioacchino Ersoch, as well as on the high quality of the material and construction (Cupelloni, 2001: 20). The attention brought by the impending demolition of the slaughterhouse can be said to have aided the introduction of the discipline of industrial archaeology in Italy and greater recognition of the country's industrial heritage (Perego, 1993: 112). Lux's contribution was to be critical, as it would sway the scholarly opinion towards the conservation of Mattatoio. Even in the local community, one could find a view in favour of preserving the area, partially due to nostalgic reasons (as many had personal relations to Mattatoio), but also for the prevailing lack of proper services in the area that could be located in the empty slaughterhouse.

The architect and left-wing politician Renato Nicolini was another important character in favour of preservation. He focused on the potential use-value of the former slaughterhouse. When the slaughterhouse closed, it had brought a crisis to the entire area, with many people losing their primary sources of income. The regeneration of the slaughterhouse could be a way by which the quality of life for the local community could be improved (Nicolini, 1976: 202–3). Nicolini also emphasised the strategic position of Testaccio in the urban tissue of Rome. The partly uncontrolled urban sprawl in Rome made this central developable district even more critical (Nicolini, 1976: 201). His proposition for the new use of the slaughterhouse was to create a multi-functional centre, with spaces for education, culture, sports or other types of activities needed by the local community. In this way, the slaughterhouse would be '… recognised as cultural heritage, not due to its "artistic" values, and not only due to its significance as a sign of the history of the city, but by its capacity to assume new urban uses and thus new values (Nicolini, 1976: 203).[3]

The emphasis is here more on the urban and social aspect of the area, even if the historic and artistic values are recognised. As Francesco Perego states, this debate resulted in the historicisation of the former slaughterhouse of Testaccio, affirming its position as an essential part of the city's cultural heritage and its potential value for reuse (Perego, 1993: 109). It is within this context that the first proper plans of regeneration of the area would be developed.

The formal authorisation of Mattotoio's position as a cultural heritage was concluded by its listing in 1988 (within the law no. 1089).

To conclude, the notion of aesthetic appreciation and potential reuse of the slaughterhouse complex was not apparent during the period of its closing but needed a process of negotiation to defend its future conservation. The changing attitudes towards the slaughterhouse were closely related to the contemporary progress of industrial archaeology on a European scale. The case for industrial remains was predominately a professional discourse, although there was also growing support for preservation in the local community. The asserted heritage values were mainly aesthetic and historic qualities. However, we have also seen indications of a rising urbanist approach to the strategic reuse of the former industrial area. Even this is in line with the general European trend in industrial archaeology where adaptation and reuse became more widely accepted means for conservation and preservation (Cossons, 2000).

Early plans of reuse and conservation 1975–86

A few years passed before the new appreciation for the area were presented in any official plans. One early project was put forward in 1978 by the Ufficio per gli interventi del Centro Storico (the office for interventions in the historic centre). While commercial use was dismissed, the plans were in line with the ideas of Renato Nicolini, who had become Councillor of Culture in the municipal government. The design included a cultural centre for the industrial heritage and science, as well as spaces for educational activities, while the former cattle market was to be redesigned as a park. Buildings in the near vicinity of the slaughterhouse were also intended to be restored (Menichini, 1986: 78). Still, there was some disagreement between the planners and the local community concerning the scope and target groups of the future complex. While official plans viewed the slaughterhouse in relation to the city as a whole, the representatives of the local community wished the complex to remain an asset primarily for the neighbourhood of Testaccio (Menichini, 1986: 78; Perego 1993: 118). Although at least 3.5 billion lire had been earmarked for the realisation of this project, the actual accomplishments were limited (Perego, 1993: 118).

An urban laboratory and a city of science and technology

The early plans were limited in scope. Even if the 1978 project included educational activities, it was not until the more elaborated plans were presented in the 1980s that the university also played a more prominent role.

In 1982 architect Carlo Aymonino, also a professor at the architectural school at La Sapienza, created a 'laboratory' for strategic areas of urban development in Rome, with a specific focus on the Esquiline and Testaccio (Caruso, 1986: 10). The work on Testaccio was done in close collaboration with Luigi Caruso. Caruso was responsible for the Testaccio plan from 1982, and he also held assignments from the Ministry of Education for the restructuring of the La Sapienza. As Ranaldi points out, the creation of a laboratory coincided with the final closing of the adjoining industries in Ostiense in 1984, thus creating a vast abandoned industrial area in a central location of the city, stretching from Testaccio southwards (Ranaldi, 2014: 138). The overarching goal was a general upgrading of the entire area, the reinforcement of the local identity, while Testaccio simultaneously would become better integrated with the rest of the city (Aymonino, 1986: 7).

Three main points of interest were presented: the residential area, traditional craftsmanship, and archaeological and modern cultural heritage. Operations included the renovation of the residential area, construction of a new piazza at the vacant lot next to Monte Testaccio, restoration and reuse of the slaughterhouse complex, improvement of the space between Monte Testaccio and Via Marmorata, and restoration of the caves in Monte Testaccio.

Besides the upgrading of the residential area, the proposed interventions in the urban fabric were quite radical. The former Prati del Popolo Romano – in between Monte Testaccio, the non-Catholic cemetery and Via Marmorata – would be completely reorganised. The area consisted of small-scale buildings with a great variety of workshops. Referencing the history of this particular area as an important public place in Rome, the entire site would be transformed into a centre of leisure and sports. The ambition was to embrace the contemporary cultural heritage of the area: a large sports field in the centre recalled the former Campo Roma, the football field of the team AS Roma (Murgia and Salanitro, 1986: 58). Only workshops considered to be of value due to their craftsmanship (traditional crafts such as blacksmiths and carpenters) were intended to be relocated within the area. Surrounding the sports field were 'laboratories' for these craftsmen, as well as a nursery school and some additional housing (Murgia and Salanitro, 1986: 58).

The slaughterhouse was the very heart of the regeneration plan for the area. Mattatoio was envisioned to become a *Città della Scienza e della Tecnica* – a centre for science and technology. Included in this centre would be space for advanced research, exhibitions and educational activities (Consiglio Nazionale delle Ricerche, 1986: 80). The university, La Sapienza, was an essential partner in the project, and there were plans to locate the Department of Architecture to the site (Marroni, 2017: 79), a forerunner to the present location of the Architectural School of Roma Tre. The architect in charge was the university professor Paolo Portoghesi, responsible for the material restoration and restructuring of the slaughterhouse. Principal for the project was the Consiglio Nazionale delle Ricerche (the National Research Council).

The project would not only highlight the slaughterhouse as an innovative piece of industrial heritage; it aimed to define and market Rome as a city of innovation and technology and emancipate it from the image of a conservative and bureaucratic capital (Portoghesi, 1986: 81). It was supposed to strengthen Rome's position within an international and competitive context with the new millennium approaching (Consiglio Nazionale delle Ricerche, 1986: 80, Portoghesi, 1986: 81).

Figure 10.4 Città della scienza al mattatoio, Roma. Paolo Portoghesi, 1983. © Accademia Nazionale di San Luca, Roma

So, besides the restoration of the slaughterhouse pavilions, an entirely new building was proposed on the side facing the Tiber (see Figure 10.4). The appearance of this new building would be a reference to iconic architectural forms in a Roman tradition, modern as well as classical, in a post-modern play with architectural tradition, recalling designs associated with the university. In Portoghesi's words:

> In this ... is inserted symbolical allusions and historic memories: the cupola of the Sapienza as a symbol of the *Studium Urbis*; the spiral as a symbol of research, the anatomical theatre and the spherical amphitheatre of Leonardo, imagined as *locho dove si predica*. (Portoghesi, 1986: 81)[4]

Facing the river would be a long and compact façade, with a concave part creating a small piazza and interrupting the otherwise closed appearance of the building. The façade facing the inside of the slaughterhouse would take on a lighter appearance divided into steps, letting the building gradually rise upwards.

The other half of the complex, the cattle market (Campo Boario), was planned to contain a cultural centre. The paving would be redone for cultural events, and the surrounding buildings restored to house various establishments: a restaurant, a small museum with archaeological remains from the area, an archive and library for the Soprintendenza ai

Monumenti Moderni (Murgia and Salanitro 1986: 82). Compared to the 1978 project, the budget had grown substantially, and covered both two parts of the area (Perego, 1993: 128).

A period of crisis

While the future of Testaccio and the slaughterhouse complex were debated and various plans put forward, very few actual interventions were carried out. Some suggestions as to why the ambitious projects never came to be realised are given by Perego, who states that these plans coincided with a period of political uncertainty in the government of the municipality of Rome (Perego, 1993: 147). The left, who had been supporting the plans, lost their majority and as public finances were poor, other priorities were made. Another cause could be found within the project itself, where the ambitious and overarching plans had limited anchoring in the concerned institutions (Perego, 1993: 125). Only one organisation decided to move to the slaughterhouse during this period, within legal boundaries: the Scuola Popolare di Musica di Testaccio (the Popular School of Music of Testaccio). This school was founded with openly left-wing political ambitions and had strong support in the local community (Ranaldi, 2014: 133).

All in all, the political restructurings during this period restrained most new initiatives and made it difficult to carry out even those previously planned. As we have seen, the process in Ostiense and Testaccio would gain new momentum in the early and mid-1990s with heavy involvement of the new university, Roma Tre. In this process, some of the old ideas were discarded, but continuity and new ideas also influenced things to come. Between the mid-1980s and the early 2000s, when the new formal planning process gradually got off the ground, an informal occupancy commenced that could be characterised as an alternative process of heritage-making in the area.

An area in waiting

Moving forward to the 1990s, the complex of Mattatoio was more-or-less abandoned by the municipality of Rome and began to be spontaneously used by various groups in need of space, who found a suitable location on the premises of the slaughterhouse (see Figure 10.5). Few traces of the ambitious and expensive plans previously put forward by the municipality could be seen. Despite this, the abandoned spaces of the slaughterhouse slowly began to be used by people in need. Immigrants and refugees found a temporary – or in some cases quite permanent – home within the premises of the Campo Boario. At one point, the area would house both Somalian and Senegalese immigrants, among others, and a Roma-Kalderashi camp set up their caravans in the old cattle market. Besides these groups, coachmen used some of the old stalls to keep their horses and coaches, and a local gym was established in one of the buildings of the Campo Boario. The use of the slaughterhouse complex was continuously developing and would take on different forms during this time.

Villaggio Globale

There was one restoration in Campo Boario proposed by Caruso and Aynomino that was carried out. In 1987, the ex-borsa was reopened for use as a communal art gallery – primarily focused on contemporary art (Perego, 1993:147). Although inaugurated and functional during a few exhibitions in the late 1980s, no plan for its long-term use existed, and it was eventually left virtually abandoned.

The empty and recently restored building became the base of the *centro sociale* (roughly translated as social centre) Villaggio Globale when it was founded in 1990 (Perego, 1993:154). This marks one of the first organised initiatives of what we call 'unofficial actors'. They did not have any official support for their activities and spontaneously occupied parts of the complex. Villaggio Globale was born out of a local radio show, the *Radio Città Aperta,* and had a strong political orientation towards the left and arranged different manifestations during the late 1990s and early 2000s. Their activities included art exhibitions, festivals, nightclubs and education, all with a focus on international solidarity.

The *centro sociale* is an Italian phenomenon, combining a political engagement with social and cultural activities, and the centres established during the 1970s to the 1990s often consciously made use of squatted buildings. These centres can be found in several Italian cities, from the north to the south, represented by different organisations such as the *Leoncavallo* in Milan (Membretti, 2007: 252). The organisation represents a parallel force to the officially directed plans towards the slaughterhouse, with their bottom-up, grass-roots organisation rooted in a social tradition with local support (Membretti, 2007: 252–53).

The activities of Villaggio Globale seem to have had quite a wide popularity, particularly among a younger audience (Björk, 2008: 26). Although illegally squatting the buildings, the *centro sociale* was tolerated by the municipality and continued to develop their activities up until at least the 2010s.

Stalker and Ararat

Another organisation connected to the spaces of the abandoned slaughterhouse during the 1990s was Stalker. Stalker can best be described as a group of young architects who were engaged in architectural and urban experimentation and activism. The origins of Stalker can be traced to a group of students occupying the School of Architecture at the Roman University La Sapienza in 1990 (Lang, 2006: 196). This occupation was a protest against privatisation of the university system, coordinated mainly by the organisation La Pantera, which would later form the basis of Stalker (Lang, 2006: 196). Already having strong political undertones originating from their activities at La Sapienza, this group would, during the following years, arrange urban interventions directed towards forgotten or neglected places in the capital. Their strategies involved artistic interventions and activities involving the local community, such as concerts and similar events (Lang, 2006: 197). The name 'Stalker' originates from the 1979 film with the same name by Andrei Tarkovsky, where the main subject is exploring a mysterious and possibly dangerous zone. Stalker would continue arranging various activities during the 1990s, having created a manifesto stating that '[Stalker] is a collective subject that engages research and actions within the landscape with particular attention to the areas around the city's margins and forgotten urban space, and abandoned areas or regions under transformation (Stalker, n.d.).

In 1999, the activities of Stalker were located in the Campo Boario of the slaughterhouse in Testaccio. Together with Villagio Globale and Azad, a Kurdish social organisation, Stalker came to aid a large group of Kurdish refugees who had fled to Rome at the time (Lang, 2006: 201–2). What started as provisional measures of creating various social services for the refugees led to the founding and permanent residence of Ararat in the former veterinary buildings in the Campo Boario (Careri and Romito, 2005: 44f).

The foundation of Ararat increased the tension between the various groups illegally occupying the area without much interaction or cooperation (Lang, 2006: 202) (see Figure 10.5). Stalker took the role of mediator between the different groups, drawing on previous experiences and strategies to use artistic events to create social spaces and find ways of co-existing (Lang, 2006: 202). Furthermore, they started to map the

Figure 10.5 Various groups inhabiting the Campo Boario during the 1990s. Nyström, 2015

Campo Boario and develop plans of how to display values present at the site. Concerning the choice of artistic approach, Stalker says that 'Campo Boario need neither artworks nor public architecture to define its clear identity. Its characteristics are the uncertainty, the indefiniteness, and the self-organisation of its own physical and relational spaces. The challenge is to produce a public space starting from these premises' (Careri and Romito, 2005: 46).

As explained here, the specific qualities of the place already exist for those directly involved. Art was not the most crucial goal of those involved in the various projects at the Campo Boario, but rather a useful tool to facilitate the communication of the multicultural values of the place.

Two of the events arranged by Stalker were the *Pranzo Boario* (Boario Lunch) and the *Orto Boario* (Boario Garden). The *Pranzo Boario* was merely a lunch arranged in the open piazza of the Campo Boario, where the various groups residing there could meet and talk in a non-threatening, informal environment (Lang, 2006: 202–3). Likewise, the creation of a 'Mediterranean garden' in the same piazza in 2001 presented an opportunity for diverse groups to meet and create a collective and physical space (Careri and Romito, 2005: 45).

Today, Ararat remains in the ex-veterinary buildings on the premises and has been granted a legal contract (*Ararat Roma Blog*, 7 June 2011). The Roma-Kalderashi community, on the other hand, was ultimately evicted from Testaccio in June 2008, during a controversial intervention directed by the municipality (*Corriere della Sera*, 6 June 2008). The entire community of 120 people, out of which 40 were children, was moved to a more peripheral location near Tor Vergata. They had at that point been staying for 15 years, and the living conditions were described as: '… clean

Figure 10.6 Art exhibitions outside the MACRO. Photo: Maria Nyström, 2015

and well-maintained, the families were living in spacious and comfortable caravans surrounded by a large number of cars' (*Corriere della Sera*, 6 June 2008).

Building a *Città delle Arti*

In parallel to the described more-or-less informal settlements, the Ostiense-Marconi project, including Testaccio, started to take off around 2000. The project was intended to allow experiments with new and innovative urban planning strategies and included an aim to strengthen the identity of the future city (Ricci, 2001: 229; Cecchini, 2001: 222–3). Integrated into the overall scheme were cultural institutions, a science museum, a large multi-functional centre in the former Mercati Generali and various other cultural and social services (Comune di Roma, 2003: 4).

A vision for Mattotoio as *Città delle Arti* (City of the Arts) emerged. The idea was to design a multi-functional centre based on art, creativity and culture (see Figure 10.6). The project included new uses for the slaughterhouse, restoration of the buildings, historical research and valorisation of the built heritage. The establishment of a cultural centre close to the city centre was a way to modernise the city and make it more competitive on an international scale.

Roma Tre was still one of the main actors in the Ostiense-Marconi project, and Mattatoio came early on to be the location for the school of architecture. As well as being partly responsible for the regeneration plans of the complex, the university also moved into one of the first restored pavilions in 2000. Bit-by-bit, this first settlement has been expanded with student facilities, lecture halls, an aula and a library. The architectural school of Roma Tre is currently occupying the most space in the slaughterhouse complex and continues to expand.

The leading architect, Francesco Cellini, a long-time head of the architecture department, describes the 'Mattatoio model' as contrasting the idea of a campus. The aim was the opposite, to integrate the university with the city, position it alongside other institutions, open it up for the public and people passing by. It should avoid being a single-functional complex and be a university 'as a city'. The area included both public and private institutions emphasising culture and education besides other services and commercial activities. Cellini indicates that the university leadership or teachers have not always embraced this vision for the Mattatoio. The close coexistence with the public and other institutions also results in frictions in everyday activities. The intended spontaneous interactions can be seen as annoying disturbances. Another

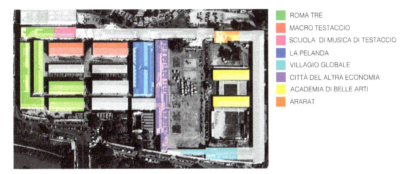

Figure 10.7 Overview of the various actors in Mattatoio 2015. Nyström, 2015

arena for disagreement in the implementation was the physical interventions and divergent attitudes towards conservation. Cellini underlines his deep interest in the built heritage but is frustrated by the deciding authorities' strict conservative attitude, wanting to protect all details from the rusty nails to the 'broken gates on the illegal shacks of the fifties' (Cellini, 2017: 80–3). According to Cellini, this resulted in many buildings becoming exposed to decay and destruction.

An early tenant in Mattatoio, alongside the architectural school, was the municipal museum of contemporary art in Rome, MACRO. It was first inaugurated in its current form in 2002, opening on two locations in Rome. In close connection to MACRO, a new exhibition space called *La Pelanda* opened in 2006. Officially under the overarching management of MACRO, this centre includes spaces for different artistic expressions with galleries, theatre halls, studios and laboratories for artists in residence, and areas for cultural activities directed towards youth and children. For the different actors in Mattatoio, see Figure 10.7.

In the former cast-iron portico facing the Campo Boario, new spaces were created for the Città dell'Altra Economia (the City of Alternative Economy) in 2007. This is a loosely based non-profit organisation to promote an alternative economy, solidarity and sustainable development. Their activities include a restaurant, an organic food store, a bookstore, and several smaller companies. The events organised by the Città dell'Altra Economia range from short film festivals to yard sales, and attract a vast number of people.

Lastly, the most recent actor to establish on the premises is the Accademia di Belle Arti, who are occupying two restored pavilions at the Campo Boario, officially inaugurated at the beginning of 2015 (see Figure

10.7). Besides these, several earlier actors remain in the slaughterhouse complex, such as the Scuola di Musica di Testaccio and Ararat, and supposedly also Villagio Globale. Neither Villagio Globale nor Ararat are frequently mentioned in the various projects by the other actors but are included in the municipality's official plan for the Ostiense-Marconi project.

A permanent provisional state: Testaccio

The long timespan from partial and gradual abandonment of the Ostiense area and Testaccio starting in the 1960s until the start of a factual redevelopment in the 1990s led to what Gabriella Olshammar (2002) has coined as 'a permanent provisional state'. The uncertainty of what was going to happen and the lack of planning decisions, combined with the magnitude of the problems at hand, led to a situation where there would be a considerable risk involved for any actor to start improving on buildings and sites on their own. On the other hand, the overall strategic plans, and more tangible development decisions, got pushed into the future. So, what seemed like a provisional state, a situation of waiting, came to continue over a very long period. In fact, due to the reasons stated above, this situation of uncertainty and waiting has also continued after the decisions on the Progetto Urbano.

Briefly outlined in this chapter, we have seen two parallel processes of heritage-making taking place in Mattatoio. One official planning process with a stark collaboration between the municipality and the university and several other actors. This planning process has been going on over a long period, sometimes interrupted and then resumed in new forms. A second process has been informal, sometimes illegal, benefiting from the slow development and the more-or-less abandoned facilities at the site. There have been overlaps and instances when these processes have met and been beneficial to each other. Some of the more spontaneous activities of Campo Boario, like Villaggio Globale and the public events, have even been integrated into the more extensive cultural programme for a *Città delle Arti* (Marroni, 2017).

One of the key officials from the municipality, Gabriella Raggi, acknowledges the creative meeting between the formal and informal settlers. She recalls a competition for 'the rebirth of the city' sponsored by the Lega delle Cooperative in the early 1980s, aiming to map already existing activities and explore new ideas. Combining 'the noble and public part (the slaughterhouse pavilions) with the private and dark world of

Campo Boario, condensed around the large and old heart of the slaughterhouse – the pelanda – transformed into a factory of culture'[5] (Raggi, 2017: 69–70).

Born out of this approach was later the often-referenced biennale in 1999. The initiative came from Luca Bergamo, a politician and university scholar, director of the organisation Zone Attive, and gained support from municipal politicians. The event – *Biennale dei Giovani Artisti del Mediterraneo* – was organised as a competition for people under 40 as an act of solidarity with the rehabilitation after the Bosnian war and gathered over 400 participants. The later implementation of the planning scheme has meant that the place and surroundings are now filled with students, the Campo Boario with concerts, and new activities have been added. Still, Raggi thinks the slaughterhouse is not 'taking off'; the planned synergies between the different initiatives are missing due to a lack of overall coordination (Raggi, 2017: 70–1).

It also looks like there is a scarcity of communication and mutual acknowledgement. Stalker writes about the biennale in 1999 as a crucial moment in their development and are disappointed over being met by indifference. However, they do not, in their turn, mention the role of the municipality in the event (Careri and Romito, 2005). Informants from the university confirm that the communication between the formal and informal settlers is limited, which is in line with Raggi's observations.

Conclusions

The process of converting provisional spaces of a living heritage on a larger urban scale to a city of culture promoted by the city has had a long life span. A slow implementation has offered possibilities to incorporate the spontaneous, bottom-up initiatives from different communities with the planned redevelopment and improvement of city space. But it also shows the tensions between actors with different sets of goals and resources.

Twenty years after the first settlement, we were sitting in the small garden in Campo Boario – the only liveable space within sight – drinking tea (see Figure 10.8). We spoke to two members of Stalker, who pointed with irritation at the wall in the background. The people from Ararat served tea, and at the same time picked vegetables for their lunch. The wall stands opposite the Kurdish settlement and the garden lies in between. The barrier covers a newly built and renovated structure for the art school in Rome. This way of separating the formal art education

Figure 10.8 The garden in Campo Boario overlooking the fence to the art school. Photo: Ola Wetterberg, 2018.

from its surroundings felt provocative for their neighbours. Stalker and Ararat's counteraction was to make a 'mural' on the wall, opposing the barrier, and in this way, appropriated the space.

The garden anecdote cannot grasp the situation's complexity and does not give justice to the positive interaction and overlays that played out for a long time. But visiting the place today, the story can symbolise some of the problems joining the place's formal and informal processes: to sustain urban life with all its contradictions or create a university 'as a city'. After his long-time engagement in the urban projects, Cellini notes that this university vision – that builds on juxtaposition and coexistence – is often hard to embrace and implement in practice (Cellini, 2017).

The Roma Tre University has all along been a principal player in the restructuring of Ostiense and Mattatoio. Not only have they been the primary developer in the area, but they have also acquired a formal role in the planning process alongside and in close collaboration with the municipality. The university has been the most enduring actor of this urban redevelopment on the institutional and economic level, while many other urban development aims have not been implemented.

On the individual level, professors of architecture and planning have committed, contributions from scholars in art history and other disciplines have also significantly impacted the outcome of the urban process. These contributions have only been indicated in this chapter. Even the informal settlement processes and critique of the overall planning strategies have included academic staff.

Taking all the complexities and struggles of a large-scale urban development process into account, it is still clear that the university has a significant possibility to impact the city. The disappointment felt by university members that other actors, including the municipality, has not fulfilled their undertakings does not change this. Nor does it diminish the responsibility that follows.

Acknowledgments

We want to thank Professor M. M. Segarra Lagunes and Professor A. L. Palazzo for arranging the workshop 'Conflicting heritage in the timeline', together with Dr Marta Rabazzo and doctoral student Romina d'Ascanio, in 2019. The event was made possible by funding from UCL Cities partnerships Programme (CpP)-Rome Hub and Centre for Critical Heritage Studies, University of Gothenburg. Key lectures were given by L. Montuori, A. L. Palazzo, M. M. Segarra Lagunes, G. Raggi, D. Cecchini, F. Cellini, G. J. Burgers and P. Desideri. Finally, we also want to thank Professor Hans Bjur for lifelong inspiration and for introducing us to the subject.

Notes

1. Programme of Works for Roma Capitale, Law no. 396 of 1990, approved in January 1992: Lecture Gabriella Raggi, 2019.
2. Planning documents of the Progetto Urbano Ostiense Marconi are available at the Roma Capitale webpage: http://www.urbanistica.comune.roma.it/progetti-urbani/citta-storica-pu-ostiensemarconi.html, read on 14 August 2020.
3. '…viene in questo riconosciuto come un bene culturale, non per i suoi valori 'artistici' e non solo per il suo significato di documento nella storia della città, ma per la sua capacità di assumere nuove funzioni urbane e dunque nuovi valori'.
4. 'Su questo (…) si innestano allusioni simboliche e memorie storiche: la cupola della Sapienza come simbolo dello *Studium Urbis*; la spirale come simbolo della ricerca, il teatro anatomico e l'anfiteatro sferico di Leonardo, immaginato come *locho dove si predica*'.
5. 'la parte nobile e pubblica (i padiglioni dei macelli) con il mondo privato e oscuro del Campo Boario, condensate attorno all'ampio e Vecchio cuore del Mattatoio – la Pelanda – trasformata in fabbrica di cultura e produzione culturale.' (Raggi, 2017: 70).

References

Ararat Roma Blog, 7 July 2011. 'Ararat 1999'. Accessed 12 December 2014. http://ararat-roma.blogspot.com/2011/07/ararat-1999.html.
Aymonino, C. (1986) 'Presentazione'. In L. Caruso (ed.), *Testaccio: Progetto per la trasformazione di un quartiere*. Rome: Fratelli Palombi Editori.
Bjur, H. (2007) 'Det dynamiska Rom/Dynamic Rome'. *Arkitektur*, 107 (8).
Björk, A. (2008) *Testaccio: En stadsdel i Rom under omvandling*. Bachelor Thesis in Architecture. Gothenburg: Chalmers.
Caruso, L. (1986) 'Cronistoria di un progetto'. In L. Caruso (ed.), *Testaccio: Progetto per la trasformazione di un quartiere*. Rome: Fratelli Palombi Editori.
Careri, F. and Romito, L. (2005) 'Stalker e i Grandi Giochi del Campo Boario'. *Building Material*, 13, 42–7.
Cecchini, D. (2001) 'Rome, a laboratory for new city planning'. *Urbanistica*, (116) 221–224.
Cellini, F. (2017) 'Ex Mattatoio Università Roma Tre: la Facoltà di Architettura'. In U. Marroni (ed.), *Roma. La rigenerazione dei quartieri industriali. Il Progetto urbano Ostiense-Marconi*. Roma: Ponte Sisto.
Città dell'Altra Economia/CAE (2005) Accessed 3 March 2022. https://www.facebook.com/cittadellaltraeconomia/
Comune di Roma (2003) 'Deliberazione n. 10. Estratto dal verbale delle deliberazioni del consiglio comunale'. Accessed 9 April 2015. http://www.urbanistica.comune.roma.it/citta-storica-exmattatoio.html.
Consiglio Nazionale delle Ricerche (1986) 'Il programma del Cnr per la 'città della Scienza e della Tecnica'. In L. Caruso (ed.), *Testaccio: Progetto per la trasformazione di un quartiere*. Rome: Fratelli Palombi Editori.
Corriere della Sera, 6 June 2008. 'Roma, sgomberato un campo nomadi vicino al Testaccio. C'erano 40 bambini'. https://www.corriere.it/cronache/08_giugno_06/roma_sgomberato_insediamento_nomadi_dcf6e2d8-3403-11dd-9532-00144f02aabc.shtml (Accessed 18th February 2022)
Cossons, N. (ed.) (2000) *Perspectives on Industrial Archaeology*. London: Science Museum
Cupelloni, L. (ed.) (2001) *Il Mattatoio di Testaccio a Roma: Metodi e strumenti per la riqualificazione del patrimonio architettonico*. Rome: Gangemi Editore.
Garano, S. (2001) 'The Subcenter System'. *Urbanistica*, (116) 259–262.
Lang, P. T. (2006) 'Stalker on location'. In K. A. Franck and Q. Stevens (eds), *Loose Space: Possibility and diversity in urban space*. New York: Routledge.
Linde Bjur, G. and Bjur, H. (2015) *Rom: arkitektur och stad*. 1. uppl. Stockholm: Balkong.
Manacorda, G. (2001) 'The university system'. *Urbanistica*, (116) 228–229.
Marroni, U. (2017) *Roma. La rigenerazione dei quartieri industriali. Il Progetto urbano Ostiense-Marconi*. Roma: Ponte Sisto.
Membretti, A. (2007) 'Centro Sociale Leoncavallo: Building citizenship as an innovative service'. *European Urban and Regional Studies*, 14 (3), 252–63.
Menichini, F. (1986) Il Mattatoio e il Campo Boario'. In L. Caruso (ed.), *Testaccio: Progetto per la trasformazione di un quartiere*. Rome: Fratelli Palombi Editori.
Murgia, M. and Salanitro, C. (1986) 'I "Prati del Popolo Romano"'. In L. Caruso (ed.), *Testaccio: Progetto per la trasformazione di un quartiere*. Rome: Fratelli Palombi Editori.
Neri, M. L., Parisella, A. and Racheli, A. M. (2000) *Industria e città. I luoghi della produzione fra archeologia e recupero*. Series: Roma Moderna Contemporanea VIII (1–2). Roma: CROMA.
Nicolini, R. (1976) 'L'esempio del Mattatoio: Il riuso della "chang città industriale" a servizio della città'. In L. Borroni and Giorgi V. (eds), *Roma Ovest lungo il Tevere: Per un disegno architettonico di parchi attrezzati e servizi sociali nel settore ovest di Roma lungo il Tevere*. Roma: Bulzoni Editore.
Nyström, M. (2015) *The Creative Industry. Regenerating industrial heritage in Rome*. MA thesis. Gothenburg: University of Gothenburg, Department of Conservation.
Olshammar, G. (2002) *Det permanentade provisoriet: Ett återanvänt industriområde i väntan på rivning eller erkännande*. Diss. Gothenburg: Chalmers.
Ottolenghi, M. and A. L. Palazzo (1997) 'Three universities in search of actors: A capital city case'. In H. Van der Wusten (ed.), *The Urban University and Its Identity: Roots, locations, roles*. Amsterdam: Kluwer Academic Publishers, 87–98.

Palazzo, A. L. (2017) 'Culture-Led Regeneration in Rome: From the factory city to the knowledge city'. *International Studies: Interdisciplinary political and cultural journal*, 19 (1), 13–27.

Perego, F. (1993) *Monumenti Differiti: Il Mattatoio di Testaccio a Rome.* Rome: CLEAR.

Pistone, S. (2007) 'Il Campo boario'. In E. Torelli Landini (ed.), *Roma: Memorie della Città Industriale. Storia e riuso di fabbriche e servizi nei primi quartieri produttivi.* Roma: Palombi Editori.

Portoghesi, P. (1983) 'Ecco la Città della Scienza'. *Roma – la Repubblica,* 24 August 1983.

Portoghesi, P. (1986) 'Progetto per la 'Città della Scienza e della Tecnica'. In L. Caruso (ed.), *Testaccio: Progetto per la trasformazione di un quartiere.* Rome. Fratelli Palombi Editori.

Rabazo, M. (2018) *Tra Infrastrutture e Città: Spazi Persi e Luoghi d'Opportunità nella Scala Intermedia del Paesaggio, Il Caso Studio del Progetto Urbano Ostiense-Marconi.* Diss. Roma: Università Degli Studi Roma Tre.

Raggi, G. (2017) 'Ex Mattatoio'. In U. Marroni (ed.), *Roma. La rigernerazione dei quartieri industriali. Il Progetto Urbano Ostiense-Marconi.* Roma: Ponte Sisto.

Ranaldi, I. (2012) *Testaccio: Da quartiere operaio a village della capitale.* Milano: Franco Angeli.

Ranaldi, I. (2014) *Gentrification in Parallelo: Quartieri tra Roma e New York.* Rome: Aracne Editrice.

Ricci, P. (2001) 'The Ostiense-Marconi urban project'. *Urbanistica,* (116).

Rossi, S. (2007) 'Il Mattatoio comunale a Testaccio'. In E. Torelli Landini (ed.), *Roma: Memorie della Città Industriale. Storia e riuso di fabbriche e servizi nei primi quartieri produttivi.* Roma: Palombi Editori.

Stalker (n.d.) 'Manifesto: Stalker Trought (sic!) the Actual Territories'. Accessed 30 March 2015. http://digilander.libero.it/stalkerlab/tarkowsky/manifesto/manifesting.htm.

Università degli Studi Roma Tre (2004) *Piano di assetto per l'attuazione del progetto urbano Ostiense-Marconi.* Roma: Kappa.

Urbanistica (2001), (biannual journal from Istituto Nazionale di Urbanistica, Italy) issue 116, 288 pages.

11
Heritage from a neighbourhood perspective: reflections from the American University of Beirut

Cynthia Myntti and Mona El Hallak

Introduction

Cities everywhere face the challenge of managing change in a way that benefits those who live and work within their boundaries while at the same time creating and publicising their comparative advantage to attract capital through investment and spending. With the ostensible purpose of improving the quality of life for urban dwellers and workers, city leaders often designate rundown historic neighbourhoods as sites for regeneration – that is, for improved housing, commercial and cultural amenities, green and blue spaces, and infrastructure, especially enhanced transport links. In recent decades, city leaders have recognised that comparative advantage can be rooted in a unique historic event, stunning natural beauty or an attractive built environment. The temptation to monetise this comparative advantage is great, and to use regeneration as the driving force. The case of Istanbul, for example, reveals a story repeated in many places: government-designated 'urban regeneration sites' become part of a municipal strategy to use upgraded historic neighbourhoods as catalysts for economic competitiveness and city marketing campaigns (Ercan, 2010). As Pendelbury and Porphyriou point out (2017: 429) the instrumental use of architectural heritage preservation in regeneration and city marketing is now a global phenomenon.

The marketing and investment imperatives are even stronger when a city is recovering from what has been termed 'urbicide', the destruction of an urban environment due to conflict (Badescu, 2017: 17). Beirut offers a complex case in point. Much of the city's historic centre was destroyed during the country's civil war (1975–1990), and its reconstruction in the 1990s was described as 'perhaps the most important undertaking in urban regeneration in the world today' (Gavin, 1998: 217). And yet for the rest of Beirut – outside the city centre – which also suffered damage and neglect during the war, government-led regeneration was almost totally absent. Public authorities did not articulate an urban design strategy or revised master plan to guide and regulate post-war development (Nasr and Verdeil, 2008: 13), nor did parliament enact legislation to define and protect the country's architectural heritage, or any other type of national heritage. In this context, more heritage buildings and sites may have been destroyed by profit-seeking real estate developers since the war than by the various parties to the conflict during the war itself.

This chapter focuses on a district of Beirut outside the city centre, one more typical of the city's post-war experience with heritage and urban development. The neighbourhood is Ras Beirut, the area of the city surrounding the American University of Beirut (AUB). AUB is the largest employer and most significant educational and cultural institution in Beirut, with a walled 25-hectare campus containing diverse architecture, stunning flora and fauna, and views of the Mediterranean. As a property-rich institution with expanding academic ambitions, the university faces complex choices between heritage and development inside and outside its walls. But as an institution that has existed in that part of Beirut since 1866, it is – in many ways – of the place. The chapter describes the work of one of the university's community outreach programmes, the Neighborhood Initiative, which takes a broad view of heritage and starts with the experiences of ordinary people.

Our context: history and heritage[1] in Beirut

Beirut, with an estimated current population of about 2.2 million, is an Eastern Mediterranean port city that has been settled since antiquity and occupied by history's conquering civilisations, among them the Phoenicians, Greeks, Romans, Persians, Byzantines, Mamluk Arabs, Crusaders, Ottoman Turks and the French. The architectural historian Nasser Rabat refers to the visible, tangible relics of the past conquerors as corporeal anchors tying contemporary Beirut to its rich and varied history (Rabat, 1998: 21).

The history of modern Beirut, and shape of its urban heritage, may be divided into five different periods (Yassin, 2012). Each of these periods is summarised here.

Ottoman heritage: 1850–1920

During this period, Beirut, as a small port city in the Ottoman province of Syria, benefited from Turkish investments in urban infrastructure. The port was expanded, roads built, other urban infrastructural developments made. By the early twentieth century, Beirut was electrified and had a private water system, tramway and postal system. Beirut benefitted from new sea trade routes to Europe, which enabled the export of its main cash crop, silk. During this time, Beirut expanded beyond its medieval walls, ringed by suburban zones with villas set in gardens. The city was transformed into a prominent cosmopolitan trading city, and Christian missionaries established a number of foreign schools and universities, including the Syrian Protestant College (since 1920, the American University of Beirut) and the Jesuit-run St Joseph University, the former on a hill in Ras Beirut to the west of the city centre and the latter on a hill in Achrafieh to the east of the centre.

When the missionaries founded AUB, they established a campus far outside the medieval city walls, on hills overlooking the Mediterranean Sea. Over the years, the city expanded, and a new district grew up around the university. The district attracted diverse residents (students and professors from all of Lebanon's sects and classes, the countries of the region and beyond) and businesses to serve them (Abunnasr, 2018: 3–4).

French colonial heritage: 1920–58

With the defeat of Turkey's allies in the First World War, the victors France and Britain divided up the Levant. France came to control an area that became Syria and Lebanon. The French continued with Beirut's modernisation, demolishing much of its walled medieval city to create a modern commercial district with wide radiating avenues named after French and British generals: Foch, Weygand and Allenby. The French put their stamp on the city's architectural heritage and urban design of the period. The city continued to grow, particularly with the arrival from Turkey of Armenian refugees in the 1920s and hundreds of thousands of Palestinian refugees in 1948.

The area around AUB developed and densified in this period. Urban villas in gardens gave way to low-rise apartment buildings, and businesses catered to the 'college town' residents: book shops, gathering places such as the famed Fayssal's Restaurant and family-owned shops providing for the needs of daily life.

Modern heritage: 1958–75

During this period, Beirut developed into an influential city for banking, services, higher education and medical care, with strong cultural and commercial ties in the Middle East and North Africa, and beyond to Europe, Africa and South Asia. The city's population exploded, with migrants from the countryside settling into poor-quality housing in poorly-served suburbs and alongside Palestinian refugee camps surrounding the capital.

Ras Beirut continued to densify, with modernist eight-storey buildings adding to the architectural fabric of the neighbourhood. These buildings typically had retail, commercial and dining or cultural spaces on their ground floors, with residential units above. Hamra Street, the neighbourhood's preeminent commercial street, became a glamorous destination due to its cosmopolitan cinemas, pavement cafés and boutiques.

Violent urbanisation and civil war: 1975–90

The tensions between the haves and the have-nots, leftist Arab-nationalist and right-wing pro-European groups, Muslims and Christians, Palestinians and Lebanese erupted into a long and violent civil war in spring 1975. The civil war divided Beirut into enclaves controlled by an ever-changing array of militias, but generally Christian East Beirut and Muslim West Beirut. A no man's land, the Green Line, running right through the heart of central Beirut, separated them. Sectarian territorialisation became Beirut's spatial reality (Nasr, 2003). Intensified inter-communal fighting, the intervention by Syria and the Israeli invasion of 1982 had left Lebanon, by the late 1980s, a shattered, tired country. Estimates vary, but range from 90,000–150,000 dead, 20,000 disappeared, 100,000 badly injured and 800,000 displaced (Haugbolle, 2011: 2).

No Beirut neighbourhood was spared from the violence, but the worst hit was the city centre. Ras Beirut suffered physical damage from the score-settling of competing militias and the bombardment from the sea by the Israelis in 1982. Many residents fled and refugees from other parts of the country squatted in vacant properties where they could feel safe.

Global glitz and the post-war urban reconstruction: 1991–2019

The peace that was agreed in Taif, Saudi Arabia, in 1990 established new power-sharing arrangements and explicitly looked forward, not backward to the causes of the war. As Yassin notes (2012: 71), 'the reconstruction plan was hugely influenced by the neoliberal peace model that assumed economic growth and recreating linkages to the liberal world system would sustain peace and bring prosperity'. Political leaders were eager to show the world that Lebanon was back in business. Rebuilding the shattered central district of Beirut became the symbol of the country's rebirth, and the grander and more glamorous the better. This meant creating a *tabula rasa*, following bulldozers in full force. A full 80 per cent of buildings downtown were designated damaged beyond repair (Makdisi, 1997: 674). The motto of rebuilding the city became 'Beirut: ancient city of the future'. Initial plans envisioned a futuristic high-rise landscape with monumental buildings and axes to the sea.

A public outcry against these plans, which were almost unanimously denounced as outrageous, forced changes to the overall design (Makdisi, 1997: 670). The new masterplan for downtown limited high-rise buildings to one corner of the downtown, and otherwise relied on low- and middle-rise sandstone buildings in the Franco-Ottoman style, popular in the so-called golden age of Beirut immediately preceding the war (Kassir, 2003: 634). But as Aseel Sawalha notes in her book *Reconstructing Beirut: Memory and space in a postwar Arab city* (2010: 29), 'although Solidere [the Lebanese company in charge of planning and redeveloping Beirut's Central District] expressed interest in preserving Beirut's heritage in its promotional literature, opponents criticized its plans for considering only physical appearance and future revenue and for ignoring the social aspects of reconstruction, public interests and needs, residents' diverse historical pasts and their memories of intimate urban places'. Indeed, architects, intellectuals, writers and activists judged the new designs harshly: a mirage (Salam, 1998: 132); a place where 'fakeness and exclusion' is the prevailing notion (Ragab, 2011: 111–12); elegant but historically ersatz structures, a projected fantasy; a Beirut that literally never was, a sanitised and safe vision of a happy, prosperous past (Fricke, 2005: 171, 173); an identikit regeneration scheme drawing on a sanitised version of localism (Nagle, 2017: 149); a visual pastiche of traditional forms, presented as pure appearance, pure surface and hardwired to the global circuits of transnational capital (Makdisi, 1997: 704); stylised conservation but amnesiac (Kassir, 2003: 635).

The deficiencies in the plans for reconstructing the city centre reveal a deeper problem: the role of capital in rebuilding the Beirut city centre. In its eagerness to signal its return to its pre-war status as the premier financial hub of the Middle East, the government and parliament authorised Solidere, a private company, to expropriate property, draw up a masterplan and commission demolition, refurbishment and new building. The billionaire Lebanese Prime Minister, Rafik Hariri, and his political allies introduced the legislation to create Solidere, a company he partially owned; this conflict of interest was noted by many critics of the company (Charlesworth, 2006: 71; Haugbolle, 2005; Larkin, 2010). External investors, mainly from the Arabian Gulf, underwrote Solidere. Despite its assurances about creating a neutral zone for mixing among civil war rivals (Kabbani, 1998), Solidere's main objective was to create attractive spaces for global investment and profit. Its demolitions and new construction displaced pre-war commercial and residential tenants and, with them, the memory of the social uses of the space. This is precisely what a group of local architects warned against in a forward-looking plan developed in the early years of the war, recommending instead maintaining the existing urban fabric whenever possible, maintaining original property tenure and encouraging previous businesses and residents to return (Salam, 1998: 130). Or, as the influential Lebanese architect Jad Tabet advised, reconstruction should 'create places that establish relationships and encourage sociation and conviviality' (Tabet, 1993).

Through its city marketing campaign and its regeneration tailored to global investment, Solidere became an internationally recognised brand, and Beirut's city centre its star project. The rest of Beirut faced a more chaotic and unplanned situation, one also following the neoliberal logic and dominated by private real estate interests with little regard for protecting the city's heritage or healing the wounds of war. Indeed, the spatial transformations of Beirut have been shaped by the interconnections among the political and economic elites, particularly those in banking and construction (Marot, 2018a; Tonkiss, 2018). Real estate-led development unfolded mainly through demolition and new construction, with internationally renowned architects adding cachet to speculative luxury towers (Marot, 2018b: 351–2). The new high-end construction was most intensely concentrated on the most valuable parcels of land, those with views of the Mediterranean or the city's rare green spaces.

In Ras Beirut, recent decades have witnessed luxury towers replacing low- and middle-rise buildings on land with views of the sea and the AUB campus. As in other parts of the city, some of those demolished were unique heritage buildings, left vulnerable in the absence of any heritage protection laws. Viewless buildings, often in block interiors and hidden from street view, persist in a decaying state.

The neighbourhood remains one of the city's most diverse in every sense: sect, class and nationality in particular. In a recent study conducted by Larkin among young Beirutis, they observed that Ras Beirut and its commercial heart, Hamra, are the opposite of Solidere with a unique urban subculture: unplanned, authentic, mixed (Larkin, 2010: 432–3). Described in the 1960s as a predominantly middleclass neighbourhood (Khalaf and Kongstad, 1973), a recent survey (Kaddour, Myntti, Salti, Abdulrahim, Wick and Zurayk, 2018) found evidence of an increasing gap between the rich and poor residents of the neighbourhood, with the wealthiest living high-security lives in the newly constructed high-end residential towers and the poorest living in crowded, poor-quality buildings nearby. Many are older people living in older, rundown dwellings with tenuous rental contracts thanks to the recent legislation removing protections for long-term tenants (Public Works Studio, 2018). Many are foreign labourers, Syrian workers and Syrian families who have fled their own civil war next door, living in precarious conditions in dilapidated apartment buildings or unrenovated commercial buildings. As Khechen recently observed, vulnerability has many faces in Ras Beirut (Khechen, 2018).

AUB: an anchor in Ras Beirut since the 1860s

Founded by American Protestant missionaries in 1866 as the Syrian Protestant College, AUB epitomised the prevailing view of the place of higher learning as a 'city on a hill', but it was never conceived of as an ivory tower, remote and disengaged from its surroundings. Since its earliest days, university leaders stressed their broad social responsibility and the requirement of community service (Myntti, Zurayk and Mabsout, 2009). Although an 'American' institution following the American model of liberal education, AUB's 150-year longevity in Ras Beirut – its well-regarded hospital, tens of thousands of loyal alumni, admired faculty that have served the Arab world as progressive public intellectuals since the early twentieth century – has made it a respected, 'almost local' institution.

In the years prior to the civil war, town and gown were inter-connected, with most university employees and students living nearby and famous meeting places for professors, poets and revolutionaries in nearby streets. The civil war cut short this golden era. AUB remained open and educating students throughout the war, but university faculty, staff and students suffered like other residents of the city. A university president was kidnapped, another assassinated, faculty were taken hostage and the main administration building was destroyed by a car bomb. These horrific events turned the university inward, and it lost many of its connections to the neighbourhood.

The Neighborhood Initiative was launched in 2007 to reknit those connections and encourage AUB faculty and students to contribute in practical ways to solving the problems of the city district just outside the campus walls. The Neighborhood Initiative became a special project of the university president and was placed administratively in his office. Working across the university's administrative and academic divisions, the Neighborhood Initiative is the university's main office for outreach to the people, businesses and institutions of Ras Beirut. The Neighborhood Initiative's main roles are connecting, catalysing and facilitating projects to address neighbourhood issues – heritage preservation among many others – capitalising upon the university's assets.

Compared to well-known university–neighbourhood initiatives in North America, and indeed the European institutions represented in this volume, AUB's engagement with its neighbourhood is modest in terms of budget (Perry and Wiewel, 2005; Rodin, 2007; Haar, 2010). (The university currently supports the salaries of two full-time staff, and private foundations and donors support its projects, often with in-kind contributions.) AUB's neighbourhood engagement has not been dictated by the need for major expansion, or to mobilise significant resources to acquire land and real estate to make that expansion possible. Nor was there an urgent need to intervene in the urban fabric to improve neighbourhood safety for members of the university community, as so eloquently described by Judith Rodin for the University of Pennsylvania. Ras Beirut bears scars of the civil war but it is not an unsafe place, surprising as that may seem.

Despite its modest budget, the Neighborhood Initiative's significance lies in its uniqueness in Beirut; it is a rare, private institutional effort to address the many problems confronting the city's urban neighbourhoods in absence of any public interventions beyond basic infrastructural maintenance. The Neighborhood Initiative emerged out of the AUB's best values in social responsibility, but the university, like any complex property-rich institution, has many conflicting needs and aspirations. This is particularly true when it comes to architectural heritage. AUB's impressive walled campus is known for its stunning landscape and architecture, but to accommodate academic and residential needs the university has demolished one modern heritage apartment building, and plans to demolish an old house, which while not of a unique architectural value, is one of the last remaining in the neighbourhood. The Neighborhood Initiative has played an advocacy role for architectural preservation with the university administration, but not always successfully. More, however, will be said below about the Neighborhood Initiative's more successful current efforts with other types of heritage preservation.

The earliest Neighborhood Initiative projects fell under three themes: 'urban environment', 'community and wellbeing' and 'protecting Ras Beirut diversity', none explicitly focused on heritage.

Under the 'urban environment' theme, the Neighborhood Initiative and its partners inside and outside AUB conducted research and then intervened to improve the physical environment surrounding the campus. Among the projects supported were: the Neighborhood Congestion Studies, led by the Civil Engineering faculty and students in consultation with a variety of stakeholder groups to analyse traffic congestion and develop solutions (Aoun, Abou-Zeid, Kaysi and Myntti, 2013; Al-Ayyash, Abou-Zeid and Kaysi, 2016); the Jeanne d'Arc[2] Rehabilitation Project, using a participatory design process to create a model pedestrian-friendly street for Beirut in collaboration with the Beirut Municipality (Myntti and Mabsout, 2014; Said, Geha and Abou-Zeid, 2020); Silence in the City, a final example, addressing the serious problem of noise. An interdisciplinary group of faculty conducted research, policy advocacy and consciousness-raising (Sawt wa Samt, 2014) and provided technical assistance for sound measurement to neighbours fighting noise from local bars and restaurants.

Under the 'community and wellbeing' theme, the initiative has supported research on the growing gap between rich and poor in Ras Beirut. The 'Ras Beirut Wellbeing Survey' (Kaddour, Myntti, Salti, Abdulrahim, Wick and Zurayk, 2018) documents the health and demographic composition of Ras Beirut and the conditions affecting wellbeing. A follow-up study is being conducted in collaboration with the Institute for Global Prosperity, UCL. The Neighborhood Initiative also launched a major outreach project addressing the wellbeing of older adults in the neighbourhood. The University for Seniors (UfS), created in collaboration with a faculty member from public health and with extensive input from older residents, is a volunteer-run lifelong learning programme that responds to their aspirations to remain intellectually challenged and socially engaged (Hachem and Vuopala, 2016). The UfS regularly offers courses in memoir-writing and the archiving of family photographs and documents.

Work under the 'protecting Ras Beirut diversity' theme responds to the economic changes that are transforming the neighbourhood from a mixed socioeconomic district to one with new development focused on new construction of luxury residential buildings, chain stores and restaurants. One of the biggest threats to the overall wellbeing of AUB students, employees and urban residents more generally is the high cost of housing close to the university, especially as older, affordable buildings are demolished – with no heritage laws to protect them – to make way for more profitable high-rise developments. The Neighborhood Initiative continues to play an internal advocacy role at AUB, to encourage university action on affordable housing in Ras Beirut, and has supported research and an international conference on gentrification.

How heritage features in the work of the AUB Neighborhood Initiative

Since 2017 and a transition in the university presidency and in the leadership of the Neighborhood Initiative itself, heritage has become a more prominent programmatic theme of the Neighborhood Initiative. The Neighborhood Initiative's activities offer a clear contrast to Solidere's instrumental use of architectural heritage for boosting the city's international reputation and marketing luxury real estate in the Beirut city centre. The Neighborhood Initiative approaches heritage by providing visibility to what matters to ordinary people on matters of collective memory, and the social use of space. Its projects bring diverse neighbours together to recognise, remember and celebrate shared experiences. Collaborating with designers, developers, local schools, non-governmental organisations (NGOs), the Beirut Municipality and related ministries, and other institutions, projects seek to reconnect the diverse residents and users of the neighbourhood to its Ras Beirut heritage through well-publicised research and tactical urban interventions, events and performances. Through classwork, workshops and guided visits for the AUB community, the Neighborhood Initiative promotes a comprehensive understanding of heritage and what can be done to protect it.

The Neighborhood Initiative's engagement with Ras Beirut heritage has three dimensions: architectural, landscape and intangible sociocultural.

Since 2008, the Neighborhood Initiative has embarked upon a low-key strategy of internal advocacy with the university's administration and trustees to consider different ways of creating more affordable housing for faculty and students in the neighbourhood. Each idea considered addresses the double challenge of tackling the affordable housing shortage and preserving the architectural heritage of the neighbourhood – urban villas, low-rise walk-up apartment buildings, and mid-rise mixed-use modernist apartment buildings (Blaik, 2008). Several ideas have been discussed. One is the use of modest resources to acquire individual apartments in modernist mid-twentieth-century buildings – buildings at risk of demolition. Through the purchase of these apartments, the university would become a member of the buildings' 'owners' committees and have a voice in future plans to maintain and renovate the properties. This would also indirectly protect the diverse social composition of these buildings, which would be lost if demolished and replaced by luxury towers. Another idea, beginning with older alumni living in the neighbourhood, is a programme to offer *rente viagere* for select dwellings near the university. This practice, used especially in France, offers a life annuity to the owner of a residential property in exchange for transfer of ownership to the annuity-holding institution – in this case AUB – upon their death.

The Neighborhood Initiative continues to advocate with the AUB administration for enhanced staffing and a comprehensive approach to real estate development in the neighbourhood through the elaboration of specific project ideas and workshops with students and local experts in preservation, planning and housing. For example, the Neighborhood Initiative has developed different investment scenarios for the adaptive reuse of modern heritage buildings in Ras Beirut. Given the current political and economic challenges facing Lebanon, this is not currently a top priority of the university administration. The hope is that when the time is right, these ideas may provide a useful starting point for an AUB strategy on housing and architectural preservation in the neighbourhood.

The Neighborhood Initiative recently organised a number of events to draw attention to the architectural and urban heritage of Ras Beirut. Public performances in empty heritage buildings give participants the opportunity to learn about their history, experience their inner spaces and appreciate their unique qualities. For example, as part of the Beirut Design Week 2018, the artistic installation *Recycling a Shell* by the Organisation de Developpement Durable – an NGO promoting sustainable development – transformed the Khalidy House, an iconic but empty villa built in 1932 near AUB, into an experimental musical path celebrating the themes of emptiness, the presence of people and new perspectives on the space (see Figure 11.1).

Because of Ras Beirut's hilly topography, stairs were constructed in the nineteenth century to connect people on foot in the upper areas of the neighbourhood to the Mediterranean Sea below, and they are a unique if under-appreciated feature of the neighbourhood's built environment. To

Figure 11.1 The artistic installation/performance *Recycling a Shell* gave people a chance to visit and experience the Khalidy House, a beautiful deserted 1932 heritage building in the neighbourhood. © AUB Neighborhood Initiative

draw attention to these stairs, the Neighborhood Initiative has sponsored various activities for the public on the stairs, among them a concert, a play and an acoustic installation. The award-winning playwright and actress Hanane Hajj Ali performed her play *Jogging* on the Van Dyck Stairs[3] (see Figure 11.2).

The Van Dyck stairs also hosted *Ode to the Sea*, a collaborative open-air concert, as part of the first 'Week of sound' in Lebanon. *Ode to the Sea* questions the city's relationship to the sea as high-rise developments block sound and sight connections. The Ain Mreisseh stairs feature *Le Souffleur*, a permanent acoustic installation by district d, a collaborative working to improve the socio-spatial quality of life in the city (Figure 11.3). The intervention honours the sounds of the sea, the stories of local fishermen and the adventures of a local collector of maritime memorabilia. Interconnected pipes offer opportunities for children to experiment with sound and transform the stairs into a vertical playground and a vibrant public space.

Ras Beirut landscape offers another dimension to the Neighborhood Initiative's heritage work. When the Syrian Protestant College was established on the rocky headlands of Ras Beirut in the second half of the

Figure 11.2 The Van Dyck Stairs packed with people during the theatrical performance 'Jogging' that brought back to life this almost forgotten part of the neighborhood's urban heritage. © AUB Neighborhood Initiative

nineteenth century, the land was sparsely settled with little vegetation beyond prickly pear hedges. In the intervening century and a half, AUB has introduced on its campus trees and plants common in other parts of the Mediterranean and sub-tropical zones. Many of the trees and plants that were initially cultivated on the AUB campus became part of the landscape of the urban villas and streets of the neighbourhood.

The Neighborhood Initiative activities have sought to educate the public about this overlooked and taken-for-granted piece of neighbourhood heritage. The Neighborhood Initiative has collaborated with a leading local landscape design studio, Greener on the Other Side, and AUBotanic, the university's programme to conserve the living environment of the campus and promote sustainability and ecosystem management. This collaborative project mapped neighbourhood trees, including the olive, orange, fig, mulberry, rubber, laurel, cypress, umbrella pine, palm, magnolia, walnut and frangipani trees, and myrtle, orchid, bougainvillea and jasmine plants, and labelled them with scientific and popular names and QR code links to the AUB trees' database. It also identified the birds nesting in neighbourhood trees, among them

Figure 11.3 The acoustic installation *Le Souffleur* transformed the Ain Mreisseh public stairs into a vertical playground. The sound of the sea, now totally blocked by recent high-rise construction, is transmitted continuously from the fishermen's port nearby. © AUB Neighborhood Initiative

the house sparrow, Palestine sunbird, bulbul, myna, graceful prinia, laughing dove and the Eurasian collared dove. This outreach and public education underlined the importance of the local ecosystem and the responsibility of the neighbourhood in protecting its landscape heritage.

Another landscape heritage activity is the Neighborhood Initiative's support of a grass-roots campaign against the development of Dalieh of Raouche, a wild section of Ras Beirut's rocky Mediterranean coastline that is popular for outings, picnics and kite flying, as well as its fishermen's port, caves, endemic flora and rich underwater life. This activism educates the public about Dalieh as a unique landscape heritage site and includes guided site visits and classroom presentations in the university and local schools. The Dalieh work fits within the wider framework of advocating for the protection of the entire coastal strip of Ras Beirut with its corniche promenade and rock formations as a cultural landscape site.

Perhaps the most overlooked dimension of Ras Beirut's heritage is the intangible sociocultural fabric that makes the neighbourhood special. The establishment of the Syrian Protestant College, and later the AUB,[4] had a profound influence not just on its physical surroundings but its sociocultural surroundings as well. Prior to the civil war, many AUB faculty and staff lived in Ras Beirut. It became known for its tolerance, religious diversity and educated middle-class values, and famous for its bookshops, cafés, cinemas, art galleries and educational institutions (Abunnasr, 2018: 4). The twentieth century witnessed the influx of educated Anglophone Palestinians, especially after 1948, and in subsequent decades political exiles from other Arab states. The early decades of the twenty-first century brought Syrians to the neighbourhood, those with money renting apartments and those with limited resources joining relatives and working for their minimal accommodation. These last decades also brought a new type of neighbour, the almost invisible, often part-time, resident of the new luxury towers. Although these developments have threatened the diversity and harmony for which the neighbourhood was known, Ras Beirut – relative to other Beirut neighbourhoods – remains an open and lively place.

The Neighborhood Initiative's work on this intangible heritage began by giving local people a voice through oral and life history. The Ras Beirut Oral History Project interviewed 80 older neighbours about their memories of life in Ras Beirut before, during and after the civil war. The interview recordings are housed in the AUB archives and form the basis of the book *"We are in this Together": An Oral History of Ras Beirut* (Abunnasr, 2021). Further life history research is planned among local fishermen; fishing along the polluted, over-fished Mediterranean coast is a struggling industry and, for many in the neighbourhood, a threatened way of life. A community museum is proposed to showcase one local fisherman's collection of maritime, antique and underwater heritage objects and document traditional fishing techniques, gear, terminology, mythology and anecdotes.

In general, the Neighborhood Initiative's work on intangible heritage aims to reinforce a sense of community by bringing visibility to shared cultural practices, while making explicit the neighbourhood's diversity, especially in terms of class, nationality and sectarian affiliation. Every Friday, the Neighborhood Initiative co-sponsors the lively *Al Jar Lil Jar*[5] farmers' market, which features fresh and dried fruits, nuts, vegetables and flowers sold by their producers and the sale of traditional homemade dishes such as *freekeh, moghrabieh, carob, halawa, kechek* and *zaatar*, the thyme-sesame mix (see Figure 11.4). Vendors prepare local flatbread specialities, including *mana'ish* and *lahm bi-ajine*, for hungry lunchtime visitors. Small artisans – Lebanese, Syrian and Palestinian – sell handmade products such as soap, jewellery and embroidery.

Figure 11.4 The legendary thyme *mana'ish* at the *Al Jar Lil Jar* farmers' market, held every Friday on Jeanne d'Arc Street, giving people a social gathering space, introducing local producers, farmers and artisans and offering homemade dishes that revive local culinary traditions. © AUB Neighborhood Initiative

Storytelling, a much-loved and remembered traditional form of entertainment, has been reconstituted as regular performances under landmark trees in the neighbourhood, in collaboration with the local publisher and creative media platform Dar Onboz. The *Hakawati*, or storyteller, weaves tales of the neighbourhood and its dwellers in Arabic into a moveable show with music, educational props and movement, to celebrate the language, revive forgotten tales and relate to all constituents of the community (see Figure 11.5).

Through *Public Tawleh* by Ramzi Alieh, the Neighborhood Initiative has created a social space on the pavement for impromptu backgammon games among friends and strangers (see Figure 11.6). In Beirut, playing *tawleh* in public has always been visible but ephemeral, with the players setting up their temporary seats and table only to remove them when their backgammon game is over. The new playing space, proposed as a model to apply elsewhere in the city, uses existing benches on the street to integrate a permanent locally-produced concrete board with a steel base as part of the street furniture to revive this traditional game.

Another project, *Les Salons de Beyrouth*, moves the attention from life in public space to life in private space. A joint architectural and

Figure 11.5 A *Hakawati* storytelling performance by Dar Onboz captures the attention of people of all ages, weaving neighbourhood memories into timeless fairy tales and celebrating our intangible heritage. © AUB Neighborhood Initiative

photographic venture by Sabine Saba and Karim Sakr, it documents the diversity of living rooms in Ras Beirut, reflecting on the great range of social habits and taste through furniture layouts, decoration, objects, flooring and window coverings. An exhibition and publication are planned.

A final example of the Neighborhood Initiative's work in the area of sociocultural heritage is its regular walking tours for new AUB faculty and students, the general public and international groups, to introduce them to some uniquely Ras Beiruti cultural spots, such as the fishermen's port and museum, the rare remaining pigeon trainers' roofs, iconic trees and endangered heritage buildings that have all been mapped on an open source online map to bring visibility to the little that remains of the neighbourhood's heritage.

Summary and conclusions

Critical heritage studies have underscored how the instrumental use of heritage in regeneration has had negative consequences, among them gentrification, deadening, and 'museumification' of cities and city neighbourhoods (Pendlebury and Porphyriou, 2017).

Figure 11.6 A father teaching his son how to play backgammon on the sidewalk in Jeanne d'Arc Street, where a concrete *Public Tawleh* board was installed on the existing benches to revive this traditional game in the public space. © AUB Neighborhood Initiative

In its post-war regeneration of its city centre by Solidere, Beirut has become the global poster child of the instrumental use of heritage by city boosters. As cited above, John Nagle, who has studied regeneration in violently divided cities such as Beirut, Sarajevo, Jerusalem and Belfast, has suggested that sanitised localism and identikit approaches to urban branding and regeneration usually yield a dangerous and temporary neoliberal peace by programming amnesia into urban spaces – never allowing a real reconciliation based on confronting the past (Nagle, 2017: 1–2). Haugbolle (2005: 192–9) has also pointed out the problems of Solidere's top-down, elitist approach, which elevates nostalgia for the pre-war golden age and installs a state-sponsored amnesia. Everyone loses by this approach, even the wealthy investors and political class who expect to benefit. A more just and durable approach is based on dedicated attention to the intimate spaces of culture, which allow people to make sense of the past and the present, in order to construct a different future (Fricke, 2005:163).

This is precisely the approach taken by the Neighborhood Initiative of AUB: emphasising the roles played by what Sawalha calls the 'ordinary practitioners of the city' (Sawalha, 2010: 11, 14) who appropriate, use, live in and, importantly, have memories about specific urban spaces. It is about a social and political conception of heritage and an inclusive approach to development that benefits all who live in and use the neighbourhood. Yes, the neighbourhood should have affordable housing and long-term tenants should have adequate protections from displacement. People do have the right to walk safely and comfortably on neighbourhood pavements and streets. Older adults should have the opportunity to learn and contribute and be sociable. Everyone should have the chance to experience the joys and community of free and open activities in public spaces. Memories should be shared and learned from, possibly even healing the wounds of war. Heritage, then, in the sense practised by AUB in Ras Beirut, fits in those informal, unconscious patterns of 'habitus'.

In Beirut, where leadership on inclusive urban development has not come from – and unfortunately cannot be expected from – government authorities, leadership has to come from other places in society: NGOs, professional organisations and engaged universities among them. Universities, where ideas are debated and examined from many perspectives, promise a comprehensive and nuanced approach to inclusive urban development and heritage protection. Whether the university is intervening as a large-scale real estate developer or with a lighter footprint through research, outreach and advocacy, the explicit focus on the public good, or at least on mutual benefit, is a strong starting point. The potential for cross-disciplinary conversations, based on evidence, is also key. The commitment to participation and inclusion means that different voices are heard, and this is essential. Finally, universities are places of critical thinking and questioning, and whether the topic is heritage, economic development or something else, urban universities are uniquely positioned to help provide the knowledge necessary for wise choices to be made by planners, designers, developers and others who shape the social and built environments of the city.

Notes

1   *Turath* is the Arabic term for heritage, derived from the triliteral root *waritha*, to inherit. In discussions following the civil war, when so many older buildings, streets and gardens were being demolished in the name of reconstruction, the term *turath* was almost always understood by Lebanese architects, planners, writers and activists to mean architectural heritage, because protecting older buildings became an urgent matter. *Turath* can include landscape heritage, archeological heritage, monuments, documents and intangible cultural heritage such as music, cuisine, storytelling and traditional rituals and games.

2   Street names in Beirut represent many influences and inspirations. The streets around AUB are named for university leaders, including Daniel and Howard Bliss, father and son and early presidents of the institution; Bayard Dodge another university president and benefactor; and influential professors Jabr Doumit, Harris Graham, George Post, Na'meh Jafet, Najib Ardati, Mansur Jurdak, Kamal Salibi and Constantine Zurayk (see Abunnasr, 2017). Beirut streets are also named after other influential men: Mahatma Gandhi, John F. Kennedy, AbdelAziz ibn Saud and General Allenby to name several. French names are found all over Beirut. Ras Beirut is graced by two women: Rue Jeanne d'Arc and Rue Madame Marie Curie. Elsewhere, French generals and political figures have streets named after them: Clemenceau, de Gaulle, Gouraud, Weygand.
3   The Van Dyck stairs were named after one of AUB's founding academics, Cornelius Van Dyck. Van Dyck arrived in Beirut in 1840 as a missionary and became Professor of Pathology and Internal Medicine at the Syrian Protestant College when it was founded in 1866. He is best known for translating the Bible from English into Arabic.
4   In 1866, Beirut was part of the Ottoman province of Syria. After the collapse of the Ottoman Empire following the First World War, the Arabic-speaking provinces of the empire were divided between France and Britain, with France taking control of present-day Lebanon and Syria. The boundaries of Lebanon, as separate from Syria, were determined by 1920–1. The Syrian Protestant College became the American University of Beirut in 1920 to reflect these political developments.
5   *Al Jar Lil Jar* is the Neighborhood Initiative's motto, and translated means 'neighbours (look out) for neighbours'.

References

Abunnasr, M. (2017) *46 Streets: AUB's imprint on the streets of Beirut*. Beirut: American University of Beirut, Neighborhood Initiative and Jafet Library Archive and Special Collections.

Abunnasr, M. (2018) *AUB and Ras Beirut in 150 Years of Photographs*. Beirut: American University of Beirut Press.

Abunnasr, M. (2021) *'We Are in this Together': An oral history of Ras Beirut*. Beirut: American University of Beirut Press.

Aoun, A., Abou-Zeid, M., Kaysi, I. and Myntti, C. (2013) 'Reducing parking demand and traffic congestion at the American University of Beirut'. *Transport Policy,* 25, 52–60.

Al-Ayyash, Z., Abou-Zeid, M. and Kaysi, I. (2016) 'Modeling the demand for a shared ride taxi service: An application to an organization-based context'. *Transport Policy,* 48, 169–82.

Badescu, G. (2017) 'Post-war reconstruction in contested cities: Comparing urban outcomes in Beirut and Sarajevo'. In J. Rokem and C. Boano (eds), *Urban Geopolitics: Rethinking planning in contested cities*. Abingdon: Routledge, 17–32.

Blaik, O. (2008) *Neighborhood Preservation and Investment* (Unpublished report to the AUB president).

Charlesworth, E. (2006) *Architects without Frontiers: War, reconstruction and design responsibility*. Oxford: Architectural Press.

Ercan, M. A. (2010) 'Searching for a balance between community needs and conservation policies in historic neighbourhoods of Istanbul'. *European Planning Studies,* 18 (5), 833–59.

Fricke, A. (2005) 'Forever nearing the finish line: Heritage policy and the problem of memory in postwar Beirut'. *International Journal of Cultural Property*, 12, 163–81.

Gavin, A. (1998) 'Heart of Beirut: Making the master plan for the renewal of the Central District'. In P. Rowe and H. Sarkis (eds), *Projecting Beirut: Episodes in the construction and reconstruction of a modern city*. Munich: Prestel, 217–33.

Haar, S. (2010) *The City as Campus: Urbanism and higher education in Chicago*. Minneapolis: University of Minnesota Press.

Hachem, H. and Vuopala, E. (2016) 'Older adults, in Lebanon, committed to learning: Contextualizing the challenges and benefits of their learning experience'. *Educational Gerontology,* 42 (10), 686–97.

Haugbolle, S. (2005) 'Public and private memory of the Lebanese Civil War'. *Comparative Studies of South Asia, Africa and the Middle East,* 25 (1), 191–203.

Haugbolle, S. (2011) 'The historiography and memory of the Lebanese civil war'. *Online Encyclopedia of Mass Violence*. 25 October, 2011 (accessed 17th February 2022) http://bo-k2s.sciences-po.fr/mass-violence-war-massacre-resistance/en/document/historiography-and-memory-lebanese-civil-war

Kabbani, O. (1998) 'Public space as infrastructure: The case of the postwar reconstruction of Beirut'. In P. Rowe and H. Sarkis (eds), *Projecting Beirut: Episodes in the construction and reconstruction of a modern city*. Munich: Prestel, 240–59.

Kaddour, A., Myntti, C., Salti, N., Abdulrahim, S., Wick, L. and Zurayk, H. (2018) *The Profile of a Neighborhood: Health and wellbeing in Ras Beirut*. Beirut: American University of Beirut Press.

Kassir, S. (2003) *Histoire de Beyrouth*. Paris: Fayard.

Khalaf, S. and Kongstad, P. (1973) *Hamra of Beirut: A case of rapid urbanization*. Leiden: E. J Brill.

Khechen, M. (2018) 'The remaking of Ras Beirut: Displacement beyond gentrification'. *City*, 22 (3), 375–95.

Larkin, C. (2010) 'Remaking Beirut: Contesting memory, space, and the urban imaginary of Lebanese youth'. *City and Community*, 9 (4), 414–42.

Makdisi, S. (1997) 'Laying claim to Beirut: Urban narrative and spatial identity in the age of Solidere'. *Critical Inquiry*, 23 (3), 660–705.

Marot, B. (2018a) 'Growth politics from the top down: The social construction of the property market in post-war Beirut'. *City*, 22 (3), 324–40.

Marot, B. (2018b) 'Developing post-war Beirut (1990–2016): The political economy of "pegged urbanization"'. PhD dissertation, School of Urban Planning, McGill University.

Myntti, C. and Mabsout, M. (2014) 'Improving walkability in Beirut: Lessons from the Jeanne d'Arc Street case.' *Sustainable Transport – Policy Brief #6*, Issam Fares Institute for Public Policy and International Affairs, American University of Beirut.

Myntti, C., Zurayk, R. and Mabsout, M. (2009) *Beyond the Walls: AUB engages its communities*. Cairo: American University in Cairo Gerhart Center Working Paper.

Nagle, J. (2017) 'Ghosts, memory, and the right to the divided city: Resisting amnesia in the Beirut City Centre.' *Antipode*, 49 (1), 149–68.

Nasr, J. and Verdeil, E. (2008) 'The reconstructions of Beirut'. In S. Jayyusi, R. Holod, A. Petruccioli and A. Raymond (eds), *The City in the Islamic World*. Leiden: Brill, 1121–48.

Nasr, S. (2003) 'The new social map'. In T. Hanf and N. Salam (eds), *Lebanon in Limbo: Postwar society and state in an uncertain regional environment*. Baden-Baden: Nomos Publishers, 143–58.

Pendlebury, J. and Porfyriou, H. (2017) 'Heritage, urban regeneration, and place-making'. *Journal of Urban Design*, 22 (4), 429–32.

Perry, D. and Wiewel, W. (2005) 'From campus to city: The university as developer.' In D. Perry and W. Wiewel (eds), *The University as Urban Developer: Case studies and analysis*. London: ME Sharpe, 3–21.

Public Works Studio (2018) *Narrating Ras Beirut through its Tenants' Stories*. Unpublished report, Neighborhood Initiative, American University of Beirut (in Arabic).

Rabat, N. (1998) 'The interplay of history and archeology in Beirut'. In P. Rowe and H. Sarkis (eds), *Projecting Beirut: Episodes in the construction and reconstruction of a modern city*. Munich: Prestel, 19–22.

Ragab, T. (2011) 'The crisis of cultural identity in rehabilitating historic Beirut-downtown'. *Cities*, 28, 107–14.

Rodin, J. (2007) *The University and Urban Revival: Out of the ivory tower and into the streets*. Philadelphia: University of Pennsylvania Press.

Said, M., Geha G. and Abou-Zeid, M. (2020) 'A natural experiment to assess the impacts of street-level urban design interventions on walkability and business activity'. *Transportation Research Record*, 258–71. https://doi.org/10.1177/0361198120921849.

Salam, A. (1998) 'The role of the government in shaping the built environment'. In P. Rowe and H. Sarkis (eds), *Projecting Beirut: Episodes in the construction and reconstruction of a modern city*. Munich: Prestel, 122–33.

Sawalha, A. (2010) *Reconstructing Beirut: Memory and space in a postwar Arab city*. Austin: University of Texas Press.

Sawt wa Samt (2014) 'Sawt wa Samt: The AUB noise and silence research group'. *Jadaliyya*, 26 February.

Tabet, J.(1993) 'Towards a master plan for post-war Lebanon.' In S. Khalaf and P. Khoury (eds), *Recovering Beirut: Urban design and post-war reconstruction*. Leiden: E. J. Brill, 81–100.

Tonkiss, F. (2018) 'Other gentrifications: Law, capital and spatial politics in Beirut'. *City*, 22 (3), 321–23.

Yassin, N. (2012) 'City profile: Beirut'. *Cities*, 29, 64–73.

12
From Red São Paulo to Brazilian neofascism: urban, political and cultural heritage in the making of a public university

Pedro Fiori Arantes

> *In memory of Father Ticão and Rodrigo Reis, leaders of the people of the East Side of São Paulo.*

Introduction: from an elitist medical school to a plural and democratic university

This chapter explores the interplay of urban politics, grassroots social movements and university development in São Paulo, the biggest metropolis in the Southern Hemisphere, through the expansion of the Federal University of São Paulo (Unifesp) across the city since the 2000s. It examines the transformation of the university's historic and symbolic identity, embedded in material and institutional heritage, from its origins as a traditional and elitist medical school in the heart of the city, to the recent creation of six new campus sites, multiplying the number of undergraduates by 10 and adopting a strong affirmative and inclusive access policy (Unifesp, 2019). It highlights the importance of the 'worker's university' model, conceived by Paulo Freire, as an inherited cultural asset that informed the expansion and democratic transition of Unifesp into a more plural, radical, multi-ethnic and decolonial institution – now partially blocked by the rise of a far-right government with neofascist features.

The expansion allowed Unifesp to reach other places, subjects and narratives of hybrid, non-white Brazilian identity, discourse and practice. The urban context of the new campuses, in working-class towns or neighbourhoods with an industrial heritage, changed the architectural and symbolic identity of the university's buildings, and stimulated the development of new programmes, a more diverse student body and strong outreach practices, some of them inspired by Paulo Freire's pedagogy of liberation and vision of what Brazil might be (Freire, 1967, 1970), challenging the hegemony of colonial and elitist narratives of national identity.

São Paulo itself provided a critical urban context for this evolution. In the late 1970s, the city saw the emergence of new political actors who pressed for an end to the Brazilian dictatorship and for living conditions worthy of human existence. In the largest industrial and financial metropolis in Brazil, the main hub of global capitalism in South America, São Paulo's 'otherness' was also born: a strong organised working class, in unions and in grassroots and civil rights social movements (Moisés, 1982; Brant and Singer, 1982; Sader, 1988), from which emerged the steelworker and union leader Lula da Silva, who was to become the first working-class president of Brazil (2003–10). Neighbourhood movements were also born, associated with the struggle for the 'right to the city' (Lefebvre, 1968), fighting to achieve an 'insurgent citizenship' (Holston, 2008) and supported by the progressive Catholic Church that emerged in 1970s Latin America from the 'liberation theology' grassroots communities (Brant and Singer, 1982; Sader, 1988).

São Paulo's 'East End', with a population of three million people in the 1980s, was one of the main melting pots from which new proposals for housing, health, education, transport and human rights emerged in Brazil, some of them giving rise to significant national public policies.[1] In this 'metropolis in movement', the Partido dos Trabalhadores (Workers' Party) was born in 1980. It led campaigns against the dictatorship which resulted in the election of Luiza Erundina as the first mayor of São Paulo (1989–92) – the first woman and member of the Workers' Party to hold that post in the city's 450-year-old history. Paulo Freire was her Secretary of Education, and other progressive university professors occupied other secretariats. These included, among others, the philosopher Marilena Chauí (Culture), who created Casas de Cultura to foster popular identities and traditions in the peripheries, inspired by Mário de Andrade's pioneering proposals of immaterial and symbolic culture in the 1930s, as well as the urban planning professor Ermínia Maricato, who carried out pioneering policies in favela upgrading and mutual aid housing cooperatives (Singer, 1996; Patarra, 1996; Maricato, 1996). During this time, from the late 1970s to the end of Erundina's mayoralty (1989–92), the city was referred to as 'Red São Paulo', in an allusion to its anti-fascist and left-wing politics (Arantes, 2018).

This chapter focuses particularly on the case of Unifesp's newest campus development site located in São Paulo's East End, and its Cities Institute as an institutional and spatial initiative that engages the strong participation of social movements, Freire's political and pedagogical model of the 'worker's university' from the 1980s, the heritage of São Paulo's working class in that area (with a long tradition of socialists and mutual-aid organisations, grassroots communities and a progressive Catholic Church) and the experimental approaches established by professionals and university faculty members working with them. It analyses the historical socio-political context for this initiative, and the way in which an important place in the memory of local workers – at a former steel factory where more than three thousand people worked – is being transformed and used as a site for new kinds of production: learning and knowledge seeking solutions to reduce inequality and foster urban justice through immaterial, environmental and built heritage in São Paulo's urban periphery. Finally, it considers the impact of the rise of reactionary forces with neoliberal and proto-fascist features (Ab'Saber, 2018), which have targeted public universities, such as Unifesp, due to the changes in the profile of students over the last 15 years (Arantes, 2021), and the emergence of new critical, informed and active subjects demanding transformations in Brazilian society, heritage and identity, which frighten established power and its order.

Unifesp's urban history: from the centre to the edges

Unifesp was founded in 1933 as an important private medical school (Escola Paulista de Medicina), created by the elite, so-called 'coffee barons' (see Figure 12.1). The institution was nationalised and attendance made free of charge in 1956, and in the 2000s leading medicine professors decided to broaden its fields of knowledge and develop new campuses, representing the largest and most spectacular national expansion of Brazilian public universities (Nemi, 2008; Gallian, Minhoto and Nemi, 2020).

At the time of the medical school's foundation, São Paulo had ceased to be merely the capital of the coffee export economy and instead had become one of Brazil's largest metropolises and a powerhouse for industry and finance – as well as home to an organised working class, with strong unions and grassroots social movements fighting for better

Figure 12.1a and 12.1b Paulista School of Medicine in the 1940s. This first townhouse that housed the medical school, which still exists today as its historic headquarters, became the basis for the new university logo. Reproduced with the permission of Federal University of São Paulo, CEFHI collection

living and working conditions (Porta, 2004). Like New York, the city was transformed by the in-migration of liberal professionals, workers and peasants from Europe, Asia and the Middle East and other parts of Brazil between 1900 and 1940. These migratory flows stimulated a very active and vibrant economy, a cosmopolitan and progressive culture and a high-level medical and health practice geared to caring for the middle and upper classes, with private hospitals led by immigrant communities (Portuguese, Syrian-Lebanese, Jewish, German, and so on). By contrast, the working class was afflicted by epidemics, untreated diseases and low life expectancy (Rolnik, 1997; Porta 2004; Nemi, 2008).

The medical school and its hospital (1940) were established in the Vila Clementino neighbourhood (Massarolo, 1971), which became one of the city's central areas when in 1954, in celebration of the 400 years of the city, the famous Ibirapuera Park was opened nearby, designed by Oscar Niemeyer (Alambert Jr., 2016). Vila Clementino grew around the medical school, and new buildings for research, teaching, health assistance and services gradually replaced the rows of old townhouses.

São Paulo, with 22 million inhabitants, has a concentration of wealthy neighbourhoods in its central or central-southwest region, between Paulista Avenue and the Pinheiros River, with Ibirapuera Park as its symbolic heart (or lung). It is surrounded by valued garden-city neighbourhoods, designed by the English architect and urban planner Richard Barry Parker (Wolff, 2001) and characterised by mansions and buildings with spectacular views. All the main public and private universities are close to this area, including not only the School of Medicine, but also the University of São Paulo (USP) (the best Latin American University, run by the state province). By contrast, the industrial and workers' quarters lie outside this rich and cosmopolitan historic centre, and in the cities that form the metropolitan belt, with many areas of extreme poverty and vulnerability. Unlike Rio, where favelas and rich areas are contiguous, in a complex mixing system of ghettos, São Paulo's pattern of socio-spatial inequality is more split, with different social classes in different segregated urban areas (Maricato, 1996; Rolnik, 1997; Villaça, 1998; Caldeira, 2001).

Unifesp's transformation into a multi-disciplinary public university began in 2005 (Gallian, Minhoto and Nemi, 2020). It expanded from one to seven campuses, mostly located on the outskirts of the São Paulo metropolitan area, in working-class neighbourhoods and municipalities, which previously had never had a public university campus. The teaching programmes are connected to communities and activist movements and are mostly innovative and focused strongly on public policies, critical theory and problem-solving. The number of undergraduate courses increased from five to 52, and student and staff numbers rose exponentially (Unifesp, 2019). The impact on the image and symbolic identity of the traditional medical school, embedded within the city's heritage, now transformed into a plural, democratic, inventive and spatially distributed university, has been correspondingly enormous. The profile of students changed radically thanks to the government's quota policy, which meant that in 10 years (2009–2018), students coming from public high school (mainly low-income) rose from 8 per cent to 50 per cent of the total, with Afro-descendant students increasing from 7 per cent to 30 per cent (Unifesp, 2019: 41).

The most daring and delayed initiative in this expansion was the construction of the campus in the East End of São Paulo – 'daring' because of its primary connection with activist movements, intertwining the political educational project with urban and social struggles and grassroots identities. It identified 'cities' as the main theme of its teaching–research agenda, based on the most advanced thinking in relation to inequalities in global metropolises, and mobilised São Paulo as a large laboratory (Unifesp, 2014, 2016). 'Delayed', unfortunately, because its implementation began during a period of radical political change in Brazil, resulting in the election of the ultra-rightist Bolsonaro. This greatly restricted the implementation of this emblematic and ground-breaking campus, which has become an alternative, experimental and radical training space: a sort of campus encampment symbolising the engagement of the university in class struggles in Brazil's neofascist movement, and in a significant recalibration of São Paolo's urban and colonial heritage.

The 'decolonisation' of Brazil's public university system

Democracy returned to Brazil in 1985 and, in 1988, a new Federal Constitution was approved, and a new legal framework developed with strong characteristics of a social welfare state despite Brazil's post-colonial condition. In the field of education, a National Forum for the Defence of the Public School was created and, alongside other organisations, was decisive in the struggle for redemocratisation (Saviani, 2013; Fonseca, Araújo and Vasconcelos, 2019). The Constitution and the Basic Education Guidelines Law established a commitment to the public university system and national science development, based on the principles of university autonomy and freedom in teaching and research; ethnic-racial diversity and equal conditions for access and permanence; free undergraduate and postgraduate courses; the guarantee of public funding and sufficient resources for the maintenance and development of federal institutions and national science by the central government; as well as assurance of democratic governance of public education at all levels.

In the 2000s, the governments led by the Workers' Party under Lula da Silva's and Dilma Rousseff's presidencies (2003–16) were pressured to recognise the major advances in the public university system initiated by progressive social movements (including undergraduate and postgraduate students' movements, Afro-Brazilian pro-quota movements, high-school movements against the entrance exam, faculty workers' unions, pro-science associations, NGOs and progressive intellectual and science leaders, among others). As a result of expanded access, the number of students in public universities more than tripled (in federal universities it quadrupled), the number of professors increased by 73 per cent and the public budget for higher education rose from 1 per cent to 1.8 per cent of the federal budget after 15 years. More than 200 new campuses were built in places where there was no previous relevant university presence, such as the impoverished peripheries of large cities and semi-arid, under-populated areas of the Amazon region and other less developed hinterlands (Arantes, 2021). This was accompanied by standardisation of the selection process that led to increasing access opportunities and intra-national student mobility (Andriola, 2011), with public investment in education set to increase from 5 per cent to 10 per cent of GDP in 10 years (National Education Plan-PNE, Goal 20, 2014).

The main teaching innovation for higher education was the 'curricularisation of extensionist practices', meaning that almost 10 per cent of the course credits should be derived from outreach activities and practices in areas of great social relevance (PNE, Strategy 12.7, 2014), supported by grants, extramural activities and off-campus centres in actions with communities (Corte, Gomez and Rosso, 2018). Affirmative policies significantly altered the undergraduate profile at public universities from almost exclusively white and wealthier classes (Passos, 2015; Fonaprace, 2019). The innovative Quota Law (12,711/2012) guaranteed that no fewer than 50 per cent of enrolments should be students who came exclusively from public high schools and included sub-criteria of ethnicity and income according to the population profile of each state. More recently, a complementary law has included disabled people in the quota system (n.13,409/2016). As a result, the profile of public university students today reflects that of Brazilian society as a whole in terms of income, class and race,[2] and Brazil currently has the largest public and tuition-free university system in the world, with 68 federal and 40 state universities, over 500 campuses and around two million students.[3]

International university rankings show that Brazil is an important player in higher education and research, with 14 of its universities included in the top 25 Latin American institutions, of which almost all are public. Brazilian universities are mostly 'extensionists' – that is, they build knowledge in a socially embedded way, in dialogue with communities, getting involved in actions to defend human rights, social and urban justice, environmental sustainability, local development, social technologies and so on. Nilce Monfredini considers that, although universities continue to collaborate in the expanded reproduction of capital in Brazil, the democratisation of the system 'now involves problems that arise in the effort to decolonize and rethink the production of knowledge, incorporating various social actors, in different approaches, assuming the joint production of knowledge' (Monfredini, 2019: 298). In other words, the deep connection with the poor and working classes is 'inducing the (re)creation of the university itself' (Monfredini, 2019: 299). Public universities are creating new leaders, opening up new knowledge problems and new narrative hypotheses, with significant consequences for their relationship with society and the decolonisation of the national heritage. For all the above reasons, today Brazil's far-right government has selected public universities as one of its main targets of attack.

The legacy of the 'worker's university' model

The right to access and transform the public university system has become one of the most important momentums for class struggle in twenty-first-century Brazil. Until recently, public and free universities were almost exclusively spaces for the white middle and upper classes, a mechanism for the reproduction of power and wealth in a highly unequal society (Gisi, 2006). Only in the 2000s did public universities start opening new campuses in poor working-class, immigrant and Afro-descendant neighbourhoods at the edges of the metropolis (see Figure 12.2). The first of these initiatives was that of USP in the east of São Paulo city, in 2005 (Gomes, 2005), and shortly thereafter Unifesp opened its campuses in the metropolitan region towns (Guarulhos, Diadema, Osasco and, more recently, also in East End), and the new Federal University of ABC in Santo André and São Bernardo. This new geography of university location in the outskirts was not only an initiative of the government (Lula's education minister, Fernando Haddad, proposed a metropolitan ring of new campuses) or university administrations, but also a result of direct action by social movements and grassroots communities in São Paulo (D'Agostinho, 2015; Arantes, 2017; Arantes and Santos Jr., 2017).

The choice by grassroots territorial-based movements to fight for better public education happened in the context of expansion of struggles for human rights, social welfare and urban justice at the end of the military dictatorship (1964–85) (Sader, 1988; Holston, 2008). The social movements fought not only for the right to access, but also for the reform of the curricula that reproduced an authoritarian, unequal, racist, patriarchal, economically and culturally subordinate system for central countries of the capitalist world system. They demanded a re-visioning of the university role and its function in social and public life, especially as a vehicle for building 'people power' (Mauro, 2007) and a new 'cultural identity' (Chauí, 1989). New research agendas around gender, race and class were proposed as the foundation for the formulation of radical 'southern epistemologies' and a decolonial praxis aimed at new 'civilisational transitions' and paradigms within a plural university model – 'pluriversity' (Escobar and Mignolo, 2010; Sousa Santos, 2014; Escobar, 2020).

In São Paulo, it was the popular movement itself that was first to imagine and propose a 'worker's university', to be built from the bottom up. Undoubtedly, one of the main influences for this new social and political commitment or reinvention of the role of public universities

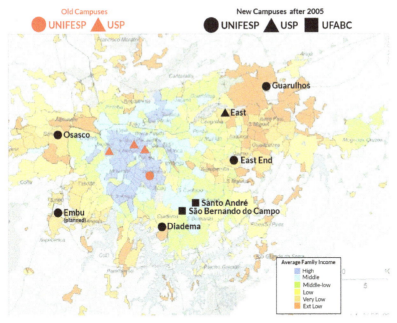

Figure 12.2 The old campuses of public universities and their expansion in new locations in São Paulo Metropolitan Region after 2005. Source: Author using income distribution map by São Paulo Subway Company Origin-Destiny research

came from contemporary reinterpretations of Paulo Freire's work and propositions – pioneered in his books *Education as a Practice of Freedom* (1967) and the *Pedagogy of the Oppressed* (1970). In both works, Paulo Freire argues that the education of the people must go beyond instrumental and decontextualised literacy; it must be a way to recognise words to better understand the world and to ultimately transform it. For this, the process of literacy and education must be socially constructed, in a deep and two-way dialogue between educators and people, embedded in their places, identities and meanings. From the material and immaterial dimensions of the community's lived experience, the 'problem-situations' and 'generating themes' of the literacy and educational processes are born, and denaturalise history not as a fatal destiny, but as a social construction, enabling subjects to recognise and free themselves from their oppressed condition (Freire, 1967, 1970).

Another key influence was Gramsci's framework for the emancipatory formation of the worker as an 'organic intellectual'

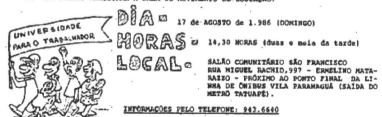

Figure 12.3 Flyer inviting the public to a meeting with Paulo Freire to debate the worker's university in the East End, 1986. The meeting place was the hall in the basement of Father Ticão's St Francis Church, in which a room was inaugurated for the education movement. Source: CEDI, 1987

(Gramsci, 1982). For Gramsci, a popular university would prioritise integrated training (humanistic, historical and technical, in parallel), without cultural downgrading of the working classes; it would recreate science in a free, cultured and living context, without detaching it from grassroots productive-organisational practices, fostering the ability to build hegemony and propagate the working-class worldview in its cultural and political dimension (Gramsci, 1982).

In 1985, the East End education movement (which emerged five years earlier in the struggle for primary education) made a proposal for the first public college in the region (CEDI, 1987; Marchioni and Ghanem, 2005). In a meeting with Paulo Freire in 1986, the movement named the proposal the 'worker's university' (CEDI, 1987: 10) (see Figure 12.3). In response, Freire, listening intently and learning from his people, proposed two mottos for the university, encapsulating two fundamental rights of the working class in their education: 'the right to know better what the people already know' and 'the right to participate in the broad production of knowledge' (CEDI, 1987: 11).

Documents of that time, collected by the Ecumenical Documentation and Information Centre (CEDI), help to reconstruct some of the bases of the original proposal. These included the right to a free, democratically run university of high standard, dedicated to the service of the working class through its teaching programmes, research, maintenance subsidies and employment opportunities (see Figure 12.4). Its purpose was to enrich the lives of workers and prepare people to actively engage in society, and it would be located at a site chosen by the people in the East End (CEDI, 1987: 10–11). The meetings took place mainly in churches and parishes inspired by 'liberation theology', the left arm of the Catholic Church (Brant and Singer, 2012). Radical priests were important popular mobilisers, including Bishop Dom Angélico Bernardino (Augusti, 2012) and the Franciscan Antonio Marchioni, known as Father 'Ticão' (Dantas and Perosa, 2013), also called 'the tractor of God' (for his ability to pressure politicians and to achieve victories for the people). As the movement gathered impetus, progressive politicians, unions and university professors joined the meetings. In August 1987, the final formulation of guidelines for the worker's university was reached, covering the following points (CEDI, 1987: 32, 33).

1. Teaching, research and extension will interact as inseparable elements (a formulation that was approved in the 1988 Constitution), since one gives meaning to the other.
2. The research will be directly relevant to the local context. The return of the educational process will be irreversibly invested in the community.
3. The university articulated through social movements takes on the role of capturing, producing and disseminating culture.
4. This knowledge, although generated within the context of a specific regional context, assumes a universal character, since it arises from a broader conjuncture that is unfolding locally.
5. The social movement must have its own project, considering that government and university elites want to reproduce the status quo. This project must be as advanced as possible, as a new university vision, within the limits of a utopia.
6. The management of the university must be in charge of those involved in its project.
7. The discussion on how to democratise access must be deepened [the Quota Law, as mentioned, was promulgated only 25 years later].
8. The university must focus on the East End's basic priorities: housing, health and education.
9. The embryo of this new university could open courses in the areas of politics, history, philosophy and education and establish an Educational Research Centre.

Figure 12.4 Cover of the East End movement's newspaper ('Lack of Education') announcing the worker's university proposal: 'at first it was a dream ...', 1987. In the dialogue between boss and worker, while the worker thinks about the worker's university, the boss replies: 'Are you daydreaming?' and 'What I want is production!' Source: CEDI, 1987

The reaction of the dominant and ruling classes to these proposals took two forms, as documented in the CEDI report. The first, more opportunistic or favourable, was from politicians interested in the votes of the millions of residents of East São Paulo or who were committed to the democratisation of the university system. These politicians decided to appropriate the East End movement proposal and commissioned competing studies for a new university in São Paulo's East End: one from the provosts of the three state universities (USP, Unicamp and UNESP); another from the staff of the governor Orestes Quércia; and a third from Mayor Jânio Quadros towards 'the first municipal university in São Paulo city'. All were, in some way, geared towards workers' demands and the university campus was likely to be located in East São Paulo, but lacked any consultation with local movements. Ultimately, the proposals were pragmatic, suggesting either an outreach 'advanced campus' connected to the main university structures (without undergraduate or postgraduate programmes), or a technical college for training East End young people in blue collar work in industries and services, reinforcing their subordinate, manual and impoverished condition.

The second reaction was strongly oppositional, driven by resentment and class hatred. Miguel Reale, a USP provost (1969–73) during the dictatorship (1964–85), ironically affirmed that, if the university of the rich was in the west of São Paulo (where the main USP campus was based), then the 'university of the poor' should be located at the 'opposite side of the city', in the East End (CEDI, 1987: 64). The traditional elites, through the editorials of their two main newspapers, violently rejected the proposal for a worker's university, disparagingly defining it as an 'alternative university' (CEDI, 1987: 46), 'university of the needy' (p. 64), 'university demagogy' (p. 64), 'the popular university circus' (p. 66), 'university of indigence' (p. 69), 'educational ghetto' (p. 70) and 'a poor university in every sense' (p. 73), among other attacks.

Notwithstanding the election of the Workers' Party's Luiza Erundina as mayor of São Paulo in 1988, and Paulo Freire's appointment as Secretary of Education, succeeded by his disciple Mário Sérgio Cortella, the project was not realised. During Erundina's mayoralty, Red São Paulo became a social laboratory for innovative political and social experiences developed in several areas, including the construction of new schools and cultural centres in all the peripheries. Universities were re-energised by redemocratisation and provided intellectual cadres for public administration. The dream of a public university on the outskirts became part of the people's imaginary, especially in East São Paulo, but the four-year mayoral term was too short to bring it into being.

In 1993, however, the movements of the East End created a new Forum for Education (Mendonça, 2003), which subsequently won a surprising battle to transform a large new prison into a college of technological and professional education (FATEC), opened in 2002. The Forum achieved a landmark victory: the space built by the state for peripheral youth would not be a new prison, but the first public institution of higher education in the East End (Costa, 2011; D'Agostinho, 2015), giving peripheral young people – mostly Afro descendants and working-class children – the resources to transform their own destiny and that of their class and the city. It is in this context that Holston proposes a 'new formulation of citizenship' (Holston, 2008: 309), defined as 'insurgent', because it not only mobilises itself for a more dignified daily life, but also acts to reinvent the city 'as a *polis* with a different order of citizenship … an unsettling yet vital terrain' (Holston, 2008: 313).

Inspired by this first conquest, the Forum for Education demanded that the great public universities open a campus in the region. After 20 years of social pressure and political agreements, USP East Campus was opened in 2005 in Ermelino Matarazzo neighbourhood, the home of Father Ticão's St Francis Church (Marchioni and Ghanem, 2005), but without any public participation (D'Agostino, 2015). In response, the forum created the Movement for the Federal University in East São Paulo in 2009 to influence the process of negotiation with the Lula Government. It delivered a 'letter of commitment' to the Unifesp commission for university expansion, demanding assurances that the university would produce positive social, economic and cultural impacts for the local community and region, improve the quality of life and build citizenship within 4, 10 and 20 years, and establish financial transparency in dialogue with the community, with potential for participatory budgeting (D'Agostinho, 2015: 97). After rounds of negotiations and pressure from the social movements, the East End entered the Unifesp expansion pipeline in 2010, as the sixth new campus site, albeit at a time when public funding for universities launched by Lula's government would start to dwindle away (D'Agostinho, 2015; Arantes, 2017, 2021).

Cities Institute at the East End Campus: reshaping the university horizon

Unifesp Cities Institute has grown out of a specific historical and geographical set of circumstances and urban heritage. The East End Campus is inserted in a complex urban context, rich in teaching, learning and intervention situations and places. It is a region that has not yet been fully consolidated, with areas of environmental preservation, a large park, small Japanese migrant farms from the 1930s, an industrial hub, informal housing settlements, large housing projects and metropolitan transport infrastructure (Unifesp, 2016). The Itaquera neighbourhood was the site of one of the 2014 football World Cup stadiums, which had an impact on rent levels and living costs in neighbouring communities, prompting land occupations and protests about the huge public expenditure on the mega football event, the new stadium and the resulting evictions (Arantes and Santos Jr., 2017).

Under the leadership of progressive university president Soraya Smaili from 2013, students and professors dedicated to Unifesp's expansion initiative finally won over the hegemony of the medical elite from the former School of Medicine (Gallian, Minhoto and Nemi, 2020).

Figure 12.5 Struggles for the East End Unifesp campus plot. Leaflet calling for an act in defence of the expropriation of the Gazarra factory, on 24 March 2012. Source: Juliana Cardoso, councillor mandate

I joined the university's administration as Vice-provost for Planning in 2013 to spearhead a political agenda of democratisation and expansion and to create a new Public Design Office to plan the new campus and buildings, especially the new East Campus (Arantes, 2017). I had first participated in meetings with the East End Movement at Father Ticão's St Francis Church in 2011 as a recently hired professor, teaching in the Art History Department at Guarulhos Campus in one of São Paulo's poorest areas. I had already worked as an architect for the housing movements in the East End for more than 10 years (Arantes, 2004; Usina, 2015), and I knew the fame of Father Ticão as the 'tractor of God'. He recounted to me a political allegory that the movement used during the fight for the university, explaining that FATEC, USP and Unifesp may be as distant as clouds on the wind – but, if the people are attentive and organised, they can pull them down to their territories. It was only years later that I found the 'pulled clouds' drawing that symbolised this allegory.

At this time, the activists, including many from the housing movement, had identified a site for the location of the new Unifesp campus – the Gazarra steel plant, which had gone bankrupt a few years earlier (see Figure 12.5). The site was finally expropriated by the public authorities at the beginning of 2013 to establish the Federal University Campus. The university set up a joint committee composed of 12 representatives of the university academy and 12 representatives of the East End social movements. It worked intensively for a year discussing the launch of undergraduate courses, university extension activities, the design of buildings and the campus development schedule and budget, so that they could be submitted for approval by Unifesp's Central Councils and by President Rousseff's Ministry of Education (D'Agostinho, 2015; Arantes and Santos Jr., 2017).

Following Paulo Freire's methodology, we agreed that the definition of a teaching framework for the campus should be based on the recognition of an important regional 'problem-situation', which was identified as the living conditions in cities, the production and transformation of urban life, the resolution of problems afflicting the Brazilian people, and poor urban infrastructure and housing conditions (Arantes, 2017; Arantes and Santos Jr., 2017). This field of knowledge corresponded with a lack of any existing courses at Unifesp in urban management, planning, architecture, geography, environment and urban design. The first draft of the so-called Cities Institute PPP (Political-Pedagogical Project), proposing eight new courses across these fields,[4] therefore drew on the heritage embedded in the urban periphery, its history of social struggle and the ideals of Paulo Freire, constituting a significant shift towards a new institutional identity and the symbolic value of Unifesp as an actor in the evolution of São Paulo as a city (Unifesp, 2014). The first 15 professors hired in 2017–18 were from different disciplines (geography, architecture, urbanism, engineering, social science, history, social psychology, law and public administration), most of them from working-class families, some born in East End São Paulo. They were not just traditional scholars, but researcher-activists, previously involved in human-urban rights NGOs or progressive public sector administrations, with links to different social movements. With the support of more than a dozen more experienced professors from other campuses, the team from the East Campus began offering an undergraduate degree in geography in 2020 and is preparing to launch an interdisciplinary master's in 'cities'.

When the Ministry of Education and the University Council authorised the opening of the East Campus, its Cities Institute and five undergraduate courses in 2014, for the first time in Unifesp history several leaders and activists from the Education Forum and the Social Movement of East São Paulo were welcomed to the council session.[5] Luís França, one of the main social leaders, declared that he firstly 'brings a greeting on behalf of Father Ticão' (who could not attend) and stated that:

> The movement of São Paulo's East Side is one wing, Unifesp is the other wing, and together we will fly and lift the university so it is stronger and safer. ... The university will arrive in São Paulo East and together we will transform reality. It will not solve problems directly, we know, ... but it will be on our side, stimulating debate, provoking governments, indicating that it is necessary to transform reality. (Luís França)

Valter Costa, who was also a member of the joint committee for campus planning, recalls that in the proposal:

> There were a lot of people involved, a lot of interest, a lot of expectations, a lot of dreams. ... The East End deserves to have a public university the size of Unifesp. After many years we succeeded, thanks to all the efforts. ... It is an Institute that thinks a more human city for all. (Valter Costa)

Another leader, Waldir Augusti, made his speech highlighting that 'people's power' drives social transformation (or in Holston's terms, 'insurgent citizenship'):

> In the East End, we learned over time that nothing, nothing, absolutely nothing that comes from the Government got there without the movements organising, fighting and demanding that their rights need to be respected. Nothing, from a nursery to a police base, from the university to whatever it is. ... We had moments of fierce clashes [with Unifesp in the struggle for the campus]. The movement wanted to guide. And guided what East End expects with the installation of a new Federal Campus. ... Today, when I saw the Cities Institute presentation, I was very moved, I must confess. I recognise that it is another historic achievement, which is part of the curriculum of the suffering, struggling and forgotten population of the city. We conquered. Unifesp did its part, presenting the project. But we will never forget – this is the result of a community that regardless of who is in power, fights for their rights and will continue to fight. (Waldir Augusti)

From the institution's side, it is worth noting how the traditional School of Medicine councillors were positively surprised by the participatory planning process. The first professor of the School of Medicine to speak, Dr Nestor Schor, observed that:

> We have always been criticised as a university distant from society. The interaction was very fragile, the university was crystallised with little chance of modification. And this project, which is innovative, shows that this is possible. … The university is changing, it is interested, it has social interaction, it responds to society. (Dr Nestor Schor)

In the same vein, the Dean of the Paulista Medical School, Dr Antonio Carlos Lopes, stated that:

> This project is really remarkable … we are impressed because we are imbued with these political-proactive activities. … The speeches of the people from the East End here in this session are really moving. It was very important [their presence]. Society needs to be respected, the academy is not sovereign at all, and then the community must also participate. The academy is not only science, it is not just the production of papers. The academy is also a social commitment for what society needs. In such a way, Provost Soraya, I congratulate the university's direction with regard to the elaboration of this project. I followed the others [campus projects], and this is the first time that the university produces a project that is really elaborated, with knowledge, with technicians and with the obligation of all those interested. (Dr Antonio Carlos Lopes)

Since then, in close collaboration with the new Cities Institute professors, a number of local activist organisations have been responsible for organising diverse activities on campus, from participatory housing design and urban agriculture, to sanitation, participatory urban management and theorising the right to the city (see Figure 12.6). They have sought the Cities Institute as a partner for research, planning and action on urban and environmental challenges in vulnerable territories, such as Jardim Helian, a small neighbourhood close to the campus (Barros, 2019). Two of the most promising initiatives running on campus at the moment are the São Paulo East End Memory and Heritage Centre and the Centre for Peripheral Studies, dedicated to recording testimonies and collecting data from social

Figure 12.6 One of the activities carried out at the East End Unifesp Campus since 2016. Field study on environmental sanitation problems in the Jardim Helian community, accompanied by grassroots leader Rodrigo Reis (in the centre, tragically deceased in 2019). Photo: the author, 2017

movements and their leaders to document and map the history of the working-class neighbourhoods. Young local activists, mostly Afro descendants and residents of deprived neighbourhoods, have defined an action research agenda drawing on decolonial theories, studies of subalternity and radical black critical theory little known in Brazilian academia. The objective is to formulate other political, subjective and testimonial narratives about their urban and social presence in the metropolis.

In a broad sense, the political and pedagogical project of the Cities Institute is based on learning through different contexts and scales of urban dynamics and its conflicts, mapping territorial inequalities and social insurgencies to theorise and propose practical solutions and public policies. The Institute is developing training through innovative didactic practices such as the use of social cartography, games, dramatisations, multimedia means of communication, models and prototypes, and also by the interaction of students and professors in integrated teaching spaces, organised in thematic laboratories and

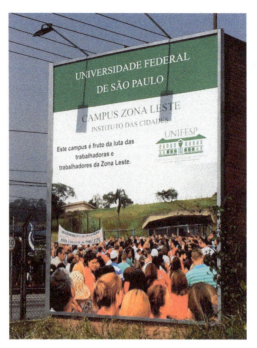

Figure 12.7 Plaque at the entrance to the campus with the words: 'This campus...' Photo: the author, 2016

workshops (under construction). Its educational project is based on public vocation guided by social demands for urban justice, equality and sustainability, and an emphasis on the history and quality of the built environment as an inseparable principle for the progressive transformation of cities.

In terms of the physical facilities, the East End Campus masterplan establishes a clear dialogue with the material and immaterial, the environmental and built heritage of the place (Arantes, 2017). The guideline established by the Public Design Office was to approach the new campus as an experimental site for testing the production and management of cities. This includes testing new construction technologies and innovative spatial forms; reflecting on the campus' relationship with the urban context and landscape, including renovation of its conservation area (APP) and springs, and development of urban agriculture to supply the university restaurant; reduction of the campus' ecological footprint through environmental and waste management policy, monitoring of emissions, water recycling and energy efficiency; combining and switching study time with 'work' time (in the workshops created inside the renovated factory building, which occupies an important place in the workers' memory); undertaking pilot actions for the maintenance and recovery of the campus buildings, furniture and equipment; and running workshops for the mapping, planning and management of the campus, as an exercise in managing a small town. All this is directed towards the goal of realising a sustainable, constructively innovative, welcoming and democratic campus (Unifesp, 2016; Arantes, 2017).

The Yellow Pavilion is the first building to be renovated on campus, containing academic and administrative spaces, but, most strikingly, a display of tribute plaques that commemorate deceased East End social leaders (Zorilda Maria da Silva, Waldermar Rossi, Orisson Saraiva and Rodrigo Martins dos Reis). This is a common practice among the landless and homeless movements, when they 'baptise' their conquests, settlements, schools and housing projects with the name of their leaders or intellectuals. It is a strategy of memory and identity, which the landless movement-MST considers part of the 'mystique' of its class belonging and worldview. At the entrance to the Yellow Pavilion, there is another sign, which names the building in honour of the former workers at Gazarra, followed by a well-known poem by Bertolt Brecht: 'In praise of fighters'.

At the main entrance of the campus site, there is another symbolic novelty. The campus is not only presented as belonging to the university and under its management – with a giant photo of a 2012 demonstration in front of the future site, when the expropriation was still being fought for – but the insignias of the university are accompanied by the following sentence: 'This campus is the result of the struggle of the workers of the East End' (see Figure 12.7).

In 2018, Unifesp would enshrine this participation in the creation of The University-Society Strategic Council-CEUS, with 60 representatives from different parts of civil society and government, forming an innovative space for social dialogue and collective thinking about the future of the university and its connection with social demands (Unifesp, 2019) (see Figure 12.8). I coordinated this initiative and I have been the secretary of CEUS until now. Of the 60 representatives, about one-third are East End activists or NGOs who work there – and at meetings, they are the most active in presenting proposals and new horizons for the university as a whole, rather than just for the new-born campus. The 'worker's university' idea thus shapes new developments and possibilities, embedded in the strategic decision-making process which supports Unifesp's visioning of its future in Brazilian society.

Figure 12.8 Leaflet inviting candidates to the University-Society Strategic Council in 2018. Design by the author with illustration by Mariana Zanetti

Conclusion: regression or resistance in dark times

The history of Unifesp's East Campus is, however, an interrupted construction, a victim of the course of Brazilian history over the last five years. Following the economic and political crisis in Rousseff's second mandate, her impeachment and the paralysis of the public sector, the public budget for funding the maintenance of 68 Federal Universities (staff expenditure excluded) has decreased by 32 per cent (Brazilian National Treasury, 2019). At the same time there has been a drop of 48 per cent in federal resources for Research and Post-Graduation (Brazilian National Treasury, 2019). The impact has been destructive for the entire system and following Bolsonaro's election in 2018, the situation has worsened dramatically.

The Bolsonaro government's overall agenda, including its relation to higher education, exemplifies a convergence of neoliberalism and neoconservatism that has resulted in an antidemocratic citizenry or forces of 'dedemocratisation' (Brown, 2019). It has driven a major reduction of the state's budget and personnel cuts to public universities, inexorably pushing for internal privatisation, intra-system predation and even destruction, as was seen decades ago with the public elementary education system (World Bank, 2017; Leher, Giolo and Sguissardi, 2020). All of these measures recall the privatising and commodifying turn in US

Figure 12.9 Unifesp students demonstrating against the cuts imposed by the government in August 2019. On the posters, the students of Unifesp Campus Guarulhos (of Humanities) tell the passers-by of the inclusion and outreach actions of the university, all free of charge: a theatre course offered by the Caminho Velho group; music and percussion with the Mala Guetta Drums; 'arteoke', art and singing activities; maths course with elementary school children; Portuguese course for immigrants; internship and partnership with public schools; the acquisition of more bus lines to serve the campus surroundings. Photo: Samara Akemi Saraiva

public universities since the late 1970s, a turn whose disastrous consequences are well-known (Newfield, 2016).

The neoconservative 'ideological agenda', which seems to be an irrationalist, fundamentalist and anti-science stance, is part of a much more complex cultural and political turn. The Bolsonaro government is also engaged in what James Hunter (1991) calls a 'culture war' against the influence of progressive, multicultural and cosmopolitan thinking. In the past two decades, public universities – with the increasingly popular, plural and multi-ethnic character of their student body – have become one of the main sites of intellectual, cultural and political progressivism. For this reason, they have also become one of the main targets of attack in the cultural warfare waged by the neoconservatives, since they are geared strongly toward the humanities and the legacy of Paulo Freire, in addition to what neoconservatives more generally identify as 'cultural

Marxism'. For the neoconservatives, their opponents in the cultural battle pose a threat to the white, Christian and patriarchal family. Brazil is experiencing a moment of polarisation and conflict – with class struggle on one side and urban warfare on the other – growing politicisation and rampant despair (see Figure 12.9).

Deprived of funding and staff, the Unifesp East End Campus remains in an embryonic stage in terms of infrastructure and operating conditions. Despite all, the Cities Institute is very lively, with innovative initiatives, extension courses, research groups, memory centres and cultural performances, etc. The East End Campus thus remains a kind of trench or barricade of imaginative knowledge and practice, built on the distinctive urban heritage of the worker's university ideology. It is this that, in the face of the huge regression Brazilians are experiencing, continues to support social resistance in the present and envision another possible future.

Notes

1. I chose to translate 'Zona Leste' as 'East End' for three reasons. Firstly, combative grassroots organisations and communities in the 1970s were far more present in São Paulo's Far East than in the central Near East (a more middle-class area) – and they were also more mobilised because the East End faced the most serious lack of access to basic rights that guaranteed better living conditions. Secondly, the title honours (and is a possible analogy of) Friedrich Engels' description of London's East End in the mid-nineteenth century, the world's largest and most wretched working-class district at the time, marked by misery but also by the emergence of strong workers' organisations. Thirdly, UCL is planning to open its new campus in the East End of London and this chapter, which narrates and problematises the creation of the new Unifesp campus in East End São Paulo, could be useful for an interesting discussion of similarities and differences – which I will refrain from here. Clare Melhuish, with whom I have been collaborating, has been working on a comparative analysis of both East End campuses in London and São Paulo.
2. The numbers collected by the Brazilian National Forum of Deans of Community and Student Affairs (Fonaprace) are impressive: in 15 years (2003–18), the number of undergraduate students from lower- or lower-middle income families (less than $350 per capita per month) grew from 42.8 per cent to 70.1 per cent; those from public high schools grew from 36.5 per cent to 60.4 per cent; students of colour (Afro and indigenous descendants) grew from 36.2 per cent to 53.5 per cent. The total number of black students grew by a factor of 5.3, and the number of brown ('pardos') students by 3.5 in the same period.
3. I will not develop an analysis of Brazilian higher education private sector expansion, which in the same period grew twice as much as the public sector. The private sector currently accounts for more than 75 per cent of undergraduate students (five million people). For a broader assessment of the expansion and democratisation of higher education in Brazil and the turnaround under Bolsonaro, see Pedro Arantes 'Higher education in dark times', in *Policy Reviews in Higher Education* (2021).
4. Public administration (with an emphasis on city and metropolis management); architecture and urbanism (in Brazil, by law, architecture and urbanism are two built-in courses); geography (bachelor's degree and teacher training for a basic education network); civil engineering; environmental and sanitary engineering; urban mobility and transport engineering; public design (with an emphasis on communication, urban services and public facilities); and tourism (with a focus on sustainability, city history and city working class culture and heritage).

5   In the session of 17 December 2019, the transcription of the speeches was carried out by the scholarship holder Isabel Barboza da Silva, from the Institutional Observatory of the Zona Leste Campus, and translated into English by the author.

References

Ab'Saber, T. (2018) *Michel Temer e o Fascismo Comum* [Michel Temer and the Common Fascism]. São Paulo: Hedra.

Alambert, Jr., F. (2016) *Parque do Ibirapuera: 60 anos | Ibirapuera Park: 60th anniversary*. São Paulo: Brasileira (bilingual edition).

Andriola, W. B. (2011) 'Doze motivos favoráveis à adoção do ENEM pelas IFES' [Twelve reasons in favour of adopting the National High School Exam by Federal Higher Education Institutions]. *Ensaio: Avaliação e Políticas Públicas em Educação*, 19 (70), 107–126. https://doi.org/10.1590/S0104-40362011000100007.

Arantes, P. F. (2004) 'Reinventing the building site'. In A. Forty and E. Andreoli (eds), *Brazilian Architecture in the XX Century*. London: Phaidon Press.

Arantes, P. F. (2017) 'The creation of a public design office at the Federal University of São Paulo and its Cities Institute at the East Zone Campus'. In A. Delijaicov (ed.), *Building Spaces, Spaces That Build*. São Paulo: FAUUSP.

Arantes, P. F. (2018) 'From red São Paulo to Brazilian neofascism: Workers Party, grassroots movements, experimental architecture and the current conservative shift' (unpublished lecture in Architectural Association AA London).

Arantes, P. F. (2021) 'Higher education in dark times: From the democratic renewal of Brazilian universities to its current wreck'. *Policy Reviews in Higher Education*, 5 (2) 131–57. https://doi.org/10.1080/23322969.2021.1872412.

Arantes, P. F. and Santos Jr., W. R. (2017) 'Instituto das Cidades: uma construção conjunta da Unifesp e dos movimentos sociais da Zona Leste de São Paulo' [Cities Institute: a joint construction of São Paulo Federal University and the social movements of São Paulo East]. São Paulo: ANPUR. Accessed 2 August 2021. http://anais.anpur.org.br/index.php/anaisenanpur/article/view/1882.

Augusti, W. A. (2012) *Dom Angélico Sândalo Bernardino: Bispo Profeta dos Pobres e da Justiça*. [Dom Angélico Sândalo Bernardino: Bishop and Prophet of the Poor and the Justice]. São Paulo: Acdem.

Barros, M. (2019) Transformações socioespaciais na Região do Jacu-Pêssego: Zona Leste de São Paulo [Socio-spatial transformations in the Jacu-Peach Region: East Zone of São Paulo]. Doctoral Thesis. São Paulo: USP.

Brant. V. and Singer, P. (eds) (1982) *São Paulo: O Povo em Movimento* [São Paulo: the People in Movement]. Petrópolis: Vozes.

Brazil National Treasury (2019) https://www.tesourotransparente.gov.br/temas/estatisticas-fiscais-e-planejamento/resultado-do-tesouro-nacional-rtn-conteudos-relacionados (accessed 17th February 2022).

Brown, W. (2019) *In the Ruins of Neoliberalism: The rise of antidemocratic politics in the West*. New York: Columbia University Press.

Caldeira, T. P. R. (2001) *City of Walls: Crime, segregation, and citizenship in São Paulo*. Berkeley: University California Press.

Castro Rocha, J. C. (2021) *Guerra Cultural e Retórica do Ódio: Crônicas de um Brasil pós-político* [Cultural War and Rhetoric of Hate: Chronicles of a Post-Political Brazil]. Goiânia: Caminhos (Kindle edition).

CEDI Centro Ecumênico de Documentação e Informação (1987) *Dossiê Universidade da Zona Leste*. São Paulo: Acervo ABONG. Accessed 5 August 2021. http://www.bibliotecadigital.abong.org.br/bitstream/handle/11465/1807/66.pdf?sequence=1.

Chauí, M. (1989) *Conformismo e Resistência: Aspectos da cultura popular no Brasil* [Conformism and Resistance: Aspects of popular culture in Brazil]. São Paulo: Brasiliense.

Corte, M. G. D., Gomez, S. R. M. and Rosso, G. P. (2018) 'Creditação da extensão universitária no currículo dos cursos de graduação: estado do conhecimento' [University extention credit in undergraduate courses: knowledge state]. *Políticas Educativas*, 11 (2), 17–36.

Costa, V. A. (2011). Política Educacional para o Ensino Médio e Educação Técnica no Estado de São Paulo – Expectativas dos Estudantes de Quatro Unidades Escolares da Zona Leste da Capital e a Disputa Ideológica na Educação [Educational Policy for High School and Technical Education in the State of São Paulo – Expectations of Students from Four School Units in the East Zone of the Capital and the Ideological Dispute in Education]. Master Thesis. São Paulo: USP.

D'Agostinho, J. P. S. S. (2015). Em busca da Universidade Pública: A criação e a participação do Movimento pela Universidade Federal na Zona Leste do Município de São Paulo na implementação dos Programas de Expansão das Universidades Federais. [In search of the Public University: The creation and participation of the Movement by the Federal University in the East Zone of the Municipality of São Paulo in the implementation of Federal University Expansion Programs]. Master Thesis. Santo André: UFABC.

Dantas, A. S. and Perosa, G. Z. (2013) 'Participação política na periferia leste de São Paulo: memória de antigos moradores (1940–1980)' [Political participation in the East periphery of São Paulo: memory of former residents (1940–1980)]. *Resgate*, 21 (1), 27–38). https://doi.org/10.20396/resgate.v21i25/26.8645751.

Escobar, A. (2020) *Pluriversal Politics: The real and the possible*. Durham: Duke University Press.

Escobar, A. and Mignolo, W. D. (2010) *Globalization and the Decolonial Option*. London: Routledge.

Fonaprace, Brazilian National Forum of Deans of Community and Student Affairs (2019) *5ª Pesquisa do Perfil Socioeconômico e Cultural dos Estudantes de Graduação* [5th Research on the Under Graduate Student's Socioeconomic and Cultural Profile Report]. Accessed 15 August 2021. http://www.fonaprace.andifes.org.br/site/wp-content/uploads/2019/06/V-Pesquisa-do-Perfil-Socioecono%CC%82mico-dos-Estudantes-de-Graduac%CC%A7a%CC%83o-das-U.pdf.

Fonseca, L. S., Araújo, R. D. and Vasconcelos, E. C. (2019) 'O ANDES-SN e a defesa da educação pública: O encontro nacional de educação como espaço de resistência' [The ANDES-SN and the defense of public education: The national education as meeting space of resistance]. *Trabalho Necessário*, 17 (33), 111–137. https://doi.org/10.22409/tn.17i33.p29371.

Freire, P. (1967) *Educação Como Prática de Liberdade* [Education as a Practice of Freedom]. São Paulo: Paz e Terra.

Freire, P. (1970) *Pedagogy of the Oppressed*. London: Penguin books, 1996 edition.

Gallian, D., Minhoto, M. A. and Nemi, A. (eds) (2020) *Unifesp 25 Anos: Histórias e reflexões* [Unifesp 25 years: Stories and reflections]. São Paulo: Editora Unifesp.

Gisi, M. L. (2006) A educação superior no Brasil e o caráter de desigualdade do acesso e da permanência [Higher education in Brazil and the inequality of access and permanence]. *Diálogo Educacional, (6)*(17), 97–112. https://doi.org/10.7213/rde.v6i17.6740.

Gomes, C. (ed.) (2005) *USP LESTE: A Expansão da Universidade de São Paulo de Oeste para Leste* [Expansion of the University of São Paulo from West to East]. São Paulo: EUSP.

Gramsci, A. (1982) *Os Intelectuais e a Organização da Cultura* [Intellectuals and the Organisation of the Culture]. Rio de Janeiro: Civilização Brasileira.

Holston, J. (2008) *Insurgent Citizenship: Disjunctions of democracy and modernity in Brazil*. Princeton: Princeton University Press.

Hunter, J. (1991) *Culture Wars: The struggle to define America: Making sense of the battles over the family, art, education, law, and politics*. New York: Basic Books.

Lefebvre, H. (1968) 'The right to the city'. In E. Kofman and E. Lebas (eds), *Writings on Cities*. Cambridge, MA.: Wiley-Blackwell, 1996 edition.

Leher, R., Giolo, J. and Sguissardi, V. (2020) *Future-se: Ataque à autonomia das instituições federais de educação superior e sua sujeição ao mercado* [Future-se: Attack on the autonomy of federal higher education institutions and their subjection to the market]. São Carlos: Diagrama. https://www.diagramaeditorial.com.br/project/future-se/ (accessed 15 September 2021).

Marchioni, A. L and Ghanem, E. (2005) 'A USP Leste e a contribuição de comunidades locais para a inovação das comunidades universitárias' [USP Leste and the contribution of local communities to the innovation of university communities]. In C. Gomes (ed.), *USP LESTE: A expansão da Universidade de São Paulo de Oeste para Leste*. São Paulo: EUSP.

Maricato, E. (1996) *Metrópole na Periferia do Capitalismo: Ilegalidade, desigualdade e violência* [Metropolis on the Periphery of Capitalism: illegality, inequality and violence]. São Paulo: Hucitec.

Massarolo, P. D. (1971) *História dos Bairros de São Paulo: O bairro de Vila Mariana*. [History of the Neighborhoods of São Paulo: The Vila Mariana neighbourhood]. São Paulo: Prefeitura de SP/DPH.

Mauro, G. (2007) 'A dialética das lutas socialistas: O MST e as novas formas de contrução do poder opular na América Latina' [The dialectic of socialist struggles: The movement of landless rural workers-MST and the new forms of building popular power in Latin America]. *Revista em Paula*, 19, 107–33.

Mendonça, M. (2003) *O Fórum de Educação da Zona Leste: Participação e cidadania na luta por uma escola de qualidade*. Doctoral Thesis. São Paulo: USP.

Moisés, J. A. (ed.) (1982) *Cidade, Povo e Poder* [City, People and Power]. Rio de Janeiro: CEDEC and Paz e Terra.

Monfredini, I. (2019) 'A universidade viva na relação com as classes populares' [The university alive in relation to the popular classes]. *Revista da Avaliação da Educação Superior*, 24 (1), 278–304. https://doi.org/10.1590/S1414-407720190001000015.

Nemi, A. (2008) *A Universidade Federal de São Paulo aos 75 anos: Ensaios sobre história e memória* [The Federal University of São Paulo at 75: Essays on history and memory]. São Paulo: Editora Unifesp.

Newfield, C. (2016) *The Great Mistake: How we wrecked public universities and how we can fix them*. Baltimore: Johns Hopkins University Press.

Passos, J. C. (2015) 'Relações raciais, cultura acadêmica e tensionamentos após ações afirmativas' [Race relations, academic culture and tensions after affirmative actions]. *Educação em Revista*, 31 (2), 155–82. https://doi.org/10.1590/0102-4698134242.

Patarra, I. (1996) *O governo de Luiza Erundina: Cronologia de quatro anos de administração do PT 1989-1992*. [The government of Luiza Erundina: Chronology of four years of the Worker's Party administration 1989–1992]. São Paulo: Geração Editorial.

PNE Brazil National Education Plan 2014–2024 13.005/2014 Law (2014). Accessed 10 August 2021. http://www.planalto.gov.br/ccivil_03/_ato2011-2014/2014/lei/l13005.htm.

Porta, P. (ed.) (2004) *História da Cidade de São Paulo: A cidade na primeira metade do século XX* [History of the City of São Paulo: The city in the first half of the twentieth century]. São Paulo: Paz e Terra.

Rolnik, R. (1997) *A Cidade e a Lei: Legislação, política urbana e territórios na cidade de São Paulo* [The City and the Law: Legislation, urban policy and territories in the city of São Paulo]. São Paulo: Fapesp/Studio Nobel.

Sader, E. (1988) *Quando Novos Personagens Entraram em Cena: Experiências, falas e lutas dos trabalhadores da grande São Paulo, 1970–80* [When New Characters Entered the Scene: Experiences, talks and struggles of workers in greater São Paulo, 1970–80]. Rio de Janeiro: Paz e Terra.

Saviani, D. (2013) 'A educação na Constituição Federal de 1988' [Education in the 1988 Federal Constitution]. *Revista Brasileira de Política e Administração da Educação*, 29, 207–21. https://doi.org/10.21573/vol29n22013.43520.

Singer, P. (1996) *Um Governo de Esquerda para Todos* [A Left Government for All]. São Paulo: Brasiliense.

Sousa Santos, B. (2014) *Epistemology of the South: Justice against epistemicide*. London: Routledge.

Unifesp (2014) 'Federal University of São Paulo, East Zone Campus: Political Pedagogical Project – Cities Institute' (First Version – Bilingual). São Paulo: Unifesp. Accessed 4 September 2021. https://www.unifesp.br/campus/zonaleste/images/campus_zona_leste/documentos/Projeto_Pedagogico/PPP/Unifesp_Projeto_Poltico_Pedagogico_Instituto_Das_Cidades.pdf.

Unifesp (2016) *Projeto Político-Pedagógico do Instituto das Cidades* (versão final) [Cities Institute Politica-Pedagogial Project – final version]. São Paulo. Unifesp. Accessed 5 September 2021. https://www.unifesp.br/campus/zonaleste/images/campus_zona_leste/documentos/Projeto_Pedagogico/PPP/PPP_InstitutodasCidades_AprovadoCG_Versao_102016.pdf.

Unifesp (2019) Relatório de Gestão Unifesp-2018 [Report of activities and management Unifesp-2018]. São Paulo. Accessed 5 September 2021. https://www.unifesp.br/reitoria/proplan/publicacoes/publicacoes/destaques/236-relatorio-de-gestao-unifesp-2018-tcu.

Usina Group (2015) *Usina: entre o canteiro e o desenho*. [Usina: Between construction site and design]. São Paulo: Aurora. Accessed 15 August 2021. https://issuu.com/usinactah/docs/usina.

Villaça, F. (1998) *Espaço Intra-Urbano no Brasil* [Intra-Urban Space in Brazil]. São Paulo: Studio Nobel.

Wolff, S. F. S. (2001) *Jardim América: O primeiro bairro-jardim de São Paulo e sua arquitetura* [Jardim América: São Paulo's first garden-city district and its architecture]. São Paulo: Imprensa oficial.

World Bank (2017) *A Fair Adjustment: Efficiency and equity of public spending in Brazil*. Washington: WB Report. Accessed 20 September 2021. https://www.worldbank.org/en/country/brazil/publication/brazil-expenditure-review-report last

Postscript: a collective reflection by the contributors

This book has brought forward the field of urban heritage as a lens through which to understand the complexities of universities' engagement in urban development, understood as the construction of new buildings and spaces by universities in urban settings, in response to evolving institutional needs. But its ambition is also to frame this more broadly as a reflection on how such initiatives contribute to a re-imagining of what cities can and should be. Its contributors share an understanding of the role in which universities can, and should, play a part in promoting economic, social and ecological sustainability in urban contexts, addressing spatial inequalities and social injustice, and making cities better and more equal environments for human habitation. We see universities as key agents, not just in the delivery of higher education but also in processes of integrated and sustainable urbanism. Across the chapters of this book, we frame this complex interplay of inheritance, rights and future aspiration to a 'good life' as a broad field of urban heritage, across a variety of social and geopolitical urban contexts, in which universities are involved not only as developers of real estate but also as intellectual leaders, innovators and agents of diversification and widening participation in urban futures.

However, as the manuscript was being finalised, the COVID-19 pandemic hit, plunging human society into a liminal state of chronic uncertainty and suspended activity from which it is yet to emerge. For universities, the immediate implication has been an almost overnight and radical shift to online activity enabled by rapidly overhauled digital interfaces, and a steep learning curve for academics in the use of remote platforms for teaching, research, public engagement and pastoral care. For many academics, the academic year 2020–1 has been one of remote working, with little or no access to physical campus sites and university buildings, and by extension, to the intellectual and institutional heritage enshrined in those sites and meeting places that plays a powerful role in binding university communities together. Similarly, exclusion from those sites has compounded the loss of access to public urban spaces and engagement with fellow urbanites in surrounding neighbourhoods and more widely that has been experienced by city dwellers all over the world.

The historic conceptualisation of the university as an inward-looking, self-contained community, segregated from the surrounding urban fabric, has shifted in the last century or more to embrace a vision of permeability, accessibility and integration with the wider city at different scales, from local neighbourhood to global communities, which has had significant architectural and urban design implications for the planning and design of twenty-first-century university facilities and urban contexts. If the university is visualised as a beacon looking out to the city, engaging with, shaping and being shaped by its urban heritage, it is worth considering as a historic point of reference the model of Patrick Geddes' Outlook Tower in Edinburgh (1892), which he described as 'an educational museum in every city and village for social cohesion and public betterment', 'scientific but practical', and designed for 'practical civic work' that could contribute to the evolution of cities: 'the iconic urban observatory for the modern age' (Tewdwr-Jones, Sookhoo and Freestone, 2019: 3). But with the partial dissolution of space and place brought by the pandemic, through the emptying of public buildings, streets and gathering points, and the recalibration of social interactions and communities through digital networks, it is hard to evaluate the importance of buildings and material infrastructures in the future of universities. Even while construction has continued apace at sites such as UCL East in London's Olympic Park, and Campus Näckrosen in Gothenburg, the planning of academic programmes and research for the coming years is set to embrace the shift to online and blended forms of learning which had been in development for decades but only actualised, at speed, on a global scale in the 12 months from Spring 2020 due to the catalysing impact of COVID-19.

How then might we speculate about the forms new architecture will take as we learn to live with the experience of pandemic, and what are the longer-term institutional and spatial implications likely to be for urban universities and the cities in which they are embedded? From a British perspective, it will be framed by 'policy versus pragmatics', a scenario wherein developers are stuck between trying to maintain a business model based on risk, with the need to socially distance and maintain public health infrastructure, while the issue for the university is not so much COVID-19 itself (socially distanced campuses, hybrid learning), but the fact that the pandemic seems to have energised the sector into accelerating changes that have been agonised about for years, reversing the established trend towards massification, sacrificing the humanities, and moving full steam towards lecture capture and remote student engagement. Top-down restructurings, with zero consultation, have become an increasing cause for concern within university communities, while construction of new buildings is proceeding apace, demonstrating a reliance on 'disaster capitalism' to drive the economy – which is not confined to the UK – and in many instances a scant regard for shared narratives and experiences of urban heritage.

From a more positive perspective, it may be that there is hope to be invested in the long-term urban impact of the pandemic on the de- and re-construction of urban CBDs and local high streets, so that public place-making potentially becomes much more anchored in popular (and possibly populist) urban practices of congregation, rather than the corporate strategies of urban impression management which have driven urban regeneration for many years. This has direct implications for understandings of urban heritage and the responsibility of universities to contribute to the creation and maintenance of shared spaces of urban encounter and interaction between diverse communities and cultures, which are not regulated by corporate ambitions, profit margins or securitisation. In this context, it is vitally important to recognise the position of both universities and heritage at the centre of the current 'culture wars' fuelled by social, political, racial and environmental inequality, division and intolerance, which have played out in parallel with the pandemic through mass protests in urban spaces mounted by Black Lives Matter, Extinction Rebellion and a multitude of other protest and worker-led movements. Universities will need to draw on the wealth of intellectual resources and influence which they wield to negotiate these divisions and broker understanding and positive change as the world's cities navigate the realities of trite political campaigns for 'building back better' through the pandemic; to draw attention to the embedded structural violence and disproportionate economic and health consequences of the pandemic that further aggravates the precarity of the historically marginalised, oppressed and excluded.

In the present, however, the pandemic has brought about a series of new practices that fundamentally undermine what 'public space' is about – the non-negotiability of the encounter with people other than oneself and, as such, a symbol for an open society. With the pandemic came restrictions for social gathering, fear of public transport and an increased search for single family homes. In workplaces, including the university, a shift to web-based meetings has been the rule, and thus social distancing has not only been a governmental prescription, but has also become a habitual practice, and an individual *modus vivendi* setting up a completely different target for life: one that favours seclusion, privacy and (possibly) individualism over inclusion, openness and encounter. What can the city be, what is heritage, what is the university if inclusion, openness and encounter are set aside or even reversed as goals? The university will have to re-think and re-work its agenda for research and education in response to the restructuring of the map, and the increasingly angry demands of the disenfranchised for parity of access to the city, to a participatory and representative heritage, and a shared future anchored in environmental stability and protected livelihoods.

It is painfully evident that the impact of the pandemic is not, and will not be, equal or comparable across all regions and cities of the world, even from the relatively restricted vantage points of this book's contributors. In Lebanon, for example, the impact of the pandemic has come on top of an already dire and deteriorating situation facing the country, a perfect storm of compound crises. Mass protests against the country's corrupt political class and a banking shutdown in October 2019 led to a compound financial, fiscal, debt, banking and economic crisis described by the World Bank as one of the world's worst three depressions since the mid-nineteenth century. The Lebanese lira lost 90 per cent of its value, leading to skyrocketing prices, severely limited electricity, shortages in basic commodities (including fuel and medicines) and the increasing impoverishment of the majority of the Lebanese population. Many families are going hungry. Adding to the general despair, the cataclysmic explosion in Beirut's port in August 2020 killed hundreds, injured thousands, devastated nearby neighbourhoods and damaged buildings throughout the city. Lebanon has been without a government since the blast, but many believe, according to David Gardner (2021) writing in the *Financial Times*, that public officials are colluding in a 'deliberate depression'. It is hard to predict when the country will hit rock bottom.

Like all Lebanese institutions, AUB has been deeply affected by the national crisis, with increased operational costs and reduced revenues from student fees and unpaid bills to the university's medical centre, among others. The AUB president wrote in May 2020 that the university was confronting its greatest crisis since its founding in 1866, forced into survival mode with staff reductions and only mission-essential programmes continuing. The Neighborhood Initiative has continued with reduced support and adjusted emphases; only those activities with an immediate impact on the daily lives of neighbours are now priorities. The Neighborhood Initiative coordinates a programme to collect donations from AUB faculty and staff for the most vulnerable neighbours, and has partnered with NGOs to raise funds to rehabilitate houses in the neighbourhood damaged by the port blast. Thanks to Neighborhood Initiative networking, older neighbours are now receiving free consultations and medications from the university's primary health care centre. Other activities now being explored or planned include connecting students who need housing with older neighbours needing extra income and a little company, borrowing unbuilt land in the neighbourhood for a community garden, creating a system of shared transport to optimise vehicle use, and using a barter system to link neighbours with the food-producing farmers who used to sell their produce in the weekly farmers' market.

In Brazil, the emergence of public universities as a special place for the reinvention of practices, identities and narratives has scared the traditional white elites, and they are currently facing multiple attacks on higher education, including cuts in public funding and attempts to limit universities' autonomy, freedom of thought and internal democracy (Arantes 2021). This is driven by the neofascist government's condemnation of public universities as a hotbed for a leftist proliferation of 'Cultural Marxism' that should be exterminated. This is part of a broader attack on science itself, especially on scientific evidence that contradicts increasingly environmentally-predatory policies and actions, and an attack on the rights of indigenous populations, minorities and human rights, which the government carries out itself or permits. More recently, the attacks on science have been associated with the government's criminal stance in relation to the COVID-19 pandemic.

The COVID-19 pandemic, with its unequal and destructive impact on different social classes and their territories, is deepening the social and economic crisis in Brazil, with an increase in unemployment, misery and hunger. This will bring the country either to the brink of collapse and barbarism or to a progressive and radical turn. Undoubtedly, it will be up to those who recently entered public university, mostly from the coloured working class and poor, in different regions of Brazil, to defend public institutions, decent living conditions and wellbeing for all. It is important to note that the two major national demonstrations in defence of public education (in May and August 2019) have been the main mobilisations against the Bolsonaro government until today. Although this is a dark moment, deepened by the COVID-19 pandemic, it is still possible to believe that in recent decades, influenced by various progressive currents of thought, public universities have been, and still are, redefining the terms of debate about conflict, identity and heritage in Brazilian society and cities, and creating a generation of new intellectual and scientific leaders that can shake the structure of domination in one of the most unequal and violent countries in the world.

Turning back to the European context, many cities are facing the immediate challenge of new demographic trends shaped by the pandemic, with a significant dispersal of inner-city dwellers moving away from hollowed-out central areas in the expectation of being able to work remotely part-time, long-term, as well as the establishment of more local patterns of commerce and exchange within urban neighbourhoods due to the vast reduction in commuting. For universities, the impact of these changes, which also bring greater freedom for international staff and students never to relocate to – or join – communities in host cities, is still unclear. As noted, the big construction projects continue as if nothing has happened, even while the urban tourism and cultural sectors have shut down.

Yet the pandemic has provoked a valuable discussion of the way in which different spatial spectra and facilities correspond to different forms of knowledge production and how these spectra might be organised in a more strategic and resourceful way. Undoubtedly, it has opened up new kinds of opportunities, particularly in relation to new forms of engagement and audiences reached as different kinds of public formats have been explored under the physical constraints imposed by the pandemic. So, both the geographies and heritage of the university have been extended in interesting ways when the physical campus, the material infrastructure itself, is no longer in focus. But alongside these new challenges and opportunities there is also a shared growing concern about the nature of the university as a workplace and community during and post-COVID-19, and the extent to which the pandemic might be used to effect merciless rationalisation.

There is a question of legacy here, and also perhaps a recalibration to be undertaken. It is arguable that the university is not widely recognised within university communities as a historically privileged and unsustainable type of institution, and perhaps the pandemic, for better or for worse, has provided a timely reminder that the university apparatus cannot float above the economies and geographies it stands on, as a protected (and privileged) sphere, but must re-ground itself. Yet there is also certainly a high risk that all the necessary changes that the universities will have to undergo to become sustainable and relevant, prompted by demographics, climate crisis and COVID-19, can be reduced to new public management. Most alarming is the way in which the key intersecting issues of globalisation, capitalism, pandemics and the climate crisis are still being kept apart in the official discourses that frame public policy, action and, especially, education and its infrastructures. In this context, the rich and complex institutional and intellectual heritage of universities should be recognised as offering an invaluable resource for the cities in which they are located, towards a better holistic understanding of the significant challenges society faces in the coming decades of the Anthropocene, and the mutual achievement of better alternative futures shaped by narratives of shared urban heritage.

Transdisciplinary critical heritage investigations into the infrastructures of the 'universe-city' offer a means to re-decentre humans from their world, making/breaking responsibilities in the Anthropocene. This becomes an uncertain and indeterminate act of caring for the multi-plurality and temporal flows of agents that inhabit the world, in order 'to repair damaged places and make flourishing multi-species futures' (Haraway, 2016: 146). This may provide a response to a fundamental desire to humanise the uncaring universe and provide operational tools that we can use in making a world in which there is the possibility of happiness. So, rather than precarity and controversy being seen as misunderstandings and problems that need to be avoided, they can be embraced as the matters of concern in a mode of exploration for a creative response to inhabiting uncertain worlds with generosity and curiosity (Conolly, 2011). The elevation of disciplinary humility and doubt over certainty and hubris of professional arrogance provides a counterpoint to the egocentric reinforcements of privileged specialists secure in their expertise; the lack of professional certainty makes choices only credible when subject to broader justifications (Cassam, 2018).

Some provisional certainties can be secured from the disciplinary uncertainty of researching the bipolarity of urban universities as they are dissolved into the swirling coming together of the complexity of the city. A professional response can be conceived that is guided by asking diverse questions in hybrid fora, which enables change in unforeseeable ways. This requires creative listening to stories told in otherwise muted registers that avoid human exceptionalism, to detect previously unrealised common agendas. From this it is possible to make common cause with other human, non-human and non-animate actors to co-create more liveable, more-than-human cities, co-deciding with those who will bear the precarity of the consequences (Callon, Lascoumes and Barthe,

2011: 28). As such, world-making collaborations are good for some but not all; the benefits need to be identified to compensate for what is lost (Tsing, 2015: 255). The contribution offered by transdisciplinary critical heritage investigations into the infrastructures of the urban and its universities becomes the aim of making permanently provisional, preferable, good-enough cities.

References

Arantes, P. F. (2021) 'Higher education in dark times: From the democratic renewal of Brazilian universities to its current wreck'. *Policy Reviews in Higher Education*, 5 (2) 131–57. https://doi.org/10.1080/23322969.2021.1872412.

Callon, M., Lascoumes, P. and Barthe, Y. (2011) *Acting in an Uncertain World: An essay on technical democracy*. Cambridge: The MIT Press.

Cassam, Q. (2018) 'Epistemic insouciance'. *Journal of Philosophical Research*, Online First: 29 August 2018. https://doi.org/10.5840/jpr2018828131.

Connolly, W. E. (2011) *A World of Becoming*. Durham and London: Duke University Press.

Gardner, D. (2021) 'Sanctions could force Lebanon's politicians to govern'. *Financial Times*. 23 June 2021.

Haraway, D. (2016) *Staying with the Trouble: Making kin in the chthulucene*. Durham: Duke University Press.

Tewdwr-Jones, M., Sookhoo, D. and Freestone, R. (2019) 'From Geddes' city museum to Farrell's urban room: Past, present, and future at the Newcastle City Futures exhibition.' *Planning Perspectives,* 35.

Tsing, A. L. (2015) *The Mushroom at the End of the World: On the possibility of life in capitalist ruins*. Princeton: Princeton University Press.

Index

Page numbers in italics are figures and/or information in captions.

Accademia di Belle Arti 241, *241*
Addie, J.-P. 22
agnotology 95
Ågren, Lars 85
Ahmed, Sara 9, 134, 151, 152
Ain Mreisseh stairs 259, *261*
Akademika Hus (Sweden) 31
Al Jar lil Jar (farmer's market) (Beirut) 262–3, *263*
Albert, Prince Consort 167
Albertopolis 166, 167–9, 171, 186–7
Almqvist, Helge 72
Ambasz, E. 25–6
ambivalence 79–80
American University of Beirut (AUB) 248–9, 254–7
 history 250–1
 and the Neighborhood Initiative 255–66, *259–61*, *263–5*, 299–300
Anthropocene 48, *48*, 63, 133, 178, 180, 302
Ararat 237, 238, *238*, 240, *241*, 242, 243
archaeology
 Olympic Park (London) 159–61, 193
 Testaccio (Rome) 228, 230, 231
architectural renderings 90–3
 and disruption/permanence 93–5
 and fragment and world 104–6
 and from now to when 109
 and function/sign 101–4
 and future/past 106–9, *107*
 and knowledge/location 98–100
 and photograph/data 95–8, *97*
 and representation/production 100–1
Arthur, Michael 45, 46, 156
attraction, imaginary geography of, and Haga (Gothenburg) 70–2, *71*, 86–7
Augusti, Waldir 285
Authorised Heritage Discourse (AHD) 18, 50, 61
autopoietic/sympoietic systems 48–9
Aymonino, Carlo 232, 236

backgammon 263, *265*
Baudrillard, J. 101, 104, 108, 108–9
Beirut (Lebanon) 248–51, 299
 see also American University of Beirut
Bell, David 98
Bender, Thomas 18, 19, 188
Benevolo, Leonardo 230
Bergamo, Luca 242
Betancourt, M. 91, 97–8, 103
biennale, Rome 243
Big Science 200, 215–17
Bologna 124, 204, 205

Bologna Process 140
bonding capital *see* bridging/bonding capital
Bose, S. 27
Bostadssociala utredningen (Sweden) 77
Boyer, M.C. 104–5, 106, 108
Brazil
 São Paulo 270–1, 273
 university system 274–82, *277–8*, *280*, 290–2, 300–1
 see also Federal University of São Paulo (Unifesp)
Brecht, Bertolt 289
Brexit 170
bridging/bonding capital 190–2
Bridle, J. 95, 102
Brighenti, A.M. 209
Building Information Management (BIM) 100

Cambridge colleges 124, 204
Campo Boario (cattle market, Rome) 229, 234–5, 236, 238, *238*, 242–4, *244*
campus (term) 124, 204
Carpenters Estate 156, *157*, 164
Caruso, Luigi 232, 236
Cellini, Francesco 225, 240–1, 244
Centre for Critical Heritage Studies (CCHS) (University of Gothenburg) 2, 114, 188
centro sociale 236
Chalmers University of Technology (Gothenburg) 82, 84–5, 117–18, 119, *120*, 127–8
Chalmers, William 117
Cities Institute *see* Federal University of São Paulo (Unifesp)
Città della Scienza e della Tecnica (Rome) 233–5, *233*
Città delle Arti (Rome) 229–30, *239*, 240–2, *241*
climate change 179
Cochrane, A. 21
Cole, Henry 167
colonialism 18–19
commemoration, imaginary geography of, Haga (Gothenburg) 73–5, *73*, 86–7
competition 21
connectivity 52
conservation 17, 46, 47, 48–9, 52
 heritage 50–1
contested heritage 183–4
Cornell, Elias 82–3
Cortella, Mário Sérgio 281
Costa, Valter 285
COVID-19 pandemic 12, 170, 178–80, 296–301
Critical Conservation Practice 52
Critical Heritage Practice 53, 62
Crystal Palace *165*, 167, 168–70, *169*

crystallisation, and Lund University 208–12, *210*, *212*, 216
Curating the City 2, 3, 4, 59
curating (term) 52–3

Dalieh (Beirut) 261
Dar Onboz 263, *264*
de Certeau, M. 55
Debord, G. 98, 101, 104
deferred heritage (term) 91
democratisation, spatial 23–6
design education 132–4
  changes in orientation 147–52
  and the city 144–6
  past 135–42
  transformation of 142–5
designation, heritage 68–9
development, and heritage discourse 27–39, 30, *32–3*, *37–8*
digital capitalism 97–8
digital renderings 95–8, *97*
Dilnot, Clive 132–3, 151
disaster capitalism 298
discursive formation 80
disruption 91–2, 93–5, 99, 103–4, 108, 194
disruptive thinking, and UCL 164, 172
Drucker, Peter 98

East Bank project 46, 155, 158, 163, 165, 170, 171–2, 187, 193
East End movements (Brazil) 278–81, *280*, 283, 284
economic growth 20–2
Education Faculty (Pedagogen, University of Gothenburg) 121–3, *121–2*
Ekman, Oscar 116
Ericsson 127
Ernst and Young 93, 109
Ersoch, Gioacchino 228–9, 230
Erundina, Luiza 270, 281
European Spallation Source (ESS) 201, *202*, 203, 206, 207, 208, 211, *212*, 213–15, 217
Evans, Graeme 163, 168
experience economy 17

fauxtomation 94
Federal University of São Paulo (Unifesp) 19, 269–71, 276, *277*, 282–92, *283*, *287–9*, *291*
  history 271–4, *272*
Festival of Britain (1951) 166, 170, 171
Fontana-Giusti, G. 209
Forum for Education (Brazil) 281–2
Foucault, M. 27, 80
Frampton, Hollis 105–6
França, Luís 284–5
France 25
  Université 2000 project 123–4
Freire, Paulo 269, 270, 271, 277, 281, 284, 291
funding 23

gambling 92
Geddes, Patrick 297
gentrification 36, 43, 46, 58, 68, 187–8, 257

glitch 95, 101–3
globalized identity, and universities 19
Goddard, J. 21–2
good neighbour concept 43, 46, 58, 62–3
Gothenburg Exposition 29, 32–3
Gothenburg Historical Museum 74, 75, 83, 85
Gothenburg (Sweden)
  Haga 66–7
    imaginary geographies 69–85, *71*, *73*, *76*, *81*
  and Slöjdföreningens skola 144–6
  University of see University of Gothenburg
Gramsci, A. 278
Grant, Malcolm 156
Gravesen, Cecilie 59–60
Great Exhibition of 1851 155–6, 165–7, *165*, 171
Gurmund, L. 119

Hadid, Zaha 95, *96*, 97, 101, 102, 103, 108
Haga (Gothenburg) 66–9, 115
  imaginary geographies 69–85, *71*, *73*, *76*, *81*
Hajj Ali, Hanane 259, *260*
Hall, Stuart 28
Haraway, D. 48–9
Harding, Alan 21
Hariri, Rafik 253
Hårleman, Carl 204–5, 211
Harvey, D. 20
heritage (defined) 47–50, *47–8*, 155
heritage designation 66, 67–8
heritage discourse 155–6
  and university development 27–39, *30*, *32–3*, *37–8*
heritage places 43–4, *44*, 50–1, 61–3
  co-curating change 51–3
  and critical heritage 45–6
  hidden sites/out of site out of mind 59–60
  House Mill 43, *44*, 56–9, 60–1
  redefining heritage 47–9, *47–8*
  spaces and places 53–6, 62155
heritagisation 10, 50, 53, 167, 203, 216, 221, 229–30
  Haga 84
  Mattatio 229
  Ostiense 221
Hidden Sites Research Workshop 59–61
HIGAB 137, 141, 143, 144, 145, 149
HKPU see Innovation Tower (Honk Kong)
Högskolan för Design och Konsthantverk 133, 139–43, 149
Holston, J. 26
Holtorf, C. 50
House Mill (Bromley-by-Bow) 43, *44*, 56–9, 60–1
hysterical materialism 177–80, 193

identity 26
  national 17, 24, 26, 28
  and university development 27–8
imaginary geographies
  Haga (Gothenburg) 69–85, *71*, *73*, *76*, *81*, 86
indigenous peoples 184
Innovation Tower (Hong Kong) 97, *97*, 99, 101, 108
Institute for Global Prosperity 256
Jaffe, R. 27

James, L. 98–9
Jockey Club Innovation Tower (Hong Kong) 97, *97*
Johnson, Boris 155, 165–6, 187

Karsten-Wiberg, E. 78
Khalidy House (Beirut) 258, *259*
Khan, Sadiq 170, 187
Kitchin, R. 96
Kjellin, Maja 72
knowledge, archaeology of 69, 80
knowledge economy/knowledge-based economy (KBE) 6, 9, 19, 20–1, 35, 92
and architectural renderings 98–100
knowledge production
future *see* architectural renderings
and Haga (Gothenburg) 67, 70, 85, 86, 88
Kristinelundsgatan 6–8 (Slöjdföreningens skola) 135, 137, 141, 149–50, 152
Kurek, Jacob 213–14

La Sapienza (university, Rome) 220, 222, 224, 230, 232, 233
and *Città della Scienza e della Tecnica* 233–4, *233*
and Stalker 237
Larsson, Ursula, *Landshövdingehus och trähus i Göteborg* 85
latency 59
Latham, Ian 107–8
Lebanon 299
see also Beirut
Lefebvre, H. 25–6
Letchimy, S. 25
Liedman, S.-E. 113–14
Lindahl, Göran 82
Liseberg Amusement Park (Gothenburg) 29
lockdowns 178–9
London Docklands Development Corporation (LDDC) 158, 163
London Legacy Development Corporation (LLDC) 35, 36, 156, 158, 161
Lönnroth, Gudrun, *Landshövdingehus och trähus i Göteborg* 85
Lopes, Antonio Carlos 286
Lula da Silva, Luiz Inácio 270, 274
Lund University (Sweden) 200–18, *202*
and Big Science 200, 215–17
crystallisation and heritage 208–12, *210*, *212*
heritage and public visibility 212–15
history 204–5, *206*
spatial expansion 203–8
Lux, Simonetta 230

McCann, E. 21
Macedonia (North Macedonia) 104
MACRO (Rome) *239*, 241, *241*
maintenance, imaginary geography of, and Haga (Gothenburg) 80–8, *80*
'making' (term) 186
Manovitch, Lev 101
Marchioni, Antonio (Father 'Ticão') 279, 282, 283
Marroni, Umberto 220
Mattatoio (slaughterhouse) (Testaccio) 227–42, *228*, *234*, 238–9, *241*
MAX IV (synchrotron) 201, *202*, 206, 206–7, 208, *210*

Meyer, Michael W., 'Changing Design Education for the 21st Century' 147, 148
Monfredini, Nilce 275
multiversities 125, 188
Mumford, Lewis, *The City in History* 204

Näckrosen project (University of Gothenburg) 28–9, 31–4, *32–3*, 36, 106, 128, 129, 141
Nya Konst 137, 138, 142, 144, 151
Nagle, John 265
Nalbantoglu, G.B. 25
nation building 11, 16–20, 28
national heritage discourses 16–18, 24–5, 28, 39, 249, 275
Neighborhood Initiative (Beirut) 255–66, *259–61*, *263–5*
neoliberalism 20
New Aesthetic 95, 102
Nicolini, Renato 231, 232
Norman, Don, 'Changing Design Education for the 21st Century' 147, 148
Nya Konst (Gothenburg) 137, 138, 142, 144, 151

Oberg, Johan 34
'Objects of the Misanthropocene' (Speculative Design Project) 63
Ohio State University 27
Olausson, L. 113–14
Olympic Delivery Authority (ODA) 159–60
Olympic Park (London) 28–9, *30*, 31, 35, 43, *44*, 46, 157–9, 171, 185–6
archaeological work 159–61, 193
heritage trail/Groundbreakers project 193–5
and UCL East 162–5, 185, 187–8
Olympicopolis 156, 166, 170, 187
Olympics (2012) 157–9, 171, 185
as legacy 184–9, 190–3
Oral History Project (Beirut) 262
Oriel College (Oxford) 184–5
Ostiense (Rome) 221, *221*, 223, 232
Ostiense-Marconi project 223–5, 227, 240–2
'Out of site out of mind' workshop 44, 59, 59–61
Oxford colleges 124, 204
and Cecil Rhodes 184–5

Palazzo, Anna 227
pandemic *see* COVID-19 pandemic
Perego, Francesco 231
permanent provisional state 222, 242–3
photography
and architectural rendering 95–8, *97*, 104–6, 109
Piano Regulatore Generale (PRG) (Rome) 223–4, 230
places and spaces 53–6, 62
Portoghesi, Paolo 233–4
postcolonialism 25, 26
postmodern nomadic subject 188
private-public partnerships 16, 22, 27
prosthetic heritage 181, 183, 184, 187
public service 22
Putnam, Robert 190

Queen Elizabeth Park *see* Olympic Park

Raggi, Gabriella 242–3
Reale, Miguel 281
Recycling a Shell (artistic installation) 258, *259*
Rhodes, Cecil, and Oriel College (Oxford) 184–5
right to the city 16, 26, 270, 286
Robbins Report (1963) 24
Röhsska Muséet (Gothenburg) 72, 136, 137, 147–8
Roma Tre University (Rome) 220–7, *221*, *227*, 244–5
   Mattatoio (slaughterhouse) (Testaccio) 227–42, *228*, *234*, *238–9*, *241*
Roma-Kalderashi community 236, 238, *238*, 240
Romantic movement 188
Romdahl, Axel 72
Rome, planning/development 222–4
Rosenthal, M.A. 92
Roth, Stig *73*, 75
Rousseff, Dilma 274, 290
Roy, A. 21

Saba, Sabine 264
Sakr, Karim 264
Salons de Beyrouth, Les (project) 264
sanitisation, imaginary geography of, Haga (Gothenburg) 75–9, *76*, 86–7
São Paulo (Brazil) 270–1, 273
   'worker's university' model 276–7, *277*
Save Britain's Heritage 17
Sawalha, Aseel 252
Schor, Nestor 286
Science Road (Lund) *202*, 203, 206, 208–9, 211, 215
Science Village Scandinavia 201–3, *202*, 207, 208
slaughterhouse *see* Mattatoio (slaughterhouse) (Testaccio)
Slöjdföreningens skola 133–52
   as Högskolan för Design och Konsthantverk 133, 139–43, 149
Smaili, Soraya 282
Smith, Laurajane 18
Solidere 252–3, 257, 265
Souffleur, Le (acoustic installation) 259, *261*
South Kensington *see* Albertopolis
South Bank complex 163, 170–1, 172
spallation (defined) 213–14
spatial democratisation 22–6
   see also development
spatial expansion *see* Lund University
Speculative Design Project 63
Stalker 236–40, 243
Stein, Robin 60
Strategic Regeneration Framework 185
Stratford (London)
   UCL Stratford scheme 156, *157*, 164
   see also Olympic Park
Strohmayer, U. 160
Swansea University Bay Campus 106–8, *107*
sympoietic/autopoietic systems 48–9
Syrian Protestant College 259–60, 262

Tabet, Jad 253
Tafuri, Manfredo 100
Taleb, Nassim, *The Black Swan* 96
Tange, Kenzo 104

Taylor, Astra 94
temporality 49, 63
Testaccio
   as a permanent provisional state 242–3
   see also Mattatoio (slaughterhouse) (Testaccio)
Thrift, Nigel 216–17
Ticão, Father *see* Marchioni, Antonio (Father 'Ticão')
tramways
   Beirut 250
   Lund *202*, 203, 207, 209, 216
transdisciplinary approach 1–5, 302–3

Unifesp *see* Federal University of São Paulo (Unifesp)
United Kingdom 23–4
   heritage 17–18
   public service 22
   university development 28
   see also University College London
United States of America 19, 20–1, 23, 124
   Ohio State University 27
   University of Virginia 24
Université 2000 project (France) 123–4
University College London (UCL) 19, 35–6, 45, 154
   and the community 182–3
   East 28, 29, *30*, 31–2, 33, 35–6, *37–8*, 46, 155–7, *157*, 162–5, 166, 170, 171–2, 187–8, 189
      archaeology 159–61
   as heritage maker 180–1
   Institute of Archaeology, and the House Mill Trust 58–9
   and the Institute for Global Prosperity 256
   Stratford scheme 156, *157*, 164
University of East London (UEL) 188–9
University of Gothenburg *32*, 33–4, 38, 113–14
   Centre for Critical Heritage Studies (CCHS) 188
   city university 123–5
   cluster units 126–8, *126–7*
   compared to Chalmers 117–18, 119, *120*
   dispersed and multi-sited 118–20, *120*
   early history 114–17, *115*
   Education Faculty/Institute of 121–3, *121–2*
   globalized identity 19
   and the heritage discourse 129–30
   Project Näckrosen 28–9, 31–4, *32–3*, 36, 106, 128, 129
   and the Slöjdföreningens skola 138, 143, 145, 149
University of Toronto 108
University of Virginia, Academical Village 24
Urban Laboratory (UCL) 3, 36, 38
urbicide 248–9

Vallance, P. 21–2
Van Dyck Stairs 259, *260*
vectorialism 91–2
Victoria & Albert Museum (formerly South Kensington Museum) 168, 185
V&A East 186–7
Vidotto, Andrea 224

Villaggio Globale (Rome) 236–7, *238*, *241*, 242
Virginia, University of *see* University of Virginia
Volvo 127, 144

Ward, K. 21
Wark, McKenzie 91–2
Weston, Edward 105
Widéen, Harald 75
William-Olsson, Tage *76*
windmill, Lund 211, *212*
Wong, C.T. 25
'worker's university' model, Brazil 269, 271, 276–82, *277–8*, *280*

Yassin, N. 252

Zettervall, Helgo 205, *206*
Zevi, Bruno 230

Lightning Source UK Ltd.
Milton Keynes UK
UKHW020406290722
406518UK00001B/20